BATTLEFIELD INDIA

25 YEARS OF POLITRICKS AND ECONOMIX

Shobha Warrier

Vitasta

Published by
Renu Kaul Verma
Vitasta Publishing Pvt Ltd
2/15, Ansari Road, Daryaganj
New Delhi - 110 002
info@vitastapublishing.com

ISBN 978-93-90961-30-6

First Edition 2023

MRP ₹795

Editor: Papri Sri Raman
Cover by Somesh Kumar Mishra
Layout by Ram Kumar
Printed by Chaman Enterprises, New Delhi

To

Maya, my sunshine

THE TIMES OF INDIA

Distant Destiny

Parliament re-enacts freedom at midnight

President calls for war against corruption, casteism, criminalisation

A nation on the march at India Gate

The partition before independence in 1947 was an unforgettable tragedy. Despite this, within three years, India declared itself as a Republic. Tragically, by 1997, it had nothing different in governance to show.

Thank you, Google.com; Thank you, India Today; Thank you, Times of India.

They know the truth
Yet they tricked the truth
They see the truth
Yet they are blind to the truth
They hide the truth
They have phobia for truth
Always denying the truth
They preach truth
Their truth is veiled
Laded with politricks
That is their truth
So, read their lips
When they speak the truth

—**Babatunde Aremu**

We thought everybody would be like Mahatma Gandhi or Jawaharlal Nehru or Rajaji — C Subramaniam

They dreamt of Free India together.
In 1947, their ideals were, however, different.
Nobody had any clear vision about an ideal India, said Poornam Viswanathan.
'Rama Rajya' is a concept first projected by Mahatma Gandhi. His ideal state would be Rama Rajya. That Ram Rajya in 2022 continues to be elusive.
Thank you, National Herald.

We have reached Mars.
'More than anything else, it was the charisma of Dr Sarabhai, the gleam in his eyes when he described his plans and his sincerity which attracted me', said R Aravamudan, one of the first scientists picked up by Vikram Sarabhai to launch ISRO at Thumba in Thiruvananthapuram.
https://www.globalindian.com

Contents

PART 3

1999-2004

Ruling Party: The National Democratic Alliance (NDA)

Prime Minister: Atal Bihari Vajpayee (BJP)

PART 4

2004-2009

Ruling Party: The UPA (United Progressive Alliance)

Prime Minister: Dr Manmohan Singh (Congress)

PART 5

2009- 2014

Ruling Party: The United Progressive Alliance (UPA)

Prime Minister: Dr Manmohan Singh (Congress)

PART 6

2014-2019

Ruling Party: The National Democratic Alliance (NDA)

Prime Minister: Narendra Damodardas Modi (BJP)

Author's note

It was one of those casual meetings I had after my walk with my neighbour in the evenings. He, a regular reader of Rediff.com, liked to discuss India's economy based on the interviews I had done. One day he asked me, why don't you compile your interviews? My response was, 'they are very topical. Who will be interested in reading after a few years?' 'Think about it', he said.

That was the beginning of this book. This was in 2019.

The idea remained in my mind without taking any shape. Then my son Siddhu said, 'you should have a story to tell through your interviews.'

That was the eureka moment.

One of the most exciting times of my career as a journalist was interviewing people who had witnessed India's independence. I thought, why not start the story from 1997, when India celebrated 50 years of independence?

The pandemic gave me the opportunity to tell the story till India celebrated 75 years of independence.

That is, 25 years of India's story; from 1997 to 2022; from when India celebrated 50 years of independence to when it is celebrating 75 years of independence.

Of course, I have not recorded every single event that happened in these 25 years through my interviews. But then I felt there was a story.

I was fortunate to have spoken to some of the very interesting and extremely knowledgeable people who could talk to me about the political, economic and social happenings in the country authoritatively.

And that is the story behind this book!

Insights into Policy-making in New India

Ever wondered what the real thinking was that lay behind the sometimes surprising and sometimes shocking speeches or actions of the decision-making elite in India?

This is a book that can act as a primer in your journey towards that.

Why it works as a decoder is because the author, Shobha Warrier, has made it a point to interview these movers and shakers not in their prime but when they reached their 80s, a period of life where one tends to be reflective and look at the larger shape of things.

Take for example R Venkataraman, who was 86 at the time of the interview, and had come to live in Chennai after completing his five-year term as the President of India. He said, 'The motive in politics is self-interest now. The days when people jumped into the freedom movement, sacrificing their career, properties, family, are all over. Today, politics is like any other profession. And everybody wants to come up in politics like everybody wants to come up in law, medicine, education, engineering etc'.

We are living in a period when the BJP appears to be extending its appeal to many parts of the country and even in parts of South India. What could the party's intrinsic appeal be? We can gather many insights about that from the author's interview with O Rajagopal, vice president of the BJP in its early days where he says, for example, that 'Rama Rajya is a concept first projected by no less a person than Mahatma Gandhi. When he was asked about the ideal state, he talked about Rama Rajya'.

The events that led to Rajiv Gandhi's assassination by a Tamil woman has always been a mystery to me but the author's interview with K Mohandas, the then Director General of Police (DGP), throws a lot of light on the motivations of the various parties involved. He was often described as 'MGR's eyes and ears', the only man ever to have arrested the LTTE leader V Prabhakaran two times and had been an eyewitness to the Indian government's sponsorship of the Tamil Tigers. Nobody had as much knowledge about the Indian government-LTTE nexus, and the sordid events that led to the assassination of Rajiv Gandhi.

Can there be an alternative viewpoint to the all-encompassing Atma Nirbhar Bharat Abhiyan programme? The author's interview with Gurcharan Das, in 1998, then a member in the Vajpayee government's Foreign Investment Promotion Council where he analyses India's potential and predicts where it will be by 2020 and 2050 presents a different point of view on this: the view that the Swadeshi ideology is an ideology which betrays inferiority complex.

I have narrated above just a glimpse of the wide variety of insights across the many different interviews in this book.

What is in common across all the stories in this book is author Shobha Warrier's gentle questioning that makes all these famous personalities present a truthful and frank insight into the New India of the 1997-2022 years.

—Ajit Balakrishnan, Founder, Rediff.com

PART 1

1997

Ruling Party: The United Front

Prime Minister: I K Gujral (JDU)

Shankar Pillai (1902-1989) and Abu Abraham (1924-2002) were two famous cartoonists from the 1960s to 1980s.

In the first drawing here, Abu shows Gandhi's spectacles on the Elephant. We look at the elephant as India, a very intelligent mammoth with a long life and long memory, which even Alexander could not figure out. The Idea of India is ephemeral. Unfortunately, we Indians too have not figured India out yet; we continue to dither and after 75 years of independence, have not managed to fix our goal – exactly what do we want for this nation state?
http://cartoonexhibition.blogspot.com/2010/10/abu.html

Cartoonist Kesava Shankar Pillai was very active in the 1960s and '70s. He founded Shankar's Weekly *in 1948;* Children's Book Trust; Shankar's International Dolls Museum. *What he drew in the early 1980s is still true today, there is price rise and party politics in equal measure.*
https://alchetron.com/K-Shankar-Pillai

Chaos, Freedom and Change

15 AUGUST 1997.

A momentous occasion for India.

A special day. In fact, it is a special year.

It was 50 years since the country became independent.

But for the people of India, 1997 was not one of those years to feel cheerful about. Instead of cheer, people felt that the entire political system had decayed and was crumbling. There seemed to be only unpredictability, volatility and uncertainty in India's political scene.

If we are to talk about the 50th year of India's independence, we have to go back a few years to understand why people felt frustrated when they should have been in a mood to celebrate.

Actually, the turmoil began with the 1989 election for the 9th Lok Sabha (the lower house of the Indian Parliament).

Rajiv Gandhi, who had a mammoth victory in the 1984 elections after the assassination of his mother and the then Prime Minister Indira Gandhi, sadly lead a government that was marred by many corruption charges and numerous scandals – starting with the Bofors scandal to unabated terrorism in Punjab, and with India taking an unwarranted active part in the bloody war in neighbouring Sri Lanka.

When the party that won a mammoth 414 seats in 1984 was reduced to just 197 in the 1989 elections, Rajiv Gandhi felt it was not morally right to stake claim to form the next government.

Next in line was the National Front that had 141 seats. V P Singh of the Janata Dal was chosen as the leader of the National Front to form the next government, with outside support from the BJP that had 85 seats. For the first time, the BJP tasted real power as a ruling partner.

V P Singh as the Prime Minister of India did not last long. Reason: L K Advani, the leader of the BJP, was arrested on the 30th of October, 1990 after his Rath Yatra to Ayodhya was prohibited from entering the site.

The angry BJP withdrew support, and the V P Singh government fell, losing the vote of confidence on 7 November, 1990.

Chandrasekhar, who had broken away from the Janata Dal along with 64 other MPs and had formed the Samajwadi Janata Party in 1990, became the next Prime Minister of India with outside support from the Congress.

The Chandrasekhar government also did not last long. He took charge on the 10th of November 1990 but his government also fell in no time when the Congress withdrew support, alleging that the government was spying on Rajiv Gandhi. But he continued to head the caretaker government till the next election in 1991.

The legacy left behind by the V P Singh government was the implementation of the Mandal Commission report which gave legitimacy and legality to the traditionally divided Indian society on caste lines.[1]

And the demolition of Babri Masjid by right wing Hindu activists on the 6th of December 1992 resulted in the country getting divided on religious lines too.

So, the 1991 elections were fought on the Mandal-Mandir issue. It was also for the first time that a general election took place in a phased manner.

But 1991 will be remembered for the assassination of Rajiv Gandhi by the LTTE (a Lankan separatist force called the Liberation Tigers of Tamil Eelam) in retaliation for his decision to send the Indian Peace Keeping Force (IPKF) to fight on the Sri Lankan soil against the Tamil Tigers, during his tenure as the PM.

Despite the tragedy, there was no sympathy wave for the Congress and the party won only 244 seats. While the Bharatiya Janata Party (BJP) under L K Advani won 120 seats, the National Front that had created chaos in the country came out only a distant third.

The Congress chose P V Narasimha Rao as the Prime Minister of India when Rajiv's wife, Sonia Gandhi, refused to listen to the pleas of Congressmen to lead the party. For the first time in the history of the Congress, a non-Nehru-Gandhi family member was chosen to rule the country.

Narasimha Rao will be remembered as the Prime Minister who opened up the Indian economy and changed the destiny of the

---

1 The Mandal Commission, the Socially and Educationally Backward Classes Commission, was established in India in 1979 by the Janata Party government under Prime Minister Morarji Desai to 'identify the socially or educationally backward classes' of India. It was headed by B P Mandal.

nation. Unfortunately, the image of his government was that of a corrupt one.

In the 1996 Parliamentary elections, for the first time, the BJP, a non-Congress party, became the single largest party with 161 seats.

The emergence of the BJP as the single largest party can be termed as the beginning of a fundamental shift in the body language of politics in India, from left of centre to the right.

Though the BJP did not have the numbers to form the government, the then President, Shankar Dayal Sharma invited Atal Bihari Vajpayee to form the government, following the Westminster model of calling the single largest party. Vajpayee was sworn in on the 15th of May 1996 as the first BJP Prime Minister of India.

Facing a confidence motion before the 31st of May, Vajpayee could not garner support from more than 200 members. In those days, the BJP was still an untouchable party! So, after 13 days, he resigned instead of facing the confidence vote.

Congress, the second largest party with 140 seats, declined the offer to form the government. The party decided to be the kingmaker instead, by supporting the United Front which was a coalition of the Janata Dal and a group of other smaller parties, with Deve Gowda as the Prime Minister. On hindsight, it was axing the branch on which it sat.

With the Congress giving outside support and the Marxists within the government, as expected, frequent ideological clashes occurred between the Congress and the United Front.

Just 18 months had passed when the Congress threatened to withdraw support. It resulted in a constitutional crisis, and the country was facing yet another election in a matter of months.

This was the India that was going to celebrate 50 years of independence.

What is the Future?

It was just before 15 August 1997 that I spoke to the former President of India, ***R Venkataraman*** *(1987-1992), who had to face many critical moments during his term as the President of India.*

Venkataraman, once an ardent Congressman, had come to live in Chennai after completing his five-year term as the President of India. He was accessible, and even at 86, he was extremely sharp and agile both mentally and physically.

I had the privilege of interviewing him quite a few times when India faced political and constitutional crises, and he was there to give his well-founded opinion.

This was one time I found him extremely pessimistic and agitated over the political uncertainty the country was facing, especially when we were to celebrate 50 years of independence in a few months' time.

PRESIDENT Shankar Dayal Sharma (1992-1997) has given the Prime Minister (Deve Gowda) time till 11 April (1997) to prove majority in the Lok Sabha. Will it not result in horse trading?

Constitutionally, the President has done the correct thing by asking the Prime Minister to take a vote of confidence in the House.

A similar situation arose when I was the President of India also, when the BJP withdrew support to V P Singh's government (in 1990). When the BJP came and reported to me that they had withdrawn the support, I told them that the government had to prove its majority in the House. Since the majority had to be established in the House, it was appropriate that it was tested in the House by a motion of confidence or a motion of no-confidence.

Suppose the Deve Gowda government does not win the vote of confidence, can the President call the Congress to form a government? The Congress is the second largest party in the Lok Sabha.

Normally, the President should ask the parties according to their strength. And the BJP, according to its strength, stands above the Congress. But the President may not ask the BJP once again because he has already given them a chance, and they have not been able to form a government. The next in order of strength is the Congress. He can ask the Congress to form a government.

But when the BJP government (Atal Bihari Vajpayee as the Prime Minister) resigned after being unable to muster strength, the Congress itself said, the President may call the United Front. Therefore, it could be interpreted that the Congress had itself declined on the earlier occasion.

So, it rests completely with the discretion of the President whether to call the Congress or not.

Had you been in that position, would you have called the Congress?

See, it is difficult to say. I am not in touch with the parties. It all depends on various factors. If I felt that the Congress was in a position to form a viable government, then I might invite them.

If I came to the conclusion that the Congress was not in a position to form a viable government, and like Charan Singh, they would accept the office and call for the dissolution of the House, I may not agree.[1]

It depends on the political situation at the Centre with which I am not personally familiar (today).

Will this kind of situation not lead to defections? No single party can form a government now, and if anybody wants to prove its majority, it can do so only by accepting members from other parties.

Technically, defection is breaking away of a group from within the party. And, under the anti-defection law, it will not be defection if the defection is more than one third of the members of the party. Therefore, you cannot foresee what the situation could be.

You said the President might not call the BJP again because it could not form a government earlier. In your time (1987-1992), when V P Singh resigned, you called the Congress once again and when they declined, you called the BJP and then the Left Front. It came to Chandra Shekhar

---

[1] Many parties had split and reconstituted in the meanwhile. Charan Singh was sworn in as the Prime Minister on 28 July 1979, with outside support from Indira Congress. Just before he was to prove majority in Lok Sabha, Indira Gandhi withdrew support to his government, and he had to resign on 20 August 1979, after just 23 days. But before resigning, he advised President Neelam Sanjiva Reddy to dissolve the Lok Sabha, thus becoming the first Prime Minister who failed to face the parliament.

only when he came to you with the backing of the Congress. Why did you follow that pattern then?

At that time, I felt the Congress would be able to form a viable government, if given an opportunity again. It was for them to decide whether they would be able to form a viable government or not. Even when I called the Congress, I knew that they would not accept the offer, nor would the BJP accept the offer, nor would the Left Front accept the offer.

How did you assess the situation then?

When you are in actual touch with all the parties, the leaders and so on, then you know what the situation is. I was in touch with every one of the political parties. I was in touch with the leaders of the political parties, and they had a lot of confidence in me. So, they used to come and tell me what their position was. Therefore, I was able to take a decision then.

If the Deve Gowda government does not win the vote of confidence (with Gowda as the prime minister), and if he then asks the President to dissolve the House, while the other parties are staking their claim, does the President have to follow the Prime Minister's recommendation and dissolve the House?

It is a very important legal question. In England, for the last two hundred years, the advice of the prime minister to dissolve the House, whether in office or defeated in the House, has always been accepted by the Crown. In India, people argue that the President must examine whether any viable alternative can be formed.

I am a man who was a textbook President.

You must make a distinction between a Constitutional President and an Executive President. If you are an Executive

President, you can decide whether you can dissolve the House or cannot dissolve the House. But if you are a Constitutional President, you must accept the advice of the Prime Minister whether he is in office or defeated.

He *has to?*

I don't say he has to. He should. That is the Constitutional position, if you follow the British Constitution. This question has not been settled in India. For instance, Chandra Shekhar was not defeated in the House, but after giving his resignation, he advised me to dissolve the House. I accepted the resignation but asked him to continue till further arrangements were made.

As far as the decision to dissolve the House was concerned, I wanted some time to think. The question was, whether his advice was binding on me or not.

But there was another factor in that case. No other party was ready to form the government. Therefore, I said the Prime Minister recommended that the House be dissolved, and that no other party was prepared to shoulder the responsibility of forming the government. Then I dissolved the House.

So, in this changed scenario, what should the President do?

Constitutionally the President has to accept the advice of the Prime Minister, if you follow the British Constitution. Ever since the days of Queen Anne, who once refused to accept the advice of the prime minister, the prime minister's advice for dissolution has always been accepted.

As a senior citizen of India, and a former President, how do you assess the present-day uncertainties?

I may be a pessimist now. I think nobody will be able to form a government and we are heading towards a general election. Any other hotchpotch arrangement will be so unstable that economic development will become a casualty. All the time they would be striving to survive, so, they will have no time to serve the people or the country.

Do you feel sad about the way the Congress, a party you were associated with, has behaved? The general public feel they acted very selfishly.

The motive in politics is self-interest now. The days when people jumped into the freedom movement, sacrificing their career, properties, family, are all over. Today, politics is like any other profession. And everybody wants to come up in politics like everybody wants to come up in law, medicine, education, engineering etc

Soon after the 1996 parliamentary election, when I interviewed you, you told me that there was a halo around politicians who participated in the freedom struggle which was lacking in today's political leaders. You also told me that in such circumstances, the chances of any single party coming to power were very slim. Do you still feel so?

The chances are fewer. That's why I talked about coalition governments. But this 13-party hotch-potch is not a real coalition. The constituent parties today assert their views against the government's decision. There is no feeling of joint responsibility.

Is it good for the country to have a coalition government formed after the election?

If you ask, what is ideal for the country, I will say, a two-party system.

Will it happen?

It will not. Because the tendency among people to form splinter groups whenever there is a difference of opinion, has become a habit. It was not as if there was no difference of opinion earlier. But the mere fact that there was some difference of opinion did not lead them to split the party and form another group. Today at the drop of a hat, you get out of the party and form another group.

Some political analysts are talking about a two-party system featuring the BJP and Congress at the Centre in the future. Do you foresee anything of that sort?

I think this country will not elect a single party to power. There will be a large number of splinter parties.

That means we will have to face this kind of situation quite often.

Yes, it will be the same.

But that is not good for the country.

No, it is not good for the country. I have a number of solutions to offer. But who will accept it (laughs)?

One is that the party which gets the least number of votes in the general election must be eliminated. Then, five parties will become four and four parties will become three, and in the next election, the three parties will become two.

For this solution, you must also not allow future registration of any parties. You should also provide that the party which gets the least number of votes in each general election must be disbanded until the number is reduced to two parties. These are my suggestions. Some people may say that it offends Article 19 of the Constitution, the Freedom of Association.

Today, the electorate does not realise that at a general election, they are electing a government for themselves. They look upon it as an occasion to exercise patronage in favour of a particular caste, co-religionist, a neighbour and so on.

If an electorate refuses to elect a criminal, if an electorate refuses to elect a person who hops from party to party, if an electorate refuses to elect a person with a bad reputation, a corrupt man or a bad man, then politics will be cleansed. But the electorate continues to elect a person who is a criminal, continues to elect a person who has the reputation as a corrupt man.

So, what is really required is the education of the electorate. They should realise that they are electing a government for themselves, and they are not distributing a favour. It will take a long time to educate the electorate.

We are talking about United Kingdom and Europe, but they had also gone through all these trials and tribulations for 800 years. A prime minister like Walpole said, every man has his price. From that position, they have reached maturity. Now a Walpole cannot be elected.

Now we see regional parties with a regional outlook coming to the Centre. Is it because a party like the Congress – which has a national perspective – has deteriorated that people are voting for regional parties at the Centre?

As I said earlier, the electorate must feel that they must have a strong Centre. Today, the electorate is feeling that more power should be given to the State, from there to the panchayat and so on. So long as this attitude stays, it will be very difficult to have a strong Centre.

The electorate must be able to synthesise these two ideas. Decentralisation with a strong Centre to defend the country, manage foreign affairs, manage the currency, manage the economy through planning is needed. In other matters like education, health etc, the States should have more power. Even politicians are not clear about this. Either they swing to one side or to the other.

What we conceived at the time of framing the Constitution was a centralised federalism, a federalism in which the Centre is strong. That is not realised by our people.

You said you are a pessimist and foresee a fresh election. Suppose no single party gets a majority, will this not be repeated?

You should go on holding elections.

Till the electorate understands?

Yes, till the electorate understands. If a general election is called in three months' time, politicians will have to go to the electorate again. People will ask, 'We voted for you only three months back. Why do you come back?' Then, the parties will have to explain that they did not vote for a majority to a single party, and then nobody could form a government.

Soon after the election, when we had a hung Parliament, you spoke about a national government as an alternative. Why is it that no politician is interested in this?

Because everybody wants to be the prime minister when we can have only one prime minister.

I think the only solution for the present crisis is a national government. You cannot say that one party is untouchable. What has happened today is that some people say the BJP is untouchable while to some others, the Left Front is untouchable. The result is, we break into groups.

On the other hand, the crisis is such that it calls for a great deal of abnegation on the part of politicians. They should sink all their differences and come together. It can be done in one way. Informally, the Speaker can call the members of Parliament and ask them to elect a leader by a single transferable vote or, ask them to vote for whomsoever they want to.

And if nobody gets 51 per cent of the votes, we can have a run-off between the first two top candidates so that one of them will be chosen. He may become the prime minister and he can approach the President with an offer to form a government.

How will he pick the ministers?

I will come to that. Like the Public Accounts Committee or the Estimates Committee which are elected on proportional representation, the Council of Ministers can be elected in the same manner. That is, in proportion to the strength of the party in the House. If this is done, the prime minister will have the authority to allot the portfolios. Nobody can dictate to him.

Decisions in the council of ministers will be taken by a majority of the ministers. If they try this experiment for a year or two, and when the situation becomes normal or when people think it is time to seek a mandate from the people, they can agree among themselves and ask for the dissolution of the House.

Can we afford to have elections at such short intervals?

Elections are the only way of educating the electorate

But elections are a very costly affair, and we are still a poor country.

Democracy is costly.

In the end, India did not have to face another election. On 21 April 1997, the Congress agreed to support I K Gujral as a compromise candidate for the prime minister.

Prime Minister Gujral continued in the office for more than 11 months, including 3 months as the caretaker prime minister.

To my question whether we would have two parties, the BJP and the Congress dominating the political scene in India, Venkataraman had replied, 'I think this country will not elect a single party to power'.

In 2019, for the first time after 1984, a single party got absolute majority. The BJP under Narendra Modi won 303 seats.

Wish the former President of India was alive to analyse the present situation.

Does India's Constitution Need Review?

As the talk of the role of the President under the Constitution of India, and whether a review of the Constitution was the need of the hour, raged on, I spoke to the only person who was alive in 1997 to talk on the Constitution of India.

It was the former Union Minister ***C Subramaniam*** *who was a member of the Constituent Assembly when India won independence and had a hand in the framing of the Constitution of India.*

Though he served as the minister of Education, Law and Finance for Madras State from 1952 to 1962 under the chief ministers C Rajagopalachari and K Kamaraj, he was well known as the man behind the Green Revolution when he was the Minister of Agriculture from 1964-66 under Lal Bahadur Shastri as the Prime Minister.

It was my good luck that he was alive to analyse the Constitution for us.

He was one of those amicable and welcoming politicians I have met, though with a serious demeanour.

YOU had said a year ago that the time had come to review the functioning of the Constitution. Are you happy that people have started talking about it now?

Yes, I think we must review the Constitution now. Otherwise, we will continue to be in the same muddle. See, we have reached a stage where we cannot even form a stable government.

What are the problematic areas in the Constitution which have to be reviewed?

The main problematic area is our electoral system.

In the electoral system, the party system has to play a very crucial role. Now there is absolutely no control over the political party system. Unless there is a healthy parliamentary party system, you can't function as a parliamentary democracy. Therefore, we have to regulate the formation and functioning of the parties, their collections, accounting, etc

More than that, the parties should prepare their members to become good legislators and good ministers. Now everybody goes to the Parliament without any training, without understanding the various problems. That is why today you find the debates in the Parliament are not at all informative. It is mere shouting. We very rarely see any informed speech on any subject. That is because they have not been prepared for that.

So, parties should not be merely election-running organisations. On the other hand, they should prepare their members to hold various offices of positions and responsibility, starting at the panchayat level, district level, State level and national level.

Taking into account the diversity of and the vastness of India, do you feel India should have the parliamentary

system? Or, should we switch over to the presidential system?

In my view, we have to continue with the parliamentary system. It is not necessary to switch over to a new system altogether, with which we are not conversant. Even during the British times, we had some sort of a democratic parliamentary system. I don't see any advantage in shifting to a new system and finding ourselves in an uncharted sea.

Of late, in India, the parliamentary system has produced hung parliaments and unsuccessful coalition governments.

That is why I am asking, what is the reason for that? It is mainly because of the existing electoral system and the multiplicity of parties. Today you have 18, 20 parties in the government and in the opposition, another 20 parties. This is not the way a parliamentary democracy should function.

What can be done to reduce the number of parties that are there in the fray?

For example, Germany has constitutionally reduced the number of parties. No party will be recognised unless they poll a certain percentage of votes in a national election. Here anybody can start a party and can get elected from a constituency where they have a caste advantage or a linguistic advantage. Then, even a one-member party man can also become a minister. So, this is not the way to function.

We should only have three or four, at the most five strong parties. Four is a good number. So, the coalitions will be of strong parties, not splinter groups like these.

We have had so many amendments in the Constitution. At present, should we rewrite the whole Constitution, or just make some more amendments?

No, it is not necessary to rewrite. There are certain areas which have to be reviewed and investigated. One area is the electoral system or the party system.

Then, the Centre-State relations. We should review not only the relations between the Centre and the State, but also between the Centre, State and Panchayat Raj institutions. The political and fiscal relationship should also be looked into.

Then, what should be looked into is the formation of the government itself. There should be some guidelines. Now there is absolutely no guidelines.

The president's powers also have to be reviewed. He can't just be a dummy.

What, according to you, are the drawbacks of the presidential system?

In a presidential system, there is a difficult balance between the legislature and the executive. The USA has now one party in power (1997) in the legislature, and the president is from another party. Naturally there are conflicts. So, even now, they have not evolved a proper arrangement where they do not have these conflicts.

Apart from that, personality conflicts also could arise. Whereas here, the ministry is within the Parliament and responsible to the Parliament. So, this is a better system, in my view.

This was discussed in detail in the early days, and we came to the conclusion that the parliamentary system is the best, particularly taking into account the vastness of the country with different linguistic, cultural, social and religious groups.

Therefore, one person certainly cannot represent the entire India. There is always the possibility of a person becoming a dictator as it happened in Italy and Germany in the past.

In a democracy like the United States, is not the presidential system functioning well?

They have two hundred years of experience! But we will be getting into the waters without knowing to swim. So, we will have to be struggling in a new system. In addition, we will have to see whether one person can represent the whole of India. Whereas now we have a Cabinet where ministers have powers to function.

In a presidential system, won't the people know who is going to lead the country? During the United Front experiment, nobody expected Deve Gowda or I K Gujral to become prime ministers of India. So, don't you think people should get a chance to elect the leader directly?

Now we have a president, in any event. So, we should see that the president should have some more powers. But it is the parliamentary system which is predominant all over the world. Only the USA follows the presidential system.

France has a mixture of parliamentary and presidential system. Germany has parliamentary system. Britain, of course traditionally follows the parliamentary system. All the colonies which got out of Britain also have parliamentary democracies.

Wherever the presidential system has come, like in Africa for example, presidents became dictators.

Can't we follow the German system where the government completes its term in spite of no-confidence motions?

We can also have that system. There you can't just pass a no-confidence motion. They have to name the successor. So, when one prime minister goes, automatically another prime minister steps in. We can try that too, since we have problems in that area. These are all things for consideration.

Do you think Indira Gandhi called for an election after the Emergency only because we had a parliamentary system? Would she have continued if we had a presidential system?[1]

She would have continued.

So, was that one of the advantages of the parliamentary system?

See, ultimately whether you have a parliamentary system or a presidential system, it depends upon the people who work as a result of the Constitution. As long as we don't have good persons who are capable of functioning as the president or the ministers, we will get into the same thing. Then some cinema actor or actress may become the President of India!

In many debates, people have commented that even after reviewing the Constitution, even after changing the system itself, we are going to have the same kind of people in the political system, and corruption, poverty and unemployment are also going to be there in the country....

It is in these areas that we have to concentrate. We have to put various clauses in the Constitution, taking into account the deficiencies we have now.

---

1 The Emergency in India was a 21-month period from 25 June 1975 until its withdrawal on 21 March 1977, when Prime Minister Indira Gandhi had a state of emergency declared across the country; the Ordinance was issued by President Fakhruddin Ali Ahmed under Article 352 of the Constitution because of the prevailing 'internal disturbance'. The order bestowed upon the PM the authority to rule by decree, allowing elections to be cancelled and civil liberties to be suspended.

We thought everybody would be like Mahatma Gandhi or Jawaharlal Nehru or Rajaji. But the quality has deteriorated gradually, and corruption has crept in. So, all these will have to be taken care of constitutionally, and we should know how to deal with those who indulge in corruption. The Lok Pal and the other things should form a part of the Constitution.

Why is it that people are electing even charge-sheeted, corrupt leaders? It is not that they are ignorant about the corrupt deeds of the politicians.

For that, we should have better educational standards in the public. Sixty per cent of the people are not educated in the sense that they get carried away by slogans or personalities. So, an awakening should come.

Do you feel something concrete will come out of all these debates?

It should come out, otherwise we will continue to be in the same state of affairs. This is the situation where a change is necessary. If you don't bring about a change for the better functioning of the administration, we will continue to be in the same muddle.

How will this muddle affect the country?

It may disintegrate just like Russia. We will not have a united India, because when people get disillusioned like this, they might think a separate state might be better. So, disintegration is likely to set in. We should not delay the review any further, I feel.

That is why a commission has to be appointed, and I hope they will make good recommendations to rectify the deficiencies and defects.

Both Pakistan and Bangladesh tried their hands in the presidential system but had to revert to a parliamentary system later on. What are the major deficiencies in the presidential system?

It leads to dictatorship. That is the major problem. In Pakistan, the army plays a crucial role. That is not the case here. Here, the judiciary is the main player.

Are you in favour of the kind of judicial activism that we see today, and the power that the judiciary wields now?

Yes. The judiciary should have the power to step in whenever a crisis occurs, like scams, corruption, misuse of power, etc

Another thing that we see is various Central governments misusing Article 356.[2]

That also requires reviewing, like under what circumstances it should be used. There are a number of areas like this we have to look into.

The president should have more power in the formation of the government. Now, even when you have a ministry which does not have a majority in the Parliament, the President is bound by the advice of the Cabinet which has no parliamentary backing.

So many amendments have been made in the Constitution in the last fifty years. Still….

After identifying the weaknesses in the present system, many more and necessary amendments can be made in the Constitution.

---

[2] Under Article 356 of the Constitution of India, if a State government is unable to function according to Constitutional provisions, the Union government can take direct control of the State machinery.

Chidambaram Subramaniam was awarded the highest civilian order, the Bharat Ratna in 1998, and he passed away at the age of 90 on 7 November, 2000.

There are many unanswered questions, like even after more than seven decades, are we a mature democracy? Are people who elect their representatives mature enough or educated enough to vote for the right candidate? Are voters still swayed by caste and religion?

Wish R Venkataraman and C Subramaniam were alive today to answer some of these questions. We miss the wisdom of learned people like them.

50 Years of Independence

Finally, the day arrived. 15 August 1997.

With I K Gujral as the new Prime Minister, India began its celebrations.

But there were only very few people who were alive to narrate the stories of freedom struggle to all those who were born in independent India.

I went back to **C Subramaniam** *who was present at the midnight of 15 August 1947 with all the other leaders as the Constituent Assembly was in session then.*

I was lucky that he was alive in 1997 to narrate the story to a whole generation of Indians.

WHAT are the images that come to your mind when you think of India's freedom struggle?

I had the privilege of being present at the midnight of 14 August 1947, when India was declared a free nation. It was a thrilling moment.

The Constituent Assembly was in session, and I was one of its members.

It was on that occasion that Pandit Jawaharlal Nehru gave his historic address, 'The Tryst with Destiny'. Once the meeting was over, Sucheta Kripalani began singing *Vande Mataram.*[1]

After Jawaharlal's speech, we took an oath for the freedom of India. The Indian national flag was hoisted, and the British flag was brought down.

And free India was born.

It was a historic occasion for all of us. Not only did India become free, but it also heralded the beginning of the end of the colonial era, like so many other countries who had gained their freedom. The most unfortunate part was that free India was born only after India, as a country, was partitioned.

Was partition inevitable? We have heard that it took place because of ego clashes.

Yes, in a sense, ego was involved. In this case, I refer to the ego of Jinnah. He was very persistent in his demand for the partition of the country. And the Muslim League backed him. As a result, partition became inevitable. Otherwise, it might have been averted. We cannot now envisage what would have happened if we had not taken the offer at that time and become free.

We have also heard that, earlier the Hindus and the Muslims lived peacefully in united India, and it was only because of the divide-and-rule policy of the British that trouble broke out. Was that the truth?

Yes, yes. As a matter of fact, we have lived together amicably for a long time. It was only during Aurangzeb's rule that there

---

1 Sucheta Kripalani was an Indian freedom fighter and politician who was the first woman chief minister of a State, Uttar Pradesh.

were clashes between the Hindus and the Muslims. Even then, there were not serious differences.

But the British wanted absolute control over India, and they adopted the divide-and-rule policy. Therefore, they encouraged the Muslims in demanding special rights. Ultimately that was how the demand for special rights developed into the demand for a separate Muslim state.

Will you tell us something about the struggle that people of your generation had to undergo in order to win freedom for India?

The freedom struggle started during the last century. But it became much more active when Mahatma Gandhi entered the freedom movement. He became the leader of the Indian National Congress. Till then, it was in the hands of the liberals who only passed resolutions.

(Bal Gangadhar) Tilak also gave a positive turn to the struggle, but it was Mahatma Gandhi who converted it into a mass movement. He had an unusual non-violent weapon called *satyagraha* with which he wanted to fight the British. It was a completely unique method of confrontation with the government. You suffer, but you don't hurt the enemy. The satyagraha movement took a much more positive turn with the salt satyagraha in 1930. The struggle became much more intensive during World War II.

I had the privilege of participating in the freedom movement in the year 1932 and I was imprisoned for ten months. We had moved on to the phase of individual satyagraha, in which I had also participated. Then, we had the Quit India Movement which began on 9 August 1942. I had participated in that movement as well.

Because of Mahatma Gandhi, there arose an awakening in the masses; he was so clear that he would not tolerate foreign rule and that we would have *swaraj* (self rule). As a result, the British found it difficult to rule India; it was no longer economically advantageous for them to do so with such a mass awakening. That was how India gained her freedom.

We have only read about the salt satyagraha and the Quit India Movement. Will you share some of your personal experiences with us?

The Quit India Movement began when the Second World War (1939-1945) was at its peak. India was involved in the war without her consent, since the British government took the decision that India would also fight on behalf of the Allied Forces (the Great Britain, the United States of America and the Soviet Union).

It was in protest against this decision that we decided that we would not help them, that we would stay away from the war. Of course, with the armed force available with the British, they were able to put down the movement to a certain extent. But they could not control the thoughts of the people. We insisted that we would not cooperate, and that we wanted our freedom.

The Quit India Movement was the awakening of the nation against participation in the Second War. We also said that, if we were given freedom, we were prepared to cooperate as a free country. But they were not willing to do so at that time.

Winston Churchill was the Prime Minister of England then. He was thinking in terms of the British Empire continuing for ever. But the empire collapsed in 1947. After that, all the other colonies also became free.

Can you tell us about your personal experiences during the freedom struggle?

It was 1932. I was fresh out of college. I had picketed a toddy shop auction and was arrested and put in prison. In prison, we had more physical freedom as compared to the other prisoners, since we were under group imprisonment. All of us were kept together in a huge compound where there were sheds. We used to be locked into our cells only at night. Otherwise, we were free to move about in the compound.

We had discussions, study groups, etc during the day. We used to discuss economics, politics and social matters depending upon the inclination of each individual. There were persons who were learning music from others. I was taking lessons in yoga because there was a yoga expert present there in prison. Multifarious activities took place there.

I was in an A-class cell. So, they gave us rations, and we had it cooked. We had other ordinary prisoners helping us cook. We were also given censored newspapers, where most of the political news would be blacked out.

When I was in the Vellore jail, many other leaders were also there. So, I had the opportunity to become acquainted with them for the first time.

What motivated you to join the Congress and the freedom struggle?

Patriotism. The spirit of patriotism was instilled in the minds of people by the leaders, particularly by Mahatma Gandhi.

What do you remember about the Salt Satyagraha (1930) and the impact it had in the South?

Salt is commonly used, and everyone requires it. Mahatma Gandhi started the salt satyagraha because he felt that a commodity like salt, which was used by everyone, should also be freely accessed by everyone. It was a symbolic gesture more than anything else.

In the South too, people started manufacturing salt on the beaches. Then the police lathi-charged those who were doing it, and many of our leaders were put in prison.

We have heard that the freedom movement was more active in Bengal and the northern part of India than in the South. Is it true?

No, I don't think you can put it that way. There were pockets that were much more active than Madras. It all depended upon the leadership. For example, Rajaji (C Rajagopalachari, the freedom fighter who was the last Governor General of India) replicated Gandhiji's march from his ashram to Dandi. This had a great impact in the minds of people.

During that period, did you go to the northern part of India and meet leaders like Mahatma Gandhi, Nehru, etc?

They used to visit the Madras State and other places. I met Mahatma Gandhi, Pandit Nehru and all the other leaders when they came over here.

Otherwise, was your activity centred here?

Yes, we worked in Madras (pre-1947 Madras presidency). We used to go there (northern India) for the Congress sessions. At that time, we could meet all the leaders. The Congress session was a big meeting where delegates came from all over India. Various resolutions were passed. It was a big gathering, it used to be like a jamboree. It was an opportunity for people from various parts of India to interact with each other.

What impressed you about Mahatma Gandhi when you first saw him in person?

Mahatma Gandhi was a unique personality. I don't think such personalities come into existence very often. More than anything else, it was his simplicity that would attract everyone. He only wore a loin cloth and a towel on his shoulders. But he was one of the most attractive personalities one had ever seen. A strict disciplinarian, he also expected others to observe discipline. He not only got the cooperation but also the devotion of thousands of people. People even worshipped him as an avatar.

When did you first meet Mahatma Gandhi?

I met him for the first time when he visited Coimbatore in 1934, when he undertook a journey to popularise the Harijan movement (to eradicate untouchability). He visited one of the educational institutions run by Sri Avinashilingam Chettiar, who was a great friend of mine.

I was in the Vidyalaya at that time. Gandhiji stayed there one night. And I was given the great privilege of serving him. He used to get up by four in the morning and start working immediately. It was a great experience to be with him.

From Coimbatore, he went to Coonoor and remained there for four or five days. I accompanied him there too.

We heard that Mahatma Gandhi wanted to dissolve the Congress after independence as he felt it had served its purpose?

Now they have effectively dissolved the Congress in their own way! But this was not the way in which Gandhiji wanted the Congress dissolved. Today, the Congress is slowly disintegrating because of its attitude and performance.

Were you very hopeful about the future of India when you won independence for the country?

Yes. It was our dream. After we attained freedom, we thought it was possible for us to remove all the obstacles in our progress and make our country strong. And, more than anything else, eradicate poverty and ignorance. But we have not achieved these goals as yet.

Do you feel the dreams you people had then, were shattered and today's reality is something else?

We thought we would be able to get over many of these difficulties in the next decade. But, even after 50 years, many of them continue to persist. We leave it to your generation to find a solution, to bring about a new solution.

We fought for freedom, and we got freedom. That was our contribution. Your contribution should be to oversee the creation of an independent India which fulfils our dreams.

The work should be continued generation after generation. You cannot, in one generation, expect to achieve everything. Ultimately, the future depends upon your generation. There is no use of blaming the previous generation.

You should ask yourself whether your generation is doing everything that is necessary for solving the many problems India confronts. It is now the responsibility of the younger generation to take up the thread and fulfil those dreams.

Is it not because the leaders of free India were more interested in themselves than in the welfare of the country that we are in a situation like this today?

There is always a certain amount of selfishness in every human being. Unfortunately, that has become the dominant motive today. Just like we fought for freedom without any selfish motive, the present generation should take it up and strive without selfishness for the removal of all these difficulties.

Are you hopeful about that?

I am sure that it will happen, and it should happen.

What exactly can the present generation or the ordinary people do?

You can do a lot. For example, the student community and the younger generation should refuse to get agitated over silly matters. They should not get carried away by politicians who only have the selfish motive of getting into power. They should not encourage such divisive forces.

People of your generation were very hopeful when you won freedom for India. But if you look at today's generation, you can sense only pessimism, cynicism and disappointment in them.

That is not the way to make progress. You should develop a sense of optimism. Every individual will have to see to it that he or she does not function in a way which promotes these divisive forces. That's the only way to progress.

I am sure it is only because there is so much of poverty and ignorance here that politicians exploit these things. Caste politics does not bring you food or a better life. Today, caste has no meaning or significance at all. In the past, caste represented a particular profession. Today, if you take a particular caste, you will find that they occupy almost all possible professions in society, from the highest to the lowest. In the same way, you see people from the so-called higher caste doing menial jobs. Which is why the caste distinction is bound to go.

Then why do we have reservation according to caste, instead of economic criteria?

This is where our short-sightedness comes in. Now, it looks as if the entire nation is declared as backward! And it is a fact! This of course, is my view.

But let us move forward with optimism. We cannot progress on the basis of caste or religion; we can only do so by using science and technology and, at the same time, retaining the basic human values of love, truth and harmony. Thankfully, our spiritual movement is very strong since it is not based on caste but on spiritual values.

Where will India be in another 50 years?

It depends on you. You should give me the answer because we won't be there.

> *C Subramaniam said, 'you should ask yourself whether your generation is doing everything that is necessary for solving the many problems India confronts. It is now the responsibility of the younger generation to take up the thread and fulfill those dreams.'*
>
> *Our generation has not done that. Will the new generation after us succeed?*

Announcing to the World

Five thirty in the morning. 15 AUGUST 1947.

*'India is a free country', announced a young **Poornam Viswanathan** on the external broadcast band of All India Radio to East Asia. While doing so, he became the first Indian to announce India's freedom to the outside world on radio.*

In 1997, he was alive to narrate and relive the experience for the country that had more citizens born after 1947!

The moment was still fresh in his mind; how he cleared his throat, controlled his emotions and made the announcement that India was a free country.

Another interesting coincidence was, while he worked for All India Radio, his brother worked for the Azad Hind Radio from Bangkok for the Indian National Army (INA).[1]

And it was his sister who announced on AIR the assassination of Mahatma Gandhi!

---

[1] Indian National Army or the Azad Hind Fauj was formed in 1942 by Rash Behari Bose and Captain-General Mohan Singh. Later, it was given a new life by Subhas Chandra Bose on 21 October, 1943.

WHEN did you know that you were to broadcast the news of India's independence?

I was a newsreader for All India Radio from 1945 onwards. You can call it a strange coincidence, rather a divine coincidence. When the duty list was announced, my name was scheduled for the night of August 14.

The broadcast began at 5.30 in the morning for the East Asian listeners and I was to read the first bulletin. It was my great fortune, I must say. How did I feel then? I felt elated.

Was there a lump in your throat then?

As a newsreader I was not supposed to feel any lump at all. I controlled my feelings till I finished the news bulletin. Later I cried with joy.

Cried?

Yes, I cried for two reasons. One, India was free; two, I was selected to read the news bulletin announcing India's independence.

Do you remember the first line?

'India is a free country', was the first sentence. This was followed by repeating Nehru's *Tryst with Destiny* speech.

Did you read Nehru's speech in English or Tamil?

In Tamil.

Was it difficult to translate Nehru's words?

No, no, not at all. For one thing, Nehru spoke in simple words. Gandhiji spoke in yet more simple words. We had been translating Gandhiji's prayer speeches regularly. I translated Nehru's speech with great joy and read it with even greater joy.

We have heard that Nehru had tears in his eyes when he made the speech. Those who assembled there had also

wept. Did you feel the same way when you read the speech in Tamil?

It is true that all those assembled wept with joy. When Nehru himself cried while speaking, what about an ordinary newsreader like me? But if I cried while reading the news, the lines would have smeared. So, I controlled my emotions. I still cherish the moment, a moment that I will never experience again.

Did the bulletin begin with, 'India is a free country', or the regular, 'This is All India Radio?'

Though it was such an important occasion and formal announcements were not required, the listeners needed to know where the broadcast was coming from. So, the 'All India Radio' announcement was necessary.

Was that also in Tamil?

In 1947, we only said, 'All India Radio'. Akashvani came only later. So, I read, 'All India Radio, *seythikal vasippathu Poornam Viswanathan....*

Where were you at midnight?

We were at home listening to Nehruji's speech over the radio. I knew I had to leave home at three in the morning for the five thirty bulletin. Normally, we used to go to Birla House, collect Gandhiji's previous day's speech at the prayer meeting and then proceed to the radio station. There it would be translated into various Indian languages and read. But on the day of Independence, Gandhiji was not present in Delhi. He was in Naokhali. So, we went straight to the All India Radio station.

I stayed in Lodhi colony then. During the day, I used to go to the Broadcasting house via Birla Road. I could have chosen some other route, but I went that way just for the pleasure of seeing Gandhiji. Even during winter, Gandhiji used to lie on a cot on the lawns of the Birla House. Whenever I passed the area, I could see him.

Did you ever go near him?

Yes, I did. I attended at least ten prayer meetings of Gandhiji.

What was the experience of those prayer meetings?

Gandhiji talked on very important subjects. He referred to many national issues, duties and obligations of all Indian citizens, how we should behave, etc One speech would not resemble any other. We could sense his sincerity in all the speeches.

You were very young then. How much did Gandhiji and his speeches influence your development?

When I first saw Gandhiji, I was pleasantly surprised to see that his skin was like the skin of a child. Soft and beautiful. There were no wrinkles on his skin or hands even though he was very old.

Did you ever touch his hands?

Oh, no. I only touched his feet. In those days, almost every educated young man wanted to join the freedom movement. If I had gone my way, I would have become a freedom fighter. Since I was a student, my elders did not let me join the movement. But my mind was always there.

When I look back, the only regret I have is that I did not join the movement in a big way. All of us had only one thought in our mind; our country and its freedom. The kind of devotion we had for our country cannot be explained.

Partition must have been a traumatic experience for all those who lived during that period. How was it for you?

It was a very painful experience for all of us. We saw people coming in their thousands from Pakistan, walking all the way with whatever belongings they had. Exodus from India was on a smaller scale. We saw riots, murder and looting. But I have also seen many Hindu and Sikh families give shelter to suffering Muslim families. It is true that till the previous day, they were friends but under the new situation, a Hindu was not expected to protect a Muslim or be the friend of a Muslim.

You spoke about the kind of devotion people of your generation had for the country in those days. Do you feel unhappy about the way things are moving now?

I am very, very unhappy about the present situation. This is not the India Nehruji or Gandhiji dreamt of. In fact, Netaji wanted India under a benevolent dictatorship for some time after Independence, and then open the doors to democracy. He believed that only then people would develop a strong national character. How true he was! Unfortunately, the devotion for the country was gradually eroded because nobody had any clear vision about an ideal India.

Do you think the politicians who came later have been irresponsible?

Of course, the politicians are showing us the wrong way. But our deterioration is so fast and total that I cannot think of Indians living a normal life in my life time.

Are you so dissatisfied?

I am very, very dissatisfied. The dreams of all our freedom fighters are shattered.

What were your dreams?

Would you believe, I thought India would be the most prosperous country in the world? Nehru and Gandhiji expected all of us to work for the country with greater devotion. Unfortunately, that did not happen at all.

What must have gone wrong?

Something went wrong with the thinking of the politicians and the common man. Maybe, because of illiteracy, people did not understand the value of freedom. They thought the government would cook food and bring it home for them every day. They didn't realise that in freedom lay an enormous wealth. Now there is corruption at all levels. I blame people to a large extent for the amount of corruption in our society. Why do they bribe to get things done quickly? Again and again, I am reminded of Netaji's advice.

Were you very much influenced by Netaji?

Not exactly. Netaji sounded a different call. He had a different dream about free India. He wanted a very powerful character for India. That did not happen at all. I admire the way he led the INA.

I must tell you something. My elder brother Somasundaram was in the Indian army then. His unit went to Singapore to fight in the Second World War. In Singapore, he was caught as a prisoner by the Japanese. But he and four others escaped from the prison, and my brother had to disguise himself by growing a beard.

After the War, he used to live in Penang, and had found it difficult to get a job. One day, he accidentally met an old friend, and the meeting changed his life altogether. At his friend's place, he heard over the radio that the *Azad Hind Radio* run by the INA needed people as broadcasters. He had a good voice, so he applied for the job and got it.

See the irony, when he was broadcasting for the INA through *Azad Hind Radio* from Bangkok, I was broadcasting from Delhi, indirectly for the British, through the All India Radio. But he recognised my voice and name, and that was how we got united.

I will tell you one more thing. I had nothing but hatred for the British. When I think of the way the British behaved, I cannot but hate them.

Were you in Delhi when Gandhiji was assassinated?

Yes, I was in Delhi. I did not have a radio then. But my house owner's radio was always on, and I could hear it properly from my room. That day also, their radio was on, and I could hear the Tamil programme for East Asian listeners.

It was my sister who worked for the external services of the AIR who made the announcement in the middle of the music programme. I heard her voice saying that Gandhiji had been shot by an Indian. Immediately, I took my bicycle and rushed to the Birla House. I saw Nehru standing near the gate, and there were hundreds and hundreds of people outside trying to rush inside. Nehru appealed to the people to remain calm. He said it was a Hindu who shot Gandhiji so that there wouldn't be any anti-Muslim feeling among people.

You recently said that in those days you saluted a Gandhi cap whenever you saw one. What do you feel when you see a Gandhi cap now?

We had such respect and admiration for freedom fighters then! Every freedom fighter, however small or big, had good intentions. He was idealistic and unselfish.

I don't have any respect for today's politicians. I feel those politicians (with Gandhi caps) must be kept out of Indian politics completely. See, I have lived in those days, I have seen the freedom fighters but now I feel disillusioned and pained.

As a person who has witnessed the freedom struggle, as a person who is pained to see today's India, do you have any message for the youngsters?

We attained freedom through non-violence. In those days, the minds of the Indians were receptive to good messages. It should come again; at least in the minds of the generation that is growing up. The youngsters must think about the welfare of the country at heart. Even if they lead a normal life and have clear thinking, the result will be fantastic.

Are you optimistic about that?

That's a very delicate question. I am not very optimistic now. But we do not know what will happen tomorrow, and the day after. I know that one has to be optimistic even in the worst of times, so I would say that I am hopeful.

I would like to see a totally selfless leader leading the country once again towards an ideal state. Let us all wait for that day!

‖ *Poornam Viswanathan passed away on 1 October 2008, at the age of 87.*

The Inimitable Cho

There was nobody like **Cho Ramaswamy** *in India, a truly multifaceted personality; the editor of the Tamil political magazine* Thuglaq, *a political analyst, satirist and a former theatre and film personality.*

Unique, funny, eccentric and idiosyncratic; that is the only way I can describe him.

It was in 1996 that I first interviewed him. I was new to Chennai, Tamil Nadu politics and Cho Ramaswamy.

At that time, I had no idea that I would be talking to him many, many more times in the coming years. I went on to interview him quite regularly, rather too regularly for his liking.

The moment something happened nationally or domestically, I sought his opinion.

As the frequency increased, the moment I entered his room, he would look up and say with a serious expression on his face, 'I think I should stop editing Thuglaq *and talk to you all the time. Do you want me to do that?'*

I would reply with the same serious expression, 'No Sir, your loyal readers would murder me if I were to do that. I promise not to disturb you in the near future.'

Yet I did disturb him, again and again. His grouse was that unlike the television channels who only sought 'bytes', I made him talk for at least half an hour, and sometimes even an hour.
'You are an unkind journalist. I will never talk to you again', he would threaten me after each interview. But he never refused my requests.
Whether it was a Sunday or a Monday or a Friday, Cho would be in his office from the morning. He rarely refused to meet me in the midst of editing or writing for Thuglaq. Of course, only after reprimanding me for disrupting his work.
I also had to face questions like, 'Shobha, why don't you find somebody else to interview? Why torture me all the time?'
But I would play along. 'Is there anyone else quite like you in Chennai, Sir?'
Yes, nobody analysed Indian politics like Cho and nobody ever will. Here, Cho was not talking about the freedom struggle but about free India, a rather cynical point of view, in typical Cho style!

HOW old were you when India won freedom? What do you remember about the day?

Thirteen years. It was then that I had been given a box camera by my father. I took some photographs of the function held in my school. I remember the scene very well. Apart from that, I don't remember anything. In those days, nobody took photographs in school. So, my photographs became very popular, and I became quite important. Independence made me important!

Do you feel the Mahatma was forgotten soon after Independence? Now he is remembered only a couple of times a year, reduced to a paragraph or a photograph.

What else can a country do to persons of great eminence? What is Abraham Lincoln to America now? What is Mao Zedong to China now? Can a country follow the ideals of the Mahatma all the time? I doubt whether the Mahatma himself followed his ideals all the time, in all matters. He had to deviate now and then. In practical politics and administration, the Mahatma's ideals can be treated as a text, as a philosophy, not as law.

A philosophy which is to be followed or....

A philosophy which is to be kept in mind and followed whenever possible (laughs). Like the dictates of *dharma!*

As a political analyst and not as a patriot, how do you assess Gandhi's contributions to the country?

If it was not for Gandhi, there could not have been a democratic India. He was a man who did not speak the languages of the people of many of the States but commanded total and unquestioning faith of all of them. He demanded struggle and sacrifice from them, while promising nothing, and they obeyed. This is unimaginable. I have great admiration for him.

What would have happened if he had lived a little longer?

His advice would have embarrassed the government. It would have succeeded in doing only that. Gandhi could not expect everyone to be a Gandhi, but he did expect. In the administration of the country, it is just not possible to adopt Gandhian ideals in everything. You can as well ask a butcher to practice *ahimsa* in his profession.

Instead of Nehru, had Patel been made prime minister, how would it have been different for India?

There would have been greater discipline. After Independence, we lost sight of our duties and started remembering only our rights. With the Sardar at the helm of affairs, we would have been constantly reminded of our duties, and it would have given character to the nation.

The Mahatma felt the Congress should have been disbanded after Independence. Do you agree?

I disagree with what Gandhi said. Had the Congress been disbanded after Independence, there would have been at least three parties, one led by Nehru, one led by Patel and another led by Kripalani, Lohia and others. What is happening today might have started then itself. It would have been a difficult situation to manage soon after Independence. The nation would not have been able to put up with chaotic politics so soon after becoming free.

Now it is different. We have been made immune to chaos in politics, because we have been administered with it, in small doses, through the years.

Do you think dynastic rule did a lot more damage to the country than anything else, especially the reign of Indira Gandhi and Rajiv Gandhi?

As far as Mrs Gandhi was concerned, she did a lot of damage, definitely to the polity of the country. In fact, it was she who weakened the Congress. She could get votes with sheer charisma. But she was not prepared to tolerate leaders of stature in any State.

That is why she saw to it that Kamaraj in Tamil Nadu, Nijalingappa in Karnataka, Sanjeeva Reddy in Andhra Pradesh, S K Patil in Maharashtra, every one of them was relegated (to political insignificance), and the Congress lost many stalwarts because of that. And every State unit became totally subservient to the Centre.

The Congress leader of every State was seen as a peon of the Centre, whereas the leader of the local regional party was seen as a master. He shone brilliantly against the Congress leader. That is why regional parties started flourishing in this country. That was a disservice done by Mrs Gandhi.

She allowed free rein to the corrupt. But she was able to provide a determined leadership to the country. In Punjab, it is my belief that she encouraged Bhindranwale in the initial stages to embarrass the Janata Party. That is another disservice to the nation. As far as the Sri Lankan problem is concerned, even today we have remnants of the problem created by Mrs Gandhi. She started funding and training the Tigers.

Due to her charisma, she was acceptable to all sections of society, all parts of the country. Unfortunately, her style was followed by her successors who did not have charisma and mass appeal, and that led to the decline of the Congress.

During his reign, Rajiv was not very brilliant. When he was out of power, he was a changed man. If he had not been killed and had come back to power, I think he would have had a good stint as the prime minister. It would have been good if he had become prime minister instead of Narasimha Rao. But the Tigers thought otherwise.

Do you agree with the view that at least one good thing Rao did was that he put an end to dynastic rule? Indians had started believing that only someone from the Nehru family could rule them.

What is the big deal in that? Rao's government became totally corrupt.

Congressmen once again are going back to the Nehru family. They are after Sonia Gandhi, now that Rao is out. Do you think they feel that only she can lead the Congress?

They think the Congress can become united again only under Sonia Gandhi. I don't think they have the confidence that she would get a mandate from the people. But it is their conviction that she would get a mandate from Congressmen. I think they would like to have Sonia Gandhi to lead the Congress and allow somebody else to become the prime minister.

Will anything of that sort happen?

She seems to be very hesitant about entering direct politics.

Do you think Indians will listen to and worship only someone from the Nehru family?

Indians have been worshipping a Laloo Prasad Yadav, a Karunanidhi, an N T Rama Rao, an MGR, a Charan Singh, a Jayalalitha and a Devi Lal. Indira Gandhi was never worshipped like that. Why do you say that they always worship a Nehru or a Gandhi? An Andhra Pradesh was able to vote against Mrs Gandhi and Rajiv Gandhi. A West Bengal has been consistently voting against them. A Kerala has been doing it now and then. So, how do you say that Indians worship only that family?

The fact is that because of the Nehru legacy, because of the fact that we have not had a taller leader after him who could outshine him in his appeal to the people, there is a certain attachment to the family. But I don't say that Indians will not accept a leader who is not from the Nehru family. I don't accept the theory.

Do you agree with the view that a country called India was born only because of the British, and if it were not for them, we would have remained as small princely States?

Yes, it would have been true administratively and politically. But culturally we were one nation even before the British came to India.

The *Mahabharata* speaks of the participation of the Chola and the Pandya kings, and there is a Chera king who is reputed to have fed both the armies (Pandava and Kaurava armies). So, I don't think it was an act of kindness on the part of the British to have brought us together. We were one nation, but not administratively.

We speak different languages.

Yes, we speak different languages, but we celebrate the same festivals. We speak different languages, but we utter the same prayers. We speak different languages but have the same values.

We have problems in many parts of India – the North-East, Punjab, Kashmir. People are agitating for a separate Gorkhaland, Uttarakhand, Vidarbha, etc In spite of all this, do you think India will remain together?

India will remain one only if a national leadership of substance emerges. That is what is wanting. We don't have a real national leadership. There must be individuals in every party who would appeal to all parts of the country. We now have only regional leaders.

A Karunanidhi will appeal to the Tamils. A Chandrababu Naidu or Lakshmi Sivaparvati may appeal to the Telugus. A Bangarappa, to the Karnataka people. A Deve Gowda still is interested only in Karnataka. Laloo Prasad's territory is limited to Bihar. There is no national leadership.

A Kamaraj, though he couldn't speak Hindi or was not fluent in English, could vibe well with people of all States. A Rajaji from Tamil Nadu could do it too.

Why is it that today's leaders restrict themselves to a particular region?

It is the weakness of the leader of today that is posing the danger because he cannot operate in a wider field as he knows he is not equipped for that. Because of his incapacity, he wants to wield power in a small territory and make that as sovereign as possible. That is why people demand separate States.

A Karunanidhi cannot appeal to all of India, so he wants a separate Tamil Nadu, if possible. He won't air it now, but he would love *to do* it. Then he would be the monarch of all that he surveyed.

Does that mean we don't have many leaders who have vision and a national outlook?

Yes, it is a fact. But it is happening all over the country. Only during big crises does leadership of vision emerge. Has France got a de Gaulle now? Can even Mitterrand be compared with de Gaulle? Can Clinton be compared with Roosevelt? Can John Major be compared with Churchill?

In every country, it is only during huge, big crises that real leadership emerges. Then people forget all other issues, all other ideological differences and look towards the personality, to the strength and moral calibre of one man and place faith in him totally.

Does that mean we are doomed to have leaders of this stature for a long time to come?

Yes, yes, for a long time. Till a crisis strikes us. So, pray for a crisis! We can take solace in the fact that other countries are also facing a similar dearth of leadership. You see when the power goes off in your house, you are upset, but when you look through the window and see that your neighbour also does not have power, you are satisfied. Like that, let's be happy in the fact that others also do not have great leaders.

What, according to you, are the qualities that should be there in a leader – charisma, honesty or vision?

The ability to command the faith of large numbers of people. Leaders of different styles have functioned. Kamaraj was authoritative, he couldn't tolerate dissent for a long time. Nehru was also, I think, similarly disposed. Still, they were able to carry people with them. That is because people had faith in them. There must be some transparency in the leader.

Do you admire any leader in present day India?

Among the leaders that we have, I have great admiration for Advani and Chandra Shekhar. Both of them are great patriots and have the interests of the people at heart. They have a very clear perception of the problems we have. Their vision is not confined to any particular region of India.

Even Advani?

Yes, yes. No doubt about it. I have had several discussions with them, I have moved with them. I think, I understand them and my opinion is that these are two leaders among the lot we have now whom one would point out as leaders inspiring some confidence in people.

Do you see them ruling the country?

Advani has chances. But (for) Chandra Shekhar to emerge, the Congress must have vision. The Congress is a party without a leader, and Chandra Shekhar is a leader without a party. They can complement each other. If the Congress has vision, it should invite Chandra Shekhar. He is capable of rejuvenating the Congress.

Earlier, we had charismatic leaders like Gandhi, Nehru, Patel, Indira Gandhi and even Rajiv Gandhi. Why is it that we do not have a charismatic leader now?

I don't think charisma can be easily defined. I don't think any nation can hope to have charismatic leadership all the time. As I said, it is only during crises that people start placing immense faith in a leader, and only then does he become charismatic.

When people start questioning, it is rather difficult for a leader to enjoy charisma. When people start questioning, he stops to be big. It is happening the world over. People have become more aware, and there is no implicit acceptance of leadership.

Is it because they don't have any faith in their leaders?

It is because they have more information. During the times of the kings, people had no information. Now we are aware of our rights, and we think it is dangerous to allow the leadership to have unquestioned authority. That is our general attitude. This is not the climate in which charismatic leadership can emerge.

You named Advani and Chandra Shekhar as two leaders with vision. Does that mean, in a situation where the BJP does not come to power, and Chandra Shekhar is not invited by the Congress, we will only have leaders who cannot think beyond their territory?

We were talking about leaders who are possible candidates for the prime ministership. After all, he is only the head of an executive.

But we look at him as the leader of the nation. He keeps India one.

No prime minister all by himself can hold India together, however powerful he may be. It is the minds of the people which keeps India together. If tomorrow Karunanidhi, in spite of all his popularity, seriously advocates separatism, people will reject him.

The Dravidian movement started some thirty years ago, but they have not been able to sell the idea of division of the country to the people of Tamil Nadu. What does it show? People want this country to remain together.

Tamil Nadu is considered to be a marginal problem State in this matter. Not like Punjab or Kashmir, but people still think this State has to be watched. But the people of this State have refused to buy that idea from the DMK, which they vote to power. I tell you, they (the Dravidian parties) have been in power all the time, still they have not been able to sell the idea because the people are not for it. That is what ensures the integrity of the country, not the leadership at the Centre.

Recently at a meeting, an American asked me, 'After all, Russia has split into several countries. It has happened in Yugoslavia. Why not in India?' He said, 'even a husband and wife have got a right to separate'. I said it will not happen in India because here in India the States are brothers and there is no divorce between brothers. The relationship is not an artificially created one, like that of a husband and a wife. It is a creation of nature like between brothers. We are bound to be together.

There is much talk about autonomy for Kashmir these days. If it happens, what would be the repercussions for the other parts of the country?

I am against it. I am supposed to be highly reactionary in my thinking on certain matters. Kashmir is one example of that. If there is a demand for separatism in Kashmir, it has to be put down mercilessly, by use of force. As far as more autonomy is concerned, if Kashmir is granted that, then the other States also will start claiming it. Some of the North-Eastern States already claim that. And it may spread to States like Tamil Nadu also. Not because people want it, but because the political leadership demands it.

What will happen if regional leaders start demanding autonomy for their provinces?

I think the BJP will gain ground, if that happens. They will be the beneficiary ultimately, as they will emerge as the uncompromising champions of national integrity in such a situation.

The way things are going, do you think we will have a hung Parliament in the future too?

I think it is going to be the case for some more time. The Congress must get united. The Janata Dal must evaporate because it is a political anomaly and anachronism. It has no business to exist. They can merge with the Congress.

The Congress and the BJP must be the two parties contending for power. If that comes about, we can avoid a hung Parliament. I don't see it happening in the next five years or so. So, the next election also may produce a hung Parliament.

How do you assess the United Front government?

The Prime Minister's main job seems to be to go, meet and placate all and sundry so that his chair is intact. As far as the United Front is concerned, they don't agree with each other on many issues. Just for the sake of power, they are trying to make certain compromises and carry on. The one danger inbuilt in the situation is that foreign investors may hesitate because of the uncertainty. It will be in a confused state of affairs for some more time.

Do you think the BJP will be a major force in India?

I think so. I think it is destined to be one of the major political parties. It already is.

But even though the BJP emerged as the single largest party in the recent elections, it did not have adequate numbers to rule. Take UP, for instance.

It will take some more time for them to obtain a majority by themselves. Take the Congress, it did not attain a majority even last time. When Narasimha Rao became the prime minister, they were a minority government.

Why is it that all the other political parties see the BJP as a threat to the nation? They say the BJP is communal in outlook. At the same time, they ally with casteist parties.

The other parties are casteist. As far as communalism is concerned, the BJP is not out to harm the Muslims. In my opinion, that is not the plan or idea of the party at all. The other parties perceive the BJP as a common threat because if the other votes get split, in many northern States and probably in Karnataka, the BJP will be the largest vote getter. Not only the largest single party.

I would personally like the BJP to abandon this temple politics. It is not a very encouraging sight to see sadhus with huge big beards, holding tridents in their hands and asking you to vote for a particular party. It is not canvassing, it is threatening. The BJP should get rid of this association.

It might have helped them at a particular moment, when V P Singh was trying to divide the BJP vote by promoting the Mandal concept. He succeeded to an extent, but it recoiled on him later.

At that particular time, the temple politics might have helped them, but it is high time they give it up. And I think the BJP leadership is aware of it, particularly Advani.

Why are the so-called intellectuals and media anti-BJP?

Everyone is very much concerned about a secular image without understanding the concept of secularism. No editor would like to be called communal. The moment you support the BJP, you are branded communal.

Secularism in India is defined as an anti-BJP stance. If you are anti-BJP, you are secular. You may hobnob with the Muslim League, still you are secular because you are opposed to the BJP.

Was V P Singh's Mandal period one of the worst times for India?

V P Singh's period was an aberration. I have always been opposed to that man. So, you are at liberty to consider my views as prejudiced. From the moment he stepped out of the Congress and even before that, I was a critic of V P Singh and his politics. I had warned Chandra Shekhar, I had warned Hegde, I had warned all my friends in the Janata Party. Beware of V P Singh, beware of V P Singh.

But they thought he just wanted the Opposition to come together and replace the Congress at the Centre, and that he did not want to become prime minister. But I said, that was his game; becoming the prime minister, making others propose him and then accepting the chair with great reluctance.

I was the only journalist who wrote that Devi Lal, who betrayed Chandra Shekhar to make V P Singh prime minister, would betray V P Singh to make Chandra Shekhar the prime minister. It happened ultimately.

V P Singh serving as a minister in the Rajiv Gandhi Cabinet, spied on him by employing an outside agency. A Cabinet minister who can do this to his own prime minister must be the worst betrayer imaginable. From the moment he did it, I saw the man as dangerous. He was not a votary for reservation for the backward classes before he brought about the revival of the Mandal report.

The Mandal Commission was appointed during the Janata Party period. But the report was filed after the Janata Party government fell. When the BJP started disagreeing with him seriously, V P Singh thought that he should contain the BJP by taking away the backward classes from them. That was why he brought about the implementation of the Mandal proposals.

Don't you think he did a lot of damage to India by doing that? These days even school children talk about forward classes and backward classes.

Definitely. Yes, nowadays, in colleges, schools and everywhere caste is being talked about.

Is it not a dangerous trend?

One should blame V P Singh for this, nobody else. For his own chair, he divided Hindu society irreparably.

What is the biggest threat India faces now? Lack of morality, especially political morality, or the gap between the haves and have nots?

The greatest threat is the lack of attention to the rural areas. More than the gap between the haves and have nots, more than all the other differences, the difference between urban areas and rural areas is getting more and more accentuated. This will result in the migration of rural people to urban areas. This will pose problems to both the rural and urban areas. Not only that, it will also lead to unrest.

Development activities should be concentrated on the rural areas. I wouldn't be sorry if the government holds up for a while the development of urban areas and concentrates on rural areas.

Another *threat* is lack of good education to the deprived classes. Now they are being sent to corporation and panchayat schools. There cannot be worse places for learning. So many undesirable activities take place there. The deprived classes are not going to be benefitted by reservation. If you pamper them with reservation, it will only weaken them further. What should be done is, they must be provided with the best possible education, the kind of education that is provided to the elite.

You cannot expect them to be good at learning if they are asked to live in the slums. The moment they go back to their homes, they are going to experience things which are totally non-conducive to education, like gambling, petty thieving, rowdism etc So, they must be provided residential schools. This must be done, whatever be the financial implications.

Industrial houses will definitely come forward to help. Industrial houses which are willing to participate in this exercise should be given some concessions. If this is done, in 15 years, they will be on an equal footing with the privileged classes. And the necessity for reservations will go.

Even after 50 years of Independence, why are we not able to provide at least one square meal to thousands of people in our country?

The number one reason is population.

Even though overpopulation is the biggest problem that we have now, why is it that no political party is taking any active interest in it?

Most political parties get their votes from the underprivileged. The privileged classes do not go and vote at all. They are so privileged that they couldn't care less about what is happening to the country. The underprivileged are concerned, so they go and vote. And they abhor family planning. How could political parties dare advise them on smaller families?

Were you at any time influenced by Communism?

I have always been against Communism. In fact, one of the first series of articles which I wrote in *Thuglaq* twenty six years ago was titled, 'Moscow - our capital', taking to task the then Indira Gandhi government for being subservient to Moscow.

I have been against Communism because it is against the nature of man. A talented man cannot be asked to be satisfied with what a man totally devoid of talent is able to obtain from life. Communism makes machines of men.

But what about social equality that is advocated by Communism?

There is no equality in nature. You cannot go against it. Have the Communists themselves been able to bring about that kind of equality in society? They have provided themselves and members of the Communist Party with all comforts in Russia and in China. How then can you say that they have brought about equality?

Capitalism has always been projected as anti-society and anti-poor because it widens the gap between the members of society.

It is not anti-poor. When Capitalism thrives, the poor gets to be employed usefully and profitably.

Why are our intellectuals against Capitalism?

It is the other way around. Those who are against Capitalism are supposed to be intellectuals. Those who advocate Capitalism are supposed to be reactionaries and not intellectuals. A reactionary cannot be anything but an intellectual.

Is the path paved by Dr Manmohan Singh (as the finance minister in the Narasimha Rao government) through economic liberalisation the right one?

Definitely. It should have been done much earlier. But we must be careful about what areas we let foreign investment in.

Do you think Dr Singh achieved something for the country through his economic policies?

No doubt about it. He is the man who put us on the right track. Of course, international conditions helped him.

There is considerable criticism about the Coke culture and Kentucky Chicken culture invading India.

What is this Coke culture and Pepsi culture? Because a multinational is permitted to open a shop to sell chicken, does that mean it is Kentucky Chicken culture? Then would you call our culture, idli culture? Do we have chapati culture? Or do you want Murgi culture? By labelling something like this, you will not win an argument.

If you can have a Limca culture, you can have a Coca-Cola culture. If you can have a chapati culture, you can have a Kentucky Chicken culture too.

Do you think whatever Dr Manmohan Singh achieved through his economic policies is lost because of the new government?

I'll tell you one thing. Manmohan Singh had an advantage. No doubt he is a brilliant and honest man. He was not blocked on all sides while he was operating. He had an almost free hand whereas Chidambaram has to satisfy the Communists, he has to satisfy the Janata Dal, he has to satisfy the ill-informed criticism of V P Singh. So, he is pulled on all sides. He is answerable to all and sundry. That is his problem. In spite of it, he is operating.

Does that mean the economy is going to suffer?

It is suffering because of this government. Not because of Chidambaram, but because of this government. In spite of Chidambaram.

When did corruption originate in India?

It was systematised and institutionalised in Tamil Nadu during Karunanidhi's regime and institutionalised all over the country during Mrs Gandhi's time.

But it existed much, much before that. Kautilya's *Arthasastra* provides punishment for corrupt officials. Not only corrupt officials, but for judges who accept bribes. It would not have got mentioned in *Arthasastra,* if corruption had not existed then.

Is it part of human nature to be corrupt?

Yes, it is so. But a successful society will be able to contain it in such a way that it does not reach dangerous limits as it reached in Tamil Nadu during Jayalalitha's days.

Why is it that we, in India have started accepting corruption as a part of our lives?

That is dangerous for society. Mrs Gandhi was right when she said that it is a worldwide phenomenon. But in other countries, corrupt politicians are punished. In India it was not happening. Mrs Gandhi did not mention that crucial difference. But now they are made answerable.

'I think the BJP will gain ground... I think it is destined to be one of the major political parties.' What Cho said in 1997 has turned out to be true!

Legendary Cartoonist Abu Abraham

'G*in or beer?*'

That was the first question well known cartoonist **Abu Abraham** *asked me before we sat down to do the interview. When I said I would prefer a cup of tea, he laughed aloud. 'What? Tea at noon?' Over a cup of tea (for me) and gin (for the cartoonist), we spoke, in his magnificent abode designed by the celebrated architect Laurie Baker.*

Just like his long career that began as a reporter for The Bombay Chronicle *in 1946, and then the switch over to cartoons, our chat was also very long touching on a variety of subjects from the environment to Vietnam to Cuba! But then, you rarely meet someone who has had so much experience in life.*

It was one of the most illuminating conversations I have had in my career.

YOU left Kerala when you were 20. Why did you decide to come back after so many years?

Nostalgia, what else? I wanted to spend the rest of my life here. It proved to be a wise decision. Had I continued in Delhi,

I might have been dead by now. The city is so polluted, the intellectual life even more so.

And Trivandrum?

Here I get a lot of affection and love. The sea and all these things, I missed in Delhi.

And sea food too, I am sure! Especially sardines, right?

Yes, that's right. Then of course, I wanted to change the pace, I wanted to slow down a little bit. So, I decided to work from home.

But you are away from the place of all the political action.

In some ways, it is an advantage because you can analyse it more objectively from a distance. But I go to Delhi once or twice a year.

Do you feel satisfied with the intellectual interactions here in Trivandrum?

I don't get much interaction. But I can find people if I want to consult.... In Delhi, it is only an illusion that you can have intellectual interaction. That is one place where gossip is very unreliable.

The Kerala you left behind years ago must have been a very different one from today's Kerala. Over the years, people say, it has changed for the worse. What do think?

How can anybody say it has changed for the worse? Half the students in my primary school came without anything above their waist. Some of them used to walk 3 to 5 miles to get to school. They didn't have umbrellas. They would come holding banana leaves over their heads, come totally drenched. That sort of things do not happen now.

Then why is it that the cultural personalities and environmentalists always cry hoarse that Kerala is going from bad to worse, especially its environment?

Rubbish. Kerala is four times as green now than in my school days. Everybody is growing trees here. What do these environmentalists want? They stop dams, they do not want any power or atomic energy plants.... Nothing! They talk only about trees. No trees should be cut, so no new roads, no canals, no nothing!

Sugathakumari (the well-known Malayalam poet) tells me there should be no more dams. But what I say is, there should be a thousand more of dams and canals in the next ten years. *That* is the way to a green State. These people live in a kind of seclusion. When you go to Delhi by train, you realise how much arid land there is which can be converted. If water is brought there, you can grow trees and it can be cultivated.

It has become a very negative movement, this environmentalism. Their favourite sentence is, we don't want consumerism. Some law students came here, and they wanted me to sign some statement against atomic energy. I said I am for atomic energy. But I am against atomic bombs. Shouldn't mix up the two, I told them. Then they said, we are against consumerism. I asked what is consumerism? When eighty per cent of the people in this country don't have a decent standard of living, they are talking about consumerism!

Here there is no energy, no power, no factories, nothing.... People are anti-science and anti-technology. Even this Sastra Sahitya Prishad, which is doing very good work educating people, has joined this bandwagon.

In such a situation, what do you see for the State in the next few years?

I don't know. These people have no sympathy for science or technology. I don't think any of them studied science. They all took economics, history or law.

People like Maneka Gandhi are fanatics; they are worse than Khomeini. She is propagating vegetarianism. She has no business to do that. Let her put all your cows in the *gaushalas*! Let the cows take over! This nonsense has been going on for some time. The government has to be firm. Now anybody can go to court and stop anything. They can stop prawn cultivation, they can stop anything now. But I am sure soon there will be a reaction to that.

I think you love nature and animals a lot. You have ducks, dogs, fish and parrots here....

I have two goats too. Maneka Gandhi curses goats. According to her, one goat can create thousands of acres of desert. That's all a myth. Goats survive in deserts on thorns and other things. So, when you see a herd of goats grazing in an arid area, you think the goats created it. That's like saying camels created the Sahara desert!

All these NGOs get a lot of money from abroad. I am really suspicious about their activities. I get these people coming from London or France who are on to this racket of environmentalism. I took a person from London to Vellanad, and on the way I showed him the Karamana dam and told him we get water from this dam. He immediately asked, 'do you think it is a good thing?' You just can't argue with them. They do not want us to progress. They want to create a global village where white men will be the landlords and the browns and blacks their peasants.

Atomic energy is good for all white countries; it is good for France, England, America, Israel, but it is not good for us! This is the new colonialism!

Shall we go back to your school days? I have read that you started caricaturing your teachers when you were in school. Did they ever see those drawings?

No. I didn't show them. (Laughs). Once I did one on a black board but they didn't know who had drawn it. So, I went scot-free!

In those days, did you ever think of becoming a cartoonist?

I was totally absorbed in drawing. But I didn't know how to become a professional cartoonist. Besides, I had all the discouragement I needed from my parents and elders (laughs).

Was that why you decided to be a journalist?

I had to find a job. So, when I went to Bombay, I tried to get into a newspaper. But I had no idea how a paper functioned, how reporting was done. I used to think reporters were sent out in the morning to wander around and find news! Everything was so baffling to me initially. I was an apprentice for six months till I learnt where to find news and how to write it.

How did you find reporting? More interesting than cartoons?

I don't know. Because, during my spare time I did cartoons for *The Bombay Chronicle.*

You joined the *Shankar's Weekly* as a cartoonist later on. How did you get the job?

Shankar (himself a cartoonist) saw some of my work in *The Bombay Chronicle* and wrote to me. I was with a paper called *Bharat* started by Vallabhbhai Patel and his son. By the end of 1951, I joined *Shankar's Weekly.*

Why did you leave for England? And you stayed for a long time there, nearly 13 years.

I thought I was getting a bit stuck with *Shankar's Weekly.* Actually, I went on a visit to England just to get the feel of London. I wanted to see Paris also. In fact, I wanted to go to Paris more because I knew French and was interested in their culture.

Was it a personal visit?

Yes. I organised some money. In those days, a passage by sea cost only 53 pounds, just Rs 650! You got four meals a day for 20 days.

Why did you decide to stay back? Were you so attracted to London?

I thought my money would last for about three months. But it ran out in three weeks! Fortunately, I found I could sell my work. In the first week, I sold five cartoons, four to a tabloid called *The Sketch.* The one they rejected went into *Punch.* In those days, one could live on five pounds a week.

I continued as a freelancer for two-and-a-half years. There was a magazine called *The Eastern World* for which I used to do a bit of writing and also draw cartoons. But that was only once a month.

Then I met Michael Foot (later the Labour Party leader) who was editing *The Tribune* and showed him my work. He said, 'start on Monday'. I did two cartoons in *The Tribune.*

In the beginning of the third week, I got a letter from the *The Observer* editor saying he was interested in my work, so would I meet him? Till then, *The Observer* had never had a regular political cartoonist in its whole history of 150 years.

What about the other newspapers? Did they have regular cartoonists?

They had. *The Observer* was a very conservative paper. The editor told me he was looking for a cartoonist for three years. He said, 'Your drawings are attractive, you are not vicious, you are gentle, etc'

He didn't even know where I came from when he wrote to me! I used to sign 'Abraham'. He thought I was a central European emigrant, a Jew. That was in 1956, the time the Suez operations took place. He said it wouldn't be a good idea if I signed my cartoons 'Abraham' because I would be misunderstood. People would assume I was Jewish.

He offered me the job in 15 minutes. He asked me to sign a contract. So, I stopped working with *The Tribune.* I was with *The Observer* for ten years.

In those days, was it very difficult for an Indian to establish himself in England?

Yes. It was sheer hard work that saw me through. It was a great strain to produce something *every* Friday. Sometimes, on Friday morning, when you have finally come up with an idea, you find somebody has already done it!

And you had to maintain a certain standard. The editor didn't mind if my opinions differed from his, but he wanted a certain quality. That helped me a lot.

That was why when I joined *The Guardian* later, I could draw much faster. I had to, as it was a daily paper.

Do you consider yourself lucky?

Lucky? Hmm... but I achieved the standard I did through sheer hard work.

Does that mean you can establish yourself anywhere in the world if you are talented and hard working?

Yes. You asked me whether I was lucky. I was lucky in the sense that throughout my career, I didn't have to apply for a job except the first time. All the others were offered to me.

The main thing about cartooning is that it is not the quantity that matters, but the quality of your ideas. You can't think up something and make news and events. You can have your opinions, but it should be based on reality.

Can a cartoonist be impartial?

There is nothing like impartiality in cartoons. I was never impartial. I always expressed a point of view. There was a lot of objection from people, even my own colleagues. It was the time of decolonisation in Africa and Asia. And then there was Cyprus and Algeria. I did some sharp cartoons on those. So, the conservatives began saying I was not fair.

Because you were an Asian?

Not really. Of course, there were some nutcases who used to write saying, 'go back to where you came from' and that kind of thing. But soon, they too got used to my work.

We have heard a lot about the British sense of humour. How different is it from the Indian version?

There are different variations, actually. There was the type practiced by Harry Sickom and two others. They used to take off on Indian pronunciation. Then there is this very dry variety... usually, a remark which you make with a straight face without laughing.

My humour was very close to the English one. After all, English had been my main language. I had read a tremendous lot.

From the day I arrived in England, I didn't waste time. I listened to all the radio programmes including *Women's Hour* and *Children's Hour* just to educate myself. When you are in a foreign country, there is a lot of work that you have to do.

So, by the time I got the job at *The Observer,* I knew the country, its socio-political history and the idioms well. That is very important.

In most of your works, it is the politicians who are at the receiving end. Were there any protests from them?

No. They knew they would be making fools of themselves if they protested. But when the cartoons indirectly flattered them, they used to ask for the original drawing. When it was sharply critical, they would just keep quiet.

There is a framed cartoon of yours in former President R Venkataraman's office room.

Is there? In Delhi?

No, in Madras (Chennai now).

About the Budget?

Yes, Venkataraman with the finance minister's briefcase in his hand, lots of lipstick marks on his face, and a woman kissing him on the cheek.

Yes, yes. Because of that, he once introduced me to somebody saying, 'He nearly caused my divorce!'

Which politicians did you find the easiest to caricature?

There was Raj Narain.[1] But in reality, no good caricature is easy. For instance, to do a good caricature of Indira Gandhi was

---

[1] Raj Narain was a politician who won the famous electoral malpractice case against the then Prime Minister Indira Gandhi, which led to her disqualification and imposition of Emergency in India in 1975. He defeated Indira Gandhi during the 1977 Lok Sabha elections.

extremely difficult because she had a very, very sensitive face. Of course, you could draw a long nose and some grey hair and call it Indira Gandhi. I have never done that.

Recently, a British cartoonist on BBC said, he would highlight Tony Blair's smile, teeth and big ears. Do you also concentrate on prominent features of a personality?

A good cartoon is not different from a portrait, except the emphasis is more on certain features. In both cases, the idea is to get the character of a face. To draw somebody always in the same way, like showing Tony Blair's teeth, becomes a boring cliché. That's the easy way. But it will become boring.

That is, there is something more to a person's personality than his features?

Yes. The exaggeration should be for the purpose of bringing out the character. There are not many good caricaturists today. No one of the stature of David Low or Shankar. Shankar was a good caricaturist. He used to *study* the face before drawing it.

The last time we met was a few months after Rajiv Gandhi's assassination (1991). I remember you were so affected by the tragedy that you could not draw cartoons anymore.

It affected me very badly. If this is the kind of politics we have, what is the point in drawing cartoons? Cartoons are supposed to create tolerance and some kind of moderation. Humour always softens the atmosphere. Of course, there are vicious cartoons also. But generally, a touch of humour is supposed to give a sense of proportion to politics.

Rajiv Gandhi's assassination was a shock to me not because he was a great friend of mine. That way, I was closer to Indira. I knew him only a little. But just the idea that this could happen was a rude shock to me.

Anyway, when one gets to my age, it is not easy to produce even sustained weekly cartoons. It takes a lot to draw cartoons... a great deal of mental effort. It can be very exhausting.

These days, I write. And that works out quite well. That gives me enough satisfaction as I can express my views.

Did Indira Gandhi's assassination also affect you the same way? After all, you were closer to her.

That was also a shock. But I knew she would die. I had said so to my friends. Even to my wife, I had said, 'She will be assassinated'.

Why? Because of Operation Blue Star?[2]

Not only that. She developed hostility from both within and out. Especially from the Americans. Even Rajiv was not in the CIA's good books. Remember the assassination of (Patrice) Lumumba?[3] Now it has come out that the CIA chief Allen Dulles approved his 'removal'. But the advantage the CIA always had was that things become public only 10 or 20 years later. So, they get away with it. People just say it is part of history and forget it.

What about your stint with the *Indian Express* during the Emergency? A cartoonist needs a lot of freedom, so the Emergency must have been a difficult time for you...?

Only in the beginning. There was pre-censorship for the first three months. In those days, I did a kind of whimsical drawing.

---

[2] Operation Blue Star was the codename of the military-operation carried out by Indian security forces between 1 and 10 June 1984 to remove Jarnail Singh Bhindranwale and his followers from the buildings of the Golden Temple.

[3] Patrice Émery Lumumba was a Congolese politician and independence leader who served as the first prime minister of the Democratic Republic of the Congo from June- September 1960. He was assassinated in January 1961.

Sometimes it had hidden meaning. In fact, I have published a book of over hundred such drawings. It is called *Games of the Emergency.* It has my unpublished Emergency cartoons too.

Once the pre-censorship was over, I acted as though there was no restriction. C V Narasimhan (the then *Indian Express* editor) also wrote freely, and we got on very well. That was when I drew the cartoon of the president (Fakhruddin Ali Ahmed was the President of India from1974-1977) in the bath which has become quite famous now. When there was a challenge like that, I tend to draw better. It was appreciated by the general public because there was so much tension in those days. So, whenever they saw a good cartoon, they just laughed loudly for a release.

What is the essential quality of a cartoonist? A fearless mind?

Fearlessness, yes. In the sense that you express only what you believe in. Cowardly behaviour is when you try to please your editor or the proprietor or anybody else and draw cartoons on subjects that you yourself don't believe in. That happens sometimes when cartoonists go from one paper to another.

If you are honest to yourself, you feel a sense of freedom and what you call, fearlessness. Cartoonists are privileged people as there are very few of them functioning at a time. A newspaper can't afford to lose a staff cartoonist. But if you start fearing, you don't take any risks.

You said cartoonists are privileged people. In what way? How different are they from journalists?

Traditionally, a cartoonist has got away with a lot of liberties. It was people like Domier and David Low who established this tradition of freedom. Without freedom, a cartoonist won't be able to really function. You will only produce second-rate work.

Cartoonists have to think with a certain amount of passion, have to respond and react to the world and local events whether it is poverty or corruption or dowry or *sati.* But if a cartoonist goes and accepts dowry, then he can't draw cartoons on that. In other words, cartoonists should be liberals and radical. All good cartoonists are like that.

You will seldom find a right-wing cartoonist. The middle group, yes. For example, Laxman, he is so liberal (and a Centerist) centre. He is not left-wing. People like O V Vijayan (Malayalam writer) are left-wing. Shankar was left-wing.

It is difficult to place them right and left. Generally, you have to have some radical thinking. But if you are for the *status quo,* what is the point in drawing?

You once said your best cartoons were drawn during the Vietnam and Bangladesh wars. Was it because you were so disturbed by the cruelty of it all?

Yes. Both were actually monstrous wars. The Americans were going to 'take Vietnam back to the stone ages'; that was the expression they used.

In Bangladesh, it was pure massacre. I went to Tripura and saw what was happening there. I wrote an article in *The Guardian* saying it was actually cowardice not to intervene in the situation which had created ten million refugees.

In Delhi, there was a controversy. It was Indira Gandhi's leadership and those who were against her were against the Bangladesh war. Then, people were being taken for a ride by the Western embassies. I remember journalists who used to come to the Delhi Press Club and say, it was all false propaganda, and that there weren't ten million refugees. I would say, I was there, and there was no doubt about it.

It was a kind of scotch-stuff policy that the Pakistanis were pursuing. There was a racist element in it. The Pakistani Punjabis believed they were the true Muslims and not the dark Bengalis.

Actually, it is the other way round. They are one of the oldest community of Muslims in the world. Conversion started in eastern India soon after Islam was established.

Did you always go to places where the action was?

I have done that. Actually, I was a Major in the American army during the Vietnam war. I was there in Saigon and they took me in their planes to various places. I did a number of articles for the *Indian Express.* I was made a Major because it gave me protection. And if anything happened to me, my relatives would be informed soon. I must have been the only Major in the US army in *kurta pyjamas*!

Did you see a lot of action?

I didn't see any action on the ground. I went on a Red Cross ship to see an exchange of prisoners. All along the coast, you could see flares dropping and bombs exploding. That was going on. But outside Saigon, you could see all these peasant girls harvesting rice while bombing was on at a distance. But the girls were not bothered.

One could see a lot of poverty and little girls begging. But they are such a dignified nation. There was so much pride in even the children who were selling flowers.

Was it why they could drive away the Americans?

They were extremely tough. They had this analogy about bamboos: The bamboo bends, but doesn't break. And they use bamboo for everything, for utensils, bridges.... The bamboo culture was perfectly suited to the war.

The Americans used to spend tonnes of bombs to destroy the bridges. But the next day, the bridges would reappear. They fought on a handful of rice and dry fish while the Americans had these air rations, sea rations, medical attention and all that. They fought because it was their country. They were fiercely nationalist. It was an amazing phenomenon.

Like in Cuba. I always wondered how Cuba survived all these years. They tried umpteen ways to kill (Fidel) Castro.

Did you see fierce patriotism in the Cubans also?

I would say so, except there was one section which Castro used to call the Cuzanos, meaning worms who were so pro-American and couldn't stand Communism. But Castro allowed them to go to America and a lot of them went. So, there wasn't much of a fifth column in Cuba. Also, that man's leadership is charismatic. People just scream at the sight of him.

When did you visit Cuba?

In 1962. I went back again.

You seem to admire Castro a lot. You have only his portraits here in your drawing room!

Sure, I admire him as a person. I was attracted to his charm and fearlessness.

http://cartoonexhibition.blogspot.com/2010/10/abu.html

> *More than two decades have passed since I spoke to him but whatever he said then, on environmentalism, colonialism, activism and even gaushalas, is interestingly relevant even today.*
>
> *Abu Abraham passed away in 2002.*

Meeting a Gandhi Peace Prize Winner

The International Gandhi Peace Prize, named after Mahatma Gandhi, is awarded annually by the Government of India to individuals and institutions for their contributions towards social, economic and political transformation through non-violence and other Gandhian methods.

The 1997 third Gandhi Peace Prize, when India celebrated its 50 years of independence, was awarded to ***Gerhard Fischer****, a German diplomat for his work in eradicating leprosy and polio, which he received in January 1998.*

The Prize was launched in 1995 on the occasion of the 125th birth anniversary of Mahatma Gandhi. A jury consisting of the Prime Minister, the Leader of the opposition, the Chief Justice of India, Speaker of the Lok Sabha and an eminent person, decides the awardee each year.

In one's career as a journalist, only once in a while you meet people you will not forget even after decades.

Meeting Gerhard Fischer (1921–2006) was one such experience for me. His life was as colourful as a fairy tale; he was a German diplomat, Ambassador and a humanitarian. Even after going through several ups and downs in his life, he had retained a wonderful sense of humour.

His travel schedule when I met him – from Germany to the other European countries, to the Himalayas and to the southern part of India – made it difficult for me to believe he was 76.

And he had granted me an appointment at 6.30 in the morning, my only interview done so early in the morning! I still remember when I reached the meeting venue at 6.20 in the morning, Fischer was all dressed and waiting under a tree to talk to me.

YOU went back to Germany soon after collecting the Gandhi Peace Prize....

I was in the Himalayas where I have built two leprosy stations when the prize was announced. From there I went to Delhi for the surprising event at the Rashtrapati Bhavan.

I generally spend only some time at the stations because they are functioning well. I don't have to be there for long.

When this news of the Prize reached me, my wife was, to put it mildly, rather sick. She has let me go to India six months at a time for the last twelve years. None of my friends' wives would have let their husbands go for six months to another country, certainly not for 12 years! So, I decided to stay back and look after her when she was ill.

How is she now?

She is better. That's why I could come back now.

I have two projects in the construction stages in the South, and I am needed with my partners to get the projects moving.

Because of my wife's illness, I had to make a break in my programme which was in a way nice. Being away from October to March, I have not seen snow in Germany for the last twelve years. I miss the winter in Germany. This time I was in the snow and my batteries are charged well.

Why do you spend six months in Germany and six months in India?

When I decided to have a second life in 1985, I looked at the period when I am needed here in India for building and running stations for leprosy and polio.

I am also a hobby farmer. So, I had to think of my tiny little farm in the southern hilly area of Germany. As we are on our own in that country, I have to work. I have to make the hay, I have to see the fields, I have to look after the horses....

Winter is a quiet time, and my wife can take care of the horses and the fields. I chose to be here then and so, I miss the German winter.

What do you farm there?

I don't really farm. It is a mountainous area, and you can't do anything there. We just graze our horses. I have been a rider for 65 years, and so I have horses.

How many?

Two and a half! The half is a pony for my grandchild. He is my daughter's son. He is seven and a keen little rider. Every morning at five thirty, the horses are fed and at six, they are saddled by me, and for two hours I ride.

When in Germany, I can be with my family. I can take care of the farm and the horses. There will be stacks of invitations from the Rotary, Lions, schools and so on, saying, 'Fischer, come and report'. So, often I have to be on the road to report to those people who have supported me throughout these years.

How much does your wife help you in your work?

My wife is a tremendous help because she runs the administration. It is a big word, even though we don't have an administration. Twelve years ago, when I quit an organised life, I decided not to have anything to interfere with my plans and work. So, we decided not to have an administration. Just the two of us.

She has a computer as she can handle it. I don't touch it. We have 175 donor friends who have helped us for the last twelve years. We have to send them the tax receipt for every paisa they contribute. She writes to them.

I don't take cheques, I don't take anonymous donations. I accept only money and I use this money to make an artificial leg. For example, for Himani Subramaniam who is one of my many, many recipients. We send our donors pictures of children like Himani Subramaniam, so all our donors know where their money goes. That's my wife's work. She sends the typed reports to all of them. Without her, nothing would have been possible. So, she deserves half this prize.

From an organised life in the foreign service, you now lead a totally different kind of life. Did you find this transition difficult?

It was not difficult at all. I am at home here, there and everywhere. I consider Germany and the Himalayas as my home. So, there was no difficulty in the transition.

I land somewhere up there in the Himalayas, and then take buses to wherever I want to go. Or I take trains. I don't drive in India because I like to have people around me! I like the country buses and trains.

It takes me eight days from my Himalayan (leprosy) station to the Kanyakumari (leprosy) station. That is part of my fascination. I like people and I like to be in with people. In an airplane, I am not with people.

I have read that you were born in Oslo, Norway. From Oslo, how did you reach Germany?

My mother is a Norwegian and my father, a German. I was born in Oslo. When I was three-and-a-half, I think, that was a long time ago, my father got transferred to China. He went to China as a Sinologist, a Chinese scholar. We were there for sixteen years. I started to learn medicine at the Beijing Medical University but discontinued.

Why? Didn't you like medicine?

I always wanted to be a doctor. The medical school at Beijing University was started by Rockefeller. When the Japanese occupation began, they closed this American-sponsored school. So, there I was without a place to study!

I thought, what do I do? Should I take up dancing, or should I walk in the streets? But I wanted to be a doctor. So, I said goodbye to my parents and went to Germany as my father was a German. But right into another big war!

This is the first time I am meeting a person who had participated in the Second World War. I have only read about it till now.

Look at my white hair, dear! You don't meet many people with so much white hair any more. They have all gone.

In Germany, I was fighting for five years....

Were you forced to fight for the Nazis?

What do you mean by Nazis? No. This is a funny notion of yours. Here was a country at war. I am German. I arrive via

Siberia. Naturally all men were roped in! I could have stayed in China. What to do? I wanted to do medicine. I didn't realise that there wasn't a chance of studying medicine in a country which had just entered war. I walked into the trap. Yes, I call it a trap. Everybody has some purpose in life... maybe this was it for me.

Five years in the War. But I survived.

What was it like to be in the battlefield?

Oh, no. If I have to talk about the War, it will take days.

Did you meet Hitler any time?

How could a *jawan* meet Hitler?

It was said that Hitler used to address soldiers.

Could a jawan meet Krishna Menon in this country! No.

Did you see Hitler from afar?

I am sure Krishna Menon never came to the battlefield. Hitler never came to the battlefield. They never do that. They live far away from the battlefield. Where would he be otherwise? We stormed towards Moscow and then we stormed backwards because of the heavy snow. It was winter at its best.

We have read that even though Hitler was told about the hard Russian winter, he ordered his troops to march towards Russia.

Hitler was a painter from Austria. He was a corporal in the First World War, made himself a Field Marshal later. Hitler never took advice from the Generals who had experience. But they obeyed him. As a human being, I criticise this behaviour.

I am straight and very critical. You read my speech at Rashtrapati Bhavan, then you will understand, this man speaks like this. I saw everyone in the Cabinet sitting there. That did not deter me from talking straight.

There was my friend RV (R Venkataraman) who was the Industries Minister when I was here as a Diplomat, in the cabinet of a great man. Tell me, who is that great man? Kamaraj. And I say this to everyone, I said to Anna (Annadurai) also, that the best government that Tamil Nadu ever had was the Kamaraj Congress government with men like RV and CS (C Subramaniam) in it. RV unfortunately moved to Delhi and CS whom I always meet, unfortunately is in hospital now.

We were talking about World War II and the Russian winter.

Okay, okay. Let us go back to the Russian winter and how we stormed back.

How bad was the winter?

Toughies had a hard time. Weaklings had a harder time.

Were you a toughie or a weakling?

I have always been a toughie. Remember, I was only nineteen years old then.... Five years went by. On top of it, to make it really worse, I was a prisoner of war for two years and nine months.

Thus I wasted eight years of my life. Eight years later, I found myself free, but my parents were still in China, and I was in Germany.

Were you taken as a prisoner of war in France by the Allies? When did they free you?

It is a chapter in my life, as crazy as I am. Can you believe, they kept me as a prisoner of war for two-and-a-half years after the War was over? I say this to everyone. Conventions are on paper and nothing more. Facts in life are different from the nice things written on paper. Even though I say it is a chapter in my life which is as crazy as I am, I wouldn't have missed it because it means a great deal in life. In such dire conditions of life, masks disappear. When the bullets whiz past you, your mask will disappear and only then you will see the true person. So, it was a great experience.

Alas! It took eight years of my life to learn all that. Of course, eight years wasted.

When they decided to release me, they asked me, where do you want to go?

Where would I go? I love mountain countries.... I dreamt about being a doctor.... But then, I was a shaven-headed young man in wooden shoes with one shirt and a trouser, without a penny in the purse and parents in China. So, medicine was beyond my dreams. Without a penny to buy even a piece of bread, how could I have medical studies? So, I decided to forget about medicine.

Then, I registered to study Law but again, I did not attend classes. Instead, I did various jobs to make money. That was 1948. For three years I worked, which was again an experience. I made more and more money to put in the safe account.

What kind of jobs did you do?

I was a truck driver. Actually, I was this and that.

After three years, I had enough money. So, I went to an institution which we call a 'crammer'. It crams things into you. There was this famous legal crammer, and I said to the crammer, 'I am late, I am old, and I am in a hurry. Would you cram everything that I should have learnt at university where I had entered, but did not attend due to lack of time? Would you cram it into me and help me pass this law examination?'

Fortunately, I had a friend from the War who had avoided captivity, who knew this man, the crammer and put in a good word. He said, 'Look at this young man, He is from China and struggling in a foreign country. Take him and help him.'

China became my home country! Even then I cheekily said, 'Listen, I have only one year, and you have to teach me everything in one year'. He said, 'What? One year? You need four years'.

You were in a hurry….

At 27, with nothing under my belt, I was in a hurry.

He said, 'Okay. But 365 days without a single moment of rest'. Beggars cannot be choosers. So, I said, 'Yes'. He should have said, 'Young man, there is a door in front'. He did not. But he quoted an enormous amount. I had that much money, but I did not expect to pay that to this man. So, I said to him, 'Money back if I don't succeed'. Again, he should have said, 'Get out'. But he said, okay.

And he got me through.

What would I do after that? I had a Law degree. Coming from abroad, I wanted to be abroad, so I entered the foreign service.

And here I am, with 35 years in the Foreign Service. I had assignments all over the world.

The first two, three countries where I was assigned, had leprosy. As a student in Peking, I was once asked whether I would volunteer to nurse leprosy patients. They asked that to all students. That was before Fleming came in with the medication. So, I was in a leprosy station, and from then on, I wanted to nurse leprosy patients. I felt, these outcasts needed attention.

Outcasts… that was the word I used at Rashtrapati Bhavan. I said, 'don't treat us like outcasts. Don't treat us like the forgotten. We are also here in this country although you don't care about us.' I don't mince my words. Yes, it wasn't easy for those assembled there. But I had given a copy of my speech to the government earlier, just to be fair.

Did you enjoy your work as a diplomat?

Oh sure. Yes, I had a fabulous career. When I had had enough of Vietnam and Malaysia and India, I was given a European posting. That was a mistake. My government had three European embassies in 1985. But I decided, enough is enough. I wanted to come back to India.

Was it an instantaneous decision?

No. My wife and I had been thinking about it for a long time before I decided to leave the job.

In 1985, I wrote a letter of resignation to the foreign minister and said, 'Thank you, I am prematurely leaving the service'. And, zoom… I came back here.

Looking back, I feel I am lucky. How do you know how long you will live? It could have been only one year longer. Then I wouldn't have had the chance of doing much in leprosy. I am lucky. It has lasted for 12 years. And I hope it will last a little longer.

You may ask, why India?

No. I will ask, why did you choose a place like Chettipatti near Salem?

When I was the Consul General of Germany in Madras, to be precise in 1960, a woman came to my room, panting after climbing the steps and asked, 'Can you help me get a permit? I want to help leprosy patients'. I thought that was great. I asked her, 'Why do you want to help them?' She said, 'I have heard about a French nun nursing leprosy patients. I am a general practitioner. I have taken a crash course in English and leprosy. I have 30,000 Marks in my pocket'.

So, I took her to the minister of health, and she was given a work permit.

Then, all of us drove to Chettipatti. She, Dr Elizabeth Vomstein, still works there in Chettipatti.

For four years, we were here in Tamil Nadu. If you ask me which was my best posting professionally and personally, I will say, South India. I mean, all the four States. I admire that man, E M S Namboodiripad. I used to meet him if I passed by Kerala, even though most of my work was here in Tamil Nadu. Because of its beautiful water and good climate, there is not much leprosy in Kerala.

For four years, we watched how Dr Vomstein worked. When she came here, she stayed with us, and we went to Chettipatti often to see her and her station. This fabulous woman slowly built up what today is a model station. She is still cutting off infected fingers of her patients, and she is 81! She is someone very special.

When I resigned, I went and worked for her from 1985 to 1991. She is very, very difficult.

After six years, I said, 'Doctor, I have swallowed enough. I can't take any more'. So, I left her and started my own stations. I have nothing to do with Chettipatti anymore, even though I did a lot for her. I honour her.

In my speech in Europe, I put her on a pedestal but I also said, 'You can't work with her'. If she wasn't that type, she wouldn't have lasted 38 years. Imagine at 81, she still sits there and cuts off infected fingers!

Are leprosy patients treated the same way all over the world as they are treated here, as outcasts?

People call them lepers. I always tell this to people. Don't call them lepers, they are leprosy patients. Yes, there is a difference in this country. Again, I am straight. You say to these people, 'This is your karma! Your karma is not my concern. Mine is none of your concern too. This is a curse from God because of your former life. So, I have no concern for you'.

In my speech at Rashtrapati Bhavan, I said, 'It is not enough to have compassion, *daya, karuna* and pity for leprosy patients. We don't care about compassion. We want action'. That's the difference. In other countries, there is action because there is no karma theory. It is not their fault. It is the bloody bug that caught them.

How are they treated in other countries?

In the books of Moses, it is written, 'move out, here comes a leprosy patient'. The word 'leprosy' has a horrible connotation in other countries also. We also have leprosy, but in very small numbers. It is not very sizeable. But there, fear and stigma are enormous. Compassion in other countries is tied to action. Here you have *daya* and *karuna* and when you walk by him, you pity him and maybe throw a paisa in his bowl near a temple. That's it and nothing more.

Only two people did more. You have pictures of them, and you have heard about them. They are Christ and Gandhiji. They picked up leprosy patients, took them into their houses. That is not what is done normally. Leprosy patients themselves think, 'I am cursed by God for my karma in the previous birth. I have to go through life as a leprosy patient, honourable to the end because I am going to be in Fischer's shoes'. This is a drawback for us, in the medical sense, because it creates fatalism.

What was their reaction when you went to help them? How did they view you?

My patients are my friends. Yes, friends. There is a problem in people's minds because of the stigma and fear attached to the disease. I will accept visitors to come to my stations, but I know they can't face it. The disease is horrible physically. But it is far worse mentally to be an outcast from one's family and community.

If you work in a leprosy community, the mental anguish is supreme and it is no different for me. Every day, when I go to see them in the mornings and evenings and during the day, I touch everybody and say, '*Nalla thane irukku* (are you alright?). Come on, get up'. Everybody in my station has a small job to do.

Let me tell you, the human side is very important.

With mask and gloves, there is a barrier between me and him. No, I don't want any barrier. Yes, he has it, I may get it too. But there is no difference between us, two human beings. That is the condition for somebody who wants to work there. Others, please don't come.

After the publicity in 1985, many press people came there to see Fischer, the Ambassador who has gone to work in a leprosy camp, kicking his cushy job. Two teams arrived within two weeks. The critical moment came when they wanted to take pictures of me with the patients. They said they had powerful lenses so they would take pictures through the window. I told them, 'I will take you to the gate and say goodbye. Get out! If you want to take pictures, you are coming with me'.

In Germany, I object to television and the press peering at my farm because I don't need it there. But here I need publicity. I want to beat the drum, 'Leprosy is curable. Come and watch. Forget about the stigma. Forget about treating them as outcasts'.

Here, I am constantly shouting to make the community aware, and this Prize gives me a chance to focus the attention on 'us' who are forgotten.

Were you not scared of getting infected?

I don't think of that. I wouldn't have been here, if I ever thought that way. But then, why should I be scared? No, this is my life.

Your goal was to eradicate leprosy by 2000. Is it possible?

I'll tell you one thing, people like Sonia Gandhi were sitting in front at Rashtrapati Bhavan and I made them uncomfortable through my speech. The slogan of eradication of leprosy by 2000 by the Indian government and WHO, to my mind, is wishful thinking. Eradication by that year is stuck with dreams, notions and presumptions. But eradication is possible.

Tuberculosis is something far more dangerous nowadays. So, funds for leprosy have been shifted. Here and at WHO, the emphasis has shifted from leprosy to TB. It is most unfortunate.

When we, who are engaged in this work, go for donations, they ask, 'What are you taking about? WHO said, it is over. Government said, it is over. So, don't come and beg'. Fortunately, my donors are very loyal. So, leprosy goes on.... Because you can't immunise yourself, you can't prevent it, you can only cure it.

Are you an angry man?

No, not at all. But I love battles. I always loved battles. I battled against the head of my government. I battled against Collectors and district magistrates. I always said, don't try to fool Fischer.

Was it because of the Second World War that you became a tough man?

I think it is in my genes. My mother is a Norwegian, my father, a German. Then, of course, I am toughened by those eight years, I agree. But I think the toughness came mainly from our childhood when we grew up hearing our parents say, 'don't accept anything that is against your conviction'. It is your conviction that should decide what to do. That's what I got from my parents.

Do you believe in karma?

I believe in karma.

Do you feel you were destined to do this work for the leprosy patients?

I don't look at it as a spiritual trip. It is principles.

Now, I am waiting for another question which comes always. What drives you? Some are disappointed with my answer. My answer is, what drives me is my interest in human beings. Secondly, I need challenges in life. I could have chosen any other country for this work which would have been far, far easier. Third is, I am adventurous.

No, there is nothing spiritual in my work. No one is guiding me in my work, and I don't have a contract with Him.

Fischer passed away in 2006 in Copenhagen in Denmark at the age of 84. But hundreds of unknown and unsung volunteers in India are working with leprosy patients and rehabilitating them at his stations, believing in his legacy.

....

If you remember, the Congress had been giving outside support to the 13-party coalition that was called the United Front headed by Inder Kumar Gujral as the Prime Minister of India.

The United Front government that was installed on 21 April 1997 fell on 28 November 1997 when the Congress withdrew support.

That was how the year India was celebrating 50 years of independence ended – with another government falling and another election facing the nation!

....

PART 2

1998-1999

Ruling party: The National Democratic Alliance (NDA)

Prime Minister: Atal Bihari Vajpayee (BJP)

Atal Bihari Vajpayee, the hero of Kargil war! Thank you, Rediff.com

Another Government Falls!

The reason why the United Front government headed by Inder Kumar Gujral fell on the 28th of November 1997 was the release of the interim report of the Jain Commission.

And what is this Jain Commission?

Immediately after the assassination of Rajiv Gandhi, on the 22nd of May 1991, the caretaker Chandrasekhar government at the Centre handed over the investigation to the Central Bureau of Investigation (the CBI). The agency created a special investigation team (SIT) under D Karthikeyan to find out who was responsible for the assassination. The SIT probe confirmed the role of the LTTE in Rajiv Gandhi's assassination, which was also upheld by the Supreme Court of India.

Parallel to the CBI investigation, the government had also asked Justice Milap Chand Jain to look into the conspiracy angle of the assassination, and it came to be known as the Jain Commission.

After six years, the Jain Commission came out with an interim report which indicted the Dravida Munnetra Kazhagam (DMK), a regional party from Tamil Nadu, for colluding with the LTTE. The report said that the DMK had provided sanctuary to the LTTE, which made it easier for the rebels to assassinate Rajiv Gandhi.

And this interim report became the reason why the Gujral-led United Front government fell in November 1997.

The Congress, that was giving outside support to the United Front government, withdrew its support when the government refused to drop the DMK from the cabinet.

On 4 December 1997, the President dissolved the parliament and asked I K Gujral cabinet to continue as the caretaker government till the next elections were held.

The interim Jain Commission Report

The 1998 General elections also saw the emergence of Sonia Gandhi, who had till then refused to pay heed to the pleas of the Congress, to lead the party. Sonia Gandhi along with her daughter Priyanka started their campaign after paying tributes to Rajiv Gandhi at Sriperumbudur near Chennai, where he was assassinated in the year 1991.

With the emergence of Sonia Gandhi, the Bofors scandal which led to the downfall of Rajiv Gandhi, became alive.

It was on the 24th of March 1986 that the Government of India and the Swedish arms company Bofors signed a $285 million contract for the supply of 410 Howitzer field guns to the Indian Army.

A year later, on 16 April 1987, the Swedish Radio alleged that Bofors paid kickbacks to many individuals belonging to a number of countries including top Swedish and Indian politicians, to seal the deal.

The middleman associated with the scandal was Ottavio Quattrocchi, an Italian businessman who was reportedly close to the Rajiv Gandhi family, in other words, Sonia.

So, two names that dominated the year 1998 were the Bofors scandal and the Jain Commission report.

*It was **K Madhavan**, the former Joint director of the CBI, who cracked the Swiss bank accounts of those who allegedly received kickbacks in the Bofors deal.*

He was also the Joint Director of the CBI when the assassination of Rajiv Gandhi happened.

So, there was no better person than K Madhavan to talk about the Jain Commission report vis a vis the investigation conducted by the CBI's Special Investigation Team (SIT) and, of course, on the Bofors investigation too.

THE leaked version of the Jain Commission report blamed Karunanidhi (the DMK chief) and the DMK for Rajiv Gandhi's assassination. But you said neither Karunanidhi nor the DMK could be blamed for Rajiv Gandhi's assassination. Why did you say so?

A commission is generally appointed following an incident of national consequence like bribery, murder, etc After that a criminal investigation follows. The implication being that a criminal investigation is more thorough than a commission.

A commission is a fact-finding probe being conducted by a judge in an air-conditioned room with some people appearing before him, whereas a criminal investigation is headed by an officer of the rank of Inspector General, or someone with people going into the field, sifting through the evidence carefully, contacting maybe a thousand people and getting the relevant evidence. It is much more thorough than a commission's work.

The investigation work was already done in this case by IG Karthikeyan, DIG Raju, DIG Sreekumar, and Ragothaman, the chief investigating officer. And they have done a very thorough job. They have prosecuted 41 people. The trial is over and none of them is from the DMK, the AIADMK or the Congress. No politician is involved. They have squarely accused the LTTE for having conspired to kill Rajiv Gandhi, and killing him.

During the trial, (just) the defence lawyers and no other person ever accused the CBI or Karthikeyan of having left out any evidence. Now the judgment is pending.

At this time, Jain is coming out with a one-sided version, based on intelligence reports, that Karunanidhi and the DMK are behind the crime. He is even accusing P Chidambaram (who held the cabinet portfolios of Home, Finance and External Affairs in his various tenures) to some extent. Accusing Chidambaram is the unkindest cut of them all as Shakespeare would have put it, because Chidambaram was probably closest to Rajiv Gandhi in the political set-up, intellectually and age-wise.

To say that these people are responsible when a criminal investigation has not accused them of any offence, in my view, is a travesty of justice.

So, what I said applies not only to the DMK, but it also applies to the AIADMK and equally to the Congress too.

Jain has gone on the basis of some intelligence reports which more often than not are wrong. That is why I felt that having been a professional investigator, the public should be made aware that the facts-approach in the report is not correct.

Will it have a damaging effect on the Special Investigation Team's findings?

To my knowledge, it is not going to do any damage because no such plea has been taken in the court. The criminal conspiracy has also been looked into by the team. If it cannot be proved in court, it is taken as not proved. So, I don't think it is going to damage the investigation at all, and the trial.

Will it affect in any other way?

The trial?

Yes.

Not as of now. Unless the Commission files an affidavit before the court and says that the facts have been suppressed. And no such thing has been done till now.

You asked the public to be wary of this report. Why did you say so?

I said, you should be wary because a full-fledged criminal investigation has cleared all these people, and therefore, when somebody says X or Y or Z is guilty, the public should be careful about believing it.

Don't you think the attitude of the public to those accused by the report will be different now, mainly because of the kind of publicity the report has got?

That is why I am trying to clear it. I know a lot about commissions and investigations. See, each politician will approach it from his own angle. Each one of them has an axe to grind.

But when I speak out, I speak out as a professional. I was never in politics, and I have no intention of entering politics. So, I can be objective. I can speak the truth and appraise the public of what to believe and what not to believe.

When the politicians are shouting, will your voice be heard by the public?

I am not bothered about that. I am not bothered whether it will be heard, but at least if I initiate a discussion on the subject, I succeed. There will be other intellectuals who will follow it up. For example, I issued my press release four or five days ago (from the time of the interview). I am happy to find that all major newspapers are against the Jain Commission report in their editorials. They are saying the same things which I have said. I already stand vindicated.

Do you feel the report is politically motivated?

It is sensationalism. I would say the report of the Commission, I won't say Jain, is nothing but sensationalism.

What will the Commission achieve by sensationalising the report?

I don't know. I think you better ask Mr Jain what he plans to achieve, and what he proposes to achieve.

It took six long years for the Commission to come out with a report, that too an interim report. Could that be a reason?

I have been calling it the longest pregnancy!

Was that the reason why you called the report 'a wastage of public time and money' in your statement?

Yes, it did not require this much of time and money. And this is the first time in the world, to the best of my knowledge, that a Commission is appointed after a criminal investigation. It is usually the other way round. The order of precedence is, a Commission is appointed and they quickly go into the facts, place some *prime facie* findings. Then it is probed deeper by the investigation.

The Commission and the investigation team worked parallel to each other.

It was unfortunate. It should not have happened.

Is it good to have such commissions which work parallel to investigating agencies?

It is not good for the country. I can tell you an anecdote. One part of it is, I won't say obscene, a bit crude. But I can quote Parkinson. While on his way to India, Parkinson was asked on the plane, what is your impression about a commission of inquiry? He said, well, a commission of inquiry is like what happens in a toilet. There is a sitting, there is a report and then the matter is dropped. He said that. I am not saying it. You can say Madhavan quoted Parkinson.[1]

A couple of years ago, when I interviewed SIT chief Karthikeyan, he said it was a tremendous strain on them reporting to the Justice Verma Commission (The Justice J S Verma Commission investigated the Bofors case) **and the Justice Jain Commission while investigating the case.**

I can understand their agony because they have done a thorough and good job. I have heard that they spent sleepless nights in the first few months. But they have brought out the truth. So, it must be very painful for them that all this is happening.

Unfortunately, they are not able to speak. They won't be allowed to speak, and that is one of the reasons why I am speaking.

---

[1] Cyril Northcote Parkinson (30 July 1909 – 9 March 1993) was a British naval historian and author of the most famous book *Parkinson's Law* which states 'work expands so as to fill the time available for its completion. It is sometimes applied to the growth of bureaucracy in an organisation, but can be applicable to all forms of work'.

I have faced such situations when I was in service when accusations were made, and I had to be silent because I was in service. Now I felt, at least somebody should speak out and say what was actually happening. And that speaking out should be by a person who is not linked to politics, who is not a politician as such.

Don't you think the SIT proceedings have been going on for a very long time? Moreover, as the trial was conducted in camera, the public feel they are not doing anything.

It has been a very, very long time. Ultimately, nothing is going to happen.

It was reported then that Rajiv Gandhi was told by Intelligence Agencies that the LTTE could be believed. You yourself said earlier that intelligence reports more often than not are wrong. Why does it happen that way?

Half of the intelligence reports are motivated to please the government in power. Out of the remaining fifty per cent, thirty per cent are wrong. Only twenty per cent would be correct. See, one drawback with an intelligence report is, it is never tested in a court of law whereas the CBI report has to be tested. Every full stop and comma in a CBI report is tested and challenged in a court of law.

The Intelligence Bureau can make a saint out of a villain and a villain into a saint which the CBI cannot do.

As the CBI's joint director, were you aware of the way the LTTE was functioning in India at that time?

No, no. The CBI is not in the picture as far as intelligence is concerned. So, whatever knowledge I had about the LTTE was as a citizen of India, reading the newspapers. IB reports on such issues don't come to the CBI.

You were the joint director when the assassination happened. Under what circumstances was the SIT formed?

After the tragic murder of Rajiv Gandhi, at nine in the morning, the CBI director convened a meeting of all the IGs. Karthikeyan was not in the CBI at that time.

Vijay Karan, the CBI director, told all of us, 'Two names were considered; one was Madhavan and the other was Karthikeyan. Because Madhavan has done the Bofors case, some image was created about him *vis-a-vis* Rajiv Gandhi. So, we have decided to appoint Karthikeyan'.

Then Vijay Karan asked me, 'Is it all right with you, Madhavan?' I said, 'Sir, if you had asked me to head the team, I would have refused for the same reason. It is not proper that I head the team'.

Then I suggested that Raju should be called from J&K, because he was an excellent officer. Immediately Vijay Karan noted his name and telephoned the Home Secretary and told him that we wanted Raju to report to us from Srinagar immediately. Sreekumar, another DIG, joined the SIT. Ragothaman was the chief investigating officer. So, the cream of CBI was brought in, and they have done an excellent job.

So, it pained me when I found that a Commission sitting in an air-conditioned room after examining a few witnesses (had given) a report which more or less goes against what the CBI has found.

In your statement, you said that Rajiv Gandhi himself was responsible for his death....

No, no. I didn't say that. Fortunately, what I issued to the PTI was a written statement. So, I can't say I am misquoted. What I said was, Rajiv was rather careless about his security.

I didn't say Rajiv Gandhi himself was responsible. In law, there is a term known as 'contributory negligence'. It is a legal terminology.

An accident might have happened due to A doing something. But if B was also careless about it, then it becomes a case of contributory negligence. Like, in a highly dangerous building when everyone is wearing a helmet, you enter with bravado without a helmet and your head gets hurt. It is a typical example of contributory negligence.

Likewise, the security agencies are there to protect the PM and the others. But politicians also have a role to play. He should not discard security and run away from them or push away the constables. After all, they are mere constables.

If the prime minister or the chief minister or a leading VIP pushes them away, they get scared, they don't know how to react. If it is Britain, the constable would talk back saying, 'Sir, you have no business to do this'. But, in India, a poor constable feels, 'he is a big man, he is pushing me away. What can I do?'

It is well known that the LTTE became strong in India when MGR ruled Tamil Nadu. This is there in the Commission's report also….

In fact, the LTTE was even supported by the Congress government at the Centre. Everyone supported them. I won't say there is anything wrong in it, in the sense that the Tamils felt they were suffering. There is a communal affinity in human beings. If Keralites were suffering in the Gulf, people in Kerala have a feeling that our brethren are suffering. If the British suffer in India, let us say, the British will feel that our people are suffering. So, you can't say that feeling is bad.

In fact, I would put the sequence of events like BC and AD. I would name them as pre-Prabhakaran and post-Prabhakaran days. During the pre-Prabhakaran days, in India and Tamil Nadu in particular, there was a lot of sympathy for the Sri Lankan Tamils. His true colours came out in the post-Prabhakaran period. He started killing his rivals. Various people started doubting his *bona fides*. Therefore, a lot of sympathy was lost for the LTTE, though even now people feel for the suffering Tamils over there.

Are you happy with the way the CBI is functioning these days?

Yes and no. In the sense, in non-political cases which constitute 75 per cent to 80 per cent of the CBI's cases, they are doing well. But in cases with political overtones, here and there the CBI has had aberrations. While saying this, I would like to draw a distinction between a political case and a crime committed by a politician.

A political case is a case in which a crime is committed for the benefit of a party, never for the individual, not even for the leader. Like the Baroda dynamite case.

On the other hand, a politician taking a bribe for himself is not a political case. It is a crime committed by a politician. So, the public should know this distinction. For example, for a lay reader or a viewer to understand if a minister committing a rape on his office sofa, it doesn't mean it is a political case. It is a crime committed by a politician.

But the general public feel the CBI is being controlled by the politicians.

Yes, it is so, and in fact I have been canvassing during my CBI days within the department and after I left, outside the department, that the CBI should be removed totally from the governmental control. I have even given a set-up of who should control the CBI.

I have also said that the CBI should not be allowed to have a free hand because power corrupts, and absolute power corrupts absolutely. So, the CBI should be kept in check.

The check should be by a permanent commission headed by the Home Minister with one MP from the ruling party and one MP from the Opposition, a retired judge and a public personality who could be a journalist or anybody else. This commission should oversee the functioning of the CBI including all promotions, postings, assignments on deputation etc

The result is, the Home Minister is just one member of the commission and nothing can be done in secrecy. There will be others to watch and object. And the Home Minister can be over-ruled by the other four. Then an objectivity will surely come.

Now what is happening is that the CBI is over-ruled by a mere politician. That is why all these problems are arising.

What exactly happens? Do politicians control the CBI or does the CBI not act because they feel their hands are tied?

It happens both ways. Politicians have a tendency to control powerful organisations. Some officers also are willy-nilly helping politicians because it helps them in some way or the other. Like Kuldip Nayar (Journalist and human rights activist who was also a High Commissioner to the UK) said about journalists during the Emergency: 'When they were asked to bend, they crawled.' That is what is happening in some cases.

How should the CBI function? As a silent, behind the scenes organisation or a high-profile organisation?

I would put it like this: There is a stage in the CBI which should be between total silence and total exposure. It should inform the public about what is happening, without any attempt at sensationalism, because people would like to know what is happening. Whatever the CBI is doing, it is for the country. So, there is nothing wrong if the CBI gives out some press releases.

You mean it should not be a silent organisation?

It can't be a silent organisation. The very nature of things is such that it can't be a silent organisation. IB and RAW are silent organisations because their work is like that. The CBI's work, ultimately, is exposed in a court. It has to come before the court. So, there is nothing wrong in the CBI Director making disclosures to the press so that all sorts of false rumours are set right.

These days even for a small crime, politicians all over the country clamour for a CBI enquiry. Do you feel this puts a lot of pressure on the CBI?

Yes. It shows two things. It shows the CBI is overworked. It also shows the confidence people have developed for the CBI despite all the criticism. People still feel the CBI, by Indian standards, is a good organisation.

Yes, the CBI is understaffed. Then, you can't go by numbers. You can't say the CBI has got 500 investigating officers and it can take up a lot of cases. Out of the 500, only 40 or 50 can handle tough investigations.

It is like journalism. There are correspondents and correspondents, but only a few can handle subjects well. Others are sent on trivial beats. Within the CBI also, for important cases, good officers are selected. When more important cases come up, there is a dearth of good officers.

Did you ever feel frustrated when you were a CBI officer?

No. Except towards the end when I took voluntary retirement. I would say, I did it more in disgust than frustration. Frustration has a sense of pessimism attached to it. Disgust has a sense of anger.

I used to be bold. I used to put up the notes the way I liked and if my boss differed from me, I used to discuss it with him. But I developed one habit. That is, if my boss passes a written order over-ruling me, I will comply with it immediately. After that I have no right to question him. But if he wants to shoot over my shoulder and without a written order, if he is asking me to do a wrong thing, I wouldn't do that. I was known for that.

How did you deal with politicians? You must have encountered political interference in your career too.

I dealt with politicians with respect and firmness. I used to show respect which they deserved, but firmly make them understand that I am not the person who would do wrong things for them, whoever he may be.

You said you resigned in disgust. What made you feel disgusted?

For twenty years, I had been handling sensitive cases. It is only in the later part of my service that my name became known to the media. Even earlier I used to do a lot of big cases. In many of them, I faced a lot of interference. But I didn't succumb even on one occasion.

After twenty years, I felt it was enough. I thought if that was the manner in which everything was working, a single-man crusade would not do any purpose. I was making myself a nuisance to others also.

What really made you angry?

I was not allowed to speak at that time. That was why I couldn't talk then.

What made me angry were two things. One, the manner in which the Bofors case was transferred from me for political reasons. But at that time, I could not object because it was the director's privilege to assign any case to anyone. No one has the right to say, 'Only I can do this case, not others'. It would be very impetuous on somebody's part to say that, 'Only I can do this'.

Under whose instructions was the case transferred from you?

Obviously, there were some political instructions.

From whom?

Obviously from the party in power, the Congress. I don't know which person. But I didn't like it. Still, I continued. Then came the securities scam case. I wanted to follow a line of investigation. We wanted to trace some funds in foreign countries. Initially, my director, S K Dutta agreed. A week later, he said, 'We have decided not to do that'. I said, 'Sir, that means you are arresting some bank officers and brokers. We will not be able to go after the politicians'.

He said, 'Look here, Madhavan. I am under instructions not to follow this line'. Then I said, 'Sir, in that case, you transfer the case from me. I can't keep quiet on this'. He said, 'You have become too famous, and I can't transfer you. We faced a lot of criticism when you were transferred from the Bofors case. We do not want to do it again'. I said, 'Then Sir, you are leaving me with no alternative except to seek retirement'. He thought I was bluffing. He said, 'That's your privilege. Rules allow that'.

A week later, I gave my notice for voluntary retirement. Then he got shocked. He asked, 'what's this?' I said, 'Sir, you asked me to give it'. He said, 'No, no, take it back. I won't accept it'. I said, 'You have no other option, and I can't work under these circumstances. For the last twenty years, I was facing such tensions. I have done my bit for the organisation and the country. It is time for me to call it a day and get off. I have an alternative source of livelihood. Let me try my luck as a lawyer also'.

That was how I came out.

Were you disappointed that you were not allowed to complete the Bofors case?

No. In the sense that I shocked the bureaucracy, and I shocked the politicians by what I did. So, to that extent, I taught them a lesson: that there are people who are not bothered about their jobs, who would rather quit than do wrong things.

Yes, I was quite interested in completing the Bofors case. But it has nothing to do with Bofors alone. I was quite interested in doing my job and seeing that it reaches its logical conclusion, like any other job by any other professional. Even a barber who starts cutting your hair would like to complete it. He would not like to stop it midway.

Anyway, nothing came out of the Bofors case investigation, and the accused managed to go unscathed. That was the tragic end of one of the most high-profile corruption cases independent India had seen. The Jain Commission report, though, created a lot of political discontent. No wonder, efficient officers like K Madhavan felt frustrated.

Atal Bihari Vajpayee Returns as Prime Minister

February 1998.

People were fed up of the unstable coalitions at the Centre, and the chaotic two years of the 13-party coalition called the United Front government. In those two years (1996-98), the country had had two prime ministers, Deve Gowda and I K Gujral.

Still the results of the 1998 elections after the fall of the Gujral government, were indecisive: the BJP got 182 seats, the Congress under party president Sitaram Kesri won 141 and the ruling United Front, just 6. The United Front getting just 6 seats showed the contempt people had for the coalition that was fighting all the time.

For the second time, the BJP got a chance to rule the country.

The Atal Bihari Vajpayee-led NDA managed to gather the support of 286 members in the parliament, and Vajpayee took oath as the Prime Minister of India on the 22nd of March 1998 for the second time.

If you remember, his first stint as the Prime Minister in 1996 lasted only for 13 days.

Many people in the country were worried and suspicious of the Hindutva agenda of the BJP. Though people trusted Vajpayee as a moderate leader, the rest of the party including the party president, L K Advani did not enjoy the same confidence.

Those were the days when aligning with the 'communal' BJP was considered as political suicide.

A few months before Vajpayee occupied the chair of the Prime Minister, I spoke to the then vice president of the BJP, ***O Rajagopal****, on the ideology the party stood for, and whether the party that spoke about Hindutva all the time, was indeed a Hindu party!*

THE BJP is branded as a communal, non-secular and fundamentalist party. How do you respond to these accusations?

From the description, one thing is clear; the BJP is different from other political parties. This was the way the Congress was described before Independence. The Congress was described by the Muslim League as a Hindu communal party. So, this kind of labelling is nothing new.

These gentlemen cannot say why they describe the BJP as communal. They cannot pinpoint a single BJP programme to establish that it is communal.

We believe in a general secular polity which is guaranteed under the Constitution. In our party, we do not discriminate between any community while giving membership. If a person is 18 years old, and if he believes in the party's principles, irrespective of his religious or caste affiliations, he is welcome. A good number of people belonging to various communities, including minorities like the Christians and the Muslims, also have become members. Some of them are party office bearers too.

Not only political parties but the public also look at the BJP as a Hindu party. You talk about Hindutva.

We do talk about Hindutva.

And Hindu Rajya....

No, we don't talk about Hindu Rajya. Never.

Ram Rajya?

Yes, Rama Rajya. Rama Rajya is a concept first projected by no less a person than Mahatma Gandhi. When he was asked about the ideal State, he talked about Rama Rajya.

That was symbolic, was it not?

It is symbolic. Symbolic in the sense that under Sri Rama, there was justice for all. It is our ideal about the polity. There is nothing wrong in that.

When we talk about Hindutva, it is not as a religious concept. After all, there is no religion strictly called Hindu. A religion means an opinion, *math am.* The view of Christ is Christu *matham,* the view of Prophet Mohammed is Mohammed *matham* or Islam, the views of Buddha is Buddha *matham.* This is the way it is understood. Similarly, there is no such thing as the view of the Hindu.

We have Hindu *matham* also.

Nowadays, such a description has come into existence. It has become popular also. I do agree with you. But I am talking scientifically. Strictly, there is nothing called a Hindu religion. The word Hindu has got a very wide meaning even according to our Constitution. It includes all religious faiths except Christianity and Islam. Like the Jains, the Buddhists, the Advaitists, the Saivites, the Sikhs, etc This is the definition given according to our Hindu law.

The word Hindu is used to describe those who believe in all the faiths that have sprung up in India.

When we use the words Hindu and Hindutva, we only refer to them as cultural nationalism. What is the name of the culture of our country? Hindutva. Actually, this is accepted also by very many political observers not belonging to the BJP. I recollect what Joseph Parecattil, who was the cardinal of the Catholic Church in Kerala, used to say, 'I am by religion a Christian. But by culture, I am a Hindu'.

A few months ago, when Advaniji (he was the then BJP president) had a reception in Hyderabad, Reverend Irulappa, the bishop of Hyderabad, came to meet him and said the same thing. He said, 'By religion, I am a Christian. By nationality, I am an Indian. By culture, I am a Hindu.'

But it is not interpreted by many this way.

We are trying to make them understand. That is because the BJP is more understood by the propaganda of its opponents. They are more powerful because there are so many voices, and we are only one. Parties like the Congress, the Communists and every other party have nothing else to say about the BJP. So, they say the BJP stands for Hindutva, and Hindutva is communal!

If people have begun to like the BJP more and more now, in spite of the consistent propaganda by every other political opponent, it is because of the perception among the common people in India. They feel it is only the BJP which is there to protect the Hindus. And in a country where 85 per cent of the people are what you call religious Hindus, it doesn't do any harm for the party.

It is only the anglicised, Westernised, elitist section, the so-called intellectual section, who are much worried about that. As far as common people are concerned, they are not afraid of that.

And, in a State like Kerala, where people are quite educated, they have seen for themselves how all the other political parties like the Congress, the Communists, the Janata Dal bow before the communal forces like the Muslim League, the Christian Kerala Congress, the caste-based parties like the Nair party, the Ezhava party....

How come the BJP got this communal label?

Because this is propaganda let loose by the Communists. They are anti-religion, especially anything Hindu. Hindu is anathema for them. Probably they are following the footsteps of Mohammed Ali Jinnah. When Mahatma Gandhi and the Congress party stood for the whole country, when they fought for freedom without any distinction between one religion or the other, the Muslim League thought it fit to describe them as a Hindu communal party.

So, any party which has the perception of the whole country before them, and if they want to have policies and programmes which will have an impact on the entire population of the country, it will necessarily have a Hindu impact because 85 per cent of the people are Hindus.

When you are targeting only the 85 per cent, won't the rest feel alienated?

We are not targeting the 85 per cent. We are targeting the entire community. And in the entire community naturally, the 85 per cent form a big chunk.

Won't the others feel alienated?

We tell everybody in India, whether you believe this god or that god, or whether you are worshipping in this fashion or that fashion, so long as you love your motherland, so long as you love the traditions of this country, you are a Hindu.

What exactly do you mean by 'traditions'?

Our Congress friends say, this nation has come into existence from 1947 onwards. Therefore, somebody has been described as the father of the nation. This is one view.

Then, we have our Communists friends who say, this is not one nation and there are 17 or 18 nations; they call it a union of nations like the Soviet Union.

There is a third viewpoint which we uphold. We say this is a nation which has been in existence from time immemorial, for more than five thousand years.

Freedom in 1947 is only a new chapter in the history of the nation. So, we are carrying forward the history, the achievements and the failures, the aspirations and the goals of the people. It is a civilisational concept. Those concepts do play a major role in the psyche of the people.

Is it not true that when the British came here, we had many princely States and they remained independent of each other?

Yes, there were (several princely States). Therefore, the unity of this nation is not based on any political leadership. We had a number of kings, a number of empires, but at the same time we were one people; from the Himalayas to Kanyakumari.

Just think, so many centuries back, before any of these foreigners came to India, a boy from Kerala (Sankaracharya), from Kaladi, walked all over India, established *mutts* all over the country. He also ensured that all the *mutts* were properly maintained. He wanted to strengthen the unity of the nation like this. So, the concept of nationhood was in existence for thousands of years in spite of the fact that political entities were manifold.

There was a feeling among people even then that we had one common civilisation, and we belonged to one nation. Right from the *Vishnu Purana,* references about the subcontinent being one nation exist.

One charge against the BJP is that you do not accept pluralism. In a country like India, we have people belonging to various States, talking in different languages and following different cultures.

But we do accept pluralism. There may be many types of plants and many number of flowers of various hues and colours in a garden; but it is still a garden. Similarly, in this country of multifarious diversities, there is a common unity. If you can describe in one word the common unity pervading the entire country, it is Hindutva.

When you go from Kashmir to Kanyakumari, the same national ethos are reflected. So that does not stand in the way of various people adopting different religions, speaking different languages, worshipping differently or dressing differently. That is the beauty of India, its diversity.

Is it because people in northern India accepted the BJP first that you try to talk about Hindi and the Hindi heartland culture? At least that is the BJP's image in the South.

Yes, that is the way in which some people look at the BJP. But may I remind you of one thing? Any national current which had its impact in the entire country had its origins in the Indo-Gangetic plain. The impact was first felt in Northern India. Take any religion. Take the Congress party itself. It had its origins there and only from there did it spread to the other parts of the country. The Indo-Gangetic plain forms the heart of the nation, and every other part gets the impact later on by a slow process.

So, if the BJP first emerged as a major political force in northern India and subsequently in Southern India, it does not make any difference. We are only following the old tradition.

Do you regret what happened at Ayodhya on the 6 December 1992? Is it not true, it gave the BJP a very negative image, a black spot so to speak?

I will not describe it as a black spot. All I can say is that it was unexpected. As far as the BJP or the RSS or the VHP which organised the programme is concerned, we had not bargained for it. We had not anticipated that kind of a development. It took place.

And according to the government, there were some other forces which worked to create chaos for their own political gain. Some anti-national elements had their gains too. They worked upon the sentiments of the people.

But the fact remains that the building had to go one day or the other. What we wanted was, removing or relocating the building, honourably and in a legal manner. If the Muslim brethren felt it was a mosque which was sacred to them, we wouldn't have thought about that. We don't want to hurt their feelings. But the majority accepts the place is very sacred to the Hindus.

Will not our Christian friends feel very proud of the place where Jesus Christ was born? Will not our Muslim brethren feel proud about the place where Prophet Mohammed was born? Is it not scared for them? Similarly, as far as Hindus are concerned, they feel proud of the birthplace of Lord Rama. There was a special consideration for the place.

As far as the Muslim brethren were concerned, they don't have a kind of attachment to the place. They had attachment to the building only because it was a mosque. But it was not a functioning mosque for more than 54 years. Not a single Muslim had gone there to offer *namaz* in the disputed building. It is a fact.

Of course, our opponents have been shouting the mosque has been demolished! That is not because they had any love for the mosque, that is only because of their love for Muslims votes.

Do you regret what happened?

I don't regret it.

For what had happened on that day?

Why should anybody regret that? After all, a national humiliation had gone. If you look at the history of the building, how it came to be, you will know that it was not built for the purpose of conducting worship. It was built for the sole purpose of humiliating Hindus. It has been recorded. It is proved by historical evidence.

But many human lives were lost while you corrected a historical wrong.

It was not because of that. Subsequently, they let loose violence all over the country. I can tell you about Kerala. In the places where the Muslims were strong, where they had a majority, they destroyed many temples. In Malappuram district, some six or seven temples were destroyed, especially those belonging to harijans. Seventeen temples were destroyed in Kerala alone. It must be a few hundred in India. I will not blame the Muslims. I will blame only the political parties. They told the Muslims, 'Your mosque has been demolished'. Naturally, religious-minded Muslims felt offended. I don't blame them at all. Petty politicians with a view to corner Muslim votes exploited their sentiments.

A Muslim friend of mine from Tamil Nadu who had vociferously supported the BJP as far as the Ram Janmabhoomi was concerned told me, he felt isolated and terrified after the Babri Masjid demolition. Many people asked him to go back to his country, that is Pakistan to them. They were talking to a person who is as Indian as any of us. What do you say about this?

Because of the continued propaganda, many people were misled. But it was a historical event that took place. Yes, it should not have taken place that way. We had pleaded that the building should be relocated like it is done in many countries. Technology is available for that. If the Muslims feel so concerned about the building, there are ways by which it can be relocated. But because of the mob psychology or mob fury, it happened. It just happened.

Do you have plans to follow up the Kashi and Mathura temples?

It is not on our agenda now.

To most Indians, especially those who live in South or North-Eastern India, it does not really matter whether a temple is built at Ayodhya or Mathura. They have so many other concerns and worries.

You are quite right. After all, a temple here or a temple there or a mosque here is not such a serious consideration for many. But you see, these are all symbolic.

If you look back, you see a nation that was enslaved for about a thousand years where people had undergone great humiliation because their scared places of worship were demolished and destroyed by foreign enemies.

After the country became free, it is but natural that the patriots felt those symbols of humiliation (should be) removed. It is also a fact that there are more than 3,000 temples which were demolished by the opponent forces. Now it is difficult to see that all those things are rectified. It is not possible.

But the VHP and some great *sanyasins* have identified these three places which are of great concern as far as Hindus are concerned, like the place where Lord Rama was born, the place where Lord Krishna was born, and Varanasi, the most sacred place of Lord Siva. These three places should be returned to the Hindus. We are prepared to forget the rest. I think it is in the interest of the Muslims also.

If they hand back these three places to the Hindus, they can earn the love and respect and regard of the whole community. It will be a symbol of friendship between the two communities. Unfortunately, they are misled by petty politicians who are only concerned about votes.

Why does the BJP drag religion into politics? Is not religion very personal?

Yes, (it is) personal.

The concept of God is also very, very personal.

There are some people who do not believe in God also. There should be place for them too.

Yes, there should be a place for atheists also. But the BJP is accused of using religion to get votes.

No, we don't want to use religion to get votes. But you have to remember one thing. We have a 5,000-year-old civilisation. It has its soul, distinct in nature. And if we work in tune with our national culture, our nation's progress can be better ensured. It is better to remember what Vivekananda said, 'If you want to teach the people of India politics, economics or anything, we have to speak to them in the language they understand'. That means, the language of religion or spiritualism. It is not against this religion or that religion.

When people like Gopal Krishna Gokhale and other leaders with a Western orientation spoke to Indians in a liberal language of the West during the freedom struggle, people were not concerned. But when people like Tilak and Mahatma Gandhi spoke in their language, they understood. They organised Ganesh Utsava to inculcate the feeling of love for the country.

Is that the reason why the BJP is using religion to reach out to people?

Not religion. When we say, 'Rama is our national hero and his birthplace was conquered by foreigners and let us get it back', it creates a feeling of nationalism and patriotism and love for our tradition in the minds of people.

It is not against any religion. We are only reminding people of their own heritage. When I say I love my mother or wife, it does not mean that I hate another man's mother or wife. It is a positive concept.

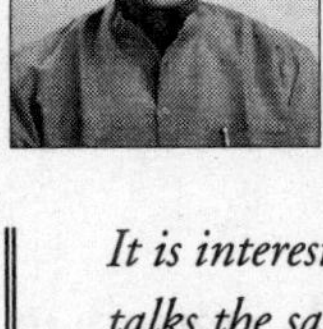

It is interesting to note that even after more than two decades, the BJP still talks the same language. O Rajagopal, the veteran BJP leader born in the year 1929, got elected as the BJP's first MLA to the Kerala Assembly in 2015, at the age of 87!

The LTTE and its India Connection

The interim Jain Commission report also led to many discussions on how the LTTE was trained on Indian soil in the 1980s.

It was believed that there were camps in Tamil Nadu when MGR (M G Ramachandran) was the Chief Minister that trained the Tamil Tigers.

One man, the so-called 'the second most powerful man' at that time in Tamil Nadu, was ***K Mohandas****, the then Director General of Police (DGP). He was often described as 'MGR's eyes and ears' and the only man ever to have arrested the LTTE leader V Prabhakaran two times.*

He was an eyewitness to the Indian government's sponsorship of the Tamil Tigers. Nobody had as much knowledge about the Indian government-LTTE nexus, and the sordid events that led to the assassination of Rajiv Gandhi.

IT is said that sympathy for Sri Lankan Tamils started in Tamil Nadu during MGR's period. You were then the DGP.

When did you realise that MGR was sympathetic to the Tamil militants?

It is not correct to say that MGR was sympathetic to Tamil militants. The political circumstances forced him to take an attitude in which he had to support the militants, particularly because of the attitude of the Government of India.

Does that mean the Centre was more sympathetic to Tamil militants than Tamil Nadu?

As I was the Chief of Intelligence in Tamil Nadu from 1977 to 1986, I was in a rather privileged position to study and analyse the twists, turns and gyrations of India's Sri Lankan policy, a policy which in all probability had a bearing on the assassination of Rajiv Gandhi.

The hallmark of India's Sri Lankan policy, which was created at the time of Mrs Gandhi and her foreign policy advisors, was what I may call for its 'consistent inconsistency'.

India first created the LTTE monster, then maintained it, and later sought to destroy it.

Had MGR no hand in the policy?

At that time, he had no hand in it. The policy was formulated by the Chairman of the Planning Committee, and the Foreign Secretary, reportedly based on inputs from the intelligence agencies, RAW and IB.

I must tell you one thing; the intelligence agencies work in such top secret fashion on such sensitive issues that there is little scope for documentary, and other evidence (being) left behind and these are normally destroyed.

Anyway, let me say that it was a dual policy. Being committed to Sri Lanka's integrity on the one hand and permitting training of militant groups on Indian soil, on the other.

No wonder Rajiv Gandhi, while inheriting the policy, had reportedly said, he had his own reservations about the inherent contradictions in the policy. He asked, 'how can we then charge Pakistan with helping militants in Punjab and Kashmir?' But the policy advisors and the intelligence agencies, who had vested interests in continuing the policy, blocked Rajiv Gandhi on some pretext or the other from putting the block back.

Who were the vested interests?

One: egoism of the top behind-the-scene men.

Two: when a person sets on a course, he is forced to continue the same line despite adverse factors arising during the course, because he is afraid that his original stand may be questioned.

Large unaudited funds were placed at the disposal of the intelligence agencies for secret operations.

There were reports in the *Indian Express* dated 9th and 10th of July 1992 that some members of the Parliament had called for the expenditure incurred by RAW to be sanctioned by a parliamentary intelligence committee in view of suspected embezzlement.

You said, political circumstances forced MGR to take a supporting attitude to the Tamil militants. But that is not the general belief. What was his real attitude to militancy?

That is not a correct thing to say. MGR, like any other person in power, was only interested in continuing in power. When the Centre said, do this, he did that. He might have had his own reservations. We are not able to say what was in his mind because he was the most difficult man to understand.

You were then in charge of the police. Didn't he ever express his feelings about militants to you?

He always gave the impression that we must follow whatever the Indian government said. What he said was, after all Tamil Nadu is a State of India and this particular policy comes under foreign affairs in which the States have no option.

It was reported that there were camps for militants here, and they were getting arms supplies too. Is it not true that people and politicians of Tamil Nadu backed the militants more than the people of any other State in India?

The influx of Tamil militants to Tamil Nadu happened firstly because of the persecution policy followed by Sri Lanka.

Secondly, this decision to bring those militants here to give them training was taken in Delhi. Whatever Delhi said, MGR followed. I told him several times that it was a very dangerous policy because Tamil Nadu was becoming a land of gun-and-bomb culture.

Was he not scared of the bomb culture that was growing here then?

That is not a right question in the sense that nobody in power is afraid of bombs and guns because they know how to protect themselves.

Do you know politicians despise the professionals?

But many leaders could not protect themselves. It boomeranged in the end. Whether it was Indira Gandhi or Rajiv Gandhi.

These are very sensitive past issues. There is no point in talking about it now. But the influx of Tamil militants was not confined to Tamil Nadu alone. They were given training in many places in North India as well.

There were more training camps in Tamil Nadu, and they got more publicity too.

It might have been so. But the quality of the training is more important than the training itself. Yes, it is all very well known. The photographs of the places where the training camps were held also got worldwide publicity.

There were training camps in Tamil Nadu, Karnataka, Uttar Pradesh and New Delhi. But they were trained by the central agencies and there were no training centres run by Tamil Nadu.

Is it news to you that the Tamil Nadu government did not run any training camps?

Yes. I thought the State government had a hand in it.

But MGR did one thing. He gave financial support to them. The training camps were done in a hush-hush manner, but he gave money to them openly. It was the government's money.

That means he was sympathetic to the Tamil militants.

You are jumping to conclusions. He gave money. You may give money to help them, you may also do it to help yourself. When people are scared, they do that.

So, MGR was scared.

I didn't say that. Just because he gave money, you cannot say that he was sympathetic. I am giving you options.

You said MGR did whatever the Centre asked him to. What was the attitude of the DMK and the other State parties to Tamil militants?

Since Prabhakaran was with MGR, the other fellows were with the other political parties.

Do you think the attitude of the politicians in Tamil Nadu changed later on, that is after MGR died? Karunanidhi

has been blamed by the Jain Commission for supporting the LTTE.

The LTTE was with MGR first, and after his death, it was with the DMK.

As far as 1989 is concerned (when the DMK was in power), I was not in the picture, so it is not fair on my part to comment about the DMK. I can only say from what I have heard. See, once an intelligence officer, always an intelligence officer!

Rajiv Gandhi thought Karunanidhi was trying to get close to the LTTE. So, he wanted to talk to them through the DMK. He was also scared because Premadasa, who had by then become the President of Sri Lanka, and the Tamil militants were getting closer, which he wanted to avoid. Premadasa was against the (*Indo-Sri Lankan*) accord.[1]

Those were the two reasons why Rajiv Gandhi wanted to use Karunanidhi and Murasoli Maran to talk to the LTTE. But Prabhakaran did not want anything or anyone to come between him and absolute power.

Yes, there appeared to be some help from the government to put down (the Eelam People's Revolutionary Liberation Front, *EPRLF, leader*) K Padmanabha. Right in T Nagar (in Chennai), 15 people were shot dead and none of the accused was arrested.

You were summoned by the Jain Commission. What is your opinion about such commissions?

These commissions usually do not get us anywhere. There is a joke in the Central Secretariat that if you cannot find anything, refer it to a commission.

---

[1] The Indo-Sri Lanka Peace Accord was an accord signed in Colombo on 29 July 1987, between the then Indian Prime Minister Rajiv Gandhi and Sri Lankan President J R Jayewardene.

The fruits of the Jain Commission appear to be highly politicised. A commission does not conduct a regular trial. I wonder why Mr Jain made a mess of the whole thing, as if he was conducting a regular trial.

The alleged leakage of the interim report made things worse. There is already a case under trial in which the judgment is slated to be delivered. It is for the legal pundits to discern, as to what extent the Jain report would affect or overlap the trial in the special court.

In fact, the conspiracy aspect and the security lapses aspect would have formed part of the whole case. The present difficulty has risen out of the fact that the conspiracy aspect and the security aspect were taken away from the main case of the trial of the accused. Worse will follow if the findings of the three judges clash with each other.

What was the atmosphere in the State when the Tamil militants were around?

Very bad. There were so many militant groups and there was rivalry among them. The first sign of the fall-out among them was a shoot-out between Prabhakaran and Uma Maheshwaran.[2] They were arrested immediately. But this shootout on 19 May 1982 in the Pondy Bazaar area brought to surface the shocking fact that the militant groups had chosen Tamil Nadu not only as a sanctuary for their political fight against the Sri Lankan government but also as an arena to settle scores among themselves. That also covers the murder of Padmanabha.

I have the gratification of having arrested Prabhakaran twice and know something of his psychology! The arrest of

---

2 A Sri Lankan Tamil rebel and founder/leader of the People's Liberation Organisation of Tamil Eelam, PLOTE, a separatist Tamil militant organisation in Sri Lanka.

Prabhakaran and Sivakumar of the LTTE, and Maheshwaran and Jyotheeswaran of PLOTE, put a momentary stop to their mutual rivalry. After the incident, we came to know that they were well trained in handling firearms.

Were the police there when the shootout started?

We were there soon. Though the Central Government was not giving us intelligence reports, we had our own intelligence apparatus.

Was MGR aware of the law-and-order situation in the State?

I had a hotline with him, and I used to inform him immediately. I was not aware whether MGR was politically informed about these activities, because whenever I conveyed the news to him, he only told me, 'Inform New Delhi'. I told him it was too serious a matter to be handled at my level. But MGR continued his sphinx-like posture.

I did write to the directors of IB and RAW but there was no proper response from them.

As far as Tamil Nadu was concerned, each training camp was a mini-Union territory completely controlled by the central agencies to which the State intelligence or the State police had no access. It was almost a takeover of chunks of Tamil Nadu territory by the Centre.

But MGR was unmoved. The news of the training camps hit the headlines all over the world and photographs of the camps with the addresses were published in the periodicals. All the while, the Government of India went on denying the existence of these camps.

Refugees, yes. But militants and training camps, no; that was the Government's persistent comment.

You arrested Prabhakaran after the first shootout in T Nagar. What conclusions did you come to after questioning him?

That he is more a terrorist than a patriot.

How did the second arrest come about?

First of November 1986. Deepavali day at Choolaimedu, right in the heart of Madras city (now Chennai). Broad daylight. A stunned and shocked State. Following a petty dispute of hiring an autorickshaw, a member of the EPRLF sprayed 60 bullets at the unarmed citizens of Madras, killing a young Dalit lawyer and injuring many others.

The perpetrators of the crime, though armed with sophisticated weapons, were quickly disarmed and taken into custody by the Commissioner of Police, Walter Devaram.

I immediately conveyed the news to MGR and repeated my concern about the activities of the militants of all hues, and the effect it was having on the law-and-order situation in the State. I told him it was high time that a fully coordinated and firm action was taken to keep them under control.

Was MGR unmoved?

He said once again, inform Delhi.

Was he not worried at all?

Looking at an actor's face, you will not be able to say whether he was worried or not. First of all, it was difficult to deal with a chief minister in the normal course of things itself. More so, if he is a film actor. They have these 'expressions' or 'no expressions'. Mostly, it is 'no expressions'!

How could he remain unmoved when such violence was affecting the State?

I should tell you frankly. Whether it is Bill Clinton or Indira Gandhi or Rajiv Gandhi or MGR, the feeling uppermost in their minds is for their own safety and their own well-being. All the rest come only later. This is my personal feeling, which I gathered from experience.

What happened after you conveyed your concern about the law-and-order situation in the State to the intelligence agencies in Delhi?

I telephoned the Additional Director, IB, at New Delhi and repeated what I had told MGR. I added that it was a serious matter and needed to be brought to the Prime Minister's notice at once.

I got a message on the 4th of November 1986, from the Home Ministry saying that SAARC (South Asian Association for Regional Cooperation) summit was going to take place in Bangalore, and they were worried because (the Sri Lankan President J R) Jayewardene was coming. See, when they want protection, they ask. Otherwise, they will keep quiet. They wanted the police and security authorities in Tamil Nadu to ensure very stringent security arrangements for the SAARC summit.

The message particularly stated that a watch should be kept on the likely movements of the Sri Lankan militants towards Bangalore as they might make an attempt to cause physical harm to Jayewardene.

Their message also stated that the IB must be requested to furnish details of the militant group activities to the DGP. So, it revealed that this information was till then not conveyed to the DGP. Another catch was that it was not the IB which was dealing with the activities of the militant groups but RAW! Their right hand apparently did not know what the left was doing.

The next day, MGR summoned me and straightaway asked me to disarm the Sri Lankan militants based in Tamil Nadu. I told the chief minister that it was an almost impossible task in view of the sophisticated weapons known to be in possession of the militants. I felt it was a matter that should be handled by the army or paramilitary forces. I also told him that it was politically unwise for the TN government to take such an action as the matter involved a foreign country.

MGR told me, the Centre was reluctant to use the army or paramilitary forces. Because in the event of an armed confrontation, there would be an international reaction to it. MGR further asked me to somehow disarm them as he had given his word to the PM. I told MGR that I had to think about it and formulate a plan which would be least risky to the police officers and men to be involved in the exercise. He asked me not to inform the IB or RAW about the information, and also the top State officials like the Chief Secretary and Home Secretary were to be kept in the dark.

Why did he want to keep it a secret from them?

Somebody told him, it should be a top secret! I told him I would not be in a position to tell even him as to when and how I proposed to strike. He agreed with his usual thumbs up sign.

I had a sleepless night thinking about the suicidal task. Finally, I thought of a plan with a large dose of psychological input, which I thought might work with good amount of luck.

The operation was slated for the early hours of 8 November. I sent small groups of policemen to go to the commander of the militants' camp and assure him of all help. See, it was the small fellows who were involved in all the shootouts. So, the policemen told the commander, 'When everyone is helping you, why do you want to shoot at ordinary people? Let us keep all your weapons safely in one place for a while so nobody will have access to your weapons. You lock the room and keep the key.' Can you believe, all of them fell into the trap?

Within 400 metres of each camp, I had specially trained commandos waiting, and they were directly in touch with me. The moment the weapons were kept inside a room, the jeeps of the commandos went right inside the camp and seized all the weapons. We disarmed everyone, including Prabhakaran.

How did MGR react?

He said, 'Hmmmmm. Oh, did you do it? How many died?' This was not the way to respond. I didn't like it. He also thought we would not do it.

That evening we were sitting in my room with my lieutenants. All the arms were spread there. I got a call from Delhi. It was the Foreign Secretary. He said he was speaking from the PM's room and the Prime Minister wanted to know why *the militants* were let free. He asked, why were they not arrested? I said, instructions were given only to disarm them and not arrest them.

He said, 'put all these people, including Prabhakaran under house arrest'. I told him, 'I cannot take orders from you'. He gave the phone to MGR who was also in the room. I checked with him. In the meanwhile, we found that there was no provision in the law for house arrest. We could only keep them under watch. MGR said, do something.

The next morning MGR came back to Madras. The first thing he told me was, 'I am going to Bangalore to attend the SAARC conference. If possible, I want to talk to Prabhakaran from Bangalore.' I assured him that it could be arranged. It was easy to convince Prabhakaran because he used to tell me, 'You are a professional. I am a professional. So, there is no problem.'

Was it true that Prabhakaran was MGR's pet?

Of all the militant groups, the LTTE was the most dedicated. That was one reason why MGR liked him.

Reason number two was, he was a very bold man. MGR appreciated dedication to the cause and liked bold men.

You were talking about MGR's desire to talk to Prabhakaran.

Yes. A special IAF aircraft was arranged to take Prabhakaran and Anton Balasingham (the LTTE ideologue) to Bangalore. I had my sources in Bangalore. So, I tried to find out what was cooking there. They had a plan to offer the chief ministership of the north (Jaffna) to Prabhakaran. Remember, they offered only the north and not the north-east. Prabhakaran said, nothing doing.

I don't know whether he met Jayewardene or not. These people thought like Indian politicians, Prabhakaran also could be lured by the offer of a chief ministership!

The next day MGR came back and at the airport itself, he shouted, 'What has this Prabhakaran done? I tried to help him by getting him something, but he didn't want that. Why is he behaving like this?' He then called me to his residence and said, 'We must teach him a lesson. Seize all the wireless systems'. I said, 'Sir, it is a foolish thing to do. We are also able to get some information about their activities because of the wireless. The IB also gets some information'. He shouted, 'No, do it immediately'. We finished the operation in an hour.

The next day Prabhakaran went on a hunger strike. He was not bothered about arms, because he knew he could always get arms. Communication was something very important to him. I was out of station at that time. The hunger strike went on and finally MGR said, 'give everything back including the arms'.

When I came back, I was shocked to see what had happened. I got wild. At least we should also get wild once in a while!

I asked him, 'What have you done? Everybody has praised the operation and now you have given back everything'. He couldn't say anything then. Then I said, 'I am resigning'. He was silent. But I did not resign because I was told I would lose some money if I resigned then. I did not tell him that. Even if I did, he would not have understood. I decided I would go on long leave. That was the end of my rendezvous with Prabhakaran and the militants.

You can see from what I have said that from 1982-83 the central intelligence agencies were actively building up and encouraging the Sri Lankan Tamil militant groups by training them in camps set up on Indian soil, funding them and also supplying them with large quantities of arms, ammunition and explosives apparently on instructions from the Prime Minister's foreign policy advisors and intelligence chiefs.

In my professional judgement, the last chance that came for putting things right was on 8 November 1986, when all the militant groups were disarmed, and Tamil Nadu was liberated from a grave menace. But the effects of the breakthrough were most unfortunately reversed within weeks. This sequence of events is, in my opinion, highly relevant to the circumstances that led to the tragic assassination of Rajiv Gandhi.

These revelations, from K Mohandas who was in the thick of what was going on in the early eighties, expose the role of both the Central and State politicians and agencies in controlling and training Tamil militants on Indian soil.

Dismiss the DMK Govt in Tamil Nadu!

The dust of the Jain commission report had not settled down when one of the supporters of the NDA, the AIADMK supremo Jayalalitha, became Vajpayee's nemesis.

She threatened to withdraw the support of her 18 party members if the Central Government did not dismiss the DMK government in Tamil Nadu. Reason: the DMK had been blamed by the interim Jain Commission report for harbouring the LTTE in the State, which resulted in the assassination of Rajiv Gandhi.

Ironically, if the DMK was the reason why the I K Gujral led United Front fell in 1997, in 1998 the same DMK became the reason behind Vajpayee's end as the Prime Minister too.

Interestingly, Tamil Nadu played a significant role in those days deciding who would rule the Centre!

I spoke to ***Murasoli Maran****, the DMK's leader in Parliament, on Jayalalitha's demand for the dismissal of the DMK government in Tamil Nadu.*

Maran was more than a nephew to M Karunanidhi, the Chief Minister of Tamil Nadu. He was Karunanidhi's contact person in Delhi, and Karunanidhi also depended on Maran for support and advice.

DO you feel threatened by the way Jayalalitha is pressurising the NDA at the Centre to dismiss the DMK government in Tamil Nadu?

It is not a question of us feeling threatened. She is threatened. So, she is threatening the BJP. Unfortunately, the BJP is depending on this lady. If the BJP leaders stop worrying about their image, they may not do anything. It is a question of following principled politics as they have been following earlier or switching over to Machiavellian tactics – the end justifying the means.

Not only India, but the whole world is watching what Mr Vajpayee is going to do. Is he going to succumb to the pressures of this lady, or is he going to stand on principles?

What do you think he will do?

I feel, finally good sense will prevail. In the sense, the BJP is not a fly-by-night party. It has achieved its goal for the first time, and they have to be on the Indian scene for a long time. If they give a go-by to the principles of democracy and federalism just for the sake of power, then I think they have to declare themselves enemies of democracy and federalism.

People will only weigh them according to that position. I feel they will think twice before taking a drastic decision. But we can't say. Because there is another lobby in the BJP, I know. There is a dignified side of the BJP represented by Vajpayee. There is another ugly face of the BJP also.

You mean the Sangh Parivar?

I don't want to name anyone. They want to stick to power at any cost. Nothing succeeds like success for them. Power at any cost. We really do not know which side will win.

If the BJP succumbs to the extremists and dismisses the DMK government, what will happen?

Then 14 other governments have to go. Bihar has to go. Rajasthan has to go, Maharashtra has to go. Orissa has to go.... Are they going to dismiss 14 State governments?

After his meeting with the PM, the Tamil Nadu chief minister said, Vajpayee would not sacrifice the DMK government to save his. Did the PM assure him about that?

I don't know. But there are certain Machiavellian attitudes in any party, not only in the BJP. The Machiavellian attitude is that the end is more important than the means. I don't know which will succeed. We are prepared for any eventuality.

If the BJP thwarts Jayalalitha and if she withdraws support, will you support the BJP?

That question does not arise now. Let us cross the bridge when we come to it. Still it is an unstable government.

At present, the instability is caused by the AIADMK front.

When I was a minister in a minority government (the United Front), I refused to go abroad. There were several occasions, but what is the use of going? You cannot fool them. If we go to the USA or UK and say, we are a stable government, they will laugh. They know more about us than we know about ourselves. You can't fool them.

Whenever I went abroad, I used to say, 'yes, ours is a minority government'. For some more time, we will have coalition governments.

At least, regarding the economic policies, there is some kind of consensus. So, you need not worry. Governments may fall, but policies will continue.

The BJP has always been against using Article 356.

It is always a test for every party. For example, when I was in the United Front government, a clamour for the dismissal of the UP government came, but I put my foot down. I was the only one who opposed it. In spite of it, the Cabinet carried the show. Then the President sent it back. I fought a lonely battle. I said, 'in that case, the DMK will quit the government'. I am sorry to say Mulayam Singh and the others walked out of the Cabinet meeting. They said, it did not matter even if we lost the government.

The argument at that time was that there were 95 cabinet members and horse trading was going on. I said, 'let the people of UP decide'. If there are 95 members in the cabinet, they will become a laughing stock. 'And next time, they can't come (to power). People will teach them a lesson. But if you kick them out now, they will become martyrs'.

I said, 'people of the State are the masters of their destiny. Who are you? Who are we? So, we should not stand on a moral pedestal. We should go by the principles of federalism'. That was how I fought.

The next day, Mr Vajpayee telephoned and congratulated me. Dr Murli Manohar Joshi wrote a beautiful letter saying, whatever I have done will go a long way in strengthening the healthy relationship between the Centre and the States. That was the position I had taken then.

So, if something is being done to the DMK government, it is okay. Ultimately people are there to judge. We are sure of coming back, if at all we are dismissed. But the image of the BJP will not be the same as before. And people all over the world are watching.

But the pressure from Jayalalitha can become too much for them to bear.

I don't think they are happy. Nobody will be happy with the way this lady is behaving. She is doing all this for her own selfish purpose. You know what the purpose is. Several cases of corruption against her are at various stages in various courts. She thinks by dismissing the government and imposing President's rule, she can put pressure on the Central Government to withdraw all those cases. But it can't be done so easily (and that) is another matter.

Her game plan is to get out of those cases of corruption. Those are not ordinary cases; they are cases of corruption worth several crores of rupees.

Do you feel Article 356 should be scrapped?

That was the DMK's opinion from the beginning. For example, do you have such a clause in America? Theoretically, President Clinton can press a nuclear button and destroy the world. But he can't dismiss the Governors of New York or California.

Such powers existed in the 1935 Constitution, because the British did not trust the *swadeshis.* Today it should have no place in the Constitution which calls itself federal.

Will any government at the Centre scrap the Article? Will they try?

It is possible. We discussed it. It was sent to the Inter-State Council, and they appointed a standing committee. I was one of the members.

Do you know who advocated scraping of this Article 356? Myself, belonging to the DMK, the Telugu Desam party, the Asom Gana Parishad, the chief minister of Rajasthan, Shekhawat belonging to the BJP and then the Shiv Sena. All five of us opposed the Article.

Do you know who wanted it to be in the Constitution? The Congress, that is, the Orissa chief minister. You will be surprised to know who the other person was. Mr Jyoti Basu.

I argued with Mr. Basu, 'Why do you want it? You are supposed to be a democrat, you are supposed to be an advocate of federalism.' He said, 'No, Mr Maran, see, tomorrow communal parties will come to power in some States. We want to dismiss those communal governments.' Then I asked him, "if communal parties come to power in Delhi, what will you do?' He said, 'No, no, it will not come. We will see.'

Now what has happened?

Even if the so-called communal parties come to power, it will be only when people vote for them. When people want some party in power, does any other party have the right to say anything against it?

That's right. That is why I said, if people want them, who are you or who am I to say otherwise?

The general impression about the DMK is that they are soft on Muslim fundamentalists. How true is this impression?

We are soft on minorities. We hate fundamentalism from any side.

By being soft on Muslims, are you not alienating the Hindus?

We are not soft on Muslims alone. We are soft on all minorities. Minorities have a role to play. We should be generous.

Won't you be alienating the majority then?

How? Do you want to throw all the minorities into the Bay of Bengal?

What will the majority feel when you are extra soft on the minorities?

Tell me one instance where we have given them anything extra? We are treating them as equals, that's all. We are not ignoring them. We are respecting their wishes. What is wrong in that?

Our party was started in the 1940s as a social reformist party to uplift the minorities and the backward classes, and not to contest elections. The purpose of our party is the development of backward classes and minorities.

In India, most political parties look at and treat backward classes and minorities as vote banks. Do you agree with that?

Every political party is for vote banks. So, if you are for the minority, you are for a bigger vote bank. Tell me one political party which does not want a vote bank? Everybody wants to have a vote bank, if possible. You cannot treat minorities as a group of mindless people. They vote according to their conscience. The idea of dubbing them just as vote bank is totally wrong. By doing so, you are treating them as sheep which blindly follow the shepherd.

Do you think the rise of the BJP is because Hindus started feeling that all the political parties are giving undue importance to the minorities?

I beg to differ. In Tamil Nadu, everybody is treated equal. We are all citizens of India. We can't give greater status to X, Y or Z.

Then, what according to you is the reason for the rise of the BJP?

Where is the alternative? The Congress has disintegrated. Sitaram Kesri has made it a big zero. In the Janata Dal, there was a lot of infighting. The Communists are restricted to West Bengal, Kerala and Tripura. We are limited to Tamil Nadu. The TDP is there only in Andhra Pradesh. People are searching for an alternative, but there is not a good alternative. So, take it from me, even today if there is a good alternative, people will accept it.

Even the BJP is a big regional party. It belongs to the cow belt. I think the future belongs to regional parties, a coalition of regional parties. A bigger regional party like the BJP, the Congress or Janata Dal may lead it, that's all.

Do you attribute the rise of the regional parties to the arrogant attitude and functioning of the Congress?

The Congress was associated with the freedom movement. After you attain freedom, people wanted economic freedom, but it was not there. The dynasty had a very big role to play. A very useful role.

Useful role?

Yes, at that time, India wanted leadership. Mrs Gandhi came, and in spite of the Emergency, she provided some kind of a leadership. Rajiv Gandhi's tenure was very short, and I don't want to comment on that. But there is no such kind of all-India leadership now. It can't be in the future also.

People evaluate each and every person and party on merit, on what they can do and what they have done. So, the future belongs to the regional parties. We have to get accustomed to coalitions.

Fast forward to 2022. The regional party, the party of the cow belt, became a national party and won majority of its own to rule the country. And the national party, the Congress, has been reduced to insignificance.

It is astonishing to see how the fortunes of various political parties change as time passes by. Some grow in size, and some disintegrate. Remember, DMK leader Murasoli Maran had said, 'if there is a good alternative, people will accept it'.

Swadeshi? No. More Reforms? Yes.

When the Indian economy was liberalised in 1991, the GDP growth was just 1.1 per cent but it grew to 5.5 per cent in 1992. The highest GDP growth was in 1995 and 1996 at 7.6 per cent and 7.5 per cent respectively. The instability at the Centre resulted in a huge fall to 4 per cent in 1997 under the United Front government!

Then the BJP, which spoke strongly about swadeshi, came to power under Atal Bihari Vajpayee. Still there was no stability to be seen. But Vajpayee spoke about some interesting futuristic projects like the National Highways.

The question in everybody's mind was, is it going to be swadeshi vs liberalisation? Will they go back to protectionism again? There was also a fear that the votaries of swadeshi might reverse liberalisation.

But many management experts warned about the repercussions if India were to reverse liberalisation and go back to protectionism. They said, what India needed was more reforms so that it could compete with the rest of the world, and not protectionism.

One such voice was that of **Gurcharan Das,** *popularly called the Management Guru.*

When I spoke to him in 1998, he was a member in the Vajpayee Government's Foreign Investment Promotion Council. Here, he analyses India's potential and predicts where it will be by 2020 and 2050.

YOU portrayed a very rosy and optimistic picture of India in the next 25 to 50 years. Do you see China and India emerging as very significant centres of economic growth and development?

Absolutely. But China will do it fast, and I expect China to be a major economic force by 2015. India is 20 years behind China. So, the south and west of India will achieve that status by 2025 and the eastern part of Uttar Pradesh, Bihar, Bengal, Orissa, the North-East will reach that level by 2050.

China is a Communist country, and it has gone far ahead of India, a democracy. Is there a relation between democracy and economic development?

Democracy actually does not help drive economic growth. Certainly, when it comes to reforms, it is much easier if you move much faster, if you have unitary command and if you have a reformer at the top like Deng Xiaoping was in China.

So, democracy has that disadvantage in making changes. But in the long run, democracy is more secure and more certain way of moving. What happens is that you have tremendous amount of debates and it takes much longer time to get a consensus. But once that consensus is achieved, it is shared by all the people. So, there is a lot more sense of shared future in a democracy. Therefore, the whole process is secure and there is little risk of it going back.

How do you compare the economic growth of China and India?

China has been growing at double the rate of India. Even this year, which is a bad year for China, it will grow at 7 per cent, and India will grow at 5 per cent. So, by and large, once we get out of this recession, we will become a 7 per cent growth economy, and we could even go up to 8 per cent once the power reforms and telecom reforms are done, and we begin to reform agriculture, education, etc

China has been growing at 10 per cent for a decade. Therefore, it has a much bigger economy than ours is. Contrary to what many people think, Indian economy is still relatively small. If you take it on absolute dollar basis, our economy is 16th in the world, about the size of Belgium, just a little ahead. If you look at the purchase parity basis, our economy is the sixth largest in the world.

China is one of the biggest trading partners of the US. Indian exports and Chinese exports were equal in 1974; they were both $13 billion. Today India's exports are roughly around $30 billion while China's exports are over $150 billion. The numbers speak for themselves.

Our market is said to be big, still....

Potentially our market is big, and it will grow big.

Any sensible person will realise that in the 21st century, India and China will be the biggest economies in the world. Because our market is big, the process of global Capitalism backed by technology will ensure that India will rise, and the people will be far better off. By 2020, I think the middle class of India will be around 50 per cent (of the population).

You described 1991 as India's second independence and we grew pretty fast for sometime. But after that, there is a slowdown. What went wrong?

The main difficulty in our foreign investment is that the major investments that were going to come were to be in infrastructure, power, telecom, roads, ports, etc We have not been able to reform ourselves to the point of being able to receive the investment. In other words, we have to create institutions, which will bring in the foreign investment.

Our State electricity boards are bankrupt. You expect foreign companies to put up power plants here. But why will they put up power plants when the customer is bankrupt? We should have worked out an arrangement, which will ensure that the new power plants get paid for the power they generate.

It is not that we do not have answers to our problems. It is not a question of what we have to do. It is a question of how we do it. It is a question of nuts and bolts. As they say God is in the details.

Our focus in the last five years should have been on the details. We were stuck. The bureaucrats were very obstructive. They were throwing the old rules at the foreign investors and the investors felt, how could we do business in India unless you change certain rules?

Who is responsible? Is it because we do not have a stable government at the Centre that this is happening?

No. I think it is a question of sitting down and doing the hard work of sorting out the issues. For example, coming back to the power sector. If we had said, okay the State electricity boards are bankrupt. So, how is a supplier going to sell to a bankrupt customer?

The first thing you have to do is to privatise our distribution of power. Once it is privatised, the bills are collected properly, and electricity is not stolen by people because a private customer will not allow stealing of electricity.

The State electricity boards would definitely have become healthier by the privatisation of distribution. Once the distribution is secure, the power provider will be happy to provide with power. But not every government wants to privatise the power sector and stop subsidies. They are scared of losing their vote banks.

That's what they think. But I personally think that's not true. I think a farmer would rather pay for secure power than have free power that he does not receive, or he receives between midnight and three in the morning.

Today, a lot of rural areas get power only in the night. So, they can water their field only in the middle of the night. Even a farmer is not happy about this.

Basically, the Indian voter is a decent voter, and if you explain to the voter that there is no such thing as a free lunch, that you have to pay for what you get, a decent person understands that.

The politicians themselves do not have the confidence that they can go to the voter and tell them honestly that you pay for what you get. If you say that, I think people will understand.

Why are the politicians not willing to do that?

I think it is just the mindset; they have got into populist politics or competitive politics where somebody promises two rupees for a kilo of rice. Now the voter will understand that when the rice costs five rupees a kilo, you cannot give it for two rupees a kilo.

It is a slow process of educating the voter. It is possible to do it. Even the uneducated understand the basic decency of life that you don't get anything free. These are things we learn from our mother as children. Even in unequal societies, people will understand.

So, it was wrong on the part of the earlier governments to start populist measures like subsidies in the name of socialism.

Yes, I think the bad habits got started because of the model of economic development of mixed economy or the 'Nehruvian Socialism' which, basically in the name of the poor, tried to take actions which involved subsidies.

These subsidies distorted our economy and for sometime, these distortions will continue, these inefficiencies will continue and these bad habits will continue. The people who will win in the future will be those who will be able to play the new paradigm and approach the voter with more transparency.

A person like Chandrababu Naidu?

Well, he certainly is a good example. Most people know only about his IT areas. They do not know that in villages, he has gone and created *shiksha samitis* (literacy units) and water management associations. He has created them at the *mandal* (basic village unit) level so that the villagers themselves can administer rather than the government. This way you take out bureaucratic corruption. Similarly in education, he is creating the parent associations so that the parents become more accountable.

Digvijay Singh has done the same thing in Madhya Pradesh where he has opened 20,000 schools in the last two years in the villages. People from the government go to a village and ask the villagers whether they want a school in their village. And if the villagers say yes, they find out how many parents want a school. If there are 25 parents who want a school, they are encouraged to form a *grama shiksha samiti.*

The government then tells them, 'Look, we are not going to give you a school, you are going to give yourself a school'.' Then the classroom. Somebody has a verandah, somebody has a godown and they offer one room for a school. The teachers are from the village itself. Anybody who has passed eighth standard can stand as a candidate, and then the parents select the teacher. The selected person is taken to the district headquarters to train him or her. After the training, they send him or her back with school materials.

These materials are created by a non-government organisation called Ekalavya, which is all about joyful learning, about learning that is relevant to a villager. The government pays Rs 500 to the teacher and if the parents want to pay more, they can do so. The cheque for the teacher is not sent directly to the teacher but to the panchayat, so that the teacher is accountable to the village.

The *swadeshi* lobby is said to be against liberalisation. Recently the Swadeshi Jagran Manch held a demonstration outside Parliament against opening up the insurance sector. Can *swadeshi* and liberalisation co-exist?

Frankly, if you interpret *swadeshi* as one thing to make a strong nation, there are much more domestic reforms that need to be done. The BJP leaders themselves said they would first do domestic reforms, but they have not yet done domestic reforms.

There are octrois that have to be removed, there is an uneven sales tax between States and you need to change it to VAT (value added tax) system and so on. All these will help create a common market first of all.

We got rid of license raj, but we have not got rid of inspector raj. A lot of inspector raj is from the Centre, that is the customs officials, the excise officials, and others. And they harass our entrepreneurs.

The argument of the *swadeshi* group is that the MNCs will eat away small Indian businessmen. Do you agree?

No, I think it is nonsense. The fact is that the total foreign investment is less than two per cent of total investment. So, what are they talking about? In China, it is 13 per cent of the total investment. So, China should be worried. But they are not worried, so why should we worry?

The Swadeshi Jagaran Manch says the MNCs will start dictating terms to the governments after sometime. If the investment of a company in Kerala was several times more than the income of the State government, they will have a say in the policies of the government, won't they?

I think it is all nonsense. *Swadeshi* ideology is an ideology which betrays inferiority complex. I feel the *swadeshi* people should have more confidence in their own business people to succeed.

I will give you an example of the Palanpuri Jains and what a success they have made in the world market. They are so successful that 60 per cent of the world market share of diamonds is with Indians now. There are many other examples of Indians succeeding.

If you have no confidence in your own people, you will talk *swadeshi.*

You take little Singapore, little, little Singapore. It has far more foreign investment than the whole of India does. Who has taken over Singapore? In fact, Singapore regularly lectures America on how to behave! But Singapore counts in the world market. Its reserves are over $60 billion. And the whole of India has only less than $30 billion reserves. Singapore has been created over foreign investment. So, what are these people worried about?

Gurumurthy of Swadeshi Jagaran Manch also talked about materialistic culture taking over Indian culture, which is spiritual. You said liberalisation is *baniya*isation of India as people are no longer guilty about making money. Are *baniya*isation and material pursuits one and the same?

I'll say again, we should have confidence. Has our culture not survived the Moghuls, the British? Don't you think it will survive Coca-Cola? I have a lot more confidence in the survival of Indian culture than they do. The important thing for us is to take benefits, take advantage of the global economy rather than looking at ourselves constantly as victims.

What are they talking about? They talk about potato chips versus computer chips. The trouble is you cannot choose between potato chips and computer chips. The global investment community is a linked one. You try to discourage Coca-Cola, you will see that your hi-tech industries also will get affected. Because India will get a bad name as a place to do business.

Remember the way we were treated when we threw out IBM and Coca Cola at one time.[1]

So, you cannot start differentiating. It is not easy to differentiate too. But then how do you do it? They say that we don't want consumer products but what is a consumer product? Is the PC a consumer product? Is that a hi-tech product or not? What about a telephone? Is the telephone a consumer product or not? Where do you draw the line? So, what happens then is, you give the power to the bureaucrat to make the decision and again you start the licence raj through that process. We will make our people corrupt again.

Let me ask you. What have we done in the last 50 years following *swadeshi*?

Where did it get us? We ended up on a dead-end street and there was no exit!

You talked about Adam's Theory of Convergence. You said, as the West was eight times richer than the rest of the world, when trade and investment take place between the rich and the not-so-rich, the poor will come up to the level of the rich. Will it not happen the other way, the rich coming down to the level of the not-so-rich?

I think to some extent that also can happen. Because the wage rates in the West are dropping. The jobs are getting transferred. The employers say that a worker in China is getting less wages. So, the American worker gets affected. A lot of American companies are laying off their workers. The workers tell them, okay, you were paying us $ 20 an hour till

---

[1] George Fernandez asked IBM and Coca Cola to leave India after he became the Industries Minister in 1977 when Morarji Desai was the Prime Minister.

now but we are willing to work for $10 an hour. Some are even working for $5 an hour so that they can preserve their jobs.

So, yes, America and the Western countries have a lot more to worry about as far as the global economy is concerned. There has been a downward movement in the wages in the West. There's no question about it.

Therefore, when a worker in India rises, the American worker may struggle. Eventually in a free market, it equalises.

Does that mean after a certain period, if all the countries are inter-linked by business, there will be some uniformity in their wages, lifestyle, etc?

Yes, there will be some degree of uniformity. I will not say that we will reach American salaries. But our people will rise a lot.

There is a view that Nigeria should have been a big economic power if the Theory of Convergence were true, as they got a lot of foreign investment and there was trade between Nigeria and the Western countries. Why did Nigeria remain poor?

Yes, Nigeria opened up. The problem was that people took their money abroad, and that was, of course, a very harmful phenomenon. So, we have to have institutions. I am not saying that the state has to disappear. The state cannot disappear. State has to liberalise its policies and gradually trust its citizens and open up.

Do you hold the state – the military regime – and the widespread corruption responsible for the country's poverty, even though it is liberalised?

Well, if Nigerians had responded by taking advantage of the investments to create wealth within Nigeria, they would not have remained poor.

You need a state to oversee all that.

You need a state, but you also need entrepreneurs. You need institutions too.

My feeling is that a lot of investments in Nigeria were never made. Money was just taken out of Nigeria. Mafia and crooks were operating there. No nation will progress that way.

You said as far as economic growth is concerned, we have reached a plateau. Why do you say so?

Currently we are in a recession. The fact is that capitalism is not a smooth ride. You don't grow year after year after year. What happens is there are business cycles.

The psychology of entrepreneurs is such that they are like a herd. After all they are passionate human beings. And they don't behave rationally all the time.

So, what happened in India partly was, between '93 and '96, we had tremendous investments. So you had excess capacity created. However, the demand did not pick up so there came a situation where supply was greater than demand. The recession was partly caused by that factor. This is what is called a business cycle.

What else are the reasons behind this recession? They say that 1999 is going to be the toughest. Do you also feel that way? How can we recover?

I am not sure whether I have the answer. I know that we will recover. I don't know when we will recover. I also know that we are currently in very serious trouble. Yes, some sectors are not doing too badly like Infotech and Pharmaceuticals.

Yes. Wherever India has a competitive advantage, we are doing well in those sectors. The demand for consumer products continues. Even for some white goods, the demand has picked up. Colour television market is strong. So, you have sectoral problems.

But by and large, it is pretty bad. I have no answer to your question as to when it will recover.

How can we recover?

The recovery will come partly with confidence. The trouble is, the economy is doing better than the confidence. The confidence is much worse. So, the businessmen have to gain confidence and start investing. Once they start investing, it will improve.

Do we need a strong government for economic growth?

I am not a 'statist'. I won't say that we need a strong government for economic growth. In the last 50 years, we thought we were practicing socialism, but it was only 'statism'. 'Statism' is overbearing bureaucracy, which obstructs the process of growth. Of course, you need the state.

Does that mean stability and strength of a government are immaterial?

Yes, stability gives confidence. And confidence will revive investment. Investment will revive jobs and growth. I believe in a small government. You need a government because you need law and order, you need judiciary, you also need an umpire. You need a state for giving primary education. You need a state for health. You need for defence. That's all. Those are very important functions.

Certainly, stability will help us. These unstable governments in the last five-six years have done more for the economy than all 50 years of stable governments in the past. Stability *per se* is not necessary. It gives confidence to people because their minds are set.

All these governments are trying to reform. The BJP government is trying very hard. The Internet policy, the whole IT policy – it's a revolution. They are trying to sort out the problems of the power sector and the telecom sector.

You said we would not go back from liberalisation. But in Russia, it has failed. People cannot withdraw their own money from the bank. There's no bread for them, no clothes and now the people say that the Communist regime was better. Will the present recession force people to go back to Nehruvian socialism?

I don't think that's going to come back in India. In Russia, they did not have institutions. They did not have the entrepreneurial class that was totally destroyed. So, they didn't have business that could respond. And they dismantled the state completely. So, you created a linkage with the global economy without any institution. In India, we have institutions.

In your speech at the *Review* function, you narrated the story of Raju, a teenaged tea-stall worker who, inspired by a television show on Bill Gates of Microsoft, nurses dream of studying computer science and starting his own firm in his village. Will this recession shatter the dreams of youngsters like Raju?

No. Certainly the process is slow. When you are growing at 7 per cent, you are creating ten million jobs. When you are growing at 5 per cent, you are creating only three million jobs. So, you are losing three million jobs a year.

Certainly, the livelihood of three million people get affected every year. There is disappointment and disillusionment. But what I have said is about the forces that have been let loose.

These forces will change the attitude of Rajus. And that attitude will not easily go.

Is that the reason why you painted a very optimistic picture of India?

I think it is not optimistic. It is realistic.

Interestingly, the BJP came back to power in 2014 under Narendra Modi and it is only the Swadeshi Jagaran Manch that talks about swadeshi, not the BJP.

But the word Aatma Nirbhar Bharat coined by Modi means exactly what Gurcharan Das said in 1998, confidence.

In 1998, the swadeshis were worried about MNCs dictating terms but today, it is said that a powerful lobby of a very few Indian industrialists influence the economic decisions of the government. How the wheels of fortune have changed!

And... the Vajpayee Government Falls, then Happens a War

17 April 1999.

Vajpayee's tenure as the Prime Minister of India ended.

If he was a 13-day old Prime Minister in 1996, he could extend the period to 13 months in 1999.

It was by just one vote that the Vajpayee government lost the confidence vote in Parliament.

This happened when J Jayalalitha, the AIADMK supremo, decided to withdraw the support of her 18 MPs after Vajpayee refused to use Article 356 and dismiss the DMK government in Tamil Nadu.

Soon after the no-confidence motion, President K R Narayanan dissolved the Parliament and called for fresh elections. The President also appointed Vajpayee as the caretaker Prime Minister till the elections were held later in 1999.

It was when Vajpayee was the caretaker Prime Minister that the Kargil war happened between India and Pakistan. The conflict that started on the 3rd of May 1999 ended on the 26th of July 1999, with India winning the war and reclaiming the Kargil sector along the Line of Control.

Will the war turn the election fortune in favour of Vajpayee? Will he get a third chance to be the Prime Minister of India?

1999 is also the election in which Sonia Gandhi lead the Congress as the party president and contested in the elections from Amethi in UP and Bellari in Karnataka. She campaigned as the party president and not as the Prime Ministerial candidate.

I turned to ***Cho Ramaswamy*** *for an analysis on the election scenario just before the 1999 General elections.*

WHAT is going to be the issue in elections '99? Will Kargil be the main issue?

Kargil will definitely be one of the issues. But the main issue will be the suitability of the two candidates, one of them openly projected and the other somewhat indirectly projected or left to be understood: Vajpayee and Sonia Gandhi.

I think the major issue in the minds of the voter is: who is going to be the prime minister? Is it going to be Vajpayee or is it going to be Sonia Gandhi?

Why is the Congress reluctant to project her as the PM?

Well, Sonia Gandhi has messed up her own image. First, she succeeded in creating a myth that she was out to serve the Congress and help rebuild it to its past glory. But when Vajpayee's government fell, the way she ran about trying to muster support for her candidature, well, shattered the myth.

Also, she openly claimed that she had the support of 272 MPs, when she had much less. All this created the impression that she was out to grab power somehow.

Number two, Vajpayee was seen as a man who had been asked to climb down for no fault of his. It was not on any big issue that he was brought down.

Later, the Kargil war happened, and the general opinion is that he handled it rather well. On the military front, Pakistan was definitely defeated. And it was a huge victory in the diplomatic front.

All these added together, even the Congressmen now realise that Sonia Gandhi may suffer terribly in comparison with Vajpayee. That is why they are not openly projecting her as the prime minister.

It was also reported that Congressmen are worried about the thin attendance of her rallies. Is it because the curiosity factor is lost?

Yes, her rallies seem to be thinly attended these days. The curiosity is definitely gone.

Vajpayee has repeatedly said that he didn't want to make Kargil an election issue. Who do you think will use it eventually, the Congress or the BJP?

The Congress has already made it an election issue by harping on it again and again and trying to fault the BJP for the alleged intelligence failure. Now that they have made it an election issue, the BJP has to respond. So, they have responded by blaming the Congress for all that had happened in Kashmir from 1947 till now.

Naturally, this has led to Kargil becoming an election issue. I think it is the making of the Opposition. They thought it was a convenient stick to beat the BJP with. But it is going to be a boomerang.

Who will benefit from using the Kargil conflict as an election issue?

I do not know whether the people are going to be swayed by the allegation that it was an intelligence failure which led to the Kargil conflict. I think the people will ultimately think that whatever may be the reason, once the conflict was there, it was handled very well.

Do you think the same passion over the Kargil conflict will last till the elections?

Since there is no other issue, I think this will remain so. But I don't think that this alone will decide the election.

One of the other factors that can play a role is: people may be unhappy with those who have caused this election. The Congress is the primary culprit there, the first accused. People will think that the Congress has been unnecessarily trying to pull down every government which was not theirs.

Generally, the economic situation seems to be brightening up, which is advantageous to the BJP.

Do you foresee another hung Parliament?

It need not necessarily be a hung one, because the BJP and their allies together may manage a majority. I am not very sure now. Who can predict all these things at this stage? Even exit polls go wrong. What I say is only my perception.

Do you feel the BJP is managing seat-sharing well? They seem to be having problems everywhere. Will it not affect the image of the NDA?

If they get it over and done with soon, people will accept it in their stride because these things always happen whenever an alliance is struck. But if it continues for a longer time, it may have its own negative impact.

If we look at what is happening in Karnataka, do you think it was right on the part of George Fernandes and Hegde to invite J H Patel (Janata Dal) to join the NDA?

Knowing fully well that the BJP had been criticising the Janata Dal government in Karnataka for the last two years, it was not right on their part to have initiated the move in this regard without the consent of the BJP.

Also, the BJP had started campaigning that the people should teach a lesson to all those who pulled down their government and Janata Dal was one of the parties which did it. Knowing all this, Hegde and Fernandes ought to have consulted the BJP before making these moves. Unfortunately, they do not seem to have consulted the BJP.

Anyway, since that's happened, the BJP at least should have taken the initiative to see to it that these things were not thrashed out in public but in private. They should have averted from (avoided) making this a public debate.

Do you feel, both Hegde and Fernandes did this to consolidate their position in Karnataka and Bihar?

Naturally. They have an advantage because their bargaining strength vis-a-vis the BJP goes up. You can't find fault with the political parties for trying to increase their bargaining strength. But they should have been able to see what kind of repercussions it would create in the ranks of the leading partner of the alliance.

In Orissa also, the BJP has problems with the Biju Janata Dal. It seems NDA has more problems than the Congress.

Problems are there with every party. The Congress did not make up its mind vis-a-vis Jayalalitha till the last moment. First, she offered five seats and the news was out. Then, emissaries after emissaries came to Tamil Nadu. Manmohan Singh and A K Antony came twice. So, this went on for quite some time. It happens because everyone feels that the position of the parties will be so tight in the next Parliament that a couple of seats more would lead to an enormous increase in clout.

Do you think people of Tamil Nadu will punish Jayalalitha for blackmailing the BJP-led government from day one?

I have not yet had any feedback from the various regions of the State. It will take some more time for me to assess the public opinion. But my desire is that they should.

In Tamil Nadu, who is in a better position now?

I think the DMK-BJP alliance has an edge along with the MDMK. Even then, I wouldn't say, it will be a sweep and all that. They are better placed, that's all. I can't venture beyond that now.

What about the situation in Maharashtra?

The Congress may stand to lose in Maharashtra because of Sharad Pawar's exit. They had a good number of seats from Maharashtra last year. I don't see the Congress improving its strength dramatically.

But in UP, it is going to be a three-way split of votes among Mulayam, the Congress and the BJP. The BJP votes will anyway be with it. The anti-BJP votes will be divided between Mulayam and the Congress. So, the BJP stands to gain because of the division of the anti-BJP votes.

With Sharad Pawar fighting the elections separately, do you feel the anti-BJP- Shiv Sena sentiment among the people won't affect the ruling alliance?

The anti BJP-Shiv Sena sentiment was there. But because of the Sharad Pawar factor, they may manage to win. There will be a division of the anti-BJP- Shiv Sena votes between the Congress and Sharad Pawar.

In the recent assembly elections, the BJP fared very badly in the northern belt. Do you expect them to perform better this time?

During the assembly elections, Jayalalitha's tantrums were at their peak. The BJP gave the impression of a very weak government. The prime minister was successfully building up an image for himself as a man groping in the dark.

On top of it, came the onion crisis. So, they suffered.

Once Jayalalitha was out of the government, the caretaker government performed more purposefully, more meaningfully than the regular government. It is only after Jayalalitha's exit that Vajpayee was seen as the prime minister. Before that, people were not sure who the prime minister was.

As of now, I don't know how things are going to change, I feel the NDA will be managing a majority in Parliament.

Why do you say, as of now? Do you feel the situation may change?

Let us see. Who knows? The attitude of the people may change due to something or the other. Maybe some alliances, may be some understandings, may be some revelations... so many things can happen in politics. How can one rule out anything? Or, some other incident happening... who expected Kargil? Who expected Coimbatore blasts last time? It did play a very crucial part in determining the vote in Tamil Nadu.

The Janata Dal leaders have been commenting that India is evolving towards a two-party system, the BJP and the Congress.

Not yet. The Congress and the BJP are not that strong. The Congress has become very weak, and the BJP is not growing that fast.

After another election, the BJP may attain the status of a party which has substantial support in all the States.

Will the BJP be able to break away from the RSS, VHP and Bajrang Dal?

The BJP is already becoming more and more independent of them. At least they have not been able to satisfy those groups. They should definitely have nothing to do with outfits like the Bajrang Dal. With the VHP, they can afford to sympathise with some of their demands, but not all. With the RSS, it is an umbilical cord, it cannot be broken. It will be there.

If that cord remains, how will they get acceptance from all people including the minorities?

The minorities will soon start accepting the BJP after one or two elections, because the BJP government is behaving well with them.

But why should they continue their connection with a Hindu organisation?

What is wrong? The RSS is not asking for the blood of the minorities.

If the umbilical cord remains, will it not affect the image of the BJP as a political party?

I don't think it will. Otherwise, they would not have grown this much. If that had been the case, a Fernandes or a Hegde or a Mamata Banerjee or a Karunanidhi would not have joined hands with them. How did they confidently enter into alliance with the BJP? It was because of the fact that the BJP is not seen as a communal outfit that they aligned with the BJP.

The minorities may have their own doubts as of now. But even that may be erased in due course of time.

You are seen as a BJP sympathiser.

Yes.

As a political analyst, when you look at certain things, won't you be biased in your conclusions?

No. Nobody castigates the BJP as I do when they do wrong. When they were dancing to the tunes of Jayalalitha, I was ridiculing them and attacking them very strongly in my journal.

The 1999 general elections were held in September and October. The voters were tired, and the country was cash starved.

Cho had said, 'I feel the NDA will be managing a majority in Parliament.'

Will his prediction come true? Will the BJP come back to power? Will Atal Bihari Vajpayee get a third chance to be the Prime Minister of the country and complete a full term?

PART 3

1999-2004

Ruling Party: The National Democratic Alliance (NDA)

Prime Minister: Atal Bihari Vajpayee (BJP)

FRIENDS AND FOES

Dancing to Jayalalitha's tunes! Thank you, News18.

DMK leader M Karunanidhi and Prime Minister Vajpayee. Thank you, Bangalore Mirror.

Trinamool leader Mamata Banerjee with Prime Minister Vajpayee. Thank you, DailyO.

The NDA, Third Time Lucky

Like Cho Ramaswamy had predicted, the National Democratic Alliance (NDA) managed to win the 1999 General Elections.

Though the Bharatiya Janata Party (BJP) won only 182 seats, the NDA managed 269 seats, enough to form the government. And with outside support from the Telugu Desam Party (TDP) that had 26 MPs, giving the NDA the majority to rule the country.[1]

So, on 13 October 1999, Atal Bihari Vajpayee was sworn in as the Prime Minister of India for the third time.

Interestingly, Vajpayee's first term lasted only 13 days (in 1996) while the second term was better; 13 months (1998-99).

The question was, will Vajpayee be able to complete five years this time?

---

[1] TDP, or the Telugu Desam Party, is a regional political party founded by N T Rama Rao in 1982, and has been active in the Southern Indian States of Andhra Pradesh and Telangana. From 1995, N Chandrababu Naidu has been its president.

Unmasking of Vajpayee! With L K Advani and Murli Manohar Joshi. Thank you, Loksatta.

Will the NDA Last Five Years?

Many naysayers predicted the fall of the NDA in no time as it was a coalition of many small regional parties. It was fresh in the memory of all what had happened to the United Front experiment.

There were many questions in the minds of the people.

Will the NDA last five years?

Will the Telugu Desam Party (TDP) also indulge in blackmail tactics, like what the All India Anna Dravida Munnetra Kazhagam (AIADMK) did to the previous Vajpayee government?

Will any other small party pull the plug?

I turned to the one and only **Cho Ramaswamy** *who had predicted the victory of the NDA and the BJP, for answers once again.*

ALTHOUGH the National Democratic Alliance (NDA) managed to get majority in the 13th Lok Sabha, many political analysts say that the government is not stable as it is constituted of several parties. Do you agree?

A coalition has an in-built problem as far as stability is concerned. That has to be conceded. But there are certain features in this set-up which give some confidence to Vajpayee about the stability of the government.

The TDP (Telugu Desam Party) has 26 MPs, and it is the next largest party after the BJP. The TDP cannot do business with the Congress (now the main opposition party) because of its politics in Andhra Pradesh. Once it joins the Congress in an effort, say, to topple this government, its political base in Andhra Pradesh will be shattered. It will have to be rebuilt on some other platform. So, they will hesitate a thousand times before joining hands with the Congress.

Now, the JD-U (Janata Dal United). The socialists have a congenital problem. They are the splitters. They are the destroyers. It has been their history throughout, and there are many socialists in the JD-U. It is a party of leaders. Sharad Yadav, Ram Vilas Paswan, George Fernandes, Nitish Kumar – you name anybody in the JD-U, and he is a leader. In their case also, they will find it difficult because their eyes are now set on the Bihar assembly elections. The alliance with the BJP has proved to be very successful in the parliamentary elections in Bihar. Of course, it has benefited the BJP also immensely, but it is mutual help. So, the JD-U will not like to sacrifice that now.

And, in Bihar, when the assembly elections come about, naturally there will be a substantial number of seats allocated to the BJP. The BJP's help may be required in the Bihar assembly and the JD-U will have to reciprocate it in Delhi in the Parliament. So, they may also not rock Vajpayee's boat.

Do you mean, they will not rock Vajpayee's boat till the Bihar assembly elections?

No, even after the assembly elections. There is going to be a substantial number of BJP MLAs in the Bihar assembly, and if they fair as well as they had faired in the parliamentary elections, the JD-U will require their help and assistance in the assembly. Maybe, for survival or maybe for smooth sailing. So, if they want the BJP MLAs to behave in the assembly, they will have to behave in the Parliament as a reciprocal arrangement. Even after the Bihar assembly elections, they may find it difficult to rock Vajpayee's boat.

We have several small parties in the NDA. Do you expect them to pose any threat? Or, will they keep quiet, as they will not be able to do anything drastic, alone?

Many of them will have to come together to pose a threat. Not one, not two, not three, not four... even more than that. So, that will be difficult.

Apart from all this, the greatest strength of this coalition, in my opinion, is the abysmal showing of the Congress in the elections and the number of seats they have in Parliament. It is only about 112.

The Congress will now feel that the electorate has not taken kindly to the toppling exercise, which they indulged in some months ago. So, they will definitely not be immediately ready to do anything to the government because it is going to be very difficult for them.

They will not be in a commanding position in any alternate arrangement too. They are very weak. In fact, their members are almost equal to the other non-BJP parties put together. Their clout in such an arrangement will be minimal. It will only be equal with the others, and the Congress is not going to tolerate that. It will be very difficult for the Congress to digest a situation where it will be an equal with somebody else.

So, the Congress also will hesitate. But if there are problems created on the issue of treatment of minorities, protection given to other religions, etc, some of the BJP allies may find it difficult to continue with them.

For example?

For example, the DMK (Dravida Munnetra Kazhagam). For example, even the Telugu Desam Party. So, if that front is managed by the BJP, it can survive.

Vajpayee has become stronger after the election. Under his leadership, do you expect the BJP to treat the minorities well?

I do expect them to treat the minorities well. But whenever there is a transgression by any organisation – whether it be the VHP (Vishwa Hindu Parishad), the Bajrang Dal (the militant youth wing of the VHP) or anybody else – I don't think any other organisation apart from these two will indulge in that (any transgression), or even the Shiv Sena and the government must come down heavily upon them. That will build confidence in these parties. If they do that, it will be pretty smooth sailing.[1]

Another plus factor emerging now is the situation in Pakistan. You have a government there, which is not going to be mature in its approach to its relationship with India. Infiltrators may be encouraged.[2]

Eventually, I think, a dangerous triangle may be formed by the Taliban men in Afghanistan, the terrorists being trained in

---

1 The Shiv Sena is a right-wing Marathi regionalist political party in India founded in 1966 by Bal Thackeray.

2 General Pervez Musharraf led a military coup in 1999 and overthrew the democratically elected government with Nawaz Sharif as the Prime Minister. He then declared himself the Chief Executive of the nation.

Pakistan and being blessed by the Pakistan military which is now in power. The third point in the triangle will be Osama bin Laden and his money.

But this triangle will pose a threat not only to India but also to many Western countries as well because of the terrorism, which they indulge in, the retributions, which Osama bin Laden seeks. In that case, one can expect the Western countries, led by the USA to cooperate with India in containing terrorism in this part of the world.

In what way do you expect the USA and India to come together to fight terrorism?

Supposing some terrorist escapes, he will be extradited if he has sought asylum in a foreign country. And the United States gather immense intelligence, and that will be passed on to India. Even the most modern techniques in tackling terrorism maybe passed on to us. Any information that they receive from their network satellites will be given to us. All these will be immense help to India. The terrorists in Western countries will be discouraged totally and they will not be allowed to indulge in propaganda or recruiting men.

What kind of repercussions will we have to face because of the military coup in Pakistan?

Because of the situation in Pakistan, because of the fact that the military will be an adventurist government, there will be problems in Kashmir. There may be problems elsewhere in India also. So, the nation will have to stand united.

The advantage the BJP has now is, when the situation in Pakistan is posing a real threat, when all the peaceful settlement of issues are going to be put in cold storage, people will hate those who indulge in petty political bickering. Whether it be a coalition partner of the BJP or the opposition parties, people are not going to take it lightly.

That will make anyone hesitate to topple the government. They know that in this period of uncertainty in our borders, anything done by them to disturb the government may not be looked at kindly by the people.

Do you feel there is a connection between the election of a stable government at the Centre after a long time, and the military coup in Pakistan?

I don't think it is connected in anyway with what is happening in India politically, but I have noted one thing. Pakistan under Nawaz Sharif had stopped some of the infiltrators entering into India and pulled them back. This perhaps might have been the last straw, as far as the military there was concerned because they did not like the withdrawal from Kargil, though they were forced to not only because of Western pressure but also by the heavy damages inflicted by the Indian military.

And for getting economic aid, Nawaz Sharif had to please the West, and he would have resumed the Lahore process. That also was not taken too kindly by the military.[3]

Everybody accused George Fernandes (the then Defence Minister) of talking nonsense when he said that Nawaz Sharif did not know at first that the Kargil intrusion was going to take place, and it was known only to the military. Now I think, he is being proved right. That is what I said even then.

---

[3] The Lahore Declaration was a bilateral agreement and governance treaty between India and Pakistan. The treaty was signed on 21 February 1999, at the conclusion of a historic summit in Lahore between the Indian Prime Minister Atal Bihari Vajpayee and the then Pakistan Prime Minister Nawaz Sharif.

I said that George, in all probability, may be right, but he should not have said it openly. Those critics of Fernandes who said that he was talking nonsense, I think, have been proven wrong.

From then on, the military has been unhappy with Sharif. The Pakistan military is a highly inimical outfit as far as India is concerned. Their base, the political platform of the military, is beat India. Whether military should have a political platform is altogether a different question. But they have one, and it is 'Hate India'. So, with that kind of a rule taking over the reins in Pakistan, we may have problems.

Do you expect problems in the economic front also because of an imminent increase in the defence expenditure?

Yes, it is a disadvantage to the Vajpayee government that an enormous amount of money will have to be spent on defence. Yes, it will affect the economy.

It will prevent the government from giving subsidies to the farm sector and many such areas. And it will lead to inflation. It will lead to higher taxes. They may be called differently, still people will be taxed.

So, you don't see a bright economic scenario for India, at least in the near future.

Well, because of this, there may be some surge also. Production may go up. Still people want everything subsidised; people want everything at a low price. They compare today's prices with the prices that prevailed ten years ago. Thank God, they don't compare it to the prices during the British rule, and say that was better!

Let us go back to the drubbing of the Congress in the election. Is it because Sonia Gandhi's charisma did not work

that the Congress lost heavily? Or is it because they did not realise the importance of coalition partners?

It is obvious that the Congress is not strong enough to win elections on its own in various parts of the country. The charisma of Sonia Gandhi, if there was one, is not enough to win votes. It was enough to draw crowds but not to win votes.

Why do people come in large numbers to her meetings?

That is just curiosity. I think people consider election-time as festival time. During the festival, you go and enjoy yourself. You see the illumination, you see the crackers bursting, you see people assembling. So, you also go and join the *tamasha* (funfare).

During the temple festivals, all kinds of people come to the temple but not all of them are driven by *bhakti* (devotion). Some of them will be real devotees. Some of them come to do some shopping. Some of them come to eat sweets. Some of them come to see balloons flying all over. That kind of an atmosphere prevails in an election too. A part of the crowd is your supporter but a considerable section of it goes to watch the fun and enjoy.

But then, why was it that only her meetings were well attended, and not the BJP's?

Sonia Gandhi is coming out in a big way only now. Others have been seen earlier too. So, the curiosity factor does not work with the others.

Well, when film actress Vijayashanthi went to Bellary (in Karnataka), the crowd was unmanageable! She drew better crowds than Sonia Gandhi! Jayalalitha drew good crowds here. Good crowds do not ensure heavy voting in your favour.

What went against Sonia Gandhi, her foreignness or lack of experience?

I don't think the foreigner issue worked in the minds of people at all. Ultimately the election, in my opinion, came to one thing in the minds of the voter: who should be the prime minister, Vajpayee or Sonia Gandhi. I think many of them decided that it was Vajpayee who deserved to be the PM again rather than Sonia Gandhi about whom very little is known.

See, she is still not known in the country. That is her very big disadvantage. Maybe when she is known, that may become an even bigger disadvantage, I do not know! Not being known may be the reason why she won 112 seats. If she is known and understood, she may get even lesser votes! I don't know. What do we know about Sonia? What do we know about her intentions? What do we know about her capacity and talent? Nothing is known about her except that the Congressmen fall at her feet!

From the way Priyanka Gandhi campaigned in Bellary (in Karnataka) and Amethi (in UP), do you expect her to come into active politics soon?

I do not know what the family is going to decide. But she perhaps takes to politics better than Sonia Gandhi herself. But I do not know what the intentions of the family are. Whom does Sonia want to anoint, Priyanka or Rahul Gandhi, I do not know.

All the senior leaders in the Congress are resigning one by one, accepting moral responsibility for the defeat – except, of course, Sonia Gandhi. Nobody dares ask for her resignation.

Maybe they thought by doing that, they may force Sonia Gandhi also to accept responsibility for the defeat. She accepts it but did not resign!

Will the Congressmen accept anybody other than a Gandhi as the Congress leader in the near future?

Sharad Pawar (former Congressman, now the leader of the Nationalist Congress Party, NCP) would have made a better leader for the Congress.

We saw both Chandrababu Naidu (TDP) and Karunanidhi (DMK) apologising and explaining at length to the minorities during the election why they chose to align with the BJP. After the election, both claimed that they have not lost the minorities votes.

They have lost the minority votes in the election. But it may come back to them later. Here, the minorities have a tendency to be with the winning side as a group because that assures them that their demands will be met. Now that they have seen that the side, which they opposed has won, they may shift their allegiance.

Karunanidhi said he would act as a bridge between the minorities and the BJP, and, thus, this may come true. But I think in the elections, both Karunanidhi and Chandrababu suffered huge dents in their minority vote. I wouldn't say it was lost in the entirety.

Do you think minorities will feel unsafe with them now?

The minorities will definitely feel safe with Karunanidhi. But they were angry with him. They did not disbelieve him. That is why they voted against him. Now they will come back to him. That's what I feel.

Chandrababu Naidu hesitated a lot but ultimately, he saw that he might not be able to contain the Congress all by himself. The post-Kargil situation in his opinion made the BJP a good vote-puller in his State. It is pure political arithmetic.

What was the best and worst parts of Election '99, according to you?

The best part is that it is over. The worst part is that it ever happened at all; that an election became necessary at all.

Like Cho predicted, the allies of the BJP did not topple the government and Atal Bihari Vajpayee completed his term as the Prime Minister of the country.

It is interesting to read his comments made in 1999 on the state of the Congress and Sonia Gandhi. They also came true!

On World Politics, he had said, 'Eventually, I think, a dangerous triangle may be formed by the Taliban men in Afghanistan, the terrorists being trained in Pakistan and being blessed by the Pakistan military which is now in power. The third point in the triangle will be Osama bin Laden and his money.

This triangle will pose a threat not only to India but also to many Western countries as well because of the terrorism, which they indulge in, the retributions, which Osama bin Laden seeks. In that case, one can expect the Western countries, led by the USA to cooperate with India in containing terrorism here'. Within a year, this too played out as he had predicted.

That is why we miss Cho Ramaswamy, the maverick, a lot....

The Unmasking of Vajpayee

Not even a year had passed after Atal Bihari Vajpayee became the Prime Minister of India, and a survey found that the popularity of the Vajpayee government had gone down.

Not only the people but the opposition also pulled him down after the comment he made in December 2000 in the Parliament on the demolition of Babri Masjid (on 6 December 1992), and the possibility of constructing a Ram temple at Ayodhya.

Vajpayee was responding to questions on the demolition of the Babri Masjid at Ayodhya. When the Opposition parties wanted the three Union Ministers (L K Advani, Murli Manohar Joshi and Uma Bharti) who were charged with culpability for the act, to resign, Vajpayee rejected the demand. Then he said that the movement for building a Ram temple at Ayodhya was an expression of national sentiments, and a task that remained unfinished.

This came to be famously described as the 'unmasking of Vajpayee'.

I spoke to the BJP's then vice president, ***Jana Krishnamurthy,*** *on the party's stand on Ayodhya.*

A survey conducted by a news magazine found that the popularity of the National Democratic Alliance has declined. Has this survey come as a shock to you?

If you read it carefully, you will find there is only a 0.6 per cent fall in NDA's popularity, and a gain of 2.65 per cent for the Congress party. That is because they have taken the opinion polls in various zones where there is this anti-incumbency factor.

They have found that the anti-incumbency factor in Kerala will affect the LDF (Left Democratic Front). So, there is a gain for the UDF (United Democratic Front). But the BJP is not in the UDF. So, they said the strength of the Congress will go up.

In Tamil Nadu, the anti-incumbency factor will affect the DMK. So, they found it will affect the BJP too. As the Congress is with the AIADMK, it gains a little.

So, what I want to tell you is that reality is not this.

The Prime Minister's statement on Ayodhya in the Lok Sabha was described by everyone as the 'unmasking of Vajpayee'. What do you think of this statement?

Like the Prime Minister stated, there are only two possible solutions for Ayodhya. One is the verdict of the highest court. The second is to have representatives of the two sides – the Hindus and the Muslims – coming together and arriving at a mutually acceptable solution. There is no third way.

The BJP has endorsed the PM's stand. Not because the Prime Minister has said it. But it was the stand of the party, not just now but earlier also.

I personally feel if we want a real solution, the political parties should keep out of the issue completely. We should allow the representatives to meet and have talks. Today, it appears to be an irreconcilable decision but given the mutual goodwill and understanding, I feel the leaders of both communities are capable of coming to a solution. But interference of political parties may aggravate things.

So, the BJP has made its opinion clear; that Ayodhya Ram temple is not on the agenda of the NDA, and we endorse the PM's view.

His statement in the Lok Sabha created such a furore, not only in Parliament, but elsewhere as well. Even the NDA partners reacted to it sharply.

There was nothing in the Prime Minister's statement. The Congress was just waiting for an opportunity, that's all. They can't digest the fact that there is an NDA government at the Centre. So, they want to bring it down.

Sonia Gandhi's advisors perhaps might have said, 'There are two points of strength in the NDA. The first one is the image of Vajpayeeji and the second one is the allies sticking together'. So, the Congress wanted to raise an issue by which they could throw some mud at the image of Vajpayee, and also create a wedge between the allies and the BJP.

The third objective was to try to get back the support of the minorities through this. These were the three objectives. Unfortunately, it boomeranged on them.

They never succeeded in dividing the NDA because Vajpayeeji's statement was crystal clear. The Congress demanded the resignation of the three ministers. Vajpayeeji said, they had not committed any crime. It was a political movement based on national sentiments, at that time. Now, a solution can be found either by a court verdict or through talks.

They do not know the facts of the case. The police wanted to file a charge sheet and the lower court permitted it. That order of the lower court was challenged in the high court. The verdict is yet to come. The very order of the lower court to allow the police to file a charge sheet has been challenged. So, there can be no charge sheet till the high court judgment comes.

So, where is the question of the resignation of these three ministers? That was what Arun Jaitley (who was a member of the BJP and also served as a union minister during 2014-2019. He passed away in 2019.) also said. He told them, 'You don't even understand the basic jurisprudence. And you want to bring in political jurisprudence?'

The Congress failed in their attempt. The allies are still with the NDA. And Atalji's image was not at all affected.

That is not exactly true....

You just wait and see. You may feel that Vajpayee's image was affected. I feel it was not. Both of us have got one vote each! Let us see what the verdict of the people is going to be.

Of course, a section of the press took it up in a big way. According to our feedback, their conclusions are not correct. If his image was affected really, then the opinion poll would not have given such a good rating for Vajpayee. There would have been a considerable fall in his popularity too. The truth is, nobody is anywhere near Atalji today. The efforts of the Congress and the Left parties have failed.

So, you do not agree with the description that it was the 'unmasking of Vajpayee'.

Absolutely not.

The Prime Minister told the House that it was in the interests of all Indians that a temple be built at Ayodhya. Do you feel that is so?

I feel this issue is being kept alive deliberately by the opposition parties. It is not an issue at all actually. From 1936 onwards, no *namaz* took place there. That is the court verdict. Nobody can deny that. From 1949 onwards, *puja* has been going on there.

These are the two basic facts. Can anybody deny that? It is only on this basis that, that the talks are going on. Why should we talk about it? Let us leave it to the persons concerned.

Is it in the national interest that a temple be built there?

Whose interest? Are you the sole custodian of national interest? Am I the sole custodian of national interest? Is the Congress the sole custodian of national interest?

Who is?

Let us hear the public opinion. Those who are interested should tell us. The VHP says there should be a temple. The Babri Masjid committee says there should not be. The talks are going on. Ultimately the two representatives will come together and settle the issue.

It was the Prime Minister who said the building of the temple was of national interest. Does it really matter to the people of Kerala or Manipur or Arunachal Pradesh that we have a Ram temple at Ayodhya?

Why do you say it is confined only to Uttar Pradesh? It matters to all those who are interested in a temple. There are so many people in India who are interested, and for them, it is the biggest thing. There are many people who want a temple there. There are people who do not want a temple there. Somebody wanted a hospital there. Our country is a democratic country. So, everybody can have his or her opinion. But I feel the issue will take care of itself.

So, you say that all political parties should keep themselves out of the issue.

Yes. And that includes my party also. I also feel the media also should keep out of the issue and allow the matter to settle down.

The VHP (Vishwa Hindu Parishad) has fixed a date for the temple construction. How will the Vajpayee government deal with that?

Why should the government deal with it so long as they are not breaking the law? If anybody tries to take law in his hands, then law will take its course, the Prime Minister has said.

Even if it is the RSS (Rashtriya Swayamsevak Sangh) or the VHP?

Whoever it is. You must also understand that the VHP has responsible leaders wedded to the interests of the country. Why do you think they will do something which is against the interests of the country?

But they said they were not concerned with the BJP's opinion. They said, irrespective of the BJP's stance, they would go ahead with the temple construction. Then?

Let us cross that bridge when we reach it. Why should they not tell us their vision? Just because you and I object to it? Let them have their vision.

The government will interfere only when they cross the law. This is a democracy. You have the freedom to criticise them. Do they not have the freedom to express their views? It is not democracy if you impose your views on somebody else.

But they say they will build a temple at Ayodhya.

Let them build. Then, we can step in. Do you know anything about how temples are constructed? I know. Construction of a temple is not a day's affair! It takes years and years. They have to collect money and they are answerable to all those from whom they have collected money.

Every village has contributed one brick for the temple, inscribed with '*Hey Ram*'. All those who have given money and bricks will ask the VHP, 'What are you doing? What are you going to do with the bricks? Are you going to build a VHP office?'

What kind of a relationship do you have with the RSS?

I consider the RSS a university. What is the relationship between a student and his alma mater? We learn things at the university, and then we go into our field. Once in a while, a meeting of all old students takes place at the university. All the students are proud of their university. I am too. All of us graduated from the RSS. But now we have our own lives.

We say, yes, we are proud that we are products of the RSS. But how far is a student connected with his alma mater after he leaves?... Except that he remembers he was a product of the university once. I consider the relationship between the RSS and the BJP like the relationship between an alma mater and its student.

But the RSS is the most vocal critic of the NDA government's economic policies.

They are free to raise their opinion.

Is there not some truth in what they say? For example, they say mindless liberalisation will adversely affect the lives of the poor.

I have publicly made a statement that we are also wedded to *swadeshi.* It is in our blood. The BJP is wedded to self-reliance. Not only Bharat but every country would like to be self-reliant. No country would like its economy to be controlled by outside forces. We accept it. But in the case of implementation of specific programmes in the present world context, we cannot insulate our economy from the world economy.

Time will not stand still. The country has to move on. We are committed to the WTO (World Trade Organisation). The WTO agreement was not signed by the BJP. The Narasimha Rao government signed it. We can't say no now. So, we are doing our best, keeping all those obligations in mind. I don't say all that we are doing is correct. We are using the trial and error method.

Isn't Indian agriculture going to suffer once the WTO agreement comes into force?[1]

Those who offering the criticism do not know what agriculture is and what the problems are.

It was Dr M S Swaminathan who said so.

Dr M S Swaminathan is a great agricultural expert. We have great regard and respect for him. You should also understand that we have to go ahead as a government. Do you know what is the present position of the food grain in the country? Once

---

[1] India became a WTO member on 1 January 1995. It was to address the government policies that distort markets and restrict trade that all the WTO members came up with the Agreement on Agriculture, which came into force in 1995. This was supposed to result in reductions in subsidies and trade barriers to make markets fairer and more competitive.

we were a deficit state as far as food grain was concerned but India has emerged as a surplus state now.

But that is what Dr Swaminathan said. He said the godowns are full, but the poor cannot get access to food. They have no money to buy food. There is availability but no accessibility.

We are trying to deal with the problem. We are consulting the experts. The government has announced free rice of 10 kilos to senior citizens. The State governments have to follow this up. We are giving 25 kilos of rice to all those who live below poverty line through the public distribution system.

The administrative machinery has been moving in a particular pace in the last 50 years. We have also said that when there was a natural calamity, no warrant should be taken against anyone's property. Nobody can be arrested then. That is why in our national executive, we have made an important suggestion of providing insurance cover to farmers.

People have given 50 years to the Congress, but they are not ready to give five years to the BJP.

On 9 November 2019, the Supreme Court ordered the land at Ayodhya be handed over to a trust to build a Ram Mandir. It also ordered the government to give an alternate five acres of land to the Sunni Waqf Board for the purpose of building a mosque. 'There are so many people in India who are interested in the temple, and for them, it is the biggest thing', Jana Krishnamurthy had said.

A Christian Missionary who Taught Hindu Philosophy

With a BJP prime minister at the Centre, topics like Hinduism, Hindu philosophy, Sanskrit, Vedas, Upanishads, etc were discussed and debated a lot in those days.

It was then that I met an English man who came to India as a Christian missionary in 1959 but took a doctorate in Hindu philosophy and started teaching Vaishnavite (devotion of Vishnu and his avatars) philosophy for 35 long years in India.

Not just in English, he was a man well-versed in Sanskrit, Telugu and Kannada.

And the man in question was ***Dr Eric J Lott.***

It was an interesting experience for me to talk to an English man who used Sanskrit words and Sanskrit slokas liberally in our conversation.

WAS it because you were interested in Vaishnava philosophy that you came to India?

Not quite. I came to India as a missionary, and I was expected to do relief work and pastoral work in Indian villages. In another sense, I was expected to teach the Christian communities.

It was when I was studying at the London University that I came across the writings of Ramanuja and I became attracted to his idea of looking at the whole world as the body of God. I felt Ramanuja's vision of the Universe is something that should be true for all religions and all philosophies. I decided then that I would come to India one day.[1]

Was it after you read Ramanuja's work that you began looking at the universe as the body of God, or had you been thinking in that direction earlier too?

The two went together. Yes, I had always been interested in the organic view of nature. My father was an organic farmer, and I too was farming for seven years before I went back to university. I was searching for an integral relationship between religious faiths and a positive view of nature.

I somehow felt there was a certain weakness in the modern, Christian view of the universe. So, when I came across this view; the vision or *darshan* of Ramanuja, I felt this was something that I, as a Christian, should take up seriously and make it a part of me.

Since then, many in America, particularly the eco-feminists – the feminists who are particularly interested in understanding

---

[1] Ramanuja was a Hindu philosopher, guru, a social reformer and one of the most important exponents of the Sri Vaishnavite tradition within Hinduism.

the whole universe and nature differently – began looking at the universe as a divine body.

You said you saw a certain weakness in the modern Christian view of the universe. Were you frustrated inside?

I think frustration is a good word, but one shouldn't take it too strongly. I also had a certain satisfaction in my religious experience.

I was very young at that time, in my early twenties, perhaps very naive. Yes, I was searching for something more. That indicated certain frustration. I felt the particular view (that of Ramanuja) satisfied my search, complemented what I had already believed about the world, life and God.

You came here as a missionary, and then you were learning and teaching Vaishnavite philosophy. Did your work as a missionary and what you pursued not clash?

Yes, there was a certain tension. Now, I am going to the whole question of fundamentalism. It is the exclusive attitudes of people belonging to all communities. The fundamentalists say they are right and you are wrong, and theirs is the right way and they can learn nothing from you. But that is not my way. I found the need for an interacting posture as a believing person.

Although I was strongly convinced of my religious faith, I still believed that to be faithful to God, who is greater than we can ever imagine, we need also to respond to other people's experience of God.

Naturally, within the Christian community, there are fundamentalists who take a very different line as within Islam and now increasingly, even within the Hindu communities. But I had the strong conviction that the Christian tradition has much to learn from the Hindu tradition. I also felt it was very much a two-way process, but very much a learning process for me.

When did you begin learning Vaishnavite philosophy seriously?

My initial reading, when I was in London, was very superficial. After I came here, I decided to take this up very seriously. So, after four years in India, I went back to the London University, learnt Sanskrit, and read much more widely about Indian traditions. That was how a serious foundation was laid to learn more about Vaishnavism.

After nearly ten years, in 1969 I went back to London to do my first research degree on 'Ramanuja and Vishisht-advaita' (the non-dualist school of Vedanta philosophy).

Was it to learn more about Hindu philosophy and read the scriptures like the Vedas and the Upanishads in the original that you learnt Sanskrit?

It is a complex reason. Yes, there was that simple need to know more about Hindu philosophy. It was also related to my Christian tradition.

I felt anyone who wished to be a part of the Indian consciousness had to learn to understand Indian culture and its traditions. You can't live in India without getting affected by the Indian imagery, like the birds, lotus, etc as they are a part of the Indian consciousness.

It is naïve to talk about a single Indian consciousness, as there are many dimensions to it. In fact, there is a great diversity in the Indian ways of looking at things, and that too one has to take seriously.

What I felt was, the Christian faith in India must have the ability to express authentically in response to the traditional perceptions and experiences of the Indian people, down through the ages. Some continuity must be there; otherwise, it will become artificial. So, in addition to the simple reason to know more about the Indian consciousness, there was a deeper need for completeness too.

Why did you go to London to learn Sanskrit? Why didn't you learn Sanskrit here in India itself?

After every five years, we go back to England for a year, and when you go back, most people have to tell the donors about their work. The support missionaries are very ordinary people, you know. We don't get any government grant or anything like that; we get only individual donations. When I went back, they said I could do research. So, every time I went back to the UK, I did some research.

When I got back to India, due to some reason the Ramanuja Research Society in Madras (Chennai) sent me a letter asking me to send my thesis. They heard from somewhere that it was good. I sent it and they published it in 1970. In 1976, I went back, did a broader study, and got my doctorate. Then I broadened it to the whole *vedantic* arena, and did a comparative study of the various aspects of Vedantic approach to God.

How much did Vedanta influence your thoughts and outlook to life?

In some ways, I ended up where I began. It is like a circle. The Indian concept of the cycle has a lot of truth in it. There was already a grounding in me for a more mystical or a more participating relationship with nature.

Even in infancy, I remember lying in a grass field, looking at the blue sky and experiencing the cool, and feeling that I am part of the field. So, there was this mysticism of nature in me already. In that sense, what I have learnt from Indian philosophy tended to conform my developing instinct for the mysticism of nature.

You taught Vaishnav philosophy at the Theological College of Religions in Bangalore for nearly 35 years.

Yes, I did. But I taught not only Vaishnavism, I taught religions generally. I taught some aspects of Sikhism, Islam, etc too. But it was understood that my main expertise was in Vaishnavite philosophy.

There are many other fields in Hindu philosophy, like the Shaivaite (worshipping Shiva) philosophy, the Vedanta (the end of the Vedas), etc What attracted you to Vaishnavite philosophy?

It is the body image that attracted me. In Sanskrit, they say *deha dehi bhava, sarira sariri bhava.* Way back in 1957 itself, this philosophy gripped me. So, I decided to focus on this particular vision of the universe. It is still with me. I still feel there is something very special, very inspiring about this *bhava* or *darshan* (vision of the superior being).

Ramanuja himself says that his approach is nothing new as the Vedas and the Upanishads teach it. In fact, he was able to quote large sections of tradition which spoke of the universe as the body of God. 'That whose body is this whole universe... that whose body is the *akasa,* that whose body is this *bhoomi....*' That is the context in which *tatvamasi* (translated as 'I am that' or 'Thou Art That') comes in. *Tatvamasi* is an *advaitik* statement, a *mahavakya* which Adi Sankara highlighted in the context of speaking about the universe as a body.

Do you believe in Advaita?

I am critical of Advaita (the non-dualistic school of thought that believes in only one truth that is Brahman).

Ramanuja was also critical of Advaita. Of course, I am critical of Advaita not because Ramanuja was.

Adi Sankara contended, and later the Advaitik tradition also contended, that everything at the ultimate level is absolute oneness, *ekatva.* And that there is no differentiation between you and me, between one body and another.

Therefore, if you perceive any difference that is of the nature of illusion, and if you interpret *maya* (illusion) in the *paramartika* (the supreme truth) sense, it is *asatya* – not the truth. If you say that, then you are undermining the whole creative process, you are undermining the reality of the universe that it is God's creation.

So, it is because of his faith in God, the creative power of God and the belief in the reality of God that Ramanuja said, the universe has got its own reality, which was not a *vyavaharic* reality but a reality that is no less than the reality of God.[2]

God is *satyasya satya,* but this is also *satya. Satyasya satya* is absolute truth. Therefore, Ramanuja was harshly critical of Sankara and the Advaitik tradition. Of course, he doesn't name Sankaracharya.

You came here as a Christian missionary. You are a Christian by faith. Did learning a Hindu philosophy in any way change your attitude to your religion and faith?

Yes, it did. It certainly did. As I said, there is a conforming factor, an enlarging, modifying, and enhancing factor in that

---

[2] Vyavaharic reality is everyday reality.

process; a critical element too. As I reflected further and further on the way of looking at the universe, it introduced a kind of critical element in me. But I think all religious people need to be self-critical.

Whichever religion you are born into, you have to learn to be critical of it. Because of our faith in God, we also need to be critical of the ways in which we have spoken about God, other human beings, other communities and the universe. Over the years, it has also affected my attitude to other religious communities.

In what way has it affected your attitude?

I am critical but only as I am critical of my own tradition and my own community. I think we are now moving into a very sensitive area, but we have to be critical. This is a crisis time in the history of India.

Do you feel the crisis is restricted to India alone? Are we not seeing it all over the world?

Yes, you are right. It is a global crisis. What is happening in India is a reflection of what is happening globally. In part, it is a reaction against the modern movement. In part, it is a reaction against globalisation. People now experience a threat, a threat about losing their identity because of a new global identity.

Can't we call it insecurity?

Yes, it is insecurity too. You look at what is happening in the former Yugoslavia, you look at what has been happening in Northern Ireland, in Sri Lanka. In all these areas, they have their local complexities and particular historical factors, but people fear about a global giant that threatens to take over the whole world. It is not only in the economic sense but culturally too. Globalisation has its dangerous cultural 'uniforming' that people fear. They fear about losing their particular identity.

Do you see one culture engulfing all the other cultures in the world?

I don't know. I am not a prophet. I only hope that there might be a backtracking in globalisation. You see, globally also, there is recognition that other identities, other cultures and other communities have their rights. There has never been such a greater sense of the value of particular identities and cultures at the intellectual level. I am afraid, at the level of global economy and global market, these factors are secondary. That is a great danger.

With the breakthrough in communication technology and the way in which India is taking a prominent role in the development of new technologies, it is possible that all manners of diverse and variant cultural values can become a part of the new human consciousness.

If those who are concerned about their particular identity can project their tradition and values globally through the new communication process in the right way, in a convincing way, then it is possible that it will make an impact.

It might have been a different India that you lived in when you first came here more than 35 years ago. As a missionary and as a person who has studied Hindu philosophy deeply, how do you react to the burning of Christian missionaries and demolition of religious places?

What the Sankaracharya of Puri said is absolutely true. I am so pleased that he said it and I hope that other important acharyas will speak out too. He said, what has been done in the name of Hindutva is in fact betraying Hindutva, the true

Hinduness. This is not the way to establish Hindu values. He has spoken out rightly and courageously.[3]

Do you feel insecure in India now?

No.

> *What Eric J Lott said twenty years ago on religious fundamentalism is still relevant, 'It is a global crisis. What is happening in India is a reflection of what is happening globally. In part, it is a reaction against the modern movement. In part, it is a reaction against globalisation. People now experience a threat, a threat about losing their identity because of a new global identity'.*
>
> *Today, we see the same insecurities, the same problems and the same reactions all around us, perhaps with more intensity.*

[3] The reference here is to the Staines burning. Graham Stuart Staines was an Australian Christian missionary, who along with his two sons, Philip (aged ten) and Timothy (aged six), was burnt to death in January 1999 in India by members of a Hindu fundamentalist group named Bajrang Dal.

‘India to be a Global Healthcare Destination’

A stable government at the Centre after a few chaotic years was music to the ears of the corporate sector and they reacted positively to the stability.

So, in the first year of Atal Bihari Vajpayee's rule, the GDP grew at 8 per cent, and there was buoyancy in the economy.

But you have to remember that India was still in the initial stages of liberalisation.

The situation was in stark contrast to the confidence India's corporate sector displayed in 2020 when an entrepreneur like Gautam Adani (the founder and chairman of the Adani Group is the second richest Indian) talked about his plan to become the world's largest solar power company by 2025, and the biggest renewable energy firm by 2030.

But twenty years ago, the mood was totally different. The Indian corporate sector had just started taking baby steps to combat the world. They were still weary of the multinational companies, and unsure about how to face international competition.

But unlike the rest of the jittery corporate sector, ***Dr Pratap Reddy,*** *Founder of the Apollo Hospitals was always confident of what India could achieve in the field of healthcare.*

Having started the Apollo Hospitals in 1983, he can be described as the torchbearer in the field of business in India.

When I interviewed him 22 years ago, in 2000, he had predicted a healthcare revolution happening in India, and India becoming a global healthcare destination soon! Words of a visionary in business!

WHEN you first started Apollo Hospital in Madras (Chennai) in 1983, the corporate hospital concept was unheard of in India. What was the motivating force behind it?

I have to go back to answer that. I was in the US for ten years, and came back due to my father's wishes. I then started a good heart hospital, but I used to send those who needed heart surgery to the US.

A young man of thirty-seven came to me after a heart attack and he was suffering from severe pain. He needed a coronary bypass surgery. Unfortunately, his employer refused to pay $30,000 which was the hospital fee for the Texas Heart Institute. Before I could make any alternate arrangements, in front of my eyes, he died. It shattered me. He shouldn't have died at all.

That was when I decided to create a hospital with international health standards in our country. I had seen in the US that professionally managed corporate hospitals were doing extremely well as far as quality of health care was concerned. Because of better management, they brought down the cost too. That was how Apollo, Madras, the first professionally run corporate hospital, was born.

How difficult was it to materialise your dream?

There are a million bricks in this building, and there were a million problems too. At all levels we had problems; you name it and we had it. But all that is behind us now. The million problems have made our bricks very strong now: call it reinforced bricks.

Can an ordinary person in India afford a hospital of these standards?

My desire is that no man should die for want of facilities in our country. But I know India. We have a small number of rich, a few upper middle class, and many middle class and poor people. We have beds to satisfy all these categories. We provide hospital facilities and doctor service free for poor people. Some organisations look after the medical consumable and disposables. If nothing else happens, we ourselves have a charitable society.

The image I had of Apollo was that of a five-star hospital. But I was surprised to see a mainly middle-class crowd inside the hospital. Do you feel the attitude of the Indian middle class towards health care has changed?

I am very happy that today patients can have facilities which they never had before. Sometimes, I walk into the lobby and talk to some of the patients about where they came from, their opinion about the care here, and how they were able to raise the amount, etc Their answers disturb me and make me very sad. At least 30 per cent of them cannot afford the charges. They borrow, they pledge and some even sell their properties to avail of these facilities.

My new mission is to create an opportunity or a situation so that people from all walks of life get access to a good quality health care system. For that we need to have two things. One, a high-quality health care network not only in the cities but in rural areas too; and two, we need a mechanism through which all of them will have access to these facilities.

Health insurance is a necessity. I have been working at it for nearly three years. Anyway, the process has started and I don't think anyone can stop it because people at all levels, whether it is the bureaucrats or the policy-makers or the politicians and most important the public, have realised that it is essential to get high quality health care.

You talked about India becoming the global healthcare destination. Where is the thrust going to be: attracting patients to India or expanding to other countries by setting up hospitals there?

Basically, we are here to take care of the healthcare needs of the people. Apollo and other private hospitals have tried to bring in the best health facilities to India. Now, most of these hospitals are in the metros. We want to take it to the smaller towns and villages.

Similarly, in some of the other countries, especially in the Afro-Asian region, there is a great need for healthcare facilities.

For example, people from Sri Lanka, Bangladesh and the other SAARC (South Asian Association for Regional Cooperation) countries have been coming to India for treatment for a long time. They are satisfied with the quality of care they are getting from Apollo.

Recently, when I went to Sri Lanka, the President was so thankful to Apollo for the type of facilities offered that when I wanted to start a hospital in Lanka, it was almost a blanket permission. This is the kind of respect, the kind of love, the kind of friendship that we are going to get from our neighbouring countries. We expect people from other countries, especially from the African and the Middle East countries also to come to India for their healthcare needs. In Afro-Asian countries alone, the overseas spending for healthcare is $17 billion.

I think we should tap that. We should make sure that a majority of that money comes to India. We offer the best care, and our cost is only a fraction of what it is in the developed countries.

We will have information centres there to let people know what is available in India, what they can expect and what the cost is, and also to assist them to come to the right centres.

So, our thrust is to make India the healthcare destination of the world. We are confident we can bring the world to Apollo.

We have to bring them to India because we can't give tertiary care of this standard in other countries. That is because we need an entire gamut of services in tertiary care.

We want to tell the world that our specialists have performed over 500,000 major surgeries and over a million other surgical procedures including cardio-thoracic, neurological, cancer, etc with success rates on par with international standards.

Our success rate in the cardiac surgeries we have done is 98.5 per cent. Our success in bone marrow transplants is 80 per cent. Our success rate in renal transplants is 95 per cent.

How much do you expect the healthcare sector in India to grow?

The numbers game is a very difficult one. Like I told you, $17 billion is the overseas spending on healthcare from the Afro-Asian countries alone.

Similarly, medical business process outsourcing is almost a $100 billion industry.

So, the question is, how much can we take? It is essential for us to build our strengths to try and get that market.

The architects of India's economic liberalisation, Rao and Singh.
Thank you, Rediff.com

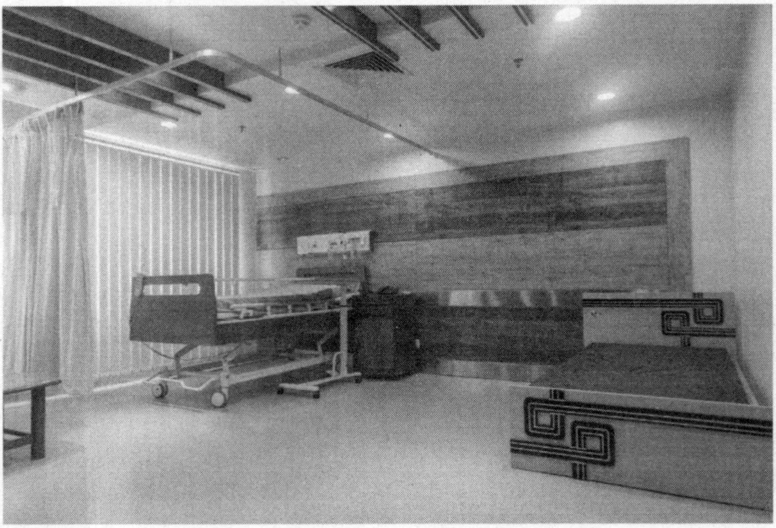

Inside a private hospital in India.
Thank you, Telegraph India.

What about medi-tourism?

When India becomes the healthcare destination of the world, health tourism also will grow accordingly. All the other industries related to healthcare also would grow with healthcare.

I must add we are the key players responsible for the emergence of medi-tourism in India.

You said, India should not lose its inherent potential as far as healthcare is concerned. To achieve that, you planned to have a test module in Goa where the best from the East would meet the best from the West, and it would offer a holistic approach to healthcare. Can you elaborate?

West means technology and adaptation in delivering healthcare. Here, we have our traditional medicines like Ayurveda, Homeopathy, Unani. We are also reversing the aging process and de-stressing people through yoga and meditation.

We plan to put all this in a package and bundle it and offer to the world.

Dr Pratap Reddy talked about those numbers in the year 2000; more than two decades have passed.

Today, India is considered one of Asia's leading medical tourism destinations with around 18 per cent of the global medical tourism market under its belt.

According to reports, India's medical tourism sector was estimated to be worth US$5–6 billion around mid-2020, soon after the pandemic struck the world.

Do You Remember the Word, e-Tailing?

It is interesting to note that in 2000, selling of retail goods on the Internet was called e-tailing. In those days, experts were worried whether it would ever be popular.

Listening to what ***Prof Nirmalya Kumar****, a Professor of marketing and e-commerce at the International Institute for Management Development in Switzerland, more than two decades ago makes us realise how technology and the way people shop has changed in such a short span of time.*

Those were the days the e-commerce giants like Amazon or Alibaba or Flipkart were unknown entities!

WHO are the customers of e-tailing in the developed world?

The customers have to be really targeted. If you are not really targeted, especially when it comes to grocery, you can never make money. The reason is that customer-acquisition costs tend to be somewhere between $200 and $700 because of brand advertising, incentives given, etc So, if the cost of acquiring a customer is $200-700, you have to have a customer who remains with you long enough for you to be able to 'recover' that initial $200-700.

Is it worth spending that much money on a customer?

It is only worth for the right customer. The right customer for grocery e-tailing is a customer who orders forty times a year on an average of $100 a year. The only people who seem to get to that level are households where, both, the husband and the wife work 100 per cent.

If the wife works 70 per cent, the first thing she does after work is grocery shopping. We find that the attitude of women who work 70 per cent towards grocery shopping through the Internet is identical to the attitude of those women who don't work at all because their mothers have taught them that buying food is a part of the meal preparation for the children, and it is a very important part of the definition of a mother.

So, we have found that e-tailing is possible only in a household where both the husband and wife work 100 per cent.

The second thing we have found is that you have to have children in the household. If you don't, the average order size is very low because children consume all kinds of stuff. Only if the order size is high, you can justify the delivery cost because the delivery costs are more or less fixed regardless of the size of the order.

So, you have to get the regular customer and that turns out to be the woman who works 100 per cent. You have to get high order size and that happens only when you have children. Only when you have this combination, you can try to get money. I don't say you can still make money, but that's where you can get close.

Is it not a very small percentage?

No. In America, it is a very big percentage. The percentage of both parents working in a household with children might be 15 per cent of all the households. It may even go beyond that. When you get 3 per cent of the population, it is called a big percentage by the e-tailing models of supermarkets selling groceries on the Internet. Only then, will you be able to break even. So, you have to get 20 per cent of the 15 per cent to break even.

Many people say it is highly unlikely that people would go for grocery shopping on the Internet.

I think it is the one place where people have the highest chance of going e-tailing. I enjoy the process of shopping books or music but it is not so when I go grocery shopping. I don't know of anybody who enjoys grocery shopping except a few housewives who have nothing else to do. If you ask most working mothers, 'what do you think of super market shopping', they will tell you, they hate it.

The need is clearly there. Whether the customer is willing to pay for the shipping cost is not clear because grocery retailing is a 25 per cent gross margin and 3-4 per cent net margin business and if the average order is $100, you make about $3-4. So, you can't afford to subsidise shipping. You have to charge the customer for the full shipping because if you subsidise shipping, you will never make money.

Many retailers like Carrefour of France talked about having e-tailing also, as a part of their business. If they do both simultaneously, will they be able to break even faster?

No. We have found that whenever retailers take on e-tailing, it is additional cost rather than additional revenue. That is because they have to run two systems and you don't have any cost savings. In the end, it will be bricks and mortar. But I think, the best retailers who are doing e-tailing may have the retailing operation separately. They have a dedicated 'hardware house' which is designed for picking individual items efficiently.

Do you think e-tailing is a passing fad and people would go back to traditional shopping once the initial excitement wears out?

No, it is not a passing fad at all. As most people are not doing it, it is not a fad as yet. Even in America, most people have not adopted e-tailing. What are you doing for the customer in e-tailing? You save them time. You give them better assortment. You save them the packing hassle. You save them the hassle of interacting with surly store clerks. It is open round-the-clock, and you can shop whenever you want rather than shop when the shop wants you to. These are the advantages of e-tailing, and these are very powerful advantages.

The only challenge for e-tailing is, we have to find a cost model which allows us to break even because the customer is willing to pay extra but not so much.

How popular will e-tailing be after ten years?

In ten years, e-tailing will be 10 per cent in America which is the most developed now in e-tailing. That is my guess. It is not based on any numbers; it is based on a complete hunch.

You have to remember that we overestimate how good technology will be in next two-three years; that is in the short run. And, we always underestimate how much people will adopt technology in the long run, which is about ten years.

When you do e-tailing, are you not losing out on the experience of shopping in a store?

Exactly. You are completely right. You will not get those customers who love the experience of shopping. You will get only the time-starved customers who don't have the time to go for these experiences. You will never get the customer who goes to a shop for the experience.

What about browsing a book in a bookstore?

I agree with you. But we can also give some things on the Internet, which you can't get from the shop. For example, we can give you user reviews. We can give you the first chapter free to read. We can give a whole lot of other things too. In the case of books, the experience will be different. It won't be a mass market. Remember we only need 3-5 per cent to make money.

What about textiles? Will people ever shop their clothes on the Net?

There is a difference between fashion items and staple items. Plain underwear on the Internet, yes. Hanky, yes. White sheets, yes. But fashion items like suits, no.

It depends on the item. Those items will not move to the Internet where the customer feels the touch-feel-see is important. Those items will move to the Internet where touch-feel-see is not important. We won't feel a handkerchief before we buy it, or a pair of black socks. But a suit, yes, I want to see how I look in it.

In India, Internet penetration is very low. Do you expect e-tailing to become popular here in India?

I don't see anything great in e-tailing in India in another ten years. We have to get the Internet penetration up. We have to get the speed of the lines up. Most people who live in the cities do not have to travel far to shop unlike in many other developed countries. Plus, the number of working wives is few in India. And, people are very price-sensitive here. I am not sure whether they are willing to pay extra for the shipping cost.

I personally think e-tailing will develop. But it is too far a step right now. It could be there in insurance, financial services, but not for grocery shopping. So, we will see both retailing and e-tailing existing side by side soon.

After some time, won't the people who shop on the Net yearn for a personal touch, like talking to a vegetable-woman or a milkman or a florist?

That personal touch is only valued by housewives who don't have anybody to talk to during the day. The working mothers, remember they are my segment for e-tailing, don't have the time to talk to the *doodhwala* (milk man), they don't have time to talk to the vegetable woman. If they have any time, they want to spend it talking to their children or to their husbands after coming home from work at six o'clock. Yes, you are right. Social interaction is very important but it is important for the housewives and not for the woman who is working 100 per cent.

Now tell me, you are a working woman. Do you have the time for such social interaction?

I like interacting with these people…

Then, I will never have you as our customer!

I cannot imagine this was what we thought about e-commerce more than two decades ago. Time was when Prof Nirmalya Kumar thought that for successful e-tailing, households needed to have children.
Cut to 2022, and it is not an exaggeration if we were to say e-commerce has transformed the way business and retail shopping is done in India. From groceries to vegetables to milk, every single household item is shopped online now, by everyone!
With a turnover of US $50 billion in 2020, India's e-commerce market has become the eighth largest in the world.

The BPO Revolution and the Y2K Crisis

The world was exposed to the abilities of India's skilled labour during the Y2K crisis, when the world moved from 1999 to 2000. Many technical glitches were anticipated, as many programmes represented four-digit years with only the final two digits, which made the year 2000 indistinguishable from 1900. Indians played a major role in fixing the programmes all over the world.

This was when, all of a sudden, the world realised that India was a country where they could get work done at a cheaper cost, or cheap labour.

No wonder, during 2001-02, Business Process Outsourcing (BPO) became the fastest growing industry in India, growing at the rate of 70 per cent.

India became the most favoured destination for multinational companies to outsource work, mainly because of the abundant skilled and English-speaking manpower India possessed. Another reason was the 12-hour time zone difference advantage the US companies had, when they outsourced work to India.

Though the communication network was not as fast as it is today, in the early 2000, India had reasonably fast Internet facilities in the cities.

The outsourcing first started as call centres, soon there were Knowledge Processing Outsourcing (KPO), Legal Processing Outsourcing (LPO), Medical Business Process Outsourcing (MPO), etc

Of course, there was a huge backlash in the US against work going out of the country.

One BPO company that made it really big in the early 2000 was Sutherland Global Services.

I spoke to **Dilip R Vellodi***, the founder of Sutherland Global Services of Rochester, in 2004 when BPO was the most important word in the Indian business circles.*

YOU launched Sutherland in 1986 as a regional start-up. It is now a global BPO company, outsourcing from India. Why did you choose India as the outsourcing centre?

We have been watching India for the last four years. In January 2002, we felt the timing was right from the BPO perspective.

The first reason was, we felt the communication infrastructure was robust enough to be able to handle what we needed for our clients, without any interruption or failure. We have got to ensure that we are taking very good care of our clients, and we cannot afford to have any kind of breakdown in our communication infrastructure, or in our data infrastructure that puts them in a bad spot. Two years ago, that was a big concern for us.

Second, India has a tremendous pool of talent, an extremely intelligent and a highly motivated workforce.

Thirdly, it is the cost factor. As far as cost is concerned, it is the manpower that makes the difference and not the infrastructure.

Did India and its workforce come up to your expectations?

Let's not forget that I am originally from India, though I have never worked in India. So, working in India is a new experience for me.

Our main concern was meshing our organisation in the US and the new one in India. The cultures and the management team should gel and work together. The way everything worked out was a little bit of a surprise for us, because we had not anticipated such a smooth change-over.

Now we have executives flying back and forth without any problem. They communicate with each other well as communication is absolutely essential in our kind of work.

I would say the workforce here has come up to our clients' expectations. They are on par with what you get in North America. But we felt there was a dearth of leadership skills at certain levels.

There is a lot of animosity against India in the US because of outsourcing. How do you react to this backlash?

You are absolutely right. BPO is an emotional issue out there. When you speak to the individual who might have been impacted, it is a very emotional issue. But if you look at it from the macro point of view, it is an economic reality that is taking place. It is something that is inevitable. It makes economic sense for companies to outsource and go offshore. This way, companies are actually getting same value for a lot less.

So, after making investments in the US, you take the decision to offshore to increase your global competitiveness.

What companies would do after that is reinvest back. This way, new jobs are created, maybe different kind of jobs, but that is really what globalisation is all about.

These countries clamour for globalisation, but when it affects them adversely, the tone changes….

Yes, you are right. What they say goes against the very tenets of globalisation, free trade and free market. But it is an election year in the US. There is a lot of political rhetoric that is going on.

Let's take the example of Sutherland itself. Offshoring helped our company to be more robust and we made our footprints globally. We became more competitive and it allowed us to reinvest and grow.

That outsourcing will help companies reinvest seems to have not reached the people there…. Otherwise, there would not have been such uproar.

When it is an emotional argument, it is very, very difficult to take a look at the reality objectively. Yes, there will have to be a programme of re-training; re-educating and setting the right expectation levels of workers.

But outsourcing will be a continuing reality?

Outsourcing and offshoring are realities. The clock cannot be turned back. The train has left the station and it will not be going back. No amount of rhetoric will stop this.

Some US States have already banned outsourcing by government-run companies. How will this affect the companies that engage in outsourcing?

Let's not forget that America happens to be a capitalist country. That is where Capitalism was born. The government will not be able to control what commercial establishments do.

Ultimately, why do companies exist? They are not non-profit organisations; you have certain responsibilities to the stakeholders, customers and employees. Outsourcing and offshoring are some of the key components that allow companies to be competitive and that cannot be controlled by the state, certainly not in the United States.

It was reported that the chairman of the National Intelligence Council of the US said that 3 million jobs might come to India by 2015 and this is a potential security risk. What is the security risk in outsourcing?

I haven't read the statement. I think he may be talking about classified information, classified data, etc Like I said earlier, if they want to have that done there, it is going to cost them more.

When the economy was boiling over, that was before 11 September 2001, a minimum of three-four jobs out of ten were going begging. They were not being filled. That has changed. Now the talent has to come from countries like India, and it's a balancing act. You know something, people over there are applying to Sutherland in India to work here.

You mean the flow of people from one country to another will take place soon….

That has got to take place. Isn't that what globalisation is all about? You are really breaking down geographic barriers, and it makes a lot of sense.

In what way will outsourcing affect the economic scene in the United States and India a few years from now?

As the economy improves over there (in the United States), there will probably be a little more of a letting up on the pricing pressure. People might be willing to pay a higher price over there but I don't believe there will be any substantial impact in terms of opportunities and growth in the foreseeable future as far as India is concerned.

From the Sutherland perspective, India is very much going to be the engine of growth. We are going to continue to grow in North America as well. The pace of growth in India will be much higher.

A report suggests that 70 per cent of the outsourcing jobs from the US will come to India, 20 per cent will go to the Philippines and 10 per cent to China. As a global BPO company, are you also looking at China?

We, as a company, will be looking at China in the future. In fact, we have looked at it but not so aggressively; but it's there on our radar screen. The fundamental challenge in China will be the workforce that knows no English, while you have a workforce that speaks English here in India. They are taking a concentrated effort now to master English. And China is a big market place.

India witnessed a huge BPO boom in the early 2000s.
Thank you, Panay News.

Out of the global outsourcing market size of US$ 232.32 billion in 2020, India continues to be the leading outsourcing destination across the world, accounting for approximately 55 per cent market share of the global services sourcing business. 'India is very much going to be the engine of growth', Dilip Vellodi had said.

As there was a lot of negative connotations attached to the work that was done in the BPOs, NASSCOM tried to change the image of the nature of work done by changing the idea of outsourcing to BPM now, which is Business Process Management (BPM). Here, the companies function as end-to-end Business Process services providers that not only process transactions but also provide business processes expertise.[1]

With over 17,000 firms and an employee strength of 1.4 million, the business process management (BPM) industry in India is the largest in the world.

The IT and BPM industry together constitute around 8 per cent of India's GDP and it is the largest private sector employer, employing around 4 million people. And the industry generated a revenue of $195 billion in 2021.

---

1 The National Association of Software and Service Companies is an Indian non-governmental trade association and advocacy group; it focuses mainly on the technology industry of India.

Muslims and the BJP

2004. As another general election neared, the country was divided on religious lines like never before, despite all the economic progress India had made.

It was then that I spoke to one of the well-known Muslim faces in India, a non-political figure, His Highness ***Nawab Ghulam Mohammed Abdul Ali,*** *the Prince of Arcot, the founder secretary general of Harmony India, an organisation that worked to promote communal amity, secularism and national integration.*

DO you feel that from the time India won independence, Muslims have been used by political parties as vote banks? Is that why there is so much tension between the Hindus and Muslims now?

Perhaps that could be a reason. India's Constitution provides equal rights to all citizens. India does not belong to one religion or one community.

It is part of Islam to be loyal and honest to the nation. Religious leaders should spell out and educate people by enlightening them to follow the true and correct religion.

This 'I am a Hindu' and 'I am a Muslim' attitude is ruining the whole nation.

Who is responsible for creating such an attitude?

Politicians, I would say. If politicians do not interfere in religion, there will be smooth sailing.

Even about Ayodhya, the matter is in court, so I should not open my mouth. But if it is left to the people, I think they can solve it.

Politicians want to take advantage of the issue, especially at election time, which I don't think is correct. In fact, Hindus and Muslims should sit together and come to a decision.

Who should be talking? The people who live in Ayodhya, or the people of India at large?

I think the people of the country as a whole. They should come forward and talk.

Do religious leaders have a place in these talks? Should they be talking or should ordinary people talk?

The leading people of that particular State or the country, who are involved in the welfare of the people, should decide. Not the politicians. If politicians come into the picture, the whole thing gets stuck. Nothing moves. From 1992 onwards, what has happened? Nothing. Now the matter is in court. We have to obey the judgment when it comes.

Even the BJP says the dispute should be amicably settled between the Hindus and the Muslims. I think it is a good idea of the BJP that they insist on both communities meeting and solving the problem.

Muslims had liberal leaders in the beginning. Do you feel they have been replaced by hardcore fundamentalists, not only in India but all over the world?

In any religion, there should not be extremists; there should not be fundamentalists. We should not become fanatics.

If I am a Muslim, let me be a better Muslim.

If you are a Hindu, you be a better Hindu.

If you are a Christian, you be a better Christian.

If all the communities in India can work together, India can be one of the leading countries in the world.

In what way are you conveying this to your community?

Whenever I go to functions and public meetings, I speak on these issues. I educate people on communal harmony, secularism, national unity, against dowry, etc Religious leaders should teach against giving and accepting dowry, which is totally un-Islamic. People go out of the way and give importance to practices, traditions, conventions, etc rather than true and correct religion. I don't think that's correct.

Do you feel the BJP is a communal party and under the BJP, Muslims in India feel threatened?

Even today, that feeling is there between the Muslims and the BJP, that the BJP is against Muslims.

Personally speaking, I don't think the BJP is against the Muslims. It's only politics. If the BJP removes from the hearts of the Muslims that they are not the enemies of the Muslims, I think it can lead the country for years and years to come.

I admire that political party, the BJP, though I am not a political person, because of their unity. If they take even the Muslims also with them, and sail together, I think that will be the best.

They should not talk about disturbing other mosques. Some vested interests are talking about around 3,000 mosques that should be brought down. That's all wrong. All this is a sheer waste of time, energy and money.

Do you feel the BJP has created a division between the Hindus and Muslims?

Not the BJP, I can say, there are some vested interests who are trying to divide the people.

What's your message to the Muslims in India?

That they should first have education, and they should join politics. By politics, I mean mainstream. We don't have Muslim leaders in the country who can take us in the right direction.

Have you ever thought of joining any political party or becoming a politician?

From childhood I have been interested in politics. But because of the pressure from my family, I am keeping away from it. I don't like to just call myself the Prince of Arcot, but do some service to society. I do service in the community in a small way.

When Rajiv Gandhi was alive, he invited me to join the Congress. I was the sheriff of Madras then. One day, the papers wrote that I had joined the Congress. The very next day I denied it. When Rajiv Gandhi met me, he said, even before becoming a politician you have become a real politician!

But I have not given a thought to joining any political party now.

You issued a statement that Muslims in India should not clamour for backward class status; instead, they should educate themselves and come up in life. When every other community in India is asking for backward class status, you sounded different. Why did you issue such a statement?

Muslims are the second largest majority in the country. Muslims are not minorities. Even in the world, Muslims are the second largest religious community. Then why should we ask for backward status, or the most backward label?

We should develop our own potentialities. We should have education and we should come up in life like any Hindu or Christian boy or girl. We should uplift ourselves in the eyes of people. We should not expect to get the tag of minority. This was my intention.

How has the Muslim community and Muslim leaders reacted to your statement?

Till now, none of the Muslim leaders have reacted to my statement, but many people have called me and congratulated me. What I feel is, our Muslim leaders are not allowing the community to come up because they are afraid, they will be sidelined. That is the reason they are not helping our community to come up through education.

I feel we should not depend on the government because Muslims are neglecting their duties. And education is a key tool for developing a community.

I want to tell you, no Indian Muslim has betrayed the country at any time. Muslims are happier in India than in our neighbouring countries. Muslims were made Presidents of India, besides Vice-Presidents, justices, Governors, Chief Ministers, Union ministers, State ministers, Cabinet secretaries, every now and then. Even in defence, there are many Muslims who hold high ranks and positions.

Only vested interests have tried to label Muslims as spies. Some say we should leave this country and go to Pakistan. It is sheer nonsense. India belongs to everybody. Muslims remained in India because we wanted to be here.

A quote from the Nawab of Arcot to remember, 'If the BJP removes from the hearts of the Muslims that they are not enemies of the Muslims, I think it can lead the country for years and years to come.'

Vaiko, the First to leave the NDA

Though Atal Bihari Vajpayee completed his term as the Prime Minister of India successfully in 2004, the NDA was not as strong as it was before.

The Marumalarchi Dravida Munnetra Kazhagham or the MDMK was the first secular, Dravidian party to align with the BJP, and it was with the NDA even in the 1998 and 1999 general elections when the BJP was an untouchable party. And its general secretary ***Vaiko*** *was one of the vocal supporters of Atal Bihari Vajpayee.*

But the relationship between the MDMK and the BJP strained when Vaiko was arrested under the Prevention of Terrorism Act, 2002 when he arrived at the Chennai airport from the USA on 11 July 2002. Thus, Vaiko became the first Member of Parliament and chief of a registered political party in the country to be arrested and jailed under POTA for one year.[1]

---

1 POTA was passed by the Parliament in 2002, to allegedly strengthen anti-terrorism operations.

In 2003, the party decided to break away from the NDA.

In 2004, it chose to fight the Lok Sabha elections as an ally of the DMK-led Democratic Progressive Alliance, of which the Congress was also a member.

Vaiko spoke to me on the reasons why he quit the NDA.

WHAT prompted you to leave the NDA?

Today, there is a threat to the secular fabric of India, which is the hallmark of our democracy. Religious fundamentalist forces are raising their threats.

Of course, we were a part of the NDA. The MDMK was one of the signatories to the NDA's National Agenda, which was a total commitment to secularism and protection of minorities.

But for the past two years, the Hindutva forces, which were lying low, have sharpened their arsenal to make India a theocratic state.

I have all respect and affection for Vajpayee, but he has become vulnerable in the hands of the Sangh Parivar.

One testimony to my charge is the Union government's decision in 2003 to file a petition in the Supreme Court to vacate the stay of the same apex court, not allowing anybody in the disputed area of Ayodhya.

Another great threat to Indian democracy is the calculated onslaught by the education ministry; to distort history, inject vicious falsehood in the text books of school children; which is more dangerous and can be branded as cultural aggression and invasion, which will ultimately destroy the unity and integrity of India.

Therefore, in prison itself, I was determined to fight these forces and come out of the BJP-led alliance.

Yet the statistics provided by the Central government indicate that communal clashes have decreased substantially over the last five years.

Communal clashes, stray incidents, do not reflect the real threat. Incidents could take place over petty things. But the real problem is when there is a deliberate attempt to inject their doctrine of Hindutva. I see it as a threat. That was not there in the initial years. They never attempted anything. We were very careful.

Did you perceive this shift in the NDA agenda after your arrest and the days you spent in jail?

It was not because I was detained; it was just a coincidence. Even before POTA was invoked against me, I had raised my voice at the NDA meetings. I had written in my party newspaper about the threat, particularly about the distortion of history in text books.

When they filed a petition in the Supreme Court (in the Ayodhya case), I wrote a strong, long letter to the Prime Minister. I quoted liberally from the national agenda and asked him several questions.

Did he respond?

He acknowledged the letter but there was no proper reply. The same letter was read at the NDA meeting by our representative, Dr Krishnan, MP. They were shocked and pleaded with him not to give out copies to anybody, particularly to the Opposition parties. Therefore, I would say I never failed in my duty.

But no one heard about this till you left the NDA.

That was because you are not a member of the NDA, madam! Since you could not attend any NDA meetings, how would you hear my voice? As a disciplined party, I raised the issues in a proper manner. I have done my duty. Since they did not change their ways, we had no other option but quit. I took that decision months ago.

Has your arrest under POTA anything to do with the decision to quit the NDA?

Even when POTA was hanging over my head like a sword, I was not perturbed. I didn't want to get any concession from the government. I was fighting my battle legally in the courts. I didn't ask them to talk to the chief minister of Tamil Nadu (J Jayalalitha) regarding POTA.

I made it very clear to George Fernandes (the then defence minister) when he came to see me thrice in jail. I told him, 'kindly tell Vajpayee not to plead with the chief minister of Tamil Nadu regarding my case. One day, she will say, Vaiko made the central government plead with me'. So, my decision has nothing to do with POTA.

But what was the promise given by the central government? That it (POTA) would not be misused. But it has been misused and abused.

Do you feel the NDA government did not help you?

I want to make it clear that I was least bothered about my detention. I was bothered only about the way they were moving (towards communalism). Even when I was in the NDA, I voted against the BJP private member's bill on a common civil code. Mr Pramod Mahajan (a BJP leader who passed away in 2006) pleaded with me saying, 'the Trinamool Congress (a political party led by Mamata Banerjee, mostly active in Bengal) has gone out of the House. You can simply go out, there won't be any embarrassment. You should not vote against the government'. I said, 'No. I will be present in the House and vote against the bill'.

In the case of POTA, at all the meetings, I analysed it section by section, and said it would strike at the root of democracy.

If you ask George Fernandes, he will tell you the truth. I think he will not hide anything.

There is another factor in my leaving the NDA. Kalaignar (DMK president M Karunanidhi) came to see me in jail. He was my mentor. I have worked with him for several years. The fraternity was cemented after the visit. We both felt there was a threat to the Dravidian movement in Tamil Nadu.

This lady, the chief minister of Tamil Nadu, under the camouflage of the Anna DMK, is trying to demolish all the cherished principles of the Dravidian movement of Anna (DMK founder C N Annadurai) and Periyar (Dravidian movement founder E V Ramasamy Naicker).

We have decided to strengthen the Dravidian movement, for which I have worked in the prime of my life. I have gone to jail 24 times. So, I decided to join Kalaignar; we would be like a double barrel gun!

In what way is Jayalalitha a threat to the Dravidian movement?

What is the necessity to have *veda pathasalas* in Tamil Nadu? What is the concept of the Vedas? It is horrible. It has not been a Tamil concept for thousands of years. Tamil is encouraged by the chief minister in the temples, (even though) she doesn't have any faith in the Dravidian ideology. Therefore, it is very dangerous. A direct enemy is easy to fight. But she is doing all this under camouflage. So, I thought I would join hands with the DMK to fight these forces.

Will your campaign be against the State government or the Central government?

Both. Now, Jayalalitha is trying to project only Vajpayee. After some time, she will say, who knows Vajpayee? People voted for me. Now, she is afraid. People are angry and upset with her. So, she is trying to project Vajpayee. She has not even said in her manifesto what she has achieved; she is just projecting Vajpayee. But we will be alert and caution people about the atrocities she has committed against people, against government servants, weavers, farmers, the press.

You recently said, like the BJP says, India is not shining, and there's no feel-good factor. As a former member of the federal government, are you also not responsible for that?

I would say we have achieved something, at the same time, there are darker areas. But our achievement started from the Nehru period. Whatever we have achieved today was because of what was started by the previous governments. Whichever government was in power, this would have happened.

The Indian economy was growing at a very slow pace; but in the last few years, the growth rate has been nearly 8 per cent.

Growth is a cycle. There were setbacks in between. Even during the period of Indira Gandhi, we grew well. Economic growth fluctuates. It happens to all countries. It is not that we have not achieved anything earlier. We have achieved then, and now also.

You can't say only the BJP can claim the credit for today's growth. IT revolution is not their brain child. It was already there. It is because of the efforts by many individual efforts (that India is growing), and not because of the government.

How did George Fernandes and you become such good friends?

I look at friendships above politics. We have been friends for the last 25 years. When he came to know that I was sick and had fainted in jail, he rushed to see me. He was concerned. Similarly, the moment I came to know that he met with an accident, I sent a telegram from the prison. I have good friends in all parties, in the Congress, too.

Did George Fernandes ever try to dissuade you from leaving the NDA?

Not at all. What he said was, you are justified in your decision.

There are no permanent friends or enemies in politics. Do you believe that?

It is not the case only in India but all over the world.

What about ideology?

Ideologies are permanent, concepts are permanent. If a politician changes his ideology, he is a hypocrite.

How do you react to the opinion polls that predict victory for the NDA?

These opinion polls fluctuate. It can change after 25 days.

Vaiko's worry in 2004 was, 'Another great threat to Indian democracy is the calculated onslaught by the education ministry; to distort history, inject vicious falsehood in the text books of school children; which is more dangerous and can be branded as cultural aggression and invasion, which will ultimately destroy the unity and integrity of India.' The same fear continues today in the minds of many.

....

After a decade of chaos, India had a Central government that lasted five whole years.

In 1999, when Atal Bihari Vajpayee took over as the Prime Minister of India, the GDP (Gross Domestic Product) growth was 8.85 per cent, it fell to 3.84 per cent in 2000 and marginally rose to 4.82 per cent in 2001. It further fell to 3.84 per cent in 2002 but there was a huge jump to 7.86 per cent in 2003.

It was a dream run for the economy from 2003 onwards mainly because of the growth in the infrastructure sector, and agriculture. The ambitious infrastructure projects initiated by Vajpayee like the Golden Quadrilateral connecting most of the industrial, agricultural and cultural centres in India, and the North-South corridor from Kashmir to Kanyakumari, created a lot of jobs which resulted in more spending by the consumers and created increased demand in the market.

There was definitely a buoyancy in the economy.

In 2004, the GDP growth rose to 7.92 per cent, giving confidence to the BJP that they could tell people that India was indeed shining!

Naturally the NDA, led by the BJP with Atal Bihari Vajpayee as the leader, went to the polls under the slogan, India Shining.

Did the people of India also agree with the BJP that India indeed was shining?

....

PART 4

2004-2009

Ruling Party: The UPA

(United Progressive Alliance)

Prime Minister: Dr Manmohan Singh

(Congress)

The kingmaker and the queen!
Thank you, Rediff.com

Dr Manmohan Singh became the Prime Minister of India.
Thank you, Wikimedia: Rashtrapati Bhavan ceremony.

The India Shining Slogan, an Election and a New Government

In the 2004 Lok Sabha elections, unlike in the last few elections, the fight was mainly between the BJP-led NDA, and the Congress and its allies. There was no third alternative of a conglomeration of small parties.

The BJP-led NDA went into the elections with a lot of confidence, expecting a second term.

After all, India's GDP grew during the NDA rule, disinvestment of public sector undertakings was on track, the Foreign Exchange Reserves stood at more than US$ 100 billion, and the service sector grew impressively producing many jobs.

No wonder, the BJP bravely and arrogantly coined the expression, India Shining!

Unfortunately, the common people did not agree with the BJP that India was shining.

They felt there was a mismatch between the India Shining slogan and the standard of their lives. Naturally, the slogan resulted in a lot of anger and frustration amongst people. And they reacted.

Proving all political analysts and opinion polls wrong, the Bharatiya Janata Party managed only 138 seats, 44 seats less than what they had won in 1999.

Sonia Gandhi led the Congress to be the single largest party with 145 seats.

With both the alliances not getting a majority to form a government, a new United Progressive Alliance (UPA) was formed with the Left, the Samajwadi Party (SP) and the Bahujan Samajwadi Party (BSP) supporting the Congress.

Sonia Gandhi was made the Chairperson of the UPA.

In a surprise move, Sonia Gandhi appointed Dr Manmohan Singh as the 13th Prime Minister of India. A Cambridge-educated Economist, he was the Finance Minister in P V Narasimha Rao's government (1991-1996), and the chief architect of India's economic liberalisation in 1991.

Of course, many expected the UPA to be a repeat of the unstable United Front experiment of the 1990s, and the new coalition crumbling in no time.

But this did not happen.

It is now Reforms with a Human Face, Folks!

With a 'reasonably' stable government at the Centre, and an Economist taking over the mantle as the Prime Minister of India, politics was pushed to the backstage, and economy took precedence over everything.

The results of the 2004 elections showed that slogans would not work unless there were positive results on the ground. People had become impatient, whether they belonged to rural India or urban India.

No wonder the medicine the UPA decided to offer was 'reforms with a human face'.

But then, how do you define 'reforms with a human face'?

I decided to talk to ***Dr Raja Chelliah****, (referred to as the 'Father of Tax reforms'), on India's economic reforms, the performance of the National Democratic Alliance (NDA) government under Atal Bihari Vajpayee, and what was expected from the United Progressive Alliance (UPA) government.*

This Padma Vibhushan award winner had also worked as the chief of the Fiscal Analysis Division of the Fiscal Affairs

Department at IMF (International Monetary Fund) from 1969-1975.

Chelliah was looked upon as a public finance expert, instrumental in bringing about early reforms in the direct taxation structure in India.

When I asked him whether it was because of the economic reforms that the NDA lost, he said, 'As an economist, I would say the NDA did not lose because they carried out reforms. Maybe the reforms did not benefit the poor or the ordinary person sufficiently; maybe it is true. But it certainly improved his position because of the lower rate of inflation, food availability, etc.'

THIRTEEN years after the economic reforms were launched, politicians are now talking about reforms with a human face. Does that mean something went wrong somewhere?

When we started economic reforms in 1991, we concentrated on the most urgent things that anyhow had to be done, like de-licensing, reform of the exchange control system, financial market reforms, and banking reforms.

We didn't have the time to sit down and think exactly what kind of a development model we needed. Thereafter, in 1994, the reforms slowed down a bit.

Then, the United Front government came to power (in 1996), and it also did not have a clear idea about what model it wanted. It only knew that the (economic) opening up had to be there, and that we had to be a part of the world. We couldn't continue in the old model of a closed economy. But further on, there was no thinking on what kind of an economic and political society we would see, and perhaps there was no agreement.

Then came the NDA government in 1999, and originally they had some problems because they also had, in the Sangh Parivar and the Swadeshi Jagaran Manch, some strong elements of economic nationalism.[1]

But I believe the thinking elements led by Prime Minister Vajpayee felt, we had to continue with reforms though it seems they also didn't have a clear idea as to how we should balance the interests of the different sections of society.

They (NDA) were clear about cutting down the size of the public sector, reforms in the telecom sector, giving a push to the IT sector, and getting more foreign investment.

But the impression seems to have gained ground that they were adopting a totally capitalistic model or the Washington model. This is not true but that was the impression.

The Left criticises that India has become a slave of the IMF (International Monetary Fund), the World Bank, etc

There are three groups in India.

One, the social activists led by Arundhati Roy (an English writer and activist) and company who say, this neo-liberalisation is leading to the impoverishment of the poor and helping only the rich.

Then there are the pure Leftists who often don't think clearly and say, we are dictated to by the IMF and the World Bank. All that is not true.

The truth is that we don't have to borrow money from the IMF or the World Bank now. We have enough reserves. We don't have any balance of payment problems. Nobody mentions

---

[1] An economic and cultural organisation founded in 1991 as an affiliate of the Rashtriya Swayamsevak Sangh, the RSS, to deal with the economic issues of the country.

this except Vajpayee. Maybe. Now Manmohan Singh too, will. We have achieved self-reliance and can grow on our own.

The ADB (Asian Development Bank) is going to borrow from the Indian market. This is an aspect of self-reliance: growth on the basis of your own exports and the capital you attract on commercial terms and not on charitable terms.

The rupee has not become a convertible currency because we don't want to make it. Otherwise, it has all the characteristics of a convertible currency. Everybody will accept it now.

The third group is a group of economists who say, these reforms do not have a human face. But not one of them has sat down and clearly examined what is wrong and where it is going.

It is obviously wrong to say that reforms have not helped, because per capita income is growing in many States and patterns of consumptions are changing. If you look at the NSO (National Statistical Organisation) consumption data, you find that in 2002-2003, there is clearly a spread of higher consumption among the lower classes.

That again is criticised by many who say that reforms are creating a consumerist society.

The fellow who criticises already has a refrigerator. Of course, I want to make this a consumer society. I don't want a Gandhian society. We want everybody to have at least the most essential goods.

But if you give freedom to people, they don't use that freedom. If you are free to consume and free to produce, you will produce the goods that people want. If they don't want to be a consumerist society, they will not buy and they will not produce.

You said, even the NDA while going ahead with the reforms, didn't have a proper idea on how to go about it. Why was it that there were no debates during that period? Why was it that at least the economists did not sit together and come out with a plan that would benefit all sections of society in some way or the other?

I wouldn't say there was no thinking on it. Yes, there was no systematic attempt to see two things; one, how to have the benefits of reforms distributed, and two, ultimately what kind of society we want to have, what model of development should we have?

Only now the present prime minister (Dr Manmohan Singh) has talked about the model of development. He has said, our model of development will be the model for the rest of the world.

Is there a tested model to fall back upon?

At the moment, many people feel we are just going along with the globalisation pattern laid down by America and its allies. It may not be true. The fear is that this may become a society dominated by the rich and the powerful and by business interests; that they will dominate to the level of dictating to the government, which they are doing in America, but not so much here.

The Left has now brought in the question whether all public sector enterprises should be got rid of. We did not want the monopoly of the public sector. This was the idea of the Narasimha Rao-Manmohan Singh (the Congress government of 1991-1996) reform package. Even then, the Left was saying, it does not want privatisation beyond 49 per cent. We were then saying competition was essential, so we must have private banks, private insurance companies, etc, all of which the Left totally opposed. I think they have a mixed economy in mind, where the private sector would compete with the public sector, and keep it on that the private sector would not become the only dominant force.

The banks are important in a poor country like ours. I also agree that we must have strong public sector banks, not so many but a good number.

When the Indian economy was opened up and the reform process started, many economists talked about the 'trickling down' effect, but the criticism today is that 'trickling down' has not taken place. After the defeat of the NDA, the argument has gained momentum. What do you say?

That is only the feeling. The 'trickling down' effect has taken place but not enough. The poor are angry because their conditions have not improved sufficiently. If you look at the consumption data, you will see that trickling down has taken place.

Also, I do not completely trust our employment data. Our employment data seems to show there is not much improvement in employment, but I don't know whether that is true.

It is also not correct to say that if you have only Information Technology (IT), there is no benefit. If I employ 1,000 IT people now, they in turn improve the lives of many connected with them because they spend on many, many things which will have secondary effect, tertiary effect and so on.

BPO (Business Process Outsourcing) companies, apart from the salaries they pay, incur expenditure. We also have increased our population in the past, which now increases the labour force. That is why there is this unemployment problem. That is because we did not grow fast enough earlier and did not control population efficiently. So, it will take another 20 to 25 years to give employment to all.

It may also be true that distribution has shifted a little more in favour of the richer classes because of the nature of the industries with which we are moving.

If there was greater thrust on the agricultural sector, may be there would have been more spread. So, two major things have to be examined now.

First, ultimately, it is what kind of a society you want to have and what kind of a model you want to follow. Should we have permanent public sector and make it efficient? If it's not efficient, we should be able to chuck out the man running it. Is that the idea?

Second, how far we should go along with the WTO (World Trade Organisation) and what the areas are, in which we will offer resistance along with other developing countries. We want to be a part of the world economy, but we want the WTO rules in such a way that they protect the weaker sections of our society. We have to think about this seriously. We also have to think about what kind of federal system we should have and how we should improve governance.

The change of government has given us an opportunity for us to re-examine all these.

The re-examination by the new government has resulted in them talking about subsidies, free power, etc once again. Is it not like going back to the old days?

If they are going back, it is not good. If they indulge in populism in the name of 'reforms with a human face', they will lead the country to ruin. It will not benefit either the rich or the poor.

Subsidies have two different important aspects. One is the redistribution aspect, that is, I am giving something at a price lower than its cost to the poorer sections. To meet that difference, I tax the richer section. That is the idea.

The second aspect is, whenever you subsidise something, its consumption goes up, and it is expected to go up. But if you subsidise it in an unlimited way, the consumption will be pushed up too much. So, if you give free power without limit, then they will misuse power.

As an economist, one has to say that absolutely free power without limit is out of the question but that was what we had in Tamil Nadu earlier.

As an economist, are you happy with the reform process India has followed?

Some reforms have been very good, and substantial. We have become self-sufficient externally. Bimal Jalan (Former Reserve Bank of India Governor) wrote a book on Indian economy in which he said that for so many years before 1991, every year we had some problem or the other with our Balance of Payments (BoP). We had the Aid India Consortium in Paris where so many countries would come together under the aegis of the World Bank and talk about how much each country would contribute to help India. We are now independent of all that kind of external aid. We have gone to a slightly higher rate of growth.

The second important thing is that we can now cope with a serious drought. In 2002-2003 we had a severe drought, still there was no great disturbance to the economy. People did not have 'lack of food' except for those whose crops failed which was an issue. It was not like 1987-1988 when everything was disturbed: rush for food from outside, prices going up and growth getting affected.

We have reached a stage where there is only moderate inflation. Low rate of inflation and higher rate of growth are some of the achievements.

The reforms are intended ultimately to benefit majority of the people. Maybe that has not been achieved. My own feeling is that a good bit of trickling down has taken place, if we analyse the consumption pattern.

Are you happy with the way the NDA went ahead with the reforms? The criticism against the previous government was that they accelerated the reforms in such a way that it helped only the rich.

I don't think so. I feel we should not blame them too much. It is not as though the earlier reformers had clear idea of the limits of globalisation.

The NDA has done some very good things. Take for instance, the reform in the telecom sector. During their regime, foreign investors increased. Some people would say they opened up too much, but that is a political idea. I don't think they were opening up recklessly.

One thing I disagree with them is in disinvesting the big profit-making public enterprises. They did not listen to the opposition in their own party. There was no reason to disinvest profit-making PSUs. Would it have accelerated the rate of growth? No.

I disagree with Arun Shourie (the then Minister of Disinvestment) in that matter. When ONGC and IOC (Oil and Natural Gas Corporation and Indian Oil Corporation; two of India's largest oil companies) are doing well, why do you disinvest them? Arun Shourie should not have wasted time on such controversies. Other than that, disinvesting a small portion was a good idea.

The moment the Left became a part of the Central government and started their criticism against disinvesting or privatising profit-making PSUs (Public Sector Undertakings), **the market started going down.**

Let the market go to hell! We need not worry about the market at all. Ultimately, they will have to come up. We don't have to bother about the market behaviour at all. If we do the right things, the market will come around.

It is true that some people will be very upset about this and therefore, they are nervous. They may wrongly conclude that the rate of growth will go down. So, the government will have to reassure them. If they say they will increase subsidies, they will give free power, they will bring ruin and they will be thrown out.

Do you feel the NDA government neglected the agricultural sector?

It is partly true. I think the weakness of the NDA government was that nobody really knew the economy, except the prime minister. Advani had no knowledge, so he did not interfere. The finance minister, poor fellow, he was an army man (Jaswant Singh, who retired as a Major from the army, was finance minister from 2002 to 2004), what did he know about the economy? He is a good, intelligent, honest man but didn't know much about the economy.

One mistake the NDA government made, mainly because of opposition from the lower rungs of the BJP and the RSS, was to throw out Yashwant Sinha (who was the finance minister from 1999 to 2002). He was following the correct policies, exactly the policies that are opposite to what the Communists want. The BJP thought they lost some by-elections because of him, but that is not true.

Yes, there was no one knowledgeable about agriculture. They didn't put enough investment in agriculture. Then, you must in all fairness say that it has to be done by the State governments. It is the deterioration at the level of the State governance that was partly responsible for the rural people not getting enough. We should not blame the Centre too much.

As an economist, I would say the NDA did not lose because they carried out the reforms. Maybe the reforms did not benefit the poor or the ordinary person sufficiently; maybe it is true. But it certainly improved his position because of the lower rate in inflation, food availability, etc

When will the poor really benefit from the reforms? When will the real trickling down take place?

Definitely, we have to change in terms of governance. We have to spend more on rural areas and agriculture. Agricultural reforms mean not just spending money, but also research, diversifying crops, looking more carefully at the questions relating to foreign trade and WTO.

I don't think the NDA neglected it. But more work was needed. The government had to clarify to the people also about the advantages and disadvantages.

As an economist, when do you feel we will cross the 'developing' status?

Production wise, we have reached the 'developed' status but not by living standard-wise or social development-wise. I think people as a whole have to participate more. They should not keep away. Non-governmental organisations have a very important role to play. They can supplement. I also have hope in the younger generation who have modern ideas. They will give up many of these older ideas and will work more sincerely.

We have to wait for them to come to power. I feel the next 25 years are very crucial.

Reading this interview after almost two decades, we realise that the problems Dr Raja Chelliah talked about still exist; even after almost three decades of the opening up of the economy.

The agricultural sector and rural India are still in distress, trickling down has not happened in the real sense, and the country has not been able to tackle unemployment effectively.

And this fear has really come true… 'The fear is that this may become a society dominated by the rich and the powerful and by business interests; that they will dominate to the level of dictating to the government, which they are doing in America.'

To Disinvest or Not...

Disinvestment of the public sector enterprises have been one of the major reforms economists and politicians across all spectrums have spoken about from the time Indian economy started liberalising.

At that time, it was famously said that governments shouldn't be making bread!

When disinvestment was not happening because of the opposition from workers' unions and the parties in opposition, the United Front government had set up a Disinvestment Commission in 1996 to look into the divestment or privatisation of public sector units.

***G V Ramakrishna** was the first chairman of the Divestment Commission.*

'GVR', as he was popularly known joined the Indian Administrative Service (IAS) in 1952 and rose to the level of the Chief Secretary to the Andhra Pradesh government in 1983.

He had also served at the Indian embassy in Washington, and was India's ambassador to the European Economic Community.

He was an advisor to the Planning Commission in 1981 and became a member in 1994.

He was of the opinion that India should have a National Shareholding Trust (NST) and a divestment fund to utilise the divestment proceeds to build rural infrastructure, schools, etc. An interesting idea that was never implemented.

YOU were the first person to head the Divestment Commission set up by the United Front government in 1996. The NDA government also had a ministry for divestment, and it pursued divestment quite actively. Were you happy with the way the NDA did the work?

The United Front government in August 1996 set up the Divestment Commission. We put forward certain general principles to be followed in the entire divestment process.

First thing we said, which we repeated three times in twelve reports, was that the proceeds of divestment should be placed in a separate fund and used for developing social infrastructure in rural areas, used for VRS (voluntary retirement scheme) of public sector employees and for restructuring the companies.

We also suggested delinking of the divestment process from the Budget. This was not followed. And, till today we do not have a divestment fund.

From 1991-92, when divestment started, if you take the first ten years, they (the government) collected Rs 20,000 crore (Rs 200 billion). It all went into the general Budget and was not used for any social infrastructure. This money, if used through a separate fund, would have helped the government build 4 million houses, which would probably accommodate 25 million people, 100,000 schools in rural areas and 5,000 primary health centres. Still, they could have a surplus of Rs 5,000 crore (Rs 50 billion) for VRS.

None of this was done. It was a lost opportunity.

Since then, the divestment proceeds have more than doubled to Rs 44,000 crore (Rs 440 billion). It could have produced double the benefits like 8 million houses, 2 lakh (200,000) schools, Rs 10,000 crore (Rs 100 billion) for VRS and 10,000 primary health centres.

But capital assets of the government have been sold to meet revenue expenditure. That is why the divestment process is seen as selling family silver to pay the butler.

The NDA talked about utilising the amount for infrastructure....

But they never made it transparent. They said they were using it for rural development through the Budget and plan allocations. In fact, from the year 1997 onwards, there has been a fall in the expenditure on rural development.

I want to say again, we lost a tremendous opportunity to show that divestment done selectively would be for the good of the rural people.

They have used the proceeds mainly to reduce the fiscal deficit. In the first ten years, the effect on the fiscal deficit was only in the second decimal place. From 5.72 per cent, it has come down to 5.70 per cent of GDP.

Where do you think the money has gone?

To the Budget. There's no mystery about it. It has gone into various expenditures; on security, on staff, etc, etc But it did not support rural development by making a net addition to the allocation for houses, etc

I would say a large number of recommendations of the Divestment Commission have not been followed. The argument is still going on as to what is divestment, and what is privatisation.

Privatisation means selling the majority shareholding, and giving management control to a private party but divestment is selling some minority shares of the government without transferring control.

Even this form of divestment has large problems because if you have the government as the largest single shareholder, with shareholding below 51 per cent, then the company is not a public sector company, and there is no accountability and no checks and balances. The minister will be using his rights as the largest single shareholder. So, I had said that this form of non-public sector company will become a private *zamindari*.

There is an alternative: you sell the shares to the people, don't keep the residual shares of below 51 per cent in the hands of the minister; hand them over to a national shareholding trust under a trust agreement.

A broad-based management of the private sector, those retired from the public sector, and some government representatives can run the trust. The government could start by entrusting the shares of a few big public sector companies to the trust. The companies under the trust will then be overseeing publicly held, professionally managed, non-public sector, non-private sector companies which can be developed into global companies.

Now that the new UPA government has abolished the divestment ministry, in what way do you think it will affect the overall Indian economy and the divestment process itself?

Divestment had started even before the ministry was formed. The concerned ministry under the guidance of the finance ministry did it. They are very clear now that, for strategic reasons you should not privatise blue-chip companies.

They say that the oil companies, NTPC (National Thermal Power Corporation), BHEL (Bharat Heavy Electricals Ltd), NALCO (National Aluminium Company Ltd), the financial institutions, etc should not be privatised.

So, the abolition of the ministry will not have any impact on disinvestment?

The mechanism of the ministry will not have any impact, but the policy and the procedures of the ministry will be quite different. The ideas are still not very clear.

Now there's a statement that ONGC (Oil and Natural Gas Corporation) and some others can raise funds from the market. They are forgetting that divestment is of government-owned shares. If the government sells the shares, the money goes to the government. But the company raising money for its own purposes is not divestment, although the percentage of government shareholding may go down.

With the Left parties announcing that the profit-making PSUs will not be divested or privatised, the market reacted adversely. Are you for the divestment of profit-making PSUs?

Everybody says PSUs should grow like global companies in a competitive environment. Compared to a private company, a PSU has several disadvantages.

Do you know the salary of the head of the largest public sector company is less than the salary of a raw graduate coming out of an IIM (Indian Institute of Management)? So, you have to provide incentives and also disincentives. You start hire and fire at the highest level.

You have to give autonomy to the public sector companies. But who will use the power if it lands the management in trouble?

There are five entities that oversee a PSU. The first is the ministry and the officials in the ministry. The second is the committees of Parliament: the Public Undertakings Committee, the Public Accounts Committee and the Standing Committee on Public Enterprises. The third is the Comptroller and Auditor General. Then there is the Central Vigilance Committee, and lastly, the Central Bureau of Investigation.

With all these five people sitting on their head, who would use any autonomy and take all the risks of being pulled up by any of these agencies?

Is that the reason why the performance of even the profit-making PSUs is much below that of private companies?

Partly that, and lack of incentives is also there. They have all the disadvantages compared to a private company. To compete in the market, you have to take quick decisions, you have to be nimble-footed, you have to take commercial decisions that entail some risks. The public sector structure does not permit all this. We are asking the public sector to compete with the private sector with one hand tied behind its back.

Today, you have the *Navaratnas* (In 1997, financial autonomy was given to nine PSUs with Navaratna, nine gems, status) but no freedom has been given to them.

Should the government start divesting profit-making PSUs because private parties will be interested only in them?

I wouldn't say, all profit-making PSUs. I said in the report itself, to keep out 20-25 companies.

The real issue is not one of privatisation. The government can raise money by the sale of shares to the public, but to get good value they have to get the company out of government control. This can be done by transferring the residual shares of below 51 per cent to the National Shareholding Trust and make them non-public sector companies.

As long as the government does not want to let go of the public sector companies, they will not get value for their shares and the companies will not grow in such a competitive environment. It will be a national loss.

Why did you suggest that some profit-making PSUs must not be divested?

Firstly, because they are already doing well, and some of them have widely held shares in India. For example, in Hindustan Petroleum Corporation, the government holds only about 51.5 per cent equity. The remaining 48.5 per cent is already out of government hands.

The oil companies hold the balance between foreign companies and private companies. They cannot compete if one of their hands is tied behind their back. So, you remove all that, let them be professionally managed. Then they can grow as well as the private sector.

In Singapore, they have a body called Temasek which holds the shares of government in over 100 companies. The companies are not under parliament's control or ministry control on a day-to-day basis. Temasek sends an annual report to the finance minister in Singapore. So, they are independent. The government people are in, private people are in and the public sector is in. So, you have a good example of companies being managed outside government control.

Share prices will not go up if the government manages a company. Why did the share market go down on the PSU stocks when the government said 'no privatisation'? If you say, we are not going to privatise, but create an NST *(National*

Shareholding Trust) and treat them de facto like privately owned companies, their share values will go up.

But various ministers say the PSUs under their respective ministries will not be divested or privatised.

It is for the government to come out with a policy. We don't know how the policies will go. Such matters are decided by a Cabinet committee.

My suggestion is, merely by paying lip sympathy, public sector companies will not grow; not unless they let go of government control. I am not saying, 'Hand them over to the private sector!' – they are strategic companies which will be held broadly by the people. But they should be allowed to be managed independently. Then they will grow.

There are more than 100 sick central PSUs in India. Who will be interested in buying them? What should the government do before trying to sell them?

These companies have their origins, very different from each other. Some of them were taken over from the private sector when they became sick. Some other companies were started in the fifties for political reasons without economic justification. These are in the sick category and each case has to be dealt with separately.

Some others, like NTPC Ltd, BHEL (Bharat Heavy Electricals Ltd), IOC (Indian Oil Corporation), NALCO (National Aluminium Company), MTNL (Mahanagar Telephone Nigam Ltd), were started by the government and have done very well. Many States competed with each other to get these companies to their States. They offered incentives, including huge tracts of land. If the company wanted 50 acres, the States offered 200 acres. This prime land fetches a lot of money now.

The NPV (Net Present Value) method should not be applied blindly. Total valuation should take into account the market value of the land apart from the NPV of the going concern. There are doubts whether this has been done in the case of the recent privatisations.

Another thing is that technological restructuring is needed in these companies, like modernisation of equipment. Managerial change can turn around a marginally sick company, provided they let it go out of government control.

A major impediment to the growth of the public sector in India has been government control. If they don't let go, it is futile to talk about autonomy, modernisation, etc But getting the government out need not necessarily mean handing it over to a private party or creating a private monopoly.

Because of the fear of the anti-incumbency factor, governments are compelled to take populist measures. Earlier it used to be said that difficult decisions can be taken soon after elections and there can be scope for populist measures before the elections. Now the situation is different and elections come every one or two years in one state or the other.

With the regional parties being a part of the central government, they are worried about elections coming more often, and the anti-incumbency factor operating. So, one can see populist policies becoming somewhat endemic.

There is a report that says all State government PSUs are running up huge losses.

Do you know almost every State had a divestment commission? They used to discuss with me about divestment when I was the chairman of the Divestment Commission. These are small enterprises and have been sick for some time. It is difficult to find buyers even for former good companies like NGEF *(New Government Electrical Factory)* in Bangalore. The State governments have to cut their losses as much as possible in a practical and transparent way.

You wrote in one of your columns that divestment is only a part of the whole process of the reform process of the PSUs.

Like I said earlier, the bigger problems are ministerial control, the control of the CBI (Central Bureau of Investigation), CAG (Comptroller and Auditor General of India) etc That is why I said, hand over the shares to a National Shareholding Trust (NST). If a PSU is under government control, share value will not be good. That is why the moment you say 'yes' to privatisation, share values go up.

As a part of its ambitious disinvestment plans, India's largest insurance firm Life Insurance Corporation of India had its IPO (Initial Public Offering) in May 2022.

The government wanted to sell 316 million shares which is about 5 per cent of its equity share as part of its plan to raise Rs 65,000 crore through disinvestment. That the IPO turned out to be a damp squib is another matter. What started off on the 1st of September 1956 as the state-owned Life insurance Corporation of India when the Indian Parliament passed the Life Insurance of India Act and nationalised over 245 insurance companies and provident societies, changed in May 2022, that is after 65 years.

Like G V Ramakrishna said, 'The divestment process is still seen as selling family silver to pay the butler'.

Farmers and Agricultural Reforms

To initiate 'reforms with a human face', the UPA made ***Dr M S Swaminathan****, the scientist behind India's Green Revolution of the 1960s, the Chairman of the National Commission for Farmers.*

Amidst strong opposition, the UPA was also planning to convert farmland into Special Economic Zones in many States. Will it spell doom for Indian farmers?

I asked Dr Swaminathan why Indian farmers were still committing suicide, and where the country went wrong.

WHEN India won independence, it was almost a starving nation. Through the Green Revolution initiated by C Subramaniam (the then minister of food and agriculture) **and you, we produce surplus food now. Fifty-seven years after independence, we once again hear about starvation deaths. Where did we go wrong?**

The great Bengal Famine happened before Independence, and starvation was largely due to lack of availability of food in the market. We had to import food from the United States,

Canada, etc Yes, we didn't have enough food for our people when we won independence.[1]

But the starvation and hunger you see today are the result of lack of purchasing power. Lack of purchasing power comes from lack of opportunities for employment or jobs. Today job famine is leading to food famine.

Our approach now has to be able to increase the livelihood security of the poor by giving opportunities for assured remunerative employment.

We have made a very extensive analysis of the three dimensions of food security: the availability of food in the market, access to food, and absorption of food in the body which is a function of clean drinking water, environmental hygiene and primary healthcare.

Today, we have made progress in addressing the first challenge in food security, namely, availability of food.

It is clear that our farmers can produce more if they have access to remunerative markets because today, markets determine whether the farmers will invest more or not. But our latest problem in food security concerns access and absorption.

Ever since India won independence, political parties and politicians are talking about rural poverty, upliftment of the poor, etc But why is it that even after almost six decades, a large chunk of India's population is below the poverty line?

There are three reasons why there is such a gap between political pronouncements and actual accomplishments.

---

[1] The great Bengal Famine occurred in colonial India just before independence, in 1942-1943. The British were engaged in World War II and their food policy in India was geared to just feeding the armed forces that fought for them. An estimated 2.1 to 3.8 million Bengalis perished, out of a population of 60.3 million, from starvation.

Number one: our population has grown a lot. When we became independent, we had 30 crore (300 million) people. Now (2004), it is more than 102 crore (1.02 billion). This population explosion has upset many of our calculations.

Number two: we have not given concurrent attention to on-farm and non-farm employment in the rural areas. If you look at China, it started its economic revolution through agricultural revolution and rural development. They started the reform process in the rural areas where they took away over 100 million people from on-farm to non-farm employment through township enterprises. We didn't have a concurrent strategy because majority of our people in the villages are landless poor. We have not given constant attention to them at all.

Number three: poor delivery systems of government programmes. Less than 50 per cent of what is intended reaches the poor.

You mention poor delivery system. In the new budget, Finance Minister P Chidambaram has allotted a lot of money for the rural sector but has not done anything to change the system. What is the point in giving more money to a system that failed?

Yes, it is a major problem. It can be refined only if you have confidence in the local democratic structures; the panchayati raj institutions, the gram sabha, etc So long as we don't have faith in them, so long as you want to run everything bureaucratically, many of our complex problems cannot be solved.

Budget is only an allocation exercise but whether that money will achieve anything or not depends upon the system.

Who should be held responsible for what rural India is now: the Congress which ruled India for decades? They had slogans like *Garibi Hatao, Jai Kisan*, but what have they actually done?

You should not mistake slogans for achievement. In our country, at the political level, there is a sentiment that once they have made a speech, they have achieved everything.

All ruling parties should be held responsible. There are so many ruling parties both in the States and at the Centre. They are all stuck with the old colonial administration.

For example, in China, even the ministers and officers are technocrats who know the subject. Their agricultural minister was the person who won the World Food Prize. But many of our political leaders, though they are elected by the people, are not trained. There should be a school to train political leaders.

But political leaders always blame the bureaucracy....

It is always easy to blame each other. This has not helped India.

Poverty in India is growing, people are suffering, and farmers are committing suicide....

We have had very good stories of successes also in this country. Punjab and Haryana have shown that our farmers are capable of producing. There are a number of good examples of non-governmental organisations working successfully. One can give a number of examples of outstanding work done in this country. How we make these unique examples more universal is the challenge.

You once said that unlike in the developed countries, farming is livelihood in India, and we have more small farmers with little land. If that is so, will doing something similar to

what Dr Verghese Kurien did in Anand (Gujarat), **starting milk cooperatives, help our small farmers?**[2]

The number of farming families in the entire OECD (Organisation for Economic Cooperation and Development) countries is hardly 10 million, while our country alone has 110 million farming families. Where is 10 million and where is 110 million? They also provide subsidies.

Regarding cooperatives, well, if they function well, they are good. Yes, not only Anand, there are other successful examples too. Unfortunately, cooperatives in many parts of the country are not functioning properly because they have been bureaucratised and not professionalised. If somebody exploits cooperatives for political purposes or personal ends, they will not function.

The present approach is to promote self-help groups. The self-help groups need not have a formal constitution; it is a group of people coming together on the basis of an agreed code of conduct. They are growing in strength, particularly among women, in technology, credit management and marketing. We have a lot of hope in these groups. The finance minister also has increased allocation to them. But unless these groups have selfless leaders, they won't succeed.

Is lack of availability of technology the main reason why our farmers produce only enough to sustain themselves?

There is a big gap between the 'know-how' and 'do-how' camps. This is why we have launched Mission 2007, that is by

---

[2] Kurien was known as the Father of the White Revolution in India. He was a social entrepreneur whose 'billion-litre idea', the Operation Flood, made dairy farming India's largest self-sustaining industry and the largest rural employment sector providing a third of all rural income.

15 August 2007, when India celebrates its 60th anniversary of Independence, we plan to take information communication technology to every village.

Our mission statement is, 'Every Village, a Knowledge Centre'. There are 600,000 villages in our country. Our villages need a lot of timely information.

The second mission is, 'Hunger Free India'. Both the missions are related, and I feel both can be accomplished, if we want.

Was it because the then government was pro-active, that you could achieve a Green Revolution in the 1960s?

Yes, there was a Green Revolution symphony then. Science, technology, public policy, input services, farmers' enthusiasm – all of them came together in a symphony. (Then Union agriculture minister) C Subramaniam was a man of action. So, we proposed the Five-year Plan in 1963 and everything fell in place.

Actually in 1963 when I proposed it first, there was no minister who would take interest. Fortunately, CS came in 1964 and he approved it immediately. Everything was done very fast. But today, paralysis of analysis is taking place.

In the 1950s, 50 per cent of the country's GDP was from agriculture. Today, it has come down to less than 20 per cent. Is this a good sign according to you?

That is because today, other economies are growing. Yes, contribution of agriculture has come down to less than 20 per cent for the first time. That is alright because we have diversified our economy.

That is not the problem. The problem is, the number of people dependant on agriculture has not come down. It has increased. There are 70 crore (700 million) people who are in agriculture who receive 20 per cent of the GDP.

Some economists say as the economy grows, the share of agriculture in the economy has to come down.

Suppose the contribution of agriculture is one lakh crore, out of 55 lakh crore or 20 lakh crore, you will have a higher percentage then. If the contribution is one lakh crore out of 100,000 lakh crore, it becomes very small.

You are against converting farmland as Special Economic Zones. You speak about Special Agricultural Zones, SAZ. Those in favour of SEZ say they are creating jobs. Do you agree with that argument?

Before they create the zones, let them publish a livelihood impact statement. The land of so many farmers has been taken away; they have not been properly rehabilitated. These people say, they are given Rs 5 lakh per acre or Rs 2 lakh per acre, but what does the small farmer do? Part of the money will be lost in drinking, part of it will go to settling their debts, and in a year, they become landless labour. If this country has 50 crore of landless labour, then even God cannot save it.

Do you see doom or hope for Indian agriculture?

I am sure Indian agriculture will bounce back. There is no other way. If agriculture goes wrong, nothing else will go right. I am optimistic about the potential but even God helps only those who help themselves! You can't eat potential; you have to convert it into production and those steps are not being taken.

Has any farmer been given any Padma award in the last 15 years? I am saying this just to show the mindset of the various governments.

The Babus call the farmers 'beneficiaries' and not even farmers. But he (the babu) will not exist if the farmer is not there!

'Punjab and Haryana have shown that our farmers are capable of producing', said Dr M S Swaminathan. Thank you, Rediff.com

Has anything changed for the farmers of India? Unfortunately, no. They still commit suicide because of the debts they incur. They still agitate in the cold winter, but their voices still remain unheard.

Even in 2020, Indian farmers sat on a dharna for months together in the cold winter in Delhi protesting against the farming reforms brought in by the Narendra Modi government!

What M S Swaminathan said on India's population is very true: 'When we became independent, we had 30 crore (300 million) people. Now (2004), it is more than 102 crore (1.02 billion). This population explosion has upset many of our calculations.' And in 2022, the number is 1.4 billion!

The Globalised World

Ever since Manmohan Singh took over as the Prime Minister of India, globalisation and liberalisation became the most discussed topics in India with the liberals supporting it, and the swadeshis opposing it.

I spoke to ***Prof John Harriss****, the then director of the Development Studies Institute (Asia Centre), at The London School of Economics and Political Sciences and also an affiliated member of the department of anthropology, on where India stood vis a vis the rest of the world as far as opening up of the economy was concerned.*

The anthropology of South Asia had always interested him, and much of his work had been done on India.

One subject that was close to his heart and research was, the impact of globalisation on Indian society.

And he could talk about the Indian economy from an outsider's unbiased perspective.

DO you feel there has been an attitudinal change about globalisation all around the world?

I think there has been a shift in the view from the 1990s to this century, more outside India than within India. There is a recognition that those kinds of neo-liberal economic policies laid out in what's called the 'Washington Consensus', which placed emphasis on trade liberalisation and integration of economies into the global economy as the means to growth, have not worked.

It has been recognised, as a result of the work of economists like Danny Rodrick at Harvard, that integration into the global economy and trade liberalisation are not the automatic keys to growth. There has been recognition that countries that have been successful in the context of globalisation are countries that have engaged in globalisation on their own terms.

China has done this on its own terms to a large extent, and India too has done it to some extent. The trickle down may be happening but is very slow. The disparities are opening up in our societies.

The arguments put forward by the protagonists of globalisation as a means to poverty-reduction is that the world is unquestionably more equal now than 15 years ago. This is because of the tremendous growth that has occurred in China and India.

They ignore the evidence that many countries elsewhere in the world, have lower incomes and higher levels of poverty now than 15 years ago. They also ignore the evidence of tremendous disparities within India and China.

You said that because of the economic growth that has taken place in the last 15 years, the difference in the life of an

average Indian or a Chinese, compared to an average citizen of the world, is diminishing. Can we say that it was because of globalisation that the economies of these two countries grew, thus improving the life of the average citizen?

The relative success of the Chinese and Indian economies is not because of globalisation but because of the policies that have been pursued in these countries. These economic policies have enabled them to engage more or less successfully with global markets.

You also talked about the need for a country to integrate into the global market for growth. Is there a global market? Is it absolutely necessary for a country to integrate into the 'global market'?

Yes, there are increasingly global markets in many commodities and services. There is clear evidence around us of the integration of markets globally in relation to many commodities and services.

We do see unquestionably the integration of markets on a global scale. But the integration into global markets does not seem to be the key to growth. This is particularly not the key to growth in the great continental economies like China, India, Brazil or the United States.

There is a great difference between the United States as the global hegemony in the 20th and 21st centuries, and Britain as the global hegemony in the 19th century. Britain encouraged free trade because it needed free trade to be economically successful, but the United States doesn't have the same kind of commitment to free trade.

What we see is the United States backtracking in different areas of trade liberalisation. The United States believes in investments in trade liberalisation because it constitutes in itself an enormous market.

India, China and Brazil too potentially constitute enormous markets. I say 'potentially' because only the surface of the domestic market of India is (has been) scratched.

I spent some days in rural Tamil Nadu after several years (in 2005), and I was pleasantly surprised to see that very little has changed. Of course, there has been penetration of certain kinds of consumer durables. People have more two-wheelers and refrigerators in their homes, but many people don't have basic consumer goods. There is a huge market, which is very largely untapped.

Indian manufacturers are more interested in exports and foreign markets. Is it because the purchasing power of majority of Indians is low?

Yes, that is an important part of the whole story. For the huge domestic market potential to be realised, millions of people must have a lot more money in their pocket.

What we see now is the result of 50 years of very significant, but skewed, industrial development. So long as the purchasing power amongst so many millions of people is so limited, Indian companies quite rightly turn to the international market. It has a positive side too: greater exposure to international competition will have a positive impact on Indian companies.

What we see today after the liberalisation and globalisation of economy is an increase in consumerism. Is it what a country or an economy really needs? Do you feel something better than mere consumerism should be taking place?

Yes, citizens have been made into consumers. The principal identity is as that of a consumer and not a citizen now. For instance, there are many more consumer goods that are readily available in countries like Russia, Hungary or Poland now than 20 years ago.

But people have lost a lot in terms of high-quality public services like transport, healthcare, education, which they enjoyed earlier. This can be described as one of the losses that people of Central Europe have experienced as a result of the liberalisation of their economies.

People of Central Europe have become consumers that they were not before and in the process, they have lost a lot as citizens. Maybe you can see the same sort of trend taking place here in India.

Is globalisation a necessary evil?

I describe globalisation as interconnectedness, and it can be in different ways across the globe. I think there is a huge amount of positive (possibilities) in that.

I come back to what I said in the beginning, which is, it is absolutely vital that countries engage in globalisation on their own terms.

In a truly globalised world, should there not be a free flow of people also than just a flow of more capital goods across countries?

I agree that free movement of people should be part of globalisation. It is important to take into account demographic trends across the world. In major European countries, there has been a decline in population, although not in Britain or in the United States.

When population will be burgeoning in one part of the world, the pressure for more free movement of people is going to become greater. But the most important aspect of globalisation is flow of money. It is extraordinary the way in which money sloshes around the world partly as a result of liquidity that is being pumped into financial markets by the United States.

You said once that instead of blurring geographies, geographies have become very distinct after globalisation. Why is it so?

I argue that one of the consequences of globalisation is, it has made us all more aware of our distinctiveness and our own identities. I referred to the ways in which people are investing in what they were not doing in the past. These are in aspects of their culture, whether material or spiritual.

Those who are most successful, for example, those in the software industry, are not necessarily going overboard to adopt Western lifestyles. They are very selective. So, in a sense, geographies are becoming more distinctive.

Is it good in the long run?

I believe it is good in the long run. The valuation of the distinctiveness of own identities, own cultures is an immensely important part of human freedom. It is also vitally important that people should be able to make choices about their cultures.

Only those amongst groups of old men feel that cultural distinctiveness becomes dangerous. They dictate what your culture should be, what you must do, and people are denied the possibility of making rational choices.

Should immigrants try to keep their distinctiveness intact or integrate with the society they live in? You also mentioned about growing violence in certain parts of the world as a result of globalisation. Do you think that maintaining a distinct

identity in an alien society would lead to violent reactions from the local community?

I think the most successful cases of immigrants are those of Punjabis in Britain. I don't want to underestimate the extent of racism in contemporary British society. I think what we see is a certain degree of give and take. Clearly, immigrant communities have to accept the responsibilities and obligations as well as taking on the rights of citizenship in another country.

I think it is perfectly possible that people can become fully integrated into another society while retaining significant aspects of their identity in terms of where they came from originally. This surely was a great triumph of the United States in the 19th century and the early 20th century.

But America is the land of immigrants....

The American society in the 19th century was very much a British society. And people came in from all over Europe into what was essentially a British culture.

Now America is an instance of truly a very successful integration of various cultures.

Slowly, the same thing is happening in Britain too. Britain is also becoming a genuinely multicultural society. London is quintessentially a global city, very cosmopolitan, and there is a recognition of the tremendous contribution made to British society by those who have come from elsewhere.

People who are very conscious of their roots in Punjab or Gujarat or Bengal think of themselves as British, but still go and cheer like mad for India at the Oval when India plays England! If it is England versus Australia, they cheer like mad for England! I think this is very healthy.

You said that India's economic growth is not sustainable because the growth is jobless. You compared this with China, and said that China realised its mistake and has started emphasising on manufacturing. Could you elaborate?

I do think that it must be a matter of huge concern for India if high rates of economic growth do not give rise to lot of productive employment.

I emphasise the need for productive employment-intensive growth, because jobs that are not productive are not good for a nation's growth. Without productive employment growth, even if there is some trickle down from those who are succeeding in the context of the new economy, the disparities in society will widen.

Increasingly high-income enclaves set in the midst of a sea of relative poverty are enormously destructive socially and politically.

The point that I was trying to make was that inclusive growth is not only important socially, but it is also important economically. Inclusive growth means growth which is balanced, and where there is realisation of the potential of the domestic market of this country.

Do you feel China could take such decisions because of the kind of system that is followed there?

I think it is important not to get too carried away with the notion that China is somehow very much more successful than India. If you look at the foreign direct investment, you will see that huge investments in China are done largely by overseas Chinese rather than by international companies.

We must also not forget the enormous population of migrant workers in China. A population of 99 million people are mobile, and are going in search of jobs. So, let's not get too carried away by the notion that China is much more successful than India.

But I do think that Chinese growth has included enormous development of manufacturing. We are now seeing wage levels rising in the coastal areas of China where industrialisation took off 15 to 20 years ago.

We should see this sort of effects taking place in India, in Bihar and Madhya Pradesh and Eastern Uttar Pradesh, and not only in Gujarat, Maharashtra and South India.

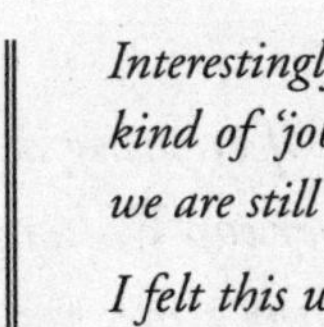

Interestingly, almost two decades ago Prof John Harriss spoke about the kind of 'jobless growth' that was happening in India then. In 2022 also, we are still debating on 'jobless growth'.

I felt this was the most interesting comment made by the Professor, 'There has been recognition that countries that have been successful in the context of globalisation are countries that have engaged in globalisation on their own terms'.

The swadeshi way?

The End of a Sandalwood Smuggler

Veerappan.

He was just a sandalwood smuggler, but he ruled the areas surrounding the Sathyamangalam forests in Tamil Nadu like a notorious criminal. If he was more like a Robinhood to the villagers, he was a criminal to the state.

He not only smuggled sandalwood and traded in ivory but also kidnapped people and demanded money in return. One of the most (in)famous kidnapping done by him was that of the Kannada film superstar, Rajkumar. The kidnapping saga went on for months with emissaries from the government visiting Veerappan at regular intervals, and him sending them back with more demands.

The Tamil Nadu government went to the extent of creating a Special Task Force (STF) headed by Tamil Nadu's super cop Walter Devaram to nab the criminal. They were so close many times yet so far.

Finally, ***K Vijay Kumar****, the man who assisted Walter Devaram, shot down Veerappan in October 2004. The operation was named Operation Cocoon.*

K Vijay Kumar soon became a national hero, and went on to write a book on his wild chase: Veerappan: Chasing the Brigand.

I spoke to the super cop two days after the success of Operation Cocoon, and the story he narrated was more thrilling than a thriller movie.

WHAT was the first thought that came to your mind after Veerappan was shot?

The first thought was to dispatch the injured persons to the hospital. I was almost sure then that they might not survive because the injuries were critical. At that moment, I thought I should somehow reach them to a hospital.

Yes, I was feeling very happy as my job was over. But along with that came the thought, 'what next'?

We had to organise ourselves very, very rapidly, and the casualties might have been more but nothing of that sort happened. So, I have to thank God for what happened.

When did you start feeling relieved and happy about your success?

It took some time for me to feel relieved because things were happening very fast, and I was very busy in the last 36 hours. Now, I feel a little bit relieved, and have started relishing the moment at last.

Today (third day) was the day we reflected with our men. There was jubilation and a good feeling in the camp. Everybody was feeling a sense of relief.

Do you consider the capture of Veerappan as the biggest achievement in your career as a police officer?

Yes, in a way, because he was a very badly wanted person for several decades. That's why I would say yes (it is the biggest achievement of my career).

You assisted Walter Devaram when he was the Head of STF in the nineties.

Exactly.

At that time, the mission did not end in success, although Devaram could reduce the gang to a handful of people. How different was this operation from what Devaram did then?

That was a different phase of the operation. I was actually with Walter Devaram for only one month during the 1993-1996 period, as I was the DIG-in-charge of the chief minister's security then. So, I had to go back after a month.

But I would say, the time I spent with Devaram was very memorable and eventful. We walked through some landmines but somehow, they did not explode. We survived. It was not very publicised then. Except for one or two encounters, the period I was with him was not very eventful. But working with him was wonderful. He was a good leader and an excellent man when it came to backing one up and boosting one's morale. I picked up a lot of things from him in the early part of my career.

Which were useful this time?

Very much, very much.

When you were appointed the chief of the STF this time, did you meet him and take any advice from him?

No, no. I was with him earlier, so there was no need to take any further advice. But I was in contact with him. But this time, my emphasis was totally on intelligence, and not merely on operation. Our operation was based mainly on intelligence. So, we had a deployment of the force everywhere, and thus we exploited every possible contact. I tried to apply a combination of technological intelligence and human intelligence. This combination was very useful.

At the press conference after the operation, you said, for about ten months you had planned everything well in advance. How exactly did you plan the operation?

We were able to plan many things in advance, depending on the kind of information that was trickling in. But finally, when the operation (actually) evolves, it will not be according to our plan; it will be according to the enemy's plans. So, our success depends on how much information we are able to gather of the enemy's plans, and how much of the enemy's ideas we can put our hands on.

But in this operation, we had certain advantages. Only thing was, we didn't know the exact date. We knew it was going to be this week. That much information was pinpointed, and we were aware of the time but not the date. Suddenly, instead of Wednesday or Friday, they advanced the date to Monday. So, we had to make arrangements fast. That's why I said the entire deployment was very rapid.

This man was the most wanted criminal for many decades, and finally, when you saw him near you, what was in your mind?

One thing I did was, I promised myself I would not get excited. I kept myself very calm because I knew if I was excited, I would make mistakes. Like everybody in the group, I also wanted to get Veerappan very badly. But then this kind of hype and anxiety can affect your performance. So, I kept telling myself, 'calm down… calm down….' I also told my boys the same thing.

Finally, the vehicle arrived, and these two people, our own people came out of the vehicle and then, we started our work.

What helped you remain cool in such tense circumstances? Do you meditate or practice yoga?

I do yoga every day for about 30 minutes but not much daily meditation. My meditation is praying. So, it is more of prayers than anything else. I do physical exercises like jogging which help me keep fit.

I also read a lot, and I prefer non-fiction like international relations. That makes me sufficiently diverted from this kind of excitement.

Immediately after your success in the mission, you went to the Bannari Amman temple (near Sathyamangalam) and tonsured your head. Did you take a vow that you would tonsure your head?

Yes. It was an old vow that I had taken. We were coming and going out unsuccessfully for several years. I came here for the first time in 1994, and the second time was in 2001 and I was here for six months. This time, I prayed at the temple for the success of our mission. I took a vow that I would tonsure my head immediately after his capture.

I also took a vow that I would take a long walk from the Bannari Amman temple (in Erode district) to the Hanuman temple at Nanganallur in Chennai.

When will you start walking?

I will do that only after the chief minister's function on October 27. On the morning of the 28th, I will start from the Bannari Amman temple.

Why did you take such a vow?

Why did I take such a vow? Because it was a mission incomplete for a long time, and I have been coming here again and again. I didn't want a situation where I have to go and come back again. I wanted this to be my third and final visit as far as this job is concerned. I wanted a completion of the job, that's all.

Your wife came to Dharmapuri (in Tamil Nadu) to be with you two days before the mission. Was it to give you moral support?

Definitely. She had total faith in me. Somehow, she had a hunch that things would be developing shortly. So, she came to be with me to give me support.

How much moral support can a person, in your case your wife, give especially to someone who is always facing this kind of challenges?

Persons like us are publicly exposed all the time and leading people where we are supposed to give morale to others, but we are very lonely. But then we have our private moments, and we draw our morale from different modes and prayers. That's why you should have one or two persons to talk to, persons who understand you. And, the house is the ultimate place, and my wife is very strong that way.

Was it these kinds of challenges that attracted you to the police force?

I like the police force by instinct but not only me, most children during their adolescent days, have a fascination for the uniform, whether it is the police or the army or the navy. My fascination was a little more than that. I stuck to it, and I had a chance to go to the administrative service which I turned down and opted for the police service, the IPS.

So, both an attraction for the uniform and the kind of challenges the service offers, played a part in me joining the police force.

After his retirement, K Vijay Kumar served as the Advisor to the Governor of Jammu and Kashmir, before joining as the senior security advisor to the Ministry of Home Affairs in December 2019.

Anti-reservation Protests Rock the Nation

Year 2006 saw widespread protests against reservation all over India. This was the biggest protest India saw after the 1990 anti-Mandal protests.

Reason: Arjun Singh, the Human Resources minister in the central government led by the Congress, decided to implement reservations for Other Backward Castes (OBCs) in central and private institutes of higher education.

The government proposed to reserve 27 per cent of seats in the premier educational institutions of India like AIIMS (All India Institute of Medical Science), IITs (Indian Institute of Technology), NITs (National Institute of Technology), IIMs (Indian Institute of Management) and IISc (Indian Institute of Science) and other Central and government institutions of higher education for the OBCs.

This move led to massive protests, particularly by students and doctors of AIIMS in Delhi, claiming that the government's proposal was 'discriminatory, discarded meritocracy and was driven by vote bank politics'.

But the government stood firm on their commitment in implementing reservations which lead to the protesters calling for a 'Civil disobedience movement'. Soon traders in Delhi joined the strike by shutting down their shops.[1]

Then the Supreme Court asked the government to clarify the basis on which the reservation policy was being implemented.

In 2008 the Supreme Court upheld the law for the provision of 27 per cent quota for candidates belonging to the OBCs in IITs, NITs, IIMs, AIIMS and other premier educational institutions. But it directed the government to exclude the 'creamy layer' among the OBCs while implementing the law.[2]

***Prof P Radhakrishnan**, a well-known social scientist, and an expert on reservations, spoke to me on how reservations in various forms came to be a part of Indian society, and its ramifications.*

WHEN did reservations start in India?

It started as a part of the patronage politics adopted by the British. As the administration of that time was monopolised by a particular group, there were demands from various groups, even with very little education, for representation.

Simultaneously, the British administration also looked into the representation of Muslims (it was known as representation then, not reservation) in public services and education. That was after the publication of the book *Indian Mussalman* by W W Hunter. So, they wanted to encourage the Muslim community in some way or the other.

---

[1] The civil disobedience movement of 1930 happened when citizens of India refused to obey certain laws and rules brought in by the British. It started with Mahatma Gandhi walking from Sabarmati Ashram to Dandi to break the Salt law.

[2] Creamy layer is a term used to refer to the members of a backward class who are highly advanced socially as well as economically and educationally.

Any particular reason why the British administration stressed only on Muslims and not other communities? Divide and rule?

The Muslims were the rulers in North India before the British came. They were also backward and not taking on English education. What was happening in North India was not happening all over the country then. This was one side.

In South India, and also in Maharashtra, Brahmins monopolised the administration. In that context, the non-Brahmin movement started which was strong in the then Madras Presidency. The demand was for education and employment of non-Brahmins.

In 1926, the government introduced what was known as the Communal GO (Government Order) by which out of the government jobs available, Brahmins got some, Muslims got some and non-Brahmins got some. Unlike today, implementation was quite strict then. After five years, they even evaluated what returns each group got.

It was Babasaheb Ambedkar (who headed the committee that drafted the Constitution of India) who brought in the idea of reservations. He kept himself away from the Congress and worked on his own. In 1919, he appeared before the Southborough Committee (one of the British committees that sat in India from 1918 to 1919) and made a series of remarks. He spoke of how divided Indian society was, and what could happen if oppressed groups were left out.

So, he was the first modern Indian leader who spoke in favour of reservations?

I would say, yes. When the Simon Commission came, it was boycotted by the Congress but the oppressed classes took it as an opportunity to present their case. They thought the Congress rule would be a Brahmin rule, and it would be worse than the British rule.[3]

They made several demands like, if India were to have a Constitution, there should be constitutional safeguards for the oppressed. And that included reservations in public services. Ambedkar even specified the percentage.

At that time, why didn't they think of economic factors as the criterion for backwardness?

There was a lot of debate on the issue as some leaders wanted to have economic criterion for reservation. But 90 per cent of the Indians were poor at that time. So, the argument was that reservation for all is reservation for none. It will not become an exception. So, they decided to club social backwardness and economic backwardness. The original idea was to continue this reservation for just ten years. They thought things would change in that period.

Reservation, which was meant for just ten years, has been going on for nearly sixty years.

Ambedkar said, there was nothing called a good Constitution or a bad Constitution. The quality of the Constitution depends on the working of the Constitution. Earlier, the Constitution worked because of the quality of leaders in the Parliament. Subsequently, power went into weaker hands. Now, power is in very weak political hands. They don't have the vision the framers of the Constitution had.

Another reason why everything went wrong was because the implementation did not go right. The system which existed

---

[3] The Simon Commission was a group of seven Members of Parliament under the chairmanship of Sir John Simon who came to India in 1928 to study constitutional reforms.

during the British rule is not there now. We have provisions in the Constitution, but we don't have the mechanism to implement the programmes.

When did the idea of including Other Backward Classes in the reservation list originate?

The first commission was appointed in 1953. But there was a last minute *volte-face* by the chairman of the commission itself. He went against the recommendations of the commission. After considerable deliberation on the recommendations, the then Prime Minister Jawaharlal Nehru refused to implement the recommendations.

The decision to implement the recommendations was then transferred to the States. The Central government issued a notice to the State governments that they could do what they wanted, but reservation should preferably be on economic criteria.

South India, because of the long history of movements, became the first to implement the recommendations.

You said after Independence, economic criterion was not considered for reservation because 90 per cent of the population was poor. Today, more than 80 per cent of the population is included in the OBC category.

In Tamil Nadu, 87 to 88 per cent of the population comes under the reservation bracket. Groups are included in the list arbitrarily by the politicians in power. In each group, there is a creamy layer, and they grab all the opportunities.

Do Dalits in India feel cheated today because it is not them but the creamy layer of OBCs who are getting all the benefits of reservations?

Yes, that is a very important issue now. Nehru was indifferent to reservations to OBCs. He was also against caste-based reservations while Ambedkar was for it; but Ambedkar also wanted to discontinue it after ten years.

The fact is, Dalits have not benefited much from reservations, particularly because politicians are using the OBC category as a vote bank. Dalits are also a vote bank, but they are small compared to the OBCs.

The recommendations made by the Mandal Commission were such that they diluted whatever facilities were given to the Dalits. There is a long way for the Dalits to catch up with the advanced groups, but politicians are not bothered.

There is a system in place for their well-being but despite that, nothing much has been done.

You have to look at reservation at various levels; for Scheduled Castes and Scheduled Tribes on the one side, and OBCs on the other. In the case of OBCs, many groups have advanced. They don't need reservation. Because of them, the benefits do not reach the really needy.

And there is no calculation by the government on the population of the OBCs, and how much should be allotted to them. Instead of OBCs, they should look at only the MBCs (Most Backward Classes) and address their social problems.

Are politicians manipulating the entire issue of reservation, and dividing the country and the student community?

Students do feel that politicians are trying to divide them. Today's politicians use reservation for garnering votes. So, there is a lot of anger in the student community.

As far as reservations are concerned, the government should have made an assessment of reservation in the last six decades. Then, if necessary, they should have come up with a better alternative.

Where will this lead to?

Now, the issue is in safe hands because the Supreme Court has intervened.

The youth of today are restless and full of resentment. Is it not dangerous?

It is not dangerous. It is good. In a democracy, protests have to come out in some form or the other. I am impressed with the way they have organised the protests. It is all high-tech in tune with the globalised world.

In France, the student community protested against labour laws and won. In Athens, students are protesting but here in India, the protesting students were silenced. Is it right?

It is not right to silence students, but the Supreme Court has intervened, and they have been given an assurance. I would not approve of the government silencing the students, but the Supreme Court did it after giving them an assurance. The court did it in public interest because the government was not suffering, only the patients were. I don't think that amounts to silencing the students.

France is a developed country, and this incident shows we are still a developing democracy. Yes, the question is, how can the state suppress students who are agitating for certain legitimate demands? But the students in India did not yield to the pressures of the state but listened to the wisdom of the judiciary. That is a very important issue. They seem to have a lot of faith in the judiciary.

Students called the anti-reservation protests of 2006 a 'Civil Disobedience movement'.
'Students do feel that politicians are trying to divide them. Today's politicians use reservation for garnering votes. So, there is a lot of anger in the student community', said Prof Radhakrishnan, well known social scientist.
Thank you, Rediff.com

Like Prof Radhakrishnan said, reservation continues to be a sensitive and contentious issue.

Point to note: 'The quality of the Constitution depends on the working of the Constitution. Earlier, the Constitution worked because of the quality of leaders in the Parliament. Subsequently, power went into weaker hands. Now, power is in very weak political hands. They don't have the vision the framers of the Constitution had.'

60 Years of Independence

Year 2007. India was getting ready to celebrate 60 years of independence.

Al Seshan, that was how ***T N Seshan,*** *the legendary former Chief Election Commissioner of India (CEC) was described when he occupied the seat of the CEC (1990-1996). That was because his very name triggered fear in the minds of politicians and journalists alike. He used to bark at politicians and tease journalists mercilessly.*

When I first spoke to him in 1998, he was very cynical about India. Almost a decade later, I found him quite different; optimistic and upbeat. I was curious to know what made him change his opinion of the country.

IN 1998 when I interviewed you, you said India was at the crossroads, and if it took the right direction, it could be one of the outstanding countries in the world in the next ten years. Almost ten years have passed. Did India take the right path?

I would say if the right path was due East, we are going in the eastern direction. But we are not fully in the eastern direction;

we are a little south of east. There are still corrections to be made; there are still changes to be made. In many areas, we have not done what we should have been doing in the last eight to ten years.

Like?

Like, for example, we lost ten valuable years in making sure that all children get education. President Kalam has been speaking about it; the others have been speaking about it. There is nothing more important than all children being in school as is promised by the Constitution. We have not done that.

From a completely different angle, we should have learnt to conduct our business, particularly in the assemblies and legislatures, in a far more disciplined fashion than we do. Yes, in every country, there is a lot of noise made in the parliaments and assemblies but sometimes business is transacted. I don't know whether we could have transacted more business than we are currently doing in the parliament and assemblies.

The progress made in the clearance of arrears in the court cases is completely unsatisfactory.

Our inability to settle outstanding social and political issues by discussion and negotiation, rather than by violence and demonstration, is unfortunate.

We have not put in place an agency to combat the growing menace of terrorism and Naxalism. Terrorism is a worldwide phenomenon now; (George W) Bush is worried, (Tony) Blair is worried, and even (Vladimir) Putin is worried. But we could have put this menace in place.

So why do you still say the path taken by India is the right path?

Because democracy is still alive and kicking. The judiciary is still alive and asserting itself whenever necessary. Our education system has not improved as much as it should have, but it is no longer the privilege of the rich. Education is available to many. Where there were 10 or 15 engineering colleges, there are 300 today. Even the poorest servant's child can aspire to go into an engineering college or a medical college if he has the merit.

We have improved tremendously in healthcare. Our hospitals have improved enormously. We can get treatment for the most complicated problem with very little delay.

Ten years ago, did you expect India to grow like this?

No. I hoped it would. Did I expect it? I was not sure about expecting anything.

In 1998, I thought you were more cynical.

Yes, I was more cynical. The answer is, there is reason to be less cynical today than I was ten years ago.

Who will you give credit to for India taking the right path to development?

Well, I know people will say it is because of my prejudice. But my basic thesis is that the man who laid the foundation was Rajiv Gandhi. He didn't live to implement what he wanted to.

In his first five years of office, he got mired in unnecessary controversy and got sucked in by all kinds of forces. But it was Rajiv Gandhi who laid the foundations of the economic reforms which were implemented by Narasimha Rao and Manmohan Singh. Rajiv Gandhi had visions of modernity even in 1987, '88 and '89.

Rajiv Gandhi died in 1991, and even in 1998, you were not so optimistic.

That is because there were many reasons to be worried about then, and not all reasons to worry have come to pass.

On the other hand, many positive things have happened in the last ten years. Many Indian boys and girls have acquitted themselves remarkably well all over the world. Ten years ago, we didn't expect, or rather we didn't know, this would happen.

Ten years ago, anybody who had an IIT degree collected his degree and went away to America. Today, they are working all over the place; and they are doing fantastically well.

You told me then that a change in the attitude of the people to the country would take place through either a social revolution or a technological revolution.

Yes. Both are happening now. Everybody knows about the technological revolution. It has made them more self-confident. The young people of 2006 are far more confident than the young people of 1996.

Do you feel the insecurity young Indians felt ten years ago about many things including employment are no longer there today?

They are less insecure than they were ten years ago. I don't say they are no longer insecure. Even today, thousands of graduates have no jobs but that is less of a worry today than ten years ago. The feeling of insecurity was terrible in those days. Today, it is not that terrible.

Do you feel because of the technological revolution, the attitude of other countries to India also has changed?

Undoubtedly. China has made unbelievable progress, physically. They have built roads, they have built steel factories and they have made enormous progress in all fields. They are growing at 10 per cent per year. But today, it is not as if China is progressing, and India is not progressing at all.

When Tony Blair made a speech to the Labour conference in Manchester, he spoke about China and India. Though we have not done as well as we should have in certain sectors like manufacturing, in hardware, etc, there are other areas where we have done extremely well; like in the automobile industry, mobile technology, etc Certain industries which were on the verge of collapse like the textile industry have taken a turnaround.

What about a social revolution?

That one third of humanity is treated as second class or third class citizens is no longer valid today. Nobody asks you: Are you a Harijan, are you an Adi Dravida, are you this or that. You are taken at face value. If you can do the job, you can do the job – whether it is in journalism or IT or any such field.

Among the poorer people, people who were called the Dalits, there was, mistakenly, an aggressive attitude in some cases. If you keep that aside, most people have a healthy social attitude today.

What do you attribute as the reason behind such an attitude? There was not a visible social revolution in India.

The reason most importantly is affluence. The poorest servant has a television set, a fridge, a telephone, a mobile telephone....

So, it is not education that has brought about the change...?

To some degree, education has, but availability of jobs, income, technology, etc has brought about the change.

We spoke about education and that brings us to the most contentious issue among the middle class right now. Do you agree with reservation in higher education?

My opinion is, between the media and the rest, everybody is making too much noise about reservation. Political personalities use reservation as one more plank to catch votes. Their heart is not bleeding for the poor. Their heart is bleeding for the next election and votes.

The people who oppose reservation are doing so without understanding what it is. Please tell me, if the number of seats is adequate for everybody, where is the question of reservation hurting anybody? You say, the value of an IIT degree will come down. Listen, the man who employs can find out whether you are recruited on merit or reservation in five minutes. So, why are you making so much noise about reservation?

You mean it is unnecessary?

Yes, it is unnecessary. I need an answer to the question, is reservation necessary? They have had 15 per cent reservation for scheduled castes, and 7.5 per cent for Scheduled Tribes for the last 45 years. Have all the Scheduled Castes and Tribes come up?

That is because the creamy layer is grabbing all the reservation benefits.

So, the creamy layer has come up. The same thing is going to happen to this 27 per cent too. In the case of OBCs too, all the benefits will be cornered by a small number of people only. The other large number of people will not get any benefits.

But nobody is bothered about it because taking away the creamy layer is something even Veerappa Moily (the Congress leader heading the committee studying reservations) is not willing to do. He said, 'We have left that to the government'. I don't understand this. How can he leave it to the government? If he is asked to look into it, he must say, either there is a creamy layer problem and this is the way to tackle it, or he must say, there is no creamy layer problem.

So, my question is, has reservation done good? You have got 50 years of experience with 15 per cent of reservation for SCs and 7.5 per cent for STs. Some people got jobs, and the good people have become better people. Some fellow said the other day that it enabled K R Narayanan's (former Indian President who was a Dalit) daughter to get into the Indian Foreign Service (IFS). So, that is what is happening.

My point is, reservation is a storm in a teacup. It will neither help nor hurt.

So, should India continue with something that has not benefited the real needy for 50 years?

If the politicians want votes, they will continue.

To politicians, it is part of the political agenda to say we are giving 27 per cent to OBCs.

It is also the political agenda of the United Progressive Alliance government to have job quotas in the private sector.

Hold on, hold on. The politicisation of the agenda of reservation is done by all parties.

But it is the UPA that is talking about job quota in the private sector.

It is only one-upmanship. It is like, if you can do that, I can do this.

Where will this one-upmanship lead to?

If you compel companies to do it, and if it is a small number, companies will engage such people. But if it goes beyond a point, they will say, I cannot carry a lot of baggage.

It's like this, when they want 10 people, you are compelling them to take two on reservation. Then, they are left with only eight people to do the job. So, they will be forced to take

12 people. Therefore, the cost of manufacturing will go up. What they will do is, they will abandon India and go away to Singapore or China or wherever they feel like. And India will become less competitive globally.

Let us go back to something you said in 1998. You said the philosophy of our existence was tolerance and not fundamentalism. Is not fundamentalism on the rise now? At the slightest provocation, people flare up. There is intolerance everywhere.

First, it is easier to be intolerant than tolerant. Second thing is, the vast majority of people show tremendous tolerance whether it is in Nashik, whether it is in Bombay, or in Ahmedabad. Nobody did react and butcher the others in these places.

There is only a small, mad minority of people from a particular community who are indulging in this. But the small minority is creating disturbance in society; they are creating noise and problems.

One must analyse the roots of terrorism. Terrorism is now widespread. It is there all over the world. The purpose of terrorism is to work tremendous violence which is impossible to explain.

To perpetuate or perpetrate unthinking violence of a huge magnitude on a majority of people who have nothing to do with the cause is the methodology of terrorism. The technical methodology is RDX, ammonium nitrate, the AK 47, human bomb, etc

How does terrorism arise? Terrorism arose once upon a time by a minority thinking that they are being seriously marginalised, whether it is the Tamils in Sri Lanka, whether it is the Catholics in Ireland, whether it is the Kurds in Turkey, whether it is the Muslims in Palestine.

What does Pakistan do? It takes charge of this and teaches a number of Muslims to be jihadis. But they want to create an impression that terrorism in India is a result of Kashmiri Muslims being angry, and terrorism in Palestine is because Palestinian Muslims are angry.

In order to fight terrorism, you must reiterate the central principle of tolerance – that we will not react; eye for an eye and tooth for a tooth will not work.

Though the world knew it earlier, the United States has recently issued a statement that Islamic fundamentalism and jihadis increased because of the war on Iraq.

They are not saying that is the reason; they are saying it is going to become the reason.

I would call it the metastasis of cancer. You got cancer in some part of the body, and the doctor says, 'It is malignant. Please remove it'. When you cut and remove it, the cancer spreads all over the body. That is called metastasis.

So, Americans went into Afghanistan and Iraq because of 9/11, saying that Saddam Hussein had weapons of mass destruction (WMD). They sat there for four-five years but could not find a single WMD.

Now, the Americans think that democracy is something like giving a lollipop. No society becomes democratic merely by holding an election. Democracy requires rule of law. It requires admission by people to rule by consent. You can't do that by suppressing the minority, nor can you do that by allowing the minority to sit on your shoulder. You can take any example from the world.

In 1998 you told me that journalism is junk, the bureaucracy is junk.... Today, has the junk worsened or become better?

One of the sad features is that it has worsened. Things like journalism and the bureaucracy have not improved. Whatever be the reason, journalism has become completely, completely yellow. Most journalism has no time for intellectual in-depth analysis of what is happening.

Take any issue, take the women's issue, take the reservation issue, take the office of profit issue, nobody has the time and inclination to sit down and analyse it in depth.

As far as the bureaucracy is concerned, it is becoming more and more and more servile. It will require administrative improvement of tremendous variety which all well-meaning people have tried and failed. I think the present prime minister is trying very hard to improve the administration but it is not easy.

How do you rate Dr Manmohan Singh as prime minister?

Given the circumstances, he is doing extraordinarily well. It is not a majority government; it stands with the support of people inside and outside. The vote-pulling characteristic of the party was Sonia Gandhi.

She is said to be pulling the strings.

What strings is she pulling? It is journalistic junk to say she is pulling the strings. Yes, she expresses her opinion forcefully and forthrightly. She is supposed to. She has a certain status, which is usually not clear to the people. Manmohan Singh walked into the prime ministership fully aware of all that.

You saw her when Rajiv Gandhi was the Prime Minister. Did she show any leadership quality then?

No, she was not called upon to show any leadership quality then. She was in the shadow of her husband from where she never came out. She was only a housewife looking after her husband and children.

How would you describe the last 59 years of India?

India has done well. Today you don't feel angry when the tourism department advertises 'Incredible India'. We are incredible.

But when the BJP campaigned with the India Shining slogan, they lost the elections.

That was because the poor people were not carried away by IT (information technology) shining. What they want is to ensure their next meal. So, they must have thought, 'You are making too much noise about what other people have achieved. So, go away'.

So, a long way to go for India to shine?

Yes, we are not shining. We have a long way to go. As I said in the beginning, we are 60-70 per cent in the right direction.

Has your opinion on politicians changed?

Nothing has changed. It has neither deteriorated nor improved.

Which Indian politician do you admire the most?

Nehru, Sardar Patel, Rajaji, Kamaraj.

All of them belong to the time India just became independent. You can't name anybody who came after them?

You tell the names. I will give my opinion.

Vajpayee?

Certainly. Why not?

Rajiv Gandhi?

Very good but very naive. Did not understand how to protect himself.

Dr Manmohan Singh?

Not yet fully displayed qualities of decisive leadership.

In those days, you used to end your regular columns in a weekly with: 'Cry my beloved country.' How would you have ended if you were to write today?

Incredible India!

'We should have learnt to conduct our business, particularly in the assemblies and legislatures, in a far more disciplined fashion than we do. Yes, in every country, there is a lot of noise made in the parliaments and assemblies but sometimes business is transacted. I don't know whether we could have transacted more business than we are currently doing in the parliament and assemblies.'

This was Seshan's observation in 2007. Has anything changed in 2022? No.

When I asked him whether India was going in the right direction, he said, 'if the right path was due East, we are going in the eastern direction. But we are not fully in the eastern direction; we are a little south of east'.

I wonder if he were alive today, what would he have said…

The Great Depression of 2008

The financial crisis that happened in the year 2008 is described as the worst and the longest period of economic decline since the Great Depression of the 1930s.[1]

An entire generation was experiencing something as alarming as a financial crisis for the first time in their lives.

It all started in 2007, with the depreciation of the subprime mortgage market in the United States which soon became an international banking crisis with the collapse of the investment bank, Lehman Brothers in 2008. This devastated the financial markets of the entire world, and also the banking and real estate industries.

The crisis led to increase in home mortgage foreclosures worldwide and caused millions of people to lose their entire life savings, jobs and even homes.

Although the entire world got affected, it was more pronounced in the US and Europe.

---

1 A severe worldwide economic depression between 1929 and 1939 which began after a major fall in stock prices in the United States. What started on 4 September 1929 ended in a stock market crash on 24 October 1929 known as the Wall Street crash of 1929.

Fortunately for India, the Indian economy, still not fully opened up, escaped the great recession.

S ***Somasegar****, the senior vice president of the developer division at Microsoft Corporation and the driving force behind launching the Microsoft India Development Centre (MSIDC), the company's research and development facility in Hyderabad, spoke to me early 2009 on the then global crisis, its impact on businesses, etc*

THERE are reports from the US that the worst of the economic crisis is over. Is it true?

If you look at the last hundred or so years, recessions have occurred several times; some with a larger impact than the others. At Microsoft, we tried to analyse several of the last macro-economic downturns and found, among other things, that when the economy expands exponentially, it sometimes goes through a reset, and then takes a while to slowly get back to the original position.

Is this phenomenon cyclical?

I wouldn't call it cyclical but it has been happening every 20-30 years. We think it's a little bit different this time. We feel the economy is going through a reset; we don't think of it as just a recession.

The private debt to gross domestic product (GDP) ratio has been at an all-time high. Before the Great Depression, the ratio was 150-160 per cent. This time, it reached about 300 per cent. What it really means is, people have borrowed beyond their means, and there was extra cash because of the borrowing. In other words, they spent a lot, and their ability to pay off their debt was much less.

We feel, therefore, that the economy is resetting itself, which means it will decrease to the right level and will not quickly snap back as it did previously. Instead, you will see normal growth from now on driven by normal GDP growth.

How did you get the early signs?

We've got a pretty good listening system in place as it relates to indications of what's going on in the marketplace. We saw early signs in the small business segment, particularly when cash and credit began to really tighten up. That was the very first customer audience that really showed us an indication. When we hit the mid-September to October time frame, we saw it hit across all channels and all audiences, and it certainly was very dramatic.

You said earlier that it was the debt-driven economy that was the reason for all this. How will people all over the world look at debt after this?

When we looked at history, we found four major 'de-leveraging' that led to economic downturns: 1820, 1873, 1929 and today. The dotcom crash in 1999-2001 was largely restricted to the hi-tech industry, but these four major economic downturns spanned multiple industries and geographical boundaries.

Over the last 30-40 years, people have been borrowing more than they could or should. Anyone who was privy to the Great Depression would have surely advised a different path, but few people today had experienced that.

I would like to believe that future generations will learn from this economic climate and not make the same mistakes. This teaches us that we have a lot to learn from our own history.

What lessons can we learn from this recession?

It teaches us some good things. We have really moved from looking in the rear-view mirror and studying the past, to positioning ourselves forward to focus on what we can control and what we can do about the environment. We can't change a lot of factors that are going on from a global societal and macroeconomic standpoint, but we need to stay focused on what we can control.

Will the recovery start this time from the developing nations?

I think China and India have an advantage. The financial controls in India, for example, have always been tight. The culture of borrowing is not very prevalent in India, at least when I was growing up here. If people borrow, they borrow within their means. I don't know how it has evolved in the last 15 years, but I feel that this culture will put the country in an advantageous position in these times.

Recession in India is not as drastic as what you might see in the developed world because the hole that is dug is not that deep. So, countries like India can recover from recession much quicker.

When do you think we will see a turn around?

We believe that the rest of 2009 will continue to be tough. We think 2010 will be difficult as well. So, for the next 12-18 months, we're taking a very conservative approach in our financial planning and expecting the recovery to happen slowly after that.

How do you compare the mood in the US and in India?

Across the board, people are a little nervous and worried. People I meet in the business circuit are worried. So, there is not much difference in the way business people worry in both the countries.

From the consumer perspective, there is a little more optimism here than you see in the US. Do you think India's dominance in the IT industry will wane after the recession, with drying up of outsourcing from the US?

No, if it wanes, it will be the companies' doing. If you do not innovate, India's leadership position in the IT industry would decrease. The services industry may see a slower growth rate in the short term but in the long term, India is in a fantastic position as of now.

India and China have the best opportunity in the long term. We have a lot of human capital, and in this information-based economy, this factor is instrumental in keeping the country in a leadership position. How best we use it...only time will tell.

> *Though mostly unaffected by the global recession, the Indian economic growth had dropped to 6.7 per cent in 2008-09, but it bounced back to 8.5 per cent in 2009-10. Because of the stimulus packages offered by the government, the fiscal deficit touched 6.4 per cent of the GDP in 2009-10. But something for people of all generations to not forget: 'Over the last 30-40 years, people have been borrowing more than they could or should. Anyone who was privy to the Great Depression would have surely advised a different path, but few people today had experienced that.*
>
> *I would like to believe that future generations will learn from this economic climate and not make the same mistakes. This teaches us that we have a lot to learn from our own history', said S Somasegar of Microsoft Corp nearly fifteen years ago.*

It's Time for Another General Election

Year 2009.

Five years had passed since Sonia Gandhi appointed Dr Manmohan Singh as the Prime Minister of India. Though many experts expected the UPA government to collapse within a couple of years, it did not happen.

And it was time for UPA1 to face the people of India.

The elections were to be held in five phases from the 16th of April 2009 to the 13th of May 2009.

I spoke to the former Chief Election Commissioner ***T S Krishnamurthy*** *(from February 2004 to May 2005) on how tough it was to conduct multi-phase elections in a country like India.*

LOK Sabha elections are around the corner. Many States, including Jammu and Kashmir, also go to polls at the same time. Separatist activities are on the rise in J&K. Several serial blasts have occurred in the last few weeks in various parts of India. Is it the right time to conduct the elections?

The elections have to be conducted according to the provisions of the Constitution. Every House has a five-year tenure unless it is dissolved earlier. By the time the tenure is over, you have to conduct the elections.

The last Lok Sabha elections took place sometime in April 2004. By May 2009, we have to complete the elections as far as the constitutional provision is concerned. But if the government chooses to dissolve the House, the consequence is, there is a time limit between the last sitting of the House and the convening of the new House which cannot be more than six months. So, suppose they dissolve the House some time in November, then by May, they have to conduct the elections. So, the timing of the conduct of the elections is fairly clear.

The Election Commission (EC) normally takes into account many things like school holidays as schools are necessary for conducting the elections. Also taken into consideration are regional festivities. Like, last time, we had the Kumbh Mela at Ujjain, so we had to adjust the dates for Madhya Pradesh differently.[1]

The Election Commission doesn't like to interfere with the entrance examinations like the IIT-JEE.

We also look at the climatic considerations. For example, in Himachal Pradesh and J&K, there are practical difficulties in winter.

We have had floods in Orissa, Bihar, etc If such conditions occur when elections take place, will the Election Commission postpone the elections?

No, elections cannot be postponed because there are constitutional provisions. The only way it can be postponed

---

[1] Kumbh Mela is a major pilgrimage and festival celebrated every twelve years, at four river-bank pilgrimage sites: Allahabad, Haridwar, Nashik, and Ujjain. Millions of pilgrims from all over India assemble at the centre during the festival.

is, you impose President's Rule during the period and elections can be conducted when President's Rule is in place. So, there is very little choice as far as the timing is concerned except when a House is dissolved prematurely.

Is it that the tenure of this House cannot go beyond May?

Yes. It cannot go beyond May. By and large, this is the principle followed by the Election Commission.

Who has the say in deciding the timing of the elections? Suppose the Election Commission decides on a date and the government opposes it?

The government has very little role to play as far as timing of the elections is concerned. As I said, within the constitutional provisions, the Election Commission decides the dates. Whether it is going to be a two-phase or a three-phase election, depends on the availability of the paramilitary forces, etc

They may consult the government about the law and order situation, local holidays, etc but the final decision is that of the Election Commission.

You spoke about the law and order situation. If we take the separatist activities in Jammu and Kashmir for example, and the violence that is going on there, how will the Election Commission go about conducting the elections in such a complex situation?

We have conducted elections even in the most difficult times when the militancy was very high. It is not that elections cannot be conducted but we have to take reasonable precautions in conducting the elections.

What are the precautions?

Like people should feel free to come and exercise their franchise. If you have a situation where it is impossible for people to come, then the best remedy will be to dissolve the House and impose President's Rule. By the time the President's Rule is completed, elections can be conducted.

How do you look at the present violent situation in Kashmir? Is it conducive to elections?

Some of these happenings are political and election-oriented. Once the election is announced, all these people will fall in line. This may be some kind of tactic to say that elections cannot be conducted. But as far as the Election Commission is concerned, I am sure they will go by the dates as prescribed in the Constitution.

Unless there is a real fear that voters will not be able to come out to vote, the EC goes ahead with the polls. With the help of the paramilitary forces, we have been conducting elections. Even during the 1996 Kashmir elections, the situation was pretty bad; still we conducted the elections. Yes, the voting percentage was not very high in some places.

The EC conducts elections in five or six phases, depending upon the ground conditions there. But the Commission will not be scared of any such activities.

During your tenure as Chief Election Commissioner, which place did you find the most difficult to conduct an election?

My major election was the Parliament elections in 2004. The other was the Bihar and Haryana assembly elections. We had some difficult times there. Fortunately, we were able to conduct the elections without any major problems. There were some disturbing trends like the chief minister of Haryana being attacked, etc In Bihar, we had a lot of problems. In the end, everything went off well.

As the Chief Election Commissioner, did you have to look at different States differently?

We have to. In States like Maharashtra, Rajasthan, Himachal Pradesh, Gujarat or Kerala, we don't see much of violence or managerial problem though they make a lot of noise. But in States like Bihar and UP, we have problems.

So, in Maharashtra, Tamil Nadu, Kerala, etc sometimes we conduct elections in a single day. There has been no re-poll in Maharashtra at all so far.

So, some States are more peaceful than the others.

In some States, we had Naxalite activities. So, we had to deploy more paramilitary forces there. Sometimes, in some places in AP, Bihar, Jharkhand, etc, we took the police personnel by helicopter.

Do you generally opt for more than one-phase election when you find the situation is not peaceful?

Generally, yes. We had more than one-phase elections where we anticipated violence or political confrontation.

Even geography is one of the reasons for multi-phase general elections.

When Assam had Bihu festival for a week, we conducted the elections in more than one phase last time.

You mean it doesn't depend on the size of the State at all?

Generally, it doesn't depend on the size of the State but in the case of UP, because of its size and also because of its problems, we had to have more phases.

Is it because you need more paramilitary forces that you spread elections to many phases?

Yes, the main reason is the lack of adequate forces.

When you compare conducting elections in Kashmir and Bihar, which was the toughest?

Difficult to say. Except for the militancy-related violence and separatist groups boycotting the elections, we didn't have major problems in Kashmir.

On the other hand, in Bihar, we had a lot of political confrontation between parties. In UP also, we had similar problems.

Is it because of the fear of extremists that people do not come out to vote in large numbers in Kashmir? It always had very poor voter turnout.

In fact, in the 2004 Parliament and assembly elections, the percentage of voting was very high compared to the earlier elections. We had adopted a number of special steps so that people came out to vote. We had brought Urdu-knowing people from UP to man 50 per cent of the polling stations. For example, if there were four people manning a polling station, two were from outside the State.

We didn't have many problems, but we had special managerial problems like transporting Urdu teachers from Lucknow by Air Force planes to Srinagar and dispersing them. We had to also provide protection to these people.

When you have opinion polls and exit polls, is conducting elections in a prolonged manner good because these polls affect and influence the mindset of the people?

You are right. Ideally an election should be conducted in a day's time or a week's time. Fortunately, we still have good officers who can enforce discipline. By and large, you can say our elections are fair and free.

Thanks to Mr T N Seshan who had set up a high tradition.

Till Seshan took over, people of India were not aware of the fact that the Chief Election Commissioner (CEC) had so much power.

You are right. There is a Supreme Court judgment that the Chief Election Commissioner (CEC) cannot throw his hands up and appeal to God that he is helpless and divine help should come! The Constitution has given him all the powers to conduct free and fair elections. If there is no legal provision supporting him, whatever he says is the law. There are hidden reservoirs of powers where there is a legislative vacuum.

Mr Seshan realised the full facts of this judgement and he started exercising it. So, 1991 was the turning point.

We tried to uphold and sometimes improve upon it, and we have been able to enforce the code of conduct with a little more strictness. We received admiration from all over. It is not that we are patting ourselves on the back.

During the period of election, how do the political parties and politicians look at the powerhouse that is the Election Commission?

They know the Election Commission is powerful during that period; from the announcement of the date of elections till the announcement of the result of the elections. By and large, they behave. They do create problems too sometimes, but then immediately we assert our rights.

Do you consider Indian elections are relatively fairly conducted?

I can say by and large, it is fair and free. At least 80-90 per cent, we are fair and free. I will put it this way: among the election commissions existing in many countries, India has one of the very few ones that are very independent.

Which country, according to you, conducts the fairest elections?

Australia is one of the countries where elections are fairly well conducted. Germany also. Maybe there are other small countries too.

Though we are a subcontinent, the problems we face are continental in size! Considering the size of the population, the number of languages, communal and geographical differences and innumerable problems faced by the Election Commission, it is probably the best.

Why did you decide to write the book *The Miracle of Democracy – India's Amazing Journey*?

I thought my experiences with regard to civil servants and politicians had a message to convey. I had situations where I had to strongly differ with the ministers. At one stage, I even thought I would put in my papers. I must say the government supported me. The minister went but I didn't go! There are a number of such incidents in my career.

I feel there is an obnoxious nexus between civil servants and politicians, which I feel we should arrest.

Similarly, we have proliferation of political parties based on language, religion and what not. It is high time there are some changes in the election system. Today, whoever gets the maximum number of votes gets elected. Persons with even 10 per cent votes can get elected. So, in my book I have suggested this system should change.

In what way should it change?

It could be proportional representation, or it could be what is known as the mixed system where 50 per cent is voted on this basis and the remaining 50 per cent in the list system. It is there in Germany, Palestine etc where a national list is prepared where there will be a list of 40-50 people. You can tick and whoever gets the maximum votes will represent the country and not the constituency.

A change is necessary in India as I feel there is a threat to the unity and integrity of India. Unfortunately, political parties are not taking the need for electoral reforms seriously.

States like Bengal and UP generally witness the maximum number of election-related political violence; though the UP police say if there were 97 election-related violent incidents in the 2017 assembly elections, it came down to 33 in the 2022 elections.

Look at the way elections are conducted in UP even in 2022. The voting for the 403 UP assembly constituencies were held over seven phases, and over 70,000 UP police personnel and 250 companies of Central Armed Police Forces (CAPF) were deployed for security duty during the counting for all the seven poll phases.

Yes, what T S Krishnamurthy said is true, 'Though we are a subcontinent, the problems we face are continental in size!'

The Manmohan Singh government completed its term successfully.

And the UPA went to the polls announcing that India remained unscathed when America and Europe collapsed in the 2008 economic crisis, only because the economy was managed well by the economist turned politician, Dr Manmohan Singh.

Some of the schemes started by the UPA like MGNREGA (Mahatma Gandhi National Rural Employment Guarantee Act) providing jobs to the poor, farm loan waiver to the tune of Rs 6,000 crore, education loan waiver of Rs 2,600 crore, implementation of the Sixth Pay Commission that saw a hike of 40 per cent in the salaries of central government employees, etc won the hearts of all sections of people.

So, it was Advantage UPA!

The MGNREGA Scheme guaranteeing 100 days of employment.
Thank you, WSJ.

PART 5

2009- 2014

Ruling Party: The United Progressive Alliance (UPA)

Prime Minister: Dr Manmohan Singh (Congress)

A disaster India will never be able to forget, and the injustice that followed: the Bhopal gas tragedy.

https://theleaflet.in

Chennai
Thursday, November 11, 2010

www.expressbuzz.com

World | Page 14
Suu Kyi wants unconditional release: lawyer

The New Indian Express

LOSS TO THE NATION

₹176000000000000

A Raja deprived govt of this much money in 2G spectrum allocation: CAG report

K S Narayanan | ENS
New Delhi, November 10

INSTANT JUSTICE

House divided on 'encounter killing' of rapist

Govt defends police action, finds support only in Congress

Express News Service
Chennai, November 10

Thank you, The New Indian Express.

UPA1 is now UPA2

The General Elections for the 15th Lok Sabha were held during April-May 2009 and the United Progressive Alliance (UPA) went to the polls full of confidence.

When the results were announced, they did increase the number of seats from 145 to 206, and the BJP led by L K Advani went down from 138 to 116.

End result was, we had a UPA2.

But the confidence the UPA2 had in the beginning of the second term soon turned to over-confidence and arrogance, like it happens to all political parties that get elected the second time.

Yes, UPA2 was totally different from UPA1, with corruption charges, scandals and scams dominating the entire 5 years of its rule.

In fact, the perception of UPA2 was that of one of the most corrupt periods independent India has seen.

'Some people say power (of the state) should not be used against the Maoists. I don't agree with that. Power must be used, but properly and lawfully.' — Former Naxal K Venu.

'Nothing has changed from the day we fought for a revolution', said Philip M Prasad.

The Sukma encounter April 2021.

Thank you, Redspark.nu. Thank you, The Economic Times.

The Rise of the Naxals and the Maoists

It was just before the General elections in April 2009 that in Jharkhand, the Maoists hijacked a train with at least 300 people on board and forced it to run to Latehar district.

In November 2009, the government of India and the state's forces started a special 'Operation Green Hunt' to hunt down Naxals in the Red Corridors of India (The central, southern, and eastern parts of India covering around eleven States with emphasis on Odisha, Bihar, Chhattisgarh and Jharkhand is regarded as the Red Corridor).

In April 2010, another major attack happened in Chhattisgarh, killing seventy-six CRPF policemen and eight Maoists which was described as one of the deadliest attacks by the Maoists.

It was in this background that I met two of the most famous people associated with Maoism and Naxalism; K Venu and Philip M Prasad.

It was interesting to note that majority of the famous Naxals and Maoists of the sixties and the seventies from Kerala led diametrically opposite lives after they left their Maoist days. If Philip M Prasad became a follower of Sai Baba, K Venu managed a construction company in Thrissur.

K Venu, a Maoist ideologue of the nineteen sixties, continued to be an ideologue, and a theoretician, but from a hardcore ultra-leftist Communist, he became an advocate of free market economy.

WHEN you were young, what attracted you to the ideology of Maoism?

When I was a student, I was not politically active though I was inclined to the Left ideology all the time as my family had always been with the Left. After I completed my postgraduation in zoology in 1968, I started writing regularly in periodicals on social, political and philosophical issues. I also started talking at the youth federation meetings of the Communist Party of India-Marxist (CPI-M). I was then asked by the famous Left ideologue, the late P Govinda Pillai to join *Desabhimani*'s (the Communist Party's newspaper) book publishing house.

By then, the Naxal movement had already started. I did not join it, though I came into contact with their literature. Slowly, I got attracted to their revolutionary ideas, and started studying the ideologies of CPI (Communist Party of India), CPI-M (Communist Party of India-Marxist) and CPI-ML (CPI-Marxist-Leninist) from a scientific point of view. Afterwards, I started a publication called the *Maoist,* identifying with the Naxal upsurge in India. After that, many pro-Naxal groups started contacting me.

Was it during that period that you met Charu Majumdar?[1]

When I was vacillating between science and revolution, an incident took place in February 1970; that was the killing

---

[1] Charu Majumdar was a communist revolutionary born in a zamindari family in 1918 and later formed the militant Naxal group. His writings on the historic accounts of the 1967 Naxalbari uprising in Naxalbari in West Bengal became the ideology which guided the entire Naxal movement.

of Arikkad Varghese (known in Kerala as Naxal Varghese who fought for the Adivasis in Wayanad) by the police. That made many like me turn towards Maoism and revolution.

I started this publication called *Inquilab,* and also worked as a part-time sub-editor with a Malayalam encyclopaedia. I was also doing my PhD in science then.

I had no direct contact with any of the Maoists till somebody asked me whether my address could be used by the local party to contact the official CPI-ML in Kolkata.

When the contact man, Ambadi Sankaran Kutty, surrendered to the police, I became their contact man for a few months. Then, the members in Kannur asked me to go to Kolkata and meet Charu Majumdar. At that time also, I was not sure whether I would plunge into party politics.

What do you remember about your meeting with Majumdar?

When I reached the Howrah railway station, the contact person was waiting for me. He took me to one point and from there, another man took over. I think I met four such people before I met the 'real man'.

Finally, the moment I was waiting for happened; I saw Charu Majumdar sitting in the room looking very ill. There was a doctor with him all the time, who gave him oxygen and injections periodically. Even though he was very ill and weak, he looked a very strong personality. I still remember his magnetic eyes.

I had the opportunity to spend an hour with him while I explained to him about the activities of the Maoist groups in Kerala. He then gave me directions on what was to be done.

Did you agree with Majumdar's idea of attacking landlords?

Yes, I did. The communist ideologues had come to this decision of attacking landlords after analysing the principal contradictions in society at that time. The position of the CPI-ML was feudalism versus the masses. We believed that the feudal lords were the very basis of imperialist penetration, and we had to smash it. Except in Kerala where the land reforms had already started, landlordism was a problem the entire country faced.

Majumdar's slogan was, '1970s is the decade of Indian revolution', and we were all charged up about that.

Did all the youngsters including you believe that a revolution was possible?

Yes, of course. We expected a big revolution like the Chinese Revolution taking place in India.[2]

After you came back from Kolkata, some landlords were attacked and killed in Kerala. You were also arrested.

The truth was, I was not aware of what had happened. I came to know of it only from the morning newspapers. Three landlords were killed, and one of them was not even a landlord; only his grandfather was. This killing created a bad impression of us among people.

After the brutal killing, I was taken into custody for questioning. That was only because I was publishing

---

[2] Chinese Revolution: On 1 October 1949, the Chinese Communist leader Mao Zedong declared the creation of the People's Republic of China, the PRC and started a cultural revolution. This Cultural Revolution was to preserve Chinese communism from the capitalist and traditional elements in the Chinese society, and to re-impose Mao Zedong Thoughts, known to the outside world as Maoism.

the magazine. Later, the police came to know that I had gone to Kolkata to meet Majumdar, and that I had arranged a few local meetings of the CPI-ML. The police wanted to know where Charu Majumdar was. I refused to answer.

Did the police torture you?

Initially they didn't, but later they did. But I took the position that I didn't know where Majumdar was.

How many years were you in custody?

I was in jail for four years as an under-trial. They could not find any evidence against me. When I was in jail, I read a lot and studied classical Marxism properly. That made me convinced that Marxism, Leninism, and also Maoism were the right forms of development in the then-situation, and only Maoism gave a correct picture of the world. I was totally convinced about Maoist ideology.

When in jail, initially we were not given books on Maoism to read. I had to go on hunger strike for twenty-one days to get a pen to write. The paradox was, I was then reading a book written by C Achutha Menon when he was in British jail, and the same person was the chief minister of Kerala when I was denied a pen to write.

When you came out of jail, were you more charged up about Maoist ideology?

Yes. I came out of jail after four years in January 1975. I took a decision to go on record and work for the party openly. When in jail, we had prepared a proper document on how to build a Leninist party, and it was sent out from the jail. The document was used to rebuild the movement in Kerala.

When I came out, the party committees and proper networks were all there based on this document. I was made the secretary of CPI-ML (Communist Party of India-Marxist Leninist).

When the Emergency was declared, we decided that we must attack police stations also, along with the landlords.

Till then, you were not for attacking the police stations. Why did you change your line?

Yes, I was against attacking the police stations but during the Emergency, it was the state that clamped (down) on the freedom of people. Police is a state organ. So, we decided to attack police stations also.

You wanted justice for the poor, and the ordinary policemen work for their livelihood. How can you justify attacking police stations and killing policemen?

As you said, policemen are ordinary people, and when I took the leadership in attacking the Kayanna (a village in Kozhikode district) police station, I had told my gang not to attack or kill the policemen. Instead, we asked them to surrender and give us their weapons.

Why did you target such workers and not the powers that be?

We were not attacking people, we were attacking the police stations which are the centres of power. That was why we didn't want to kill the policemen or attack them. We asked them to obey us and give us the weapons.

We didn't attack any policeman, but I was attacked with an iron rod by the police, and we were fired at also. Ultimately, we got only two rifles from there.

The attack became famous after they arrested Rajan following the attack and later, he was killed. Rajan had actually no role in the attack.[3]

When were you arrested again?

I went underground, and I was arrested after six months. By then, most of the others had also been arrested. I was arrested in June 1976, and I was in jail till July 1979.

How much did the second jail term change you?

This time I read and studied Hegel (Georg Wilhelm Friedrich Hegel was a German philosopher.) It gave me the confidence to write the book, *The Philosophical Problems of a Revolution*. This book was first published in Malayalam and then in English. It is a good text book on Marxism and Maoism. My book gave a Maoist perspective to the whole ideology.

By 1980-81, I started thinking on my own, and analysing the whole Marxist-Leninist movement. Then I realised that feudalism was not the biggest issue in India.

When did you realise that armed revolution is futile?

Actually, from the beginning I was not convinced about an armed revolution. When I wrote my first book, I thought Communism was the highest form of democracy, which it was not! I was very much convinced by the Communist rationalisation that an *adivasi* did not have the same right as a Tata or an Ambani or a Birla, and to change that, an economic redistribution of the wealth was a must.

Many questions started coming to my mind. I had serious doubts about the Marxist, Leninist, Maoist ideologies working

---

[3] Rajan was an REC, Calicut student who was picked up by the police during the Emergency and killed while being questioned. His body was never found, and it became the famous Rajan case.

in a democratic society. I took leave for six months and started re-thinking on the whole thing.

When I was the all-India secretary of the CPI-ML, I outlined my thoughts to the others at a meeting. But I could not make them understand my point of view on the democratisation of the organisation. So, I had no option but resign from the secretary-ship, and came out of the party.

When I published a thesis on this, I was criticised for taking the bourgeois line!

Did you feel what you had followed and preached from 1969-1989 was wrong?

I look at the development of the extremist wing within the Communist movement as a historical process in the whole Communist movement. Whether I had to join it or not was a personal choice. For example, when the cultural revolution was taking place, Mao was trying to find a way out.

Personally, do you feel it was a mistake?

Looking at that phase from an overall perspective, it was a wrong period. I was honestly approaching a social problem. There was no other way I felt then. It was a rich experience ideologically and otherwise. But theoretically, I am much more advanced today.

Today, you are a businessman. Are you for a capitalist market economy now?

In 1991, I published a book on the democratic perspective of a Communist. I was trying to make the Communist movement democratic. It was a thorough criticism of Marxism, and I tried to prove that its political and economic theories were wrong. I felt the Communist dictatorship was a retrogressive historical process, but it was a part of history and necessary.

In 1991, I felt that the open market with parliamentary democracy was comparatively better than Communism. Not the best, of course. My critics and my old comrades say that I have totally joined the capitalists. It is not true.

In the last 20 years, I have been thinking a lot. Now I have come to the conclusion that social Darwinism, that is the survival of the fittest, is not applicable to human society. That is because human beings are socially organised through languages, and language is a very advanced capacity of the human brain.

What is happening in the European Union is a democratic process where people can also move freely. It is an emerging new phenomenon, and it is going to spread elsewhere too.

How do you explain many parts of Europe where market economy works, turning left?

Capitalist societies are facing this crisis between market fundamentalism and some kind of a social control system. Market fundamentalists say that market fundamentalism will solve all the problems. No, market fundamentalism has to be defeated. Some kind of a social control is necessary.

The leftism in Europe is not Communist leftism; it is democratic leftism. I support the ideology. It must be an open market, I agree but the open market has to be socially controlled. Democratic process must control the market economy.

Do you hold the market economy and the rise of a few super rich and subsequent disparity between the rich and the poor, the reason for the rise of Maoism once again in India?

Certainly. Yet it is not just because of the emergence of corporate power alone. Maoism has influence only in the most backward areas. Wherever land reforms have taken place, there are no Maoists. Wherever democratic and modern transformations are taking place, Maoists cannot exist there.

So, it is not just because of the corporate lobbies that Maoism is rising. The question is, why is the development process not spreading to all the areas? That is mainly because of the weakness in the state machinery.

So, do you hold the weakness of the state machinery as one reason for the rise in Maoism?

Yes, one main reason is that. For example, the Naxal movement was almost wiped out from Andhra Pradesh through modern transformation, and the work of the state machinery.

New states like Jharkhand, Chhattisgarh, etc have no such state machinery in the most backward and under-developed areas, and they (Maoists) have spread to these areas.

As an ideologue who was part of this movement once, do you call the young Maoists, misguided?

There is a strong ideological structure in Maoism, and it gives you hope that you can bring in a new society where everybody is equal and democratic. Maoist ideology gives that kind of a vision. That ideology has to be theoretically and ideologically opposed, and these cadres have to be reorganised ideologically.

Do you feel development is the only answer to fight Maoism?

Not the only answer. Intervention has to be in three forms. One is ideological. I feel it is very important. The leading cadres of the Maoist movement have to be convinced ideologically.

Second is economic development.

Third is a strong state machinery. Some people say power (of the state) should not be used against the Maoists. I don't agree with that. Power must be used, but properly and lawfully.

The annual report of the Ministry of Home Affairs 2018-19 stated that over 3,700 people were killed in Naxal violence in ten States since 2010. According to the report, the Maoists were the most potent among various Left-Wing Extremist (LWE) outfits in the country and responsible for more than 88 per cent of the total violent incidents and resultant deaths.

The highest number of casualties due to Left Wing Extremism (LWE) took place in Chhattisgarh between 2010 and 2018 where 1,370 people were killed in 3,769 violent incidents perpetrated by the Maoists.

In this background, we can read the present thoughts of K Venu, a former Maoist: 'Now I have come to the conclusion that social Darwinism, that is the survival of the fittest, is not applicable to human society. That is because human beings are socially organised through languages, and language is a very advanced capacity of the human brain.'

Once a Naxal, now a Sai Devotee

***Philip M Prasad** was a dreaded Naxal in the late sixties, having been a member of the group that attacked the Pulpally police camp in northern Kerala on 24 November 1968, and brutally murdered a few policemen. This came to be known as the Pulpally murder case.*

But when I met him in 2009, Prasad had devoted himself to Sai Baba and non-violence.

The former Naxal spoke frankly on what made him choose the path of violence as a twenty-one-year-old and what made him shun it later on in his life.

It was a trip down memory lane, to the 'late sixties and the early seventies'.

LET me start from the beginning, when you met Charu Majumdar in **Kolkata. Do you still remember the meeting?**

How can I forget it? Of course, I still remember the meeting as if it happened only yesterday.

The year was 1968, and I was just twenty-one years old. The first meeting took place in a flat in Kolkata. There were

30-35 people from all over India there. From Kerala, only the two of us, Kunnikkal (Kunjikal) and I were there.[1]

From Tamil Nadu, the late Appu and Jagannathan (who is a Gandhian now) attended. There were three-four people from Andhra Pradesh. The entire State committee of the Communist Party of India-Marxist of Bihar had defected, and all of them had come, led by Satyanarayan Sinha.

I think Kanu Sanyal (one of the leaders of the Naxalbari uprising) was present and listening behind the curtains during the entire meeting.

What was the first impression you had of Majumdar?

Extreme hero worship! He was ill and suffering from asthma, and on the verge of collapse. There were doctors by his side with oxygen cylinders, still he appeared so charismatic and powerful. So truthful too.

He spoke to us about the necessity of starting guerrilla groups, and the need to have a military conflict rather than a political conflict. He wanted us to start an armed struggle without any delay. That was his message to us; an armed struggle.

Basically, what he said was influenced by the Cultural Revolution of China. Mao Zedong had come out with a poster urging the youth to barge into the party headquarters. The Vietnam struggle was going on then. Armed struggle was there in Indonesia and also in Burma. All over the world, including in Latin America, there was a Maoist upsurge.

What attracted you as a young man to Maoism?

I was a Communist. Marxism teaches you not to be democratic. At that time, I even called what we followed in

---

[1] Narayanan Kunnikkal was the famous Naxal K Ajitha's father. Ajitha was with Philip M Prasad when they attacked the Pulpally police station.

India as bourgeois democracy! We were very sincere about what we preached, and we read only Lenin, Mao Zedong, and Marx. Everything we read pointed to an armed struggle against the existing establishment.

According to Mao Zedong, to rebel is justified. Even now, when I am miles and miles away from the politics of Mao Zedong, I love him philosophically because history cannot move forward without rebelling, and without foolishness.

Every revolution is foolish, and history is taken forward by foolish revolutions.

How charged were you after meeting Majumdar?

Extremely charged! When I came back, I was like a Hanuman to his Ram, ready to do anything for him and follow him blindly.

Did you start the CPI-Marxist-Leninist movement in Kerala after coming back from Kolkata?

It was founded by the All India Coordination Committee of Communist Revolutionaries. Yes, I was also a part of it. It was the precursor to CPI-ML. So, I was one of the founders of the precursor to the CPI-ML, and perhaps the only living member now. All the others either committed suicide or were tortured to death.

Was attacking the police station (at Pulpally) the first decision taken by you people after coming back from Kolkata?

Actually, the leaders of the groups determined everything. The decision to attack the police stations was taken by Kunnikal Narayanan who had an ego clash with Majumdar, and I was only Kunnikal's *chela* (accomplice) at that time.

Majumdar wanted us to attack unarmed landlords and zamindars, but Kunnikal wanted to attack only armed police stations. He was very hasty and impetuous in his decision to attack the police stations. The psychological motivation was to show that he had an edge over Majumdar. That is how I view it now.

You didn't question the decision then?

I did, and when I did, I was isolated. During the entire operation, an armed guard was posted near me.

For Kunnikal, aiming the gun at a non-armed person is against the ethics of a guerrilla war. At that time, I did not think in those terms. Today, I agree with Kunnikkal in his decision. To enter a home, call the zamindar out, and kill him in front of his wife and children is the worst thing you can do, much worse than an encounter.

But I won't say Charu Majumdar was wrong, and Kunnikal was correct.

Do you remember the Pulpally police station attack?

I remember everything. We had planned the attacks on the Thalassery and Pulpally police stations. The first was slated for 21 November 1968, and the second on 23 November.

23 November happens to be the birthday of my spiritual master Satya Sai Baba!

The attack on the 21st failed miserably. I was in the forest with five others preparing for the Pulpally attack then. There were 400 people in several groups from Kanyakumari to Kasaragod, with each group having 10-15 people who had assembled in the forest. Naturally the news of the failure frustrated all of us.

I wanted to postpone the second attack for a few more days as the first one had failed. But nobody listened to me. So, against my objections, we marched to Pulpally and attacked the police camp. There were no arms there. Sensing an attack, the government had moved all the arms to the Mananthavady (in Wayanad district) police station.

Did you also kill the policemen?

Yes, I did.

At that time, you didn't feel bad killing people?

I was extremely happy then that I killed the policemen. It was an adrenalin rush. Also, we were all charged ideologically. We thought what we believed in was right, and the whole world would be aflame with revolution. When the whole world was going to change and become heavenly, what was there in a little bit of violence, an interlude of violence? That was how we saw it.

That was the philosophy of Marxism and Maoism. You were tagging your philosophy to a utopian tomorrow, and 'now' didn't matter to you then. We pinned our hopes on a greater tomorrow.

Why did you decide to target the police stations? Even today, Maoists attack police stations and kill policemen.

Yes, even today they kill security guards. That is because this is an armed struggle against armed people.

Are they also not poor people who are just working for their livelihood?

Yes, he may be a father, a son, a brother and a husband, but he is armed. He may be poor. All army men work for their livelihood, but when you fight a war, do you spare your enemy saying they fight for their livelihood? No.

It is only an emotional argument. Does the Indian Army man say, oh that Pakistani Army man is a poor man working for his family, and spare him?

It is like this, the armed Naxalites are attacking another army, which is the armed police.

Do you feel today's young Maoists are also driven by the same ideology and philosophy which you felt more than four decades ago?

There is no difference between us and them. Like us, these young men also believe that they are going to usher in a new tomorrow. My question to them is, are you going to commit the same foolishness which we committed in the past?

Nothing has changed from the day we fought for a revolution. Today also, the issues are the same, and they are committing the same foolishness. Why should we sacrifice our youngsters by repeating the same mistake?

It has failed in Russia, it has failed in Yugoslavia, it has failed in India, it has failed in China, and it has failed even in Nepal.

Do you feel today's Maoists are also misguided?

I don't use the word 'misguided' because they are the product of the very fabric of our society. Society has been ill-treating tribals for the last sixty years. What the Maoists are doing and what the government is doing is inevitable. Nobody has any right to blame the youngsters because society as a whole is rotten. If Naxalism is an illness of society, let the doctors treat society.

If you were to address these young Maoists, what would you tell them?

I need not and will not address them. I know how to tackle the problem. The only solution is devotion to God. Even if they capture power, they will not succeed because it is human-centric. Any human-centric ideology will crumble.

The only society that will work should be based on love, and not on violence. Violence breeds violence. Violence is counter-productive. Non-violence is the only solution to all our problems.

What Mahatma Gandhi taught us was the absolute truth. The only social revolution that can be successful is the one based on Gandhian economics.

This revelation came to you when you were in jail?

Yes, first when I was in jail. It came as devotion and not ideology. Man is not an ideological being; he is an emotional being.

I wept when I was in prison. I wept because my comrades were in prison, and I could not do anything for them.

My mother had taught me prayers when I was young. It was inside me as a seed, and when I was in jail, it sprouted up as my tears. The sprouting up was due to repentance.

When did you feel repentant?

In 1973. I was in and out of jail several times in a span of ten years. I was in prison for seven years, and three years outside.

Amongst us, there was intra-group rivalry, and we were fighting against each other. Even inside the jail, we fought against each other.

During this period, China changed. Meanwhile, no change took place in Indian society. Everything remained the same. I read a lot while in prison. I read all of Dostoevsky's books. I also started introspection. That was because the revolution had failed.

Most of the Naxals and Maoists of your time turned spiritual....

Yes, most of us. That is the beauty of it. Very few are still Naxal ideologically.

Today's Maoists also will have the same revelation after a few years.

Today, do you feel what you did then was wrong?

Definitely. I repent it. I will never justify my actions.

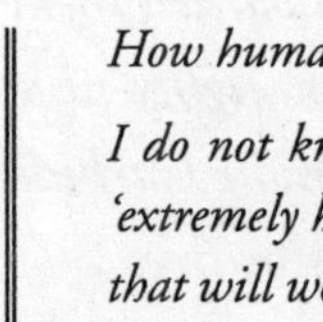

How human beings change over the years!

I do not know whether I was shocked to hear Prasad, a person who was 'extremely happy' to kill policemen in the 1970s, now say, 'The only society that will work should be based on love, and not on violence. Violence breeds violence. Violence is counter-productive. Non-violence is the only solution to all our problems. What Mahatma Gandhi taught us was the absolute truth. The only social revolution that can be successful is the one based on Gandhian economics'.

These words also were very true: 'Every revolution is foolish, but history is taken forward by foolish revolutions.'

The Bhopal Gas Tragedy: Justice Delayed and Denied

What happened in December 1984 at the Union Carbide pesticide plant in Bhopal was one of the worst tragedies in the history of the world. Over forty tons of methyl isocyanate, a poisonous gas got leaked from the plant killing nearly 3,000 people, and permanently disabling more than 50,000. On the whole, around 15,000 people might have died due to exposure to the gas.

What is even more shocking is the delay in giving justice to the affected. A quarter century after the death of over 15,000 people, a Bhopal court convicted former Union Carbide India Chairman Keshub Mahindra and seven others, and awarded them a maximum of two years of imprisonment. However, eighty-nine year-old Warren Anderson, the then chairman of Union Carbide Corporation, who resided in the United States, went scot-free.

The country was horrified when the Bhopal court announced a mere two-year jail term for the eight convicted.

It was not only justice delayed but justice denied too.

This verdict came on 7 June 2010. The tragedy had happened on 23 December 1984!

M R Sivaraman, a retired Indian Administrative Service (IAS) officer, was the finance and planning secretary of the Madhya Pradesh government when the Bhopal gas tragedy occurred on the night of 23 December 1984.

After the verdict was out, he recounted to me what happened on the night.

WHAT do you remember about the fateful night?

I was in the bungalow of the finance secretary when I heard a noise; it was around 12.45 am or 1 am. I came out of the house, and I could see people running here and there in panic and shouting, *gas leak ho gaya.*

I went to the hospital that is very close to my house around 3.30-4 am and found a lot of people there. When I spoke to the doctors, I was told that many people had taken ill, and some were frothing in the mouth, and some were complaining of pain in the eyes.

Soon, more and more people started coming in with complaints.

I told my wife to collect blankets in case the patients needed them, and I was back in the hospital. None of us, not even my children, had any complaints as we stayed quite far away from the factory.

What was the atmosphere in the hospital?

When I went back to the hospital, I found the doctors in panic as by then people had started dying. A man might be talking one moment, then would fall dead the next moment.

As I was in charge of the entire policy requirements of the government, I rushed to the main hospital, and there also, people were dying in large numbers.

Was the city in panic?

The entire city was in panic but the collector, the superintendent of police, doctors and civil surgeons were in the field carrying out their duties diligently.

By 8 am, I rushed to the secretariat but found the place completely empty. Within a few minutes, N R Krishnan, the then secretary to the chief minister came in.[1]

Somebody had to take charge of the secretariat. The chief secretary had gone to the chief minister. So, I took a personal decision and told Krishnan that I was withdrawing Rs 1 crore from State Bank of India.

I called State Bank and told the manager that I wanted Rs 1 crore in cash. Then I called 15-20 young IAS officers and told them to carry Rs 5 lakhs each to various wards and distribute the money to people who were injured and suffering after taking signatures from them.

I took the full responsibility. The poor youngsters, including a lady IAS officer who was eight months pregnant, went around distributing money to the needy. Some had to bury people, some had to cremate their near ones, some had to buy rations, medicines....

But there was no agitation in the city. There was peace as people got money for their immediate needs. I would say the city was under utter confusion in those three-four days.

People were injured, people were dying, cremation and burial grounds were full. It was chaotic. I felt, at least when people had money, they would feel less insecure.

---

[1] There was a Congress government in Madhya Pradesh in 1984 and Arjun Singh was Chief Minister.

Did the political establishment give you the freedom to take decisions depending on the situation?

The chief minister and the finance secretary told me, you do whatever you want; the government will fully stand by you.

Then, Krishnan and I took charge, and we started compiling a list of the number of people who died. It was from my room that all the coordination took place in the next two days. One officer was put in charge of cremation, another officer went around breaking open houses that were closed. Lakshminarayan (who retired as the secretary to the government of India), who went around, found people dead in locked houses. In fact, he took ill at the sight of the dead bodies.

In the hospitals, doctors and nurses were on their feet continuously for 72 hours. They were standing without eating or drinking, taking care of the ill. It was a marvellous display of commitment to a tragedy.

You talk of what (the New York Mayor) Rudy Giuliani did in the US after the 11 September attacks, but he did nothing compared to what the doctors, nurses and the young officers did in Bhopal then. At that time, there were thousands of people dying in Bhopal.

How horrifying was it when thousands of people were dying in a short span of time?

I myself recorded 1,400 deaths in four days. The photographs of all the dead were in my room, as also of those who were not identified.

Things stabilised after four days but people were still dying. Maybe a few thousands died in the next one year. Those who were alive suffered from all sorts of diseases.

The tragedy has to be seen as something that resulted in prolonged illnesses. Unlike the September 11 tragedy in the US or the tsunami of 2004, here was a grave human tragedy where people were dying slowly.

What troubled me when we started giving compensation was that those who lived far away from the factory started claiming compensation. But Krishnan and I were very strict about that.

Did you see people working selflessly when such a tragedy happened?

What I can say as the number two or number three in the government is, the kind of efforts put in by the government officers, doctors and nursing staff, was unparalleled.

I have gone to several countries in the world but never seen this kind of dedication and commitment.

After a month, I told the chief minister, we must give one month's salary to all those who worked so hard. But when I offered them that, they flatly refused. They said, 'we worked when there was a tragedy, and we will not accept anything for our work. It was our duty'. It was that kind of spirit with which the government servants worked that day.

A lot of stories were going around, some true and some false….

Those who were talking about the tragedy later and today never spoke to me, the person who first went there. Nobody ever asked N R Krishnan. That was why all sorts of false stories went around.

Dominique Lapierre (a French author who writes in English) wrote a book full of lies but never ever spoke to me. From where did all these people get the information? We were the people who were in the field. Krishnan and I were the two officers who were in the secretariat then. One day, when I write my autobiography, I will write what exactly happened that day.

Was it not unfair that it took twenty-six years for a verdict to come?

Yes. Now that the verdict is out, I feel very sad because here is a case of total negligence of the factory managers, members of the board of directors. Because of their negligence, thousands of people died and yet they got away with it. It was homicide not amounting to murder. It was criminal neglect.

Nowhere in the world would such a case take twenty-six years to come out with a verdict. By the time the verdict came, people have died and gone.

I felt extremely sad on 7 June (the day of the verdict) as I had seen people dying in front of me.

International Labour Organisation (ILO) released a report in April 2019, which dubbed the 1984 Bhopal Gas Tragedy as one among the world's major industrial accidents of the 20th century. The report stated that at least 30 tons of methyl isocyanate gas, released from the Union Carbide pesticide plant, had affected more than 600,000 workers and nearby inhabitants. Nowhere in the world would such a case take twenty-six years to come out with a verdict, pointed out M R Sivaraman.

A study by the National Library of Medicine, USA found a connection between the effects of exposure to methyl isocyanate gas and diseases like Hyperglycaemia (Diabetes), Uremia (kidney diseases), Pulmonary fibrosis, lung diseases & acidosis. The woes of those who were exposed to the gas still continues….

A Temple, a Secret Cellar and a Treasure

2011 was an eventful year as far as the Sree Padmanabhaswamy temple in Thiruvananthapuram was concerned. It became the richest temple in the world, richer than even the Vatican.

Ever since treasure in the form of gold ornaments worth crore of rupees was inventoried in the secret cellars of the temple, it became a centre of attraction. Not just journalists from all over India but from all over the world started pouring into the sleepy capital of Kerala.

And one person all of them wanted to talk to was the noted historian, ***Professor M G Sasibhooshan*** *an authority on the history of the Travancore royal family to whom the temple belonged.*

IT is said that the *Mathilakam* records mention the secret cellars and the treasures of the Padmanabhaswamy temple. Does that mean, there was knowledge of this great wealth earlier itself?[1]

---

[1] Mathilakam: Palm leaf scrolls that provide all the information on the temple and the history of the Kingdom of Travancore.

All those who have some knowledge of the history of Kerala know about the wealth of the Padmanabhaswamy temple. But only the eldest member of the Travancore royal family knew exactly how much wealth was there in the Padmanabhaswamy temple.

How far back can we go if we were to trace the history of the temple and its wealth?

There are many who say that the temple's history is as old as the Sangam period (3rd century BC to 3rd century AD in South India). In *Silappathikaram*, the epic poem in Tamil, written in the 5th-6th century AD by Prince Ilango Adigal, a sea-side golden temple called Adagamadam is mentioned. It also says the deity of the temple is Lord Vishnu in a reclining pose. Kannagi (the central character of *Silapathikaram*) is said to have come to the temple.

Many historians say that the temple mentioned is the Padmanabhaswamy temple, as its deity is Lord Vishnu in reclining pose and it is also near the sea-side. Why it was described as a golden temple was because it was a rich temple and also the one with golden *thazhikakudams* (domes on top of the *gopuram*). That is why the Adagamadam is Padmanabhaswamy temple itself.

Even in the *puranas* (religious texts) like *Varaha purana,* the temple is mentioned.

The first historical evidence about the temple is available in the Vaishnava Azhvar poet Nammazhvar's creations. These were written in the 9th century. He had written ten kirtanas in praise of this temple and the deity. His contemporary, *Thirumangai Azhvar* also had written kirtanas (lyrics in praise of divinity) about Padmanabhaswamy. These poems show without any doubt that this temple was in existence in the 9th century.

It is also mentioned in the 12th century in a Sanskrit poem by an unknown poet.

In the 13th century, there is a Malayalam creation, *Ananthapura Varnanam*.

Records show that people like Ramanuja Acharyar, Chaitanya, Guru Nanak, etc visited the temple. Guru Nanak had not started the Sikh religion then; he was a Vaishnava Goswami then. He had even written a poem on Sree Padmanabha and it is included in the Adi Granth (the sacred scripture of Sikhism).

In short, Padmanabhaswamy temple was known all over India long ago. Vaishnavites see this as one of the 108 Tirupatis.

Was it from the offerings of the devotees that this temple got its wealth, and were they kept in the secret chambers in earlier times too?

The assets of the temple were safely kept in the secret chambers all the time, that is, from the time the temple was built. Those who have learnt about the history of the temple knew there were assets, but nobody was aware of the extent or the worth. Yes, the assets were mainly the offerings from devotees, and also from the owners of the temple, that is, the Travancore royal family.

In this temple, devotees were not given much importance because it was owned by a family. In the early days, devotees from the public could only pray there and not give any offerings. That was because it was believed that if you offer anything to the God, you become the *dasa* of Sree Padmanabhaswamy (servant of the deity). Later, the family gave permission to the public to give offerings.

Was it after Marthanda Varma surrendered the state of Travancore to the temple that he became a *dasa* of Sree Padmanabha?

No, it is much before that itself. Not only the family but other kings who were their guests also started putting money in the hundi.

Did money from the state also go to the temple treasury?

No, there were three different treasuries; one for the temple, one for the state, and another personal. The personal treasury is inside the palace. The state treasury was kept outside the walls of the temple while the temple treasury was inside the premises.

Another important thing to note is, the Travancore royal family followed the matrilineal system. So, the money from the royal treasury did not go to the wife and children of the King but to his nephews and nieces. When I say royal treasury, I don't mean the revenue collection but the personal property that also went directly to the temple treasury.

How did they differentiate between the state and the temple treasury?

While revenue from the state property went to state treasury, revenue from the temple properties went to the temple treasury.

And, whatever the royal family got from their own land was their revenue. The family also contributed to the temple treasury. As rulers, they had the authority to spend one sixth of the state revenue, but this family did not spend that much because they led a very simple life.

Other than this, the Travancore family got revenue from exporting pepper to the world, and they lived on what they earned from this, though business from pepper started only in the 17th century.

The Travancore kingdom also collected land tax and that was added to the state exchequer. Land revenue went directly to the state treasury.

The temple also had a lot of property and the income from that property accrued to the temple treasury. In short, it was a rich State.

So, who does the assets found in the cellars belong to, the family or the temple?

It is the property of the temple. Though the wealth belonged to the temple, in some emergency situations, rulers could avail this for the benefit of the state, but they were bound to make restitution as soon as possible.

There was a recession in the 1930s and it is mentioned at many places that they had taken some wealth during that period, though there is no evidence to show that.

Who are the real owners of the temple property? Is there a trust?

In the old days, it belonged to the Travancore royal family. Before that, the five branches of the family had ownership rights. The senior-most member of these five families headed the trust. Later on, disputes arose between the members and the right went to two families.

There was a group of spiritual advisors to the temple, a sort of board called the *Ettara Yogam* which consisted of the Pottis (a sect of Brahmins in Kerala). There was also one Nair in the yogam. The maharaja was above the *Ettara Yogam*.

The tax collectors of the temple property were called *Ettuveettil Pillamars*. They were the children of the maharaja from his Nair wives. There were conflicts between the rulers and the *Ettuveettil Pillamars* due to which the temple was closed for fifty years or so. In fact, it was set fire to in the 17th century. It was reopened when Umayamma Rani ruled the state as the Regent Maharani.

Is there any truth in the talk that the wealth was kept in the scared chambers when Tipu Sultan started moving towards Travancore?

It was only a rumour and perpetuated by those who have no knowledge of history. Like I said, the secret chambers have always been there, and they contained the wealth of the temple.

How important is the treasure found in the chambers if you look at it from the historical, religious and cultural point of view?

From what we hear about the assets, there are no inscriptions. Yes, we can study about the diamonds, jewellery, ruby, pearls, etc they have found and movable idols, crowns, gold and silver bars.

You said earlier that the royal family conducted trade in pepper. Kerala also sold various other kinds of spices to many countries. Do you think this treasure will throw a light to Kerala's trade with the world?

The coins from those countries may be there. There are a lot of gems also in the chambers, which in all probability can be from the Deccan. As far as I know, they have not so far found anything that throws light on the kind of trade Kerala had with the world.

Today, all those who have no competence or knowledge of ancient temple history, are spouting all kinds of nonsense.

What should be done now with such a huge treasure as it is important that it has to be kept very safe?

Yes, it has to be kept safe, but you must remember that the treasure belongs to the temple and nobody else.

Is it not part of our history?

It is a part of our culture. It is a part of our pride. I consider it as a symbol of Indian pride or Hindu pride. All the other things come only later.

Should it remain inside the cellar?

For the time being, let it remain there. It should not go to the wrong hands. We should keep it safely.

Anyway, they are making an inventory under the instructions of the Supreme Court. Once the court comes out with a decision, as per the inventory, we must study the items which are of archaeological importance. This should be done under heavy security inside the temple.

There can be a beautiful museum there itself.

Do you envisage a museum of international standards coming up here like what we see in London or Paris?

Yes, it is possible. It has to be there. But you may need at least Rs 50 crore to construct such a museum. Who will fund it? The temple cannot sell this wealth and create a museum there. They should not, too. Let them take an appropriate decision at the appropriate time.

Who can take the decision?

The custodians of wealth, which is the temple right now. Also, the royal family.

But it is not the personal property of the royal family

No, it is not.

Do you think the interest world over is due to the possible history behind the wealth?

No, it is the glitter of the yellow metal that has dazzled the world. Only a minority will be interested in the historical aspect of the wealth. All the journalists who have come from all over the world have asked me questions only about the amount of wealth and the yellow metal, and not the historical aspects.

https://en.wikipedia.org

Sree Padmanabhaswamy is the richest temple in the world, richer than the Vatican. Even today, the authorities have not assessed the exact value of the treasure!
'The secret chambers have always been there, and they contained the wealth of the temple', said Prof M G Sasibhooshan.

She Rescues Girls from Trafficking

***Dr Sunitha Krishnan** is a gang-rape survivor. The incident happened when she was fifteen, but she fought the shame, fear and hypocrisies of society to start Prajwala, an organisation that rescues girls and women from trafficking.*

Even before I met her at her office in Secunderabad, she had warned me that she would have to stop the interview and run if she received a call to rescue a girl.

After all, the only mission in her life is to rescue girls from being trafficked.

YOU have rescued thousands of girls from getting trafficked. Do you think poverty is the reason that drives women to such situations?

Poverty is not a reason at all. I completely disagree with the argument that poverty and impoverishment are the reasons for trafficking. Though the reasons are multi-layered, it triggers from a situation of option-lessness which can happen in a very well-to-do broken family too.

A lonely child where husband and wife are fighting all the time can be as option-less as a child living in a labourer's family that is totally indebted and desperate to survive. Both have the same sense of desperateness, and both want to escape reality. In such a situation, not everybody gets trafficked. It is a certain personality and certain situation that makes a person vulnerable.

Across the world, you will see that hardly any physical coercion is used to exploit a person. Nobody gets kidnapped. It is largely deception through fraudulent means.

Today, the master plan of trafficking happens in such a way that the person actually feels that she is conniving in the act of getting exploited.

The biggest problem in trafficking today is that the line dividing 'I am part of the crime and I am a victim' has thinned down. The victim feels less like a victim and more responsible for what has happened to her. The whole thing is an act of deception.

The world doesn't realise that there are a huge number of organised criminals who are just looking around for vulnerable women. They are watching for the weak spot they can target. Their *modus operandi* is to make you feel part of the crime in such a way that you will never say that you are a victim.

What happens when the girl realises that she has become a victim?

By then, it will be too late. First, she is already trapped into the situation, and she is also made to believe that she is responsible for what has happened to her. And she feels guilty for what she has done. By this time, she is already inducted. The road inside is open for all.

With no exit?

I wouldn't say there is no exit; the exit is bleak.

Will a girl trapped inside be able to see the exit?

Even if she is able to see it physically, she will not see it emotionally and psychologically as she is so damn guilty to face the world. She feels responsible for what has happened to her.

What does trafficking or sex trafficking mean? It means you are raped for sure. It further means you are ashamed to face the world because you feel your body is also impure. Trafficking is a crime where your body is tortured, your spirit is broken, your determination is destroyed, and your soul is completely scarred.

So, even if all the doors are open, you will not budge. That is because you are psychologically paralysed.

When you rescue them, what kind of mental state are they in?

You won't believe when I say, we get beaten up more by the victim than the traffickers. In any other form of exploitation, the victim feels we are saving them and feels grateful for being saved, but in trafficking, the situation is different. Here, the victim doesn't want to be saved at all.

How do you manage to save them then?

Every rescue is forcibly done. That is the advantage the trafficking lobby has. They say, nobody is here by force, everybody is here by choice, and that this is a willing profession. We call it sex work to legitimise it.

But the truth is, close to 90 per cent of all women are deceived into this trade (in India). Nobody goes there as their primary choice. But those 90 per cent will not say they are deceived. This argument is used by traffickers across the country to legalise prostitution.

When the victims themselves are against you, how do you go on rescuing them?

I feel we are one of the gifted few who have sustained for so long; very few have remained in this field for this long. The hostility, the aggression, and the resistance by the victims destroy most NGOs, and that is why nobody wants to enter this field. Those who have entered go off after a while. But we have sustained for twenty-one years.

Is it your determination that keeps you going?

Yes, it is a totally individual-driven determination. I say that with all honesty and pride.

But today it is not an individual mission; the exercise is a collective effort.

Yes, in the initial years, it was a lonely battle. I have been lucky to see results in my life, and that was because I made it my goal to see the results. I did not speak in any public domain till I saw the results.

By results, do you mean rescuing and rehabilitation?

Not just rehabilitation but prevention too. If it is a young girl, our work is to give her education, get her employment and then actually integrate her back in society.

How can you prevent trafficking?

We do three things to prevent trafficking.

One is to educate girls of the crime and make them understand that there are predators walking around. Trafficking can happen to a school student, a college student, a slum dweller, a city dweller, that is, to women of all ages.

It is a demand-driven $858 billion industry! And demand is for children. So, we have a sensitising platform where our team goes to schools and colleges to sensitise girls about such a crime. We educate girls on the criminal walking around with various kinds of offers to lure girls, and how girls should spot them.

What we do next is, create community vigilance. The industry of sex trade is driven by the libido of men; it is the male demand for sex that is driving this industry.

We also target all men, talk to them, and gather them as Men Against Demand (MAD). One lakh men have pledged their support and through MAD, we are grouping the real men of the world against this crime.

Of late, we hear more and more stories of little girls, as old as three and four getting raped. Are such crimes on the rise or are they getting reported more?

It has always been there but only now are we talking about it. I feel the community as a whole has been denying this problem, and that starts with the parents to school authorities to everyone in society.

We need to understand that we are facing a real problem and the perpetrators are right within us; they are not like terrorists who come from outside.

There are women like me who give courage to many victims to talk about the crime. She doesn't have to feel ashamed to talk about it. It is the shame and fear that prevent a rape victim from talking about it.

Till the law takes its course, the girl will be in perpetual fear.

Society totally isolates such a girl....

Who is this society? Society comprises of us; you and me. Each one of us will have to contemplate; how we have become a part of the crime. Only then a change will come. Change will come only from within and not from outside.

What will you tell young girls and mothers out there?

They need to understand that it is an unsafe world, and they cannot walk around as if it is a safe world out there. So, you need to protect yourself.

For example, a three-year-old in Bengaluru who was raped, was repeatedly given chocolates by the criminal. Obviously, the mother had not told the girl not to accept chocolates from strangers and also not educated her about 'right touch and wrong touch'.

You mean we have to tell even the little girls that it is a big bad world outside?

Let us face it. It is a big bad world out there. You can't trust anyone. It doesn't mean we have to be paranoid and suspicious of everyone.

We have fantastic sensitive men and also horribly regressive women. Because there are layers and layers of grey. So, the solution also is multi-layered. There is no one answer to this diverse problem.

Today, India is perceived as a dangerous place for a woman. Is India an unsafe place for women to travel?

I will say India is as unsafe as any other city in the world. In the US, every four minutes, a woman is raped. The mechanism there is so good that the criminal gets arrested immediately and he is also punished. That is why the incident does not become big news. But I would definitely say every woman travelling in India should be careful.

The problem is, if someone behaves in a culturally inappropriate way, she gets attention. For example, if you behave in the old city of Hyderabad as if you were in Mumbai, you are in for serious trouble.

What is safety? Safety is about carrying yourself as per the context of the particular place.

Do you think the world will be a safe place for women one day?

Absolutely, it is to see that only, all of us are working day in and day out! My reason for being here is not to get name and fame; it is to see that every breath of mine is dedicated to women and children.

I can be a motivational speaker like hundreds of them out there and give *bhashans* (lectures) every day, but I prefer to be an activist and continue to do what I am doing.

Today, if I am given a Nobel Prize and at the same time, if there is a call to rescue, the rescue will be my priority and not any prize.

This mission is what I have chosen, and I will be here till my last breath.

The 2020 National Crime Records Bureau (NCRB) report says that 371,503 cases of crime against women were reported across the country in 2020 while the number of cases were 405,326 in 2019 and 378,236 in 2018. Crimes against women include cases of rape, outraging modesty, dowry deaths and harassment, acid attacks and kidnapping.

Uttar Pradesh topped the list with maximum number (49,385) of such cases followed by West Bengal (36,439), Rajasthan (34,535), Maharashtra (31,954) and Madhya Pradesh (25,640).

Another shocking part of the report was, of the total cases of crimes against women during the lockdown; there were 28,046 incidents of rape involving 28,153 victims. Out of the total victims, 25,498 were adults, while 2,655 were below the age of eighteen years.

The number of rape cases as defined in Indian Penal Code section 376, stood at 38,947 in 2016, 32,559 in 2017, 33,356 in 2018 and 32,033 in 2019.

And Dr Sunitha Krishnan continues to rescue women and girls from trafficking and getting abused!

A Raja, 2G Scam and the DMK

The 2G Spectrum Scam is described as the biggest scam independent India has ever seen.

Unfortunately, it happened under a prime minister whose image was that of an honest and clean person. When a scam of such mammoth proportions allegedly happened under his very nose, it made him one of the weakest prime ministers of India.

The 2G Spectrum Scam was about the irregularities in the allocation of Second Generation spectrum licenses for mobile communication and data transmission to telecom companies on a first-come, first-served basis in 2008 at the 2001 price level.

And the man allegedly behind the scam was the then telecom minister A Raja from the DMK.

Also allegedly involved was the DMK patriarch M Karunanidhi's daughter, K Kanimozhi, a member of Parliament.

After the opposition shouted for an investigation, the Comptroller and Auditor General of India (CAG), headed by Vinod Rai (a former IAS officer), came out with a report. It revealed that Raja had acted against the advice of TRAI, the law ministry, the finance ministry and bent the rules of the auction to benefit a few telecom players. By issuing 2G licenses at throwaway prices to some select applicants, there was a loss of Rs 1.76 lakh crore to the Department of Telecom.

A Raja who was forced to resign, was arrested in February 2011 and later in May, Kanimozhi also was arrested.

Though the DMK continued to be with the UPA at the Centre then, the relationship between the two allied parties strained after the arrests.

2011 also saw the Tamil Nadu State assembly elections where the Congress was a smaller partner in the DMK alliance.

Not only the 2G scam, the DMK was going through its worst crisis ever with many of its leaders facing corruption charges and the party confronting allegations of using money power to win the elections. Then, the DMK chief and former Tamil Nadu Chief Minister M Karunanidhi's family was accused of taking over the entertainment industry in the State.

There were troubles aplenty, but the party spokesperson ***T K S Elangovan*** *pooh-poohed all the allegations.*

WHAT is the mood of the party and its cadres after the 2G Spectrum Scam and the seat-sharing fiasco with the Congress?

All these things are part and parcel of all elections. Alliance partners will seek more seats and those who allot the seats will try to reduce the number. Finally, there will be a settlement. There is nothing new about it.

What exactly was the problem between the DMK and the Congress? You even threatened to pull out of the Union government.

When (Congress leader) Ghulam Nabi Azad came to Chennai to have discussions with our leader (M Karunanidhi), he agreed on a certain number of seats. After he went back to Delhi, the Congress changed its mind. He announced that the Congress leadership wanted a few more seats.

Instead of talking to our leader in Chennai, he announced publicly that the Congress would not agree to the number of seats we had offered. This gave our leader the impression that they were not really interested in an alliance with us.

We have always accommodated, and our leader even now tries to accommodate all our allies. We felt that one or two seats should not be a matter of contention.

How much has this incident strained the relationship between the two parties?

Whenever there's a clash between the leaders, it is the cadres who get agitated and frustrated. When we announced that our ministers were resigning, our cadres were happy! That was the mood of the party then.

Your cadres were happy when the DMK decided to withdraw from the UPA government?

It is not that our cadres are against the Congress. While the drama was going on – leaders were coming here, discussing the issue and going back – the cadres were anxiously waiting outside for a settlement. Our leader kept them posted of what was happening.

All these things were playing on their minds. So, when we said our ministers were resigning, they were happy because all the uncertainty ended then.

The DMK cadres will follow whatever instructions are given to them by the leadership. We have people and units working in all the panchayats and villages in the State. There is no doubt that the DMK will work at the grassroots level for the alliance to succeed.

How much will the 2G Spectrum Scam affect the DMK's prospects?

I must answer the question in two parts: Firstly, about the allegations and secondly about the performance of the State government.

In the last five years, Kalaignar (as Karunanidhi is referred to by DMK cadres) has done a lot for the State in the fields of industrialisation, employment generation, infrastructure development and social welfare measures. There were no compromises in these areas.

You mean because of all these measures, the 2G Spectrum Scam will not have an impact?

It will have an impact. I don't deny that. You must remember that people are not going to elect Raja; that is a different issue. The question is whether people want Kalaignar to continue or not.

Has it not damaged the DMK's image?

This has been projected as the biggest scam the country has ever witnessed, but it is not so. Other political parties are taking advantage of the situation, based on the Comptroller and Auditor General's (CAG) report. The CAG has always been critical of the government. Though it talks about the loss to the exchequer, there is no physical loss, only an estimated loss.

Raja has only followed the recommendations of the Telecom Regulatory Authority of India (TRAI). There was no violation in the allocation. Raja is very confident. He says he is clean.

Do you think the scam will have more of an impact in urban areas than rural areas?

Those in the urban areas may think about it more. But can they expect a better government from (AIADMK chief) Jayalalitha than from Kalaignar? Compared to the two tenures (when the State was ruled by the AIADMK and Jayalalitha), there was better rule when the DMK was in power.

The DMK might have hoped that the 2G scam would not have any impact in the assembly elections. But the electorate in 2014 had other thoughts. The DMK was massacred in the elections, having won just 23 seats on its own, reducing it to the 3rd largest party after the AIADMK (150) and the DMDK (29). It was one of the worst performances by the party, no matter what T K S Elangovan said.

India, an Economic Mess

In 2012, Indian economy under the economist-turned-Prime Minister went through one of the worst periods.

It had its sharpest downturn in a decade. With borrowing costs high and huge delays in government approvals, corporate investments came to a standstill. There was no cash flow in the market. Then, there was high inflation, slower hiring and dull consumer spending.

This was not what the people of India expected from Dr Manmohan Singh, the architect of India's economic liberalisation.

In fact, ***S Gurumurthy****, the Convenor of the Swadeshi Jagaran Manch remarked that the Prime Minister's economic knowledge was frozen thirty years ago!*

INDIA'S economic growth is at nine-year low now. Is it because of the global slowdown or bad management by the finance minister (P Chidambaram)?

I have three ways of responding to the question. First, the economic theories which we have adopted from the West are also responsible for this kind of situation. That is because these economic theories are based on financial capitalism. Their theory is that global capital financial flow will take care of India's economy.

So, the normal precautions we take like trade deficit, current account deficit, unguided imports, have not been taken care of in the last six-seven years. I would say the global financial capitalist theories failed in 2008.

Would you call it crony capitalism?

No. Crony capitalism is a word which the West invented to decry the Asian economies which are largely family based.

Financial capitalism is founded on the theory that money generates itself and there is no need to have a guarded approach to money. Even savings is not needed, and that credit will take care of everything. This kind of phenomenally irresponsible theories were generated in the last thirty years.

See how we applied the theory to ourselves. We relied on the funds which were flowing to the stock market and liberalised our imports, based on that. If imports are liberalised consistent with exports, that is a cautiously liberalising economy. If you are going to liberalise your imports based on stock market money, it is based on the financial capitalist model which the West generated in the last thirty years. They have admitted now that it was a wrong model.

So, my first response is, it is the financial capitalist theories which we imported wholesale from the West that did our economy in. And we felt that this financial flow will continue and kept on importing and run our economy. This was the first major mistake we did. We should have checked it sometime in 2009, maximum in 2010.

Who will you hold responsible for these decisions; the prime minister or the finance minister?

I will hold the entire UPA responsible. The commerce minister functions in a certain way, the finance minister functions in another, and the industries minister functions in yet another way. See, all these are interconnected.

Whether this financial capitalist model which makes you dependant on the global financial flows is a dependable, reliable, sustainable model is a decision one ministry cannot take; it has to be taken by the government as a whole based on consensus.

What about the role of the prime minister who is an economist?

Yes, he is supposed to be an economist though I would say that his economics knowledge is frozen thirty years ago.

Today in India, imports have increased tremendously while exports have slackened. Where will this lead to?

That is my second point. By importing irrationally, without applying our mind, we ran huge trade deficits with a country like China.

This has meant transfer of jobs from India to China. Huge power equipments in the power sector, petroleum sector, telecom sector, etc are coming from China now.

Let us assume you have a huge exports surplus, and you are throwing this money into China, then it doesn't matter. Here, you are bringing in money into the stock market and importing these goods from China. This makes no economic sense at all.

This year, we have a trade deficit of $36 billion with China. The trade deficit we have incurred with China in the last three-four years is around $120-130 billion. Overall, we have a trade deficit of $187 billion.

The trade deficit has affected the value of the Rupee and it is falling.

Yes, it has affected the value of rupee, our economy, our capital goods sector and our employment.

The third reason why India's economic growth has suffered is, you manage the economy through sentiments. This is the most foolish way of approaching an economy. While you must work on the fundamental strength of an economy, you are managing it on sentiments.

For example, it is not correct to say that because liberalisation has been put on a brake, Indian economy is going down the drain. It is because of over-liberalisation on the imports side and also on the over-dependence on the global capital finance model that the economy is under-performing. And it is not because you have not allowed the Walmart to enter the Indian retail sector.

Are you against the multi-national companies entering the retail sector?

I am against corporates entering the retail sector, but you can't ban them by law. There is only a niche population that needs big supermarkets and malls.

Are you against multinationals because the big fish will eat all the small fish?

I am against it because they promote consumerism. It will change the character of Indian families. It will have a deeper socio-economic impact.

But I know that the capacity of the Indian corporates to damage the small and medium business people is limited. Why do they want multinationals as partners? They want to comb it off like they did in the telecom sector. Why do they clamour for foreign investment when they should be protesting against it? They are only here to make money in the interim period.

What kind of impact will the entry of corporates and MNCs have on the economy?

How much investment will India get if you open the retail sector? One billion? Two billion? They say, Indian economy is in difficulty because these kind of reforms are stopped and that the rupee value has to improve if the Indian economic growth has to revive.

According to me, the word reform itself is wrong. Reform implies as if somebody has deformed the economy! Who has deformed it? The very reformers were deformers once! You are trying to repair it and call it reform. It is again another kind of deformation.

What you have to do now is, apply the most practical mode of reform.

What is the most practical form?

I will give you examples of what is not practical.

Trade is a very important sector in India. Instead of a corporate model, we follow a community model. Communities after communities are involved throughout India for hundreds of years in trade. And you want to replace these communities with corporates?

It is wrong to think that if you bring in corporates, they will rebuild your economy.

In India, we have seven crore small and marginal farming families who produce in such small quantities, and they are linked by small traders. The average size of the land holding is two hectares. Corporates can never fill in this supply chain unless there is contract farming. And, if you bring in contract farming, rural India will be destroyed. As much as 63 per cent of the agricultural produce is distributed within the villages, and only 37-38 per cent get into the market. If you make these people contract farmers, they become landless labourers and the social consequences are unthinkable.

Do you feel India is giving too much importance to the stock market when it affects only a small margin in the country?

Absolutely. Only two and a half per cent of Indian savings gets into the stock market. Only foreigners play there. And we call it our stock market.

There is no Indian orientation to our economic thinking. Our economic establishment is completely sold out to the Western model of development as it was sold out to the Soviet model 30-40 years ago.

The corporate sector is not growing and it is the non-corporate sector, which is the traditional sector, that is growing.

And Indian families are saving even today. Only because they are saving, the government is able to fund its deficits. They are able to get the capital requirements only from the Indian families. And you want to destroy the conservative nature of the families by promoting consumerism. If their savings go down, from where will the Indian government get its capital?

But has it not gone down because of inflation, price rise and the value of the rupee falling?

I agree with you. Already, there is pressure on them due to inflation. So, why do you promote consumerism?

For our capital requirement, we are getting only 2 per cent from outside India and the rest of the capital is generated within the country. And our capital investment is 32-34 per cent. We could generate that much capital only because of the savings habit of the people. And you want to destroy it.

Will you hold growing imports as the major reason for the economy slowing down?

Yes. This way, you have hit the economy at its base. In 2004, when the telecom sector grew, you should have had the far sight to invest in hardware. You began importing hardware from outside.

When you were planning huge power sector expansion, you should have ensured that the power sector capital equipments are (made) generated in India and easy to get. Instead, you made imports easy. Now, all the power plants manufacturers in India are under stress.

How do you explain the economic growth in double digits till recently?

Growth beyond 8 and 8½ per cent is because of financial capitalism. I will not take it as real growth. About 8-8.5 per cent growth is something India could achieve on its own. Once you are dependent on stock market money for financing your economy, then 8-8.5 per cent is not sustainable. India, however, can achieve 8-8.5 per cent growth on its own.

But now, it has slipped to almost 5 per cent....

That's because of the past mistakes. If they rationalise the import duty structure like put anti-dumping duty on imports of certain categories of goods from China and others, obviously, the industrial activities will pick up.

Why do you think India did not get affected in the beginning when the entire world economy slowed down?

The easy availability of capital deceived us like the Americans were deceived by the idea that the rise in the home value is going to be a permanent affair.

Why do you think the value of Indian rupee is coming down drastically?

That is because India's rupee value is linked to global economy. It's not linked to the fundamentals of Indian economy. Nobody looks at the huge capital that is generated by the savings of the Indian families and gives credit to Indian rupee. They are only looking at the exports balance sheet.

At 25 per cent depreciation of rupee value, we lost 40 per cent depreciation in the last three years. That means the rupee value of our imports has gone up by Rs 7-8 lakh crore. You are importing that much inflation into India.

How do you react to some growth rating agencies rating India poorly?

That is why I said, Indian economy runs by managing sentiments. If Standard & Poor rated India well, we are okay. If S&P threatens to rate down India, we are in trouble.

Alan Greenspan's model of managing the American and the global economy has failed with the collapse of the financial capitalism. The financial capitalist model which ran the world for thirty years, is no more a sustainable model.

Germany and France have already said that they didn't want the Anglo-Saxon financial capitalist model. It overrides all other factors in the economy, like production, distribution, capital formation, etc

Do you feel the German model of giving more importance to domestic production and distribution will be followed soon by other countries? Germany is one country that is not affected by the global slowdown now.

I will put it this way. Domestic should be the core while the external should be the additive. It cannot be the reverse. In China's case, it is the reverse. It will be a problem for China. They are running a huge risk. While domestic consumption is 57-58 per cent in India, it is only 36-37 per cent in China.

I would say India has a balanced internal economy; only its external economy is bad.

Do you feel the current economic crisis will result in a change in the way countries look at globalisation?

It is already happening but there is no debate in India. All over the world, the Anglo-Saxon model and derivatives are being discussed but is there any debate in India? Those who decide economic policies have nothing to do with India; there is a lack of understanding. That is the reason for our sharp downfall.

See, even today, people trust the rupee and save money. Most still plan a surplus budget.

Can you get a better kind of people to frame India's economic policies?

Do you feel the policy makers and economists of India look towards the West while framing policies?

Why talk about economists, what about the media? Theories from the West are sold to India and turned into convictions.

As the Convenor of Swadeshi Jagaran Manch, how worried are you to see exports coming down and imports going up?

I am really worried. Now the whole world is becoming swadeshi. Look at the way Germany is becoming swadeshi.

America is trying to turn swadeshi. What we say as swadeshi is, domestic economy, domestic savings, etc should be the core of the economy and global can only be additive.

Globalisation changed this and that is what we objected to. Each country has every right to protect its interest, like what Obama is trying to do now.

Where do you see Indian economy in the coming years?

Ultimately, the country will correct itself. The entire growth was not brought about by the government or the government's economic policies.

When the government began withdrawing the restrictions on people, they began working on their own. You know, the corporate sector has been able to add only 12 lakh jobs in the last twenty years. Government jobs have come down in this period. The rest of the growth has been because of the people of this country.

You mean, the entrepreneurs?

Yes, the entrepreneurs in the small and medium sector and the communities are generating wealth for India.

It is the families that are generating savings, but you are celebrating fund managers, stock market investors and big corporates who are doing nothing.

If you concentrate on the entrepreneurs and not on ASSOCHAM (The Associated Chambers of Commerce & Industry of India), FICCI (The Federation of Indian Chambers of Commerce & Industry) and CII (The Confederation of Indian Industry), India will produce better results. If one secretary of the government of India is deputed to take care of the 350-400 industrial clusters, they will understand India better and India will perform better.

What kind of changes you foresee globally?

Countries which are leading the world now will not lead after ten years. There will not be anything like a global order. WTO will lose all its meaning; it has already become redundant. I had said in 1994 that WTO would collapse. There will not be a single global leader; every country will be working for themselves. It will be competitive capitalism but at the national level.

'It is the families that are generating savings, but you are celebrating fund managers, stock market investors and big corporates who are doing nothing', warned S Gurumurthy, the Convenor of the Swadeshi Jagaran Manch in 2012.

Interestingly, the BJP-led Narendra Modi government which came to power in 2014 also followed the same economic policies that the UPA governments followed!

Scams, Scandals and a CBI

During the UPA2 period, innumerable scams came out in the open at regular intervals like the 2G scam, the coal scam, the Commonwealth Games scam and so on.

And the chief investigating agency in India, the CBI while investigating various scams, exposed itself as a slave of the ruling government. There was a lot of criticism about the way the CBI functioned during that period. There was also a clamour for making the CBI an autonomous body.

It was when the image of the CBI was at its lowest that I spoke to ***Dr R K Raghavan****, former director of the Central Bureau of Investigation. He belonged to the 1963 batch of the Indian Police Service (IPS). He was the Director General of Police, Tamil Nadu, when he was chosen to head the CBI.*

THE trust people had in the CBI has gone down drastically in the last six years or so, especially after the 2G scam, the coal scam, the Commonwealth Games scam, etc

I would only partially agree with you when you say the common man's trust in the CBI has gone down over the years.

It is very difficult to say accurately whether it has gone up or gone down.

More and more cases are entrusted to the CBI by the courts. There is also the demand from the public that the CBI should investigate wherever there is a controversy. So, there is a contradiction here.

On one hand, people say they no longer trust the CBI as they feel the CBI is being run by the ruling party. On the other hand, there is a demand from the public for the CBI to probe controversial happenings.

Wherever there is no politics involved, people feel the case should be handled by a neutral agency like the CBI rather than the police.

That is why I said there is a kind of contradiction here.

Where there is no direct political involvement, people still trust the efficiency of the CBI. The same applies to the courts as well.

There is basically no complaint about the quality of the CBI's work. The popular feeling is that the government's stranglehold over the CBI does not permit it to act to its full potential, independently and fearlessly.

The government's failure to accord autonomy and freedom of action has directly affected the CBI's image.

Of late, the Supreme Court has been monitoring certain cases entrusted to the CBI, asking the agency to report directly to the court....

That is because the court feels the CBI would be under pressure from the government. So, wherever the court feels the CBI is likely to be under pressure, they say they will monitor it.

This is similar to what happened to the *Hawala* case when the then Prime Minister, P V Narasimha Rao's involvement was suspected, and the court felt the agency would not be able to work independently.[1]

This arrangement has been working reasonably well, and because the court is monitoring, the investigation gains more credibility.

Because the CBI director is appointed by the government and the agency's financial needs are met by the government, the government has a stranglehold over the CBI.

If they want more cars, more travel abroad, it is the government which holds the purse strings. Naturally, the government has a huge hold over the organisation.

Has the situation always been like this?

My perception is that in the past two or three decades, there is greater and greater interference in the CBI's activities by various governments.

When did the deterioration start?

You can't specifically say when. The general impression is that it has deteriorated very badly in recent times. This is sad.

We do not know when we will have a government that is enlightened enough to reverse the drift.

Why has the situation been deteriorating like this, according to you?

That is a reflection of the nature of current politics.

---

[1] A political and financial scandal involving payments allegedly sent by politicians as black money through four hawala brokers, namely the Jain brothers. The bribery scandal implicated some of the top politicians in the country.

People get the impression that the ruling parties use the CBI to settle political scores. Is it true?

The impression that the CBI is being used to settle political ends is partially true. I would not like to name names.

Yes, the general feeling is that as the government has so much control over the CBI, it is but natural that their own people and their friends are protected by giving directions to the CBI. This is the reason why the courts have started monitoring investigations.

A Gauhati High Court ruling said, the CBI did not have the authority to arrest any accused. What kind of implications will it have on cases taken up by the CBI?

The Gauhati HC ruling did come as a bolt from the blue. Fortunately, it has been stayed by the Supreme Court. Otherwise, it would have paralysed all current investigations, and raised a big question mark on the legality of past investigations.

The Guwahati court has taken a particular view, and it has been challenged by the government. Now both of them will have to argue before the Supreme Court. Till the Supreme Court gives the ruling after hearing the petitioner and the government, we cannot say anything. We do not know whether the ruling will stay or be reversed. It is not desirable to speculate just now.

In your opinion, could the government issue an ordinance to ratify all acts of the CBI and protect its status as a police force to avoid the adverse effect from the high court ruling?

The government is well within its right to issue an ordinance, clarifying all the powers enjoyed by the CBI. However, this would have to take the form of a regular CBI Act.

In an affidavit filed in the Supreme Court, the Centre said the CBI director could not be given the *ex-officio* power

of secretary, as it would amount to vesting unbridled power in one authority.

It also opposed providing autonomy to the CBI. I am not surprised that the government has taken the position it took in denying autonomy to the CBI, and rejecting the demand that the director should enjoy the powers vested in a full-fledged secretary to the Government of India. There is a certain bias that operates here.

Recently, both the prime minister (Dr Manmohan Singh) and the finance minister (P Chidambaram) questioned the way the CBI is functioning....

Yes, it could have been avoided. It could demoralise the CBI.

The Prime Minister specifically said the CBI had no authority to question policies. What if the policies are detrimental to the country or made in a corrupt manner?

The line dividing 'policy' from a routine administrative act is thin indeed. It is very difficult for the CBI to be always conscious of this, and if it transgresses the distinction by mistake, it cannot be faulted.

Perhaps the Supreme Court can explain how exactly this happens. Ultimately, we have to get help from the court.

Where do you draw the line?

It is very difficult for me to say anything specific on this. A policy guideline is very broad and sometimes vague, but administrative acts are specific. When an administrative act violates policy, then there is a problem.

The government is not for autonomy for the CBI, but people feel the investigating agency should have autonomy....

Autonomy is not the solution for all evils. But with more autonomy, the CBI will become more professional, there will be more adherence to law, procedure and the Constitution, and it will not work in favour of the ruling party.

I won't say it will solve all problems, but it will be better than now.

How important is it for the CBI to have autonomy?

Autonomy and performance usually go hand-in-hand. These are days of complaints against people in high places inside and outside government.

If these individuals have to be investigated, there is no alternative but to ensure that the CBI is an autonomous body that exercises all the powers conferred on it by the criminal law of the land without fear or favour.

Is there any ideal situation for the CBI to function?

I have said in various fora that the power to conduct the preliminary inquiry should be with the CBI and that it should not be at the mercy of the government. Then, it should have the power to register a case without waiting for the government's approval. It should have the power to file a charge-sheet in the court against an individual without sanctions from the government. It should have the power to appeal against acquittal without depending on the approval from the government.

Can you name any such investigating agency that functions without being in the control of the government?

The FBI (the Federal Bureau of Investigation) in the US, to a large extent, has been kept out of the purview of the executive authority. I know the FBI enjoys a lot of independence and it is not at the mercy of the (American) President for any preliminary inquiry.

The Supreme Court recently commented that the CBI was a 'caged parrot'. Is it so?

The Supreme Court's depiction of the CBI was most appropriate, and no one can take umbrage at it. With the kind of constraints on it, the organisation is rightly viewed as a 'caged parrot'.

The image the CBI has is that it is an appendage of the government. Is it true?

This impression is true to a large extent. A lot depends upon the CBI leadership.

When you were director of the CBI, did you face political pressures?

Every director is subjected to some kind of pressure. Ultimately, it all depends on the individual and the maturity and sense of fair play of the director. You have to have balance. It is up to the director to cope with the pressure and if he is a man of character, he can.

How did you cope with the pressure?

You listen to people and take your own decisions according to your conscience and according to the law. There is a tendency for the government to give you instructions, but it is for you to examine the instructions and decide whether they are ethical and in accordance to the law and then take your own decisions.

The director should not blindly obey the government or blindly oppose the government. Ultimately, a lot depends on the maturity of the director and his moral fibre.

How much independence did you have when you were the CBI director?

I, as director, enjoyed a reasonable degree of independence although I would have liked to have been much more of an independent entity.

Even in 2022 when the NDA was ruling the country, the CBI continued to be called a 'caged parrot'.

'Every director is subjected to some kind of pressure', R K Raghavan had said.

It only depicts one thing; whichever party forms the government, the ruling party likes to 'cage' organisations like the CBI so that it can settle scores.

Election Time Again

From the beginning of 2014, the country was in election mode.

And the 'mother of all scams', the 2G Scam became the nemesis of UPA2.

The 2G Spectrum Scam was one of the most talked-about scandals in India, perhaps after the Bofors scandal.

According to the CBI charge sheet, several laws were violated, and bribes paid to favour certain firms in granting 2G spectrum licenses.

***P C Chacko**, the Congress MP from Thrissur, was the Chairman of the Joint Parliamentary Committee that probed the 2G Scam.*

The result of the JPC committee was that 2G Scam was not a scam at all!

When I spoke to P C Chacko, he was very confident that 2G Scam would have no impact on the elections, and that there would be a UPA3.

AT a press conference, you said the Prime Minister was responsible for the UPA getting a bad image as he never

spoke to the media or tried to talk about the good things the UPA had done. Do you hold Dr Manmohan Singh solely responsible for the UPA's bad image?

No. In fact, my statement was only partially reported. I was explaining the UPA's achievements in the last ten years. Somebody asked me why our party was on the defensive. I said, we could not sell our achievements properly. Then he asked me, whose failure is it? What I said was: From the prime minister to every member of our party, is responsible.

Our achievements should have reached the people, and if we couldn't do so, it is our failure. We were not communicative as we should have been, and it was a collective failure. I never blamed the Prime Minister.

I also said, we would form the next government, UPA3.

You spoke of the UPA's achievements. There were so many scams. Almost every day, one scam or the other was being reported.

Scams did not really happen. Whatever the others say, I am one person who can say that with all authenticity because I was investigating the 2G Scam.

The 2G Scam is no Scam. The media must have celebrated the 2G Scam, but it is no Scam.

There was some impropriety in giving licenses, irrespective of the priority of the application, and that mistake was done by (former telecom minister) A Raja. He was in jail for that failure, and the government did not defend him. He is still undergoing trial.

According to the CAG, the government's mistake was selling spectrum at a lower price and not by auction. This is totally unfounded. That is the basis of the allegation. So, I can repeatedly say that 2G is no scam at all.

A Raja said several times that the Prime Minister was fully aware of what he was doing. What does it mean?

It means that the licenses were given at a fixed price. What is 2G? Rs 1,650 crore (Rs 16.5 billion) was the price decided by the government for a pan India license, which was the fee recommended by the TRAI (Telecom Regulatory Authority of India). Whether that price should have been in the auction or not, was the question.

The Prime Minister only advised Raja to go for a transparent auction. Raja wrote back to the Prime Minister that TRAI had recommended a fixed price. He said, giving at a fixed price would increase tele-density, and that would reduce telephone charges.

Today, if India is enjoying the largest tele-density in the world, it is all because we could sell (spectrum) at a lower price. So, there is no scam as reported or celebrated by the media.

You said 2G is no scam at all, but people call it the mother of all scams.

That is your problem. The media, once they break a story, they go on and on to substantiate it. You plant a story today and what do you want to do tomorrow? You want to substantiate that. So, you call it the mother of all scams.

But do you know there is a 500-page report prepared by an inquiry committee headed by me? Why are they not demanding a discussion in the Parliament on the report? When I placed the report in the Parliament, have you heard any single Opposition leader give notice for discussion? They could have established that there was a scam. But this report says the 2G scam is no scam. Our government is suffering because of the media hype on these scams.

Now, we have to tell people the truth so that they will be the final arbiter.

Raja was in jail....

Why was Raja in jail? Because there was an impropriety in the first-come, first-serve policy. When that priority was overtaken, when the cut-off date for the application was advanced, it was found as an irregularity by the CBI. That was why criminal misappropriation or forgery was placed against Raja. That was why he was in jail and not for any scam.

The DMK has given him a ticket.

I don't have anything to say about the DMK giving him a ticket. We have nothing to do with the DMK. We severed our connection with the DMK on this issue. We said Raja was wrong on certain counts. They wanted us to defend Raja and our government did not go to that extent. Had it been the BJP or any other party, they would have defended their ally.

Why are we suffering in Tamil Nadu today? Why did we lose Raja's party? Because we put Raja and Kanimozhi in jail for impropriety, and not for the scam.

All the opinion polls paint a bad picture for the Congress.

Out of the ten predictions, five say the opposite. That is no prediction at all. The mood of the people is changing every day. You see the fight between Advani and Narendra Modi, Murali Manohar Joshi and Modi, the expelled BJP leader Jaswant Singh and Modi. When such fights are taking place in a party, do you think people will repose their confidence in them?

You compare this with a leader like Sonia Gandhi who has sacrificed all power when all the positions were available for her. And here, the veterans are fighting for a seat. So, the BJP's image is suffering.

So, I think we are gaining day by day, and the BJP is losing day by day.

Many see a Narendra Modi wave in India....

Absolutely not. It is a high charged publicity organised by Modi's media managers. Event management is propping up Modi, and this has not happened before in Indian politics. Moneybags and propaganda machinery are behind all this. Beyond that, there is no wave for Modi at all.

If he were to be the prime minister?

It is out of the question. It is something that is not going to happen.

I have four decades of political experience, and I am telling you, Modi becoming the prime minister of India is not going to happen. That is because India is a secular country, and I am not going to believe for a moment that the secular conscience of India will permit Modi, a hardcore communalist, to become India's prime minister.

He says he will develop India like he developed Gujarat.

Development of Gujarat is a bogus slogan. Kerala is far more developed than Gujarat. There are half a dozen States in India that are far more developed than Gujarat.

What Modi did in Gujarat was, he sold public property to the bigwigs of the Indian industry. It was an outright sale of Gujarat and nothing else.

Twenty years ago, we started the Narmada Dam project, and it has not yet been completed and farmers are not getting water. Child mortality, maternal mortality... you take any parameter, Gujarat is lagging behind many States in India.

What is progress? You take any socio-economic index, and Modi's State is far behind. His lies will come out and people will reject him outright.

You said recently, the Communists have become undemocratic. We get the impression that in the Congress party, all the decisions are taken by the Nehru-Gandhi family.

Absolutely not. Where was the Nehru family in the last ten years? From (the then prime minister) Narasimha Rao to Dr Manmohan Singh, all the leaders were from outside the family. The Nehru family could have captured power, and Rahul Gandhi could have become prime minister any day in the last five years. Sonia Gandhi could have become prime minister in the last ten years, had she wanted to, but did they try to do anything of that sort? No!

I am the chairman of the screening committee (to choose candidates) for Punjab, Delhi and Haryana. Soniaji told me, 'We are not going to take any decision, you decide'. We have internal democracy in our party, and we see to it that nobody takes dictatorial decisions.

What you said is an allegation, and allegations will always be there.

The impression is that the buck stops at 10, Janpath (residence of Sonia Gandhi).

That is the impression they (the BJP) want to spread. But those who know the inner dynamics of the Congress, even the journalists in Delhi, know that every decision is taken after wider consultation.

We have a Congress Parliamentary Board, we have a Central Election Committee, we have a working committee, we have a core group and all the decision-making bodies meet on a regular basis and their decision prevails.

The 2009 election campaign was spearheaded by Sonia Gandhi for the Congress. This time, it is Rahul Gandhi. Why does the party depend only on this one family?

It is not just one family; it is the conscience of the country. They are not just individuals; they are the embodiment of the spirit of nationalism and freedom struggle. So, it is natural that the family will have a certain glamour and charisma.

In the Communist party, people like A K Gopalan (one of the founding members of CPI-M) and E K Nayanar (former communist chief minister of Kerala) had the kind of goodwill which a (Sitaram) Yechury or a (Prakash) Karat cannot get. Those who cannot fight the Congress come out with such silly arguments.

You said UPA3 will rule the country. If it materialises, will Rahul Gandhi be the prime minister?

We all wanted Rahulji to take over earlier itself, but he was not very keen on taking up any position. He wanted to strengthen the party and change the political culture of this country. A totally new thinking was infused into the Congress by Rahulji. He represents the mature young leaders of the country. The Congress wishes that Rahulji takes over, as India is a country of *young* voters.

We want a generational change in the party. That is not because he is from a particular family. That is because Rahul is a young, hardworking man who has ideas on how to impress young voters.

Rahul Gandhi was in the forefront of the 2012 UP assembly election, but the Congress fared very badly. Do you

feel he doesn't have the charisma to bring the Congress back to power?

Winning and losing are part of an election. We won the Himachal Pradesh election. We won the Karnataka election. And Rahulji was the main campaigner.

You are only counting where we lost. You are not counting where we won. You don't even remember his victories. When you remember UP, you must remember Karnataka and Himachal also.

Remember what P C Chacko said in the interview, 'I have four decades of political experience, and I am telling you, Modi becoming the prime minister of India is not going to happen'.

But people had other ideas....

Is there a Modi Wave?

What surprised everyone once the 2014 general election dates were announced was the BJP announcing the name of the controversial chief Minister of Gujarat, Narendra Damodardas Modi as the prime ministerial candidate, overlooking seniors like L K Advani, Murli Manohar Joshi and Sushma Swaraj.

While the Congress boasted about a UPA3 ruling India for another five years, most of the exit polls predicted that no party would win a comfortable majority.

Except the one conducted by ***Dr Rajeeva Karandikar****, director of the Chennai Mathematical Institute, and one of India's leading mathematicians and psephologists.*

Earlier, he had predicted the DMK's success in the 2006 Tamil Nadu elections, the AIADMK's victory in 2011, Nitish Kumar winning in Bihar in 2005 and 2010, and also Mamata Banerjee's victory in 2011.

His prediction for the 2014 Lok Sabha elections was that the National Democratic Alliance (NDA) would have a comfortable win with 270 to 282 seats.

He also said that there was a Modi wave throughout the country, so also an anti-Congress wave!

Dr Karandikar spoke to me on how he and his team conducted the exit polls, and the mathematics involved in it.

ALMOST half a dozen exit poll results came out including yours. There is some difference between all of them. How much do you expect your poll results to come right because in 2004 and 2009, many exit poll results went wrong?

Yes, in 2004, it went horribly wrong, but I was not involved in the poll. In 2009, I won't say our survey was wrong as we got our indication correctly. We said 235 seats for the UPA, and they got 260. This time also, I expect the direction to be right.

The mid-point of ours is 276 for the NDA but I expect plus or minus 20 seats.

How important are such samples to get the exit poll results right?

For exit polls, the choice of sample is the most important criterion. In fact, in my opinion, an exit poll in India is very difficult. That is why we do a survey a day after the poll, and not when they come out of the polling booth.

What is the advantage in conducting a survey a day after the poll?

The randomisation and proper sampling do not work well when you do exit polls after polling. You can't stand there with a list of names and questions asking people who they voted for. We have to leave that to the enumerator; to whom to talk to.

How do you choose the sample in a diverse country like India?

First, we randomly choose constituencies. Then, we randomly choose polling booths. Then, we get hold of the voters list and randomly choose voters.

Most poll surveys decide the kind of sample they want but we choose only randomly. We do not decide the profile but randomly choose them. Many choose male and female separately, but we do not do that too. It is like you put ten names in a box, shake it and then take out a name without looking at it.

Whenever we use the random method, we generally get things right.

What about the different States in India, the conditions of which are so different from each other?

We use a technique called systematic sampling which automatically gives each State proportional number of constituencies, at least each of the big States.

If there are 130 constituencies nationwide, our systematic sampling will give me ten constituencies from Tamil Nadu automatically. This is the technical way which is statistically based. As we follow a proper methodological poll, we do not have to use our intuition. We strictly go by what our numbers say.

How much will the results go wrong if the samples are not right?

It can go completely wrong. If the samples are not right, the poll will have no meaning. Then, it will be like the 2004 situation.

How different is doing an exit poll for an assembly election and the Lok Sabha election?

Mathematically, there is no difference; it is quite similar. The methods we use are the same. The only difference is, carrying out a nationwide poll requires a lot more manpower and a lot more money.

I had 21,000 samples for the Lok Sabha elections but for an assembly election, I might have got a maximum of 5,000 to 6,000 samples.

How does a small sample of 21,000 work in a country of more than a billion people? Because you choose randomly?

Yes, that is the power of choosing by random. It is the methodology of choosing a sample randomly that works in such a huge country.

You were bang on in many assembly election exit poll results. Did you find predicting a nationwide poll tough?

In a way, yes. That is because in our country, with so much diversity, a State like Uttar Pradesh has no connection whatsoever with for example, Tamil Nadu. So, if we take each State separately, the sample size will be small for each State. That is where the challenge lies.

In a nationwide survey, I may get all States wrong but get the national picture right. That is because I may overestimate some States and I may underestimate some other States. But the overall result may come right.

If it's a State poll and let's take Tamil Nadu, if you underestimate the AIADMK by 3 per cent, that will have a huge impact on the overall result. But in the case of a nationwide poll, I may overestimate the BJP in some States and underestimate it in some other States, still, I may get the overall performance of the BJP nationwide, right. That is why the poll can be a little more reliable then. Still, our record at the State level has been very good.

In a State like Kerala, rarely do exit polls come right. We get to see totally different predictions. Is it because there are only two fronts in Kerala and a slight swing can make a huge difference in the number of seats?

I don't agree with the observation that our predictions went wrong but I would say Kerala is a psephologist's nightmare.

Generally, it is a very close fight there and the margins of victory are very narrow. That is why we can go off the mark. A couple of points' difference in the vote estimate can make a huge difference in the numbers. Yes, that is because even a small swing can change the whole scenario.

Is there any difference in the way you conduct the survey when the fight is between two fronts and when there are more than three or four fronts, like it is in Tamil Nadu now?

Yes, there is a methodology when there are only two fronts, and it changes when there are more fronts. The methodology is not the same then. We look at how many significant players are there in each constituency. It is not guess work; we follow a methodology.

Mathematics plays a major role in getting the exit poll results right.

How much does the bias of a researcher affect the results?

I can't say about the others, but it doesn't affect in my case. I try to be completely neutral, though I also have my own views. I see to it that my views don't affect the result. I try to read what people think at large and not what I think. I go with a completely open mind.

Do you see a Modi wave in the 2014 elections?

I certainly think there is a Modi wave throughout the nation, more or less.

Where the BJP has good presence like in the North and the West, the wave would be translated into more seats and in the South and the East, where the party does not have much presence, the incremental wave is not likely to give them that many seats.

The Modi, BJP wave is also superimposed by an anti-Congress wave.

While there is anger against the Congress, there is also a pro-Modi sentiment. Together, it will lead to a Modi victory.

Remember what Dr Rajeeva Karandikar said, 'The Modi wave is also superimposed by an anti-Congress wave. While there is anger against the Congress, there is also a pro-Modi sentiment. Together, it will lead to a Modi victory.'

And you know who was right when the 2014 general elections results came; P C Chacko or P C Rajeeva Karandikar!

The star campaigner for the NDA, the man brought in from Gujarat to New Delhi; Narendra Modi travelled the length and breadth of the country addressing umpteen huge, huge rallies.

For a nation tired of the scams and scandals of the UPA government, slogans coined by Narendra Modi like Achche Din aane waale hain (good days are coming), Sab ka Saath Sab ka Vikas (with everyone and development for everyone) gave them hope for a better tomorrow.

The campaigner-in-chief for the Congress was Rahul Gandhi, the son of UPA's chairperson Sonia Gandhi. It was a litmus test for Rahul, being been pitted against a great orator like Modi.

PART 6

2014-2019

Ruling Party: The National Democratic Alliance (NDA)

Prime Minister: Narendra Damodardas Modi (BJP)

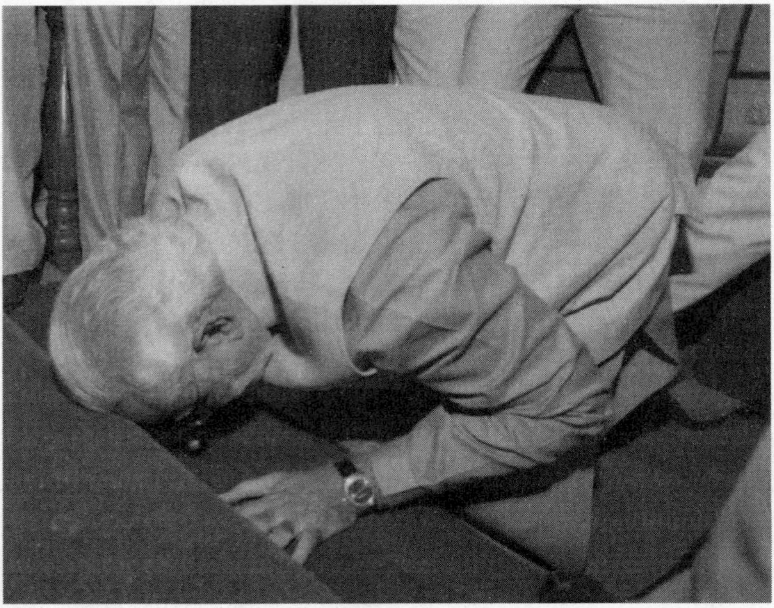

Modi pays obeisance as he enters Parliament for the first time in 2014. Thank you, DH.

Narendra Modi Wins Big!

543 constituencies. 8251 candidates and 814.5 million eligible voters.

A landmark general election it was! An election process that lasted 36 days, from 7 April to 12 May 2014.

It was a match between a seasoned politician like Narendra Modi and a reluctant and hesitant Rahul Gandhi. Naturally, the Man of the Match was Narendra Modi.

But what boomeranged for the Congress was Sonia Gandhi's description of Modi as maut ka saudagar *(merchant of death) when people saw him as a messiah who would put an end to corruption, dynastic rule and black money, and who would provide millions of jobs and develop the country.*

Then, the Congress leader Mani Shankar Aiyar ridiculed Modi by calling him a chaiwala, *after Modi talked about his humble beginnings as a tea-seller helping his father when he was a young boy. The BJP caught hold of the jibe and started* #chai pe charcha, *a discussion forum, all over the country.*

Of course, his catchy slogans Achche din aane waale hain *(good days are coming),* Sab ka Saath, Sab ka Vikas *(with everyone and development for everyone), won over the masses.*

The voter turnout of 66.4 per cent was the highest ever in the history of Indian general elections.

Globally we have seen that people come out in large numbers to vote when they are desperate for a change, and angry with the current regime. That was what we witnessed in India in 2014. They wanted to punish the corrupt UPA2 regime.

The results were declared on the 16th of May 2014, and the NDA or the National Democratic Alliance led by the BJP won by a clear margin with 336 seats. There was no confusion.

Interestingly, the 31.0 per cent vote share the BJP got was the lowest for a party that formed a majority government in India since Independence! The NDA's combined vote share was just 38.5 per cent.

But it was the largest majority government since the 1984 general elections.

Nobody, no exit poll, predicted this kind of a massive victory for Modi.

The Congress under the leadership of Rahul Gandhi got just 41 seats with a vote share of 8.1 per cent and the UPA led by the Congress won 59 seats.

The Congress did not even qualify to be the official opposition party – to become the official opposition party, a party must get 10 per cent of the seats which is 55 seats in the Lok Sabha. So, there was no official opposition party in the 16th Lok Sabha.

The Congress Party's worst-ever drubbing in the Lok Sabha election resulted in murmurs on the way Congress vice president Rahul Gandhi had led the election campaign.

Anyway, after decades of uncertainty, India finally had a majority government under the leadership of a new leader: Narendra Damodardas Modi.

And people of India waited for achche din *to come soon!*

A Prime Minister and Toilets

15 August 2014.

For the first time in independent India's history, a Prime Minister in his Independence Day address talked about the need to have toilets in every household. Till then, we had heard leaders share their vision on reaching the skies, building missiles and rockets, etc and not building toilets.

People felt, Narendra Modi, the Prime Minister of India, must definitely be applauded for this.

I thought it was the right time to talk to ***Dr Bindeshwar Pathak*** *who had been working with the most deprived class in India, the scavengers.*

After joining the Bhangi-Mukti *(scavengers' liberation) cell of the Bihar Gandhi centenary celebrations committee in 1968, he had travelled throughout India, living with scavenger families. It also became the subject of his PhD research work.*

In 1970, he founded the Sulabh International Social Service Organisation that worked to promote human rights, sanitation and waste management; said to be the largest NGO in India.

Without any doubt, we can say the Sulabh toilets changed the social condition of many poor Indians.

When two teenage girls were gang-raped and murdered in Badaun, Uttar Pradesh on 27 May 2014, Dr Pathak wrote to Prime Minister Modi explaining how rapes could be controlled by building toilets for women as women were the most vulnerable while defecating in the open.

WHY is sanitation not a priority in India, especially in rural India?

First is the cultural factor. Why I say cultural factor, it is because if you look at *Devi Puran*, it says nobody should defecate near human habitation. It says people should defecate in a pit filled with garden leaves, and they should fill the pit again with garden leaves. This cultural taboo still continues for the Hindus living in rural areas.

The second reason is the tropical climate. Had ours been a cold climate, there would have been some toilet facility inside the house. If you look at the houses in Srinagar, you see some sort of toilets inside the house.

Third, in villages, we have bushes and trees where a person could hide herself while defecating. Because of this, the practice of defecating in the open continued for centuries.

During the *Puranic* period, toilets came into existence in India, and those who were involved in carrying the excreta and cleaning the toilets became the untouchables. Both practices started in the *Puranic* period itself.

Was poverty one reason why rural India never gave importance to sanitation?

Not at all. I will tell you about my ancestral house in Bihar which was built in the 1900s. It was a very big one with every facility inside and outside the house including a well to draw water, but it didn't have a toilet inside.

You mean the toilet was outside the house?

No, there was no toilet at all. My mother, grandmother, aunties and sisters... all used to go out in the open to defecate.

What I mean is, there is no link between toilet and poverty.

What about hygiene when people defecate in the open?

Earlier, the population was very thin in the villages. So, they never used to feel the stink, and the air did not get polluted. So, they never connected defecating in the open with lack of hygiene.

Now, many know that if you put your feet on the same place where somebody has defecated, you can get bacterial infection, and the bacteria can go straight to your stomach and can give you hookworm, roundworm and severe diarrhoea.

In today's India, do you see any connection between literacy, education and sanitation?

There is a connection. Even if you give some money to an educated person to defecate in the open, he or she will not do it.

Why I asked the question was, in a state like Kerala, you don't see people defecating in the open. There was a story in the newspapers about a Kerala woman getting married to a man from Haryana, and she refusing to go there until they built a toilet inside the house.

The story is true. In fact, I have awarded quite a few women for standing up like this. One was from Madhya Pradesh and the others were from Gorakhpur and Patna. They left their husbands' houses and went to their maternal homes as there was no toilet in their husbands' houses. In the villages, it is an insult to the in-laws' family if a girl leaves the house for their mother's house for want of toilets.

I got toilets constructed in their houses and awarded those women for revolting. It needed courage to revolt like that.

In 1870, the British brought sewage system to India, first to Kolkata. In the last 144 years, only 1,600 cities out of 7,965 have sewage facilities. When you have the sewage system, manual cleaning and open defecation will end. Mahatma Gandhi wanted to end manual cleaning, but no technology could be evolved during his lifetime.

When I joined the Gandhi's centenary committee in Bihar in 1968, I was asked by the general secretary to bring human rights, dignity and respectability to the untouchables, as a tribute to Gandhi.

I said, 'I am not an engineer, I am a sociologist'. I asked him, how I could ask someone not to use bucket toilets? But he wanted me to do something about the issue.

That was when I decided to invent a new technology. Without a new technology, I knew I would not be able to end open defecation. But even after I developed the technology, there was apathy on the side of the government. They did not take much interest in the technology.

Is it not a shame that even today, in India, people defecate in the open?

It is a shame. It is a decision politicians have to make, and not the bureaucrats. I will give you an example. In 1986, the government had fixed Rs 500 to be given to a person to build a toilet. They insisted that people built it with Rs 500 and not use any extra money from anywhere. This continued till 2008 with the government increasing the amount little by little up to Rs 1,500.

In 2008, I spoke to the then minister and finally the government allowed people to make 2 pit toilets. He also raised the money to Rs 10,000. That is why I feel the politicians will have to take a decision on this, but they leave everything to the bureaucrats.

Till Jairam Ramesh took over, the entire decision on sanitation was left only to the bureaucrats.

Is giving money to build toilets enough to make people aware of sanitation?

No, giving money is not enough at all. That is why we, at Sulabh, go from house to house to motivate and educate people on sanitation. If they agree, we help them fill up a form to draw money to build a toilet. We build toilets for them and also give guarantee.

But what the government does is, just give them money. Some contractors who do not know how to build toilets take half the money and construct something that is not a real toilet.

I will give you an example. I had been to a village in Haryana. One woman who had four daughters-in-law and three daughters, told me that she had to be awake the whole night to take each of them, one by one to the fields. She also told me about a woman who had to suddenly get up when she saw a man peeping at her. After that, she had to suffer from constipation for 25 days!

After hearing the story, I saw to it that the entire village got toilets. When I found that the cost of a toilet there was Rs 15,000, I arranged a loan for Rs 12,000 and the rest of the Rs 3,000 was put in by the people. Now, every house in that village has toilets. And all the women are very happy today.

You must have spoken to many women living in villages. How uncomfortable are they about defecating in the open?

They are extremely uncomfortable. Some of them weep when they start talking about it. There is no end to their sufferings.

You go to any village, you hear the same story everywhere. But there is a solution. That is why I gave the example of the village in Haryana.

Today, when I go there, the women are all so happy; they don't complain at all. This can be replicated in the entire country but the government has to adopt a proper methodology.

The question is, if the Sulabh model created by us is successful, why not pass this to other NGOs too so that they use it elsewhere? Sulabh cannot be there everywhere. We can train other NGOs and they can work in their own area. Everybody now knows that the Sulabh model is successful.

We have found that the country needs 115 million toilets. If you train 30,000 people and ask them to take care of 25- 30 villages, in five years, we can build enough toilets for all the people. One person in charge of 25- 30 villages for five years can motivate and educate the villagers about toilets.

More important, bank loans are necessary to build these toilets because whatever is allotted in the government budget, is not enough. There are many missing links. The way the government is approaching the issue is not right.

What are the missing links?

There is no one to go from house to house to motivate and educate people. It is better to have girl volunteers to motivate women while boy volunteers can help building toilets, and also help the villagers get bank loans.

Why do you have to motivate people to build toilets, especially when women find it uncomfortable to go to the open fields?

You don't need much time to convince a woman about building toilets because they are the ones who are suffering. Men need time to get convinced as they are the ones who take decisions in a house. After that the problem is, how to get loan from the bank, how to build the toilets, etc We have to also give guarantee to them for at least two years. We have to constantly do follow ups to see that they use the toilets properly.

If we do this diligently, in five years' time, there will not be any open defecation in India.

After the horrendous rape incident in UP, you said that there was a connection between rape and lack of toilets in villages....

Politician after politician from various political parties went there, but nobody spoke of building toilets in the village so that such incidents will not happen in future. This made me angry, and I said I will build toilets.

Some women activists wrote that there was no connection between rape and lack of toilets....

I would say there is a connection between rape and absence of toilets. I am not saying all rapes are because of lack of toilets. As many as 20 to 30 per cent of rape cases happen because of lack of toilets.

I am going to tell the Prime Minister that we should train 30,000 boys and girls to work as motivators in the villages. I want these girls and boys to go to 25- 30 villages, house to house for five years. Also, 90,000 masons should be trained to build toilets. We should select girls and boys from the same area as motivators and not from outside.

The government should arrange for bank loans to families to build toilets.

There should be a national campaign by all political parties, like they do during the elections.

I am also writing to major corporates in the country like the Tatas, Birlas, Premji, Nita Ambani, etc to help us in the campaign to build toilets. I will tell them that God helped them to help somebody else. I will also tell them that if Bill Gates could give so much money to society, why not our industrialists too?

We had not taken any donation from anyone till now but for this, we are planning to take donation from the public. Then, I will build toilets in the entire country. I am not leaving the entire work to the Prime Minister. On one hand, I am requesting the Prime Minister to take some action. On the other, I am planning to do this on my own.

You feel this should be the first priority of a government?

Yes. For example, you are on your way to a temple, and you feel like going to the toilet, what will you do first? Won't you go to the toilet first?

In 1968, when I went to people with the idea of building toilets, they asked me, do you want to talk about toilets? I said, yes. Then, they would say, have tea first and then talk about toilets. But today, everybody is talking about toilets.

I am happy that newspapers and television channels are also taking interest in the subject. Till now, it was a dull subject for them. People will become aware only through the media. So, the role of the media is very important.

Gandhi got us freedom from the British. It is high time we got freedom from dirt and filth.

'Gandhi got us freedom from the British. It is high time we got freedom from dirt and filth', said Bindeshwar Pathak.

On the 2nd of October 2014, on Mahatma Gandhi's birth anniversary, the Modi government started a programme to build toilets in rural households in India under the Swachh Bharat Mission.

In October 2020, Modi announced in Ahmedabad that India was free of open-defecation, and that his government had built 110 million toilets in five years and 600 million people had access to them.

According to a survey conducted by the National Family Health Survey (NFHS) in 2022, India still has open defecation but the percentage of households practising open defecation in India has decreased from 39 per cent in 2015-2016 to 19.4 per cent in 2019-2021.

The report found that 69.3 per cent of Indian households have access to improved toilet facilities or those that are not shared.

A total of 19.4 per cent of Indian households, both urban and rural, do not use any toilet facility, which means they practice open defecation.

Bihar is at the bottom with only 61.2 per cent of households with toilet facility, followed by Jharkhand (69.6 per cent) and Odisha (71.3 per cent).

With 100 per cent of households that have access to toilet facilities, Lakshadweep is at the top with Mizoram close behind at 99.9 per cent, and Kerala at 99.8 per cent.

Ghar Wapsi!

After the BJP came to power, the Christian community, especially the missionaries became the targets of hard-core Hindu fundamentalists.

From December 2014 to February 2015, there were five attacks on churches in Delhi.

Then, some hard-core Hindu organisations organised Ghar Wapsi *(Back home) melas throughout the country to 'reconvert' Christians and Muslims to Hinduism.*

On the 15th of March 2015, the entire country woke up to listen to the shocking news of the gang rape of a 72-year-old nun and looting of the Convent of Jesus and Mary in Ranaghat in Bengal.

I met **Cardinal Baselios Cleemis***, president of the Catholic Bishops Conference of India, who had travelled to Ranaghat to meet the nun who was in the hospital and also the staff at the Convent of Jesus and Mary High School, to understand what exactly happened there.*

YOU are back from meeting the nun at Ranaghat. Was she in a state of shock?

She appeared quite calm and serene, but physically she needed some more time to come back to her normal routine.

I was surprised to learn from her conversation that she was completely free from shock. She told me she had forgiven those people, but she said it should not happen to any other woman in this country or anywhere else in the world.

Do you see communal colour to what happened to her? Is our society becoming so violent and sick that 3-year-old babies and 72-year-old women are being raped?

Something unethical has crept into our society. Incidents like these are happening in many parts of our country. But seeing a series of similar incidents, one is forced to think that this is not just a theft...

You mean the recent attacks on churches?

Yes. Because of the number of incidents that has happened in the recent past, I am forced to believe that this is not an ordinary rape case or an ordinary theft.

You feel these attacks are specifically targeted at the community?

Exactly. I am not here to talk about or judge who did it or what was the motive behind the attack. In this case, they have taken Rs 2.5 lakh from the safe, which the sisters had collected as examination fee from the students. They also ate all the food that was in the fridge.

Then, they did this shameful act. The sisters told me that when one guy wanted to take out the ring and silver chain from the sister, another stopped him saying, '*Woh bhagawan ka hai* (it belongs to God)'. So, they had full knowledge of what they were doing; yet they did the condemnable act. We do not know whether they did it on somebody else's instructions or on their own will.

The Christian community in India and people in general wonder whether this was the continuation of events that have happened in the last few months, or was it an isolated case? But it did not end with this incident; two more churches were attacked after this.

Do you feel that since the BJP came to power, churches and other minority institutions are being attacked more?

The BJP had ruled earlier too, under (Atal Bihari) Vajpayee as the prime minister, but nothing of this sort had happened then. We had a peaceful time. But this time, more aggressive-minded people have managed to twist the orientation.

I don't say the government is behind the attacks, but they don't do anything to stop the attacks. That is why we are anxious.

Julio Ribeiro, well known retired police officer, said the other day that he felt alienated as a Christian in India. Do you feel that way now?

I don't feel alienated, because this is the only country I have; this is my own country. If I feel alienated here, where will I go? I respect Mr Ribeiro's sentiments. He is a patriot. He was the face of the bold Indian! He must have been pained by some situations. I am an Indian Christian and I am happy and proud of who I am.

Incidents like these do not take away our identification with our country in any way. But there is anxiety in our minds. Is it not the government's responsibility to protect its people?

For convenience sake, you may call people of the country Christians, Hindus, Muslims and Parsis, but all of them are Indians. Based on religion, faith and attitude, can anyone say that we don't need them? The government has to clear this aspect.

During his election campaign, Narendra Modi had said, he did not differentiate based on religion, and only development mattered to him.... How do we know and judge a person? From his action. That is why we say, walk the talk.

Do you feel after he became prime minister, fringe groups are acting contrary to what Modi had said, and he remains silent and is not reining them in?

I don't want to say that all these are happening ever since he became prime minister. I would rather say, ever since this ministry was sworn in, a lot of unwanted things are happening.

The Prime Minister has to tell the perpetrators that it is not in the interest of the government that such incidents happen. The President (Pranab Mukherjee) has already warned the administration about this, and said it was necessary to respect religious freedom. He has shared his anxiety.

If this continues, we are forced to say, what we have is a helpless government.

Did you have any discussion with the Prime Minister to convey your anxiety?

I had an official meeting with him, which some political parties and Christian communities did not like. I met him as he is our Prime Minister, and also because I represent the Catholic community in India. When I expressed our apprehensions about so many issues, he was quite positive in his response. But things have not improved, and the anxiety is growing more than ever.

Do you feel had the Prime Minister given a stern message, this would not have happened?

Yes.

Do you think his silence is the reason why such attacks are repeatedly happening?

Not his silence; inaction. He should have been pro-active to maintain calm in this country.

Christians form 2.3 per cent of the population in this country. If we are not protected, what is the point in saying this is our Republic. Every single citizen should feel that the country protects him.

Do you feel disturbed?

I feel disturbed not only because of the incidents, but also because of the continuous silence of the people concerned. And also because of the speeches of some responsible people, creating confusion as well.

For example, when somebody says all Indians are Hindus, responsible people should ask him to stop and assure the country that this is not the opinion of the government. But it is not happening, and it is quite unfortunate.

You said the government should protect not only cows, but human beings too....

That was when the discussion on the ban on beef was happening. I don't side with the pro- or anti-group. My question is, are human beings not more important than the subject of these discussions? As per Christian theology and belief, the human being is the crown of creation. Hindu theology says the *paramatman* and I are the same; *Aham Brahmasmi*...

Do you look at banning beef as infringement of an individual's right to eat what he wants?

I look at this from a different perspective. Should this be the priority of India? Should we be spending our time and energy on such an issue when on another side, you are talking about India becoming a superpower in 2020 or 2030?

We should identify the priorities of the country. Let your priority be to lead India as a developed nation. I do not know how these kinds of discussions will help India achieve what it wants.

What are we aiming at? Are we aiming at a Hindu India? I know majority of Hindus are secular and they don't agree with such arguments. That is the strength of this country, and these people have to be respected for making this country what it is.

India remains a secular country not only because of the Constitution, but also because of the mindset of the people.

Some people were of the opinion that *ghar wapsi* was the reason why the Ranaghat rape incident happened. Do you think so? How do you look at *ghar wapsi*?

It questions the freedom of an individual. Do I have the freedom to choose? If I have the freedom to choose something new, I also have the freedom to go back or even choose something else. It is not confined to religion alone.

Are the political parties ready for a *ghar wapsi* in politics? Can we say all of them should go back to the first political party of this country? Then they will say it is not possible. Why? Not only in religion, personal freedom is applicable in every matter.

Those people who practice *ghar wapsi* in the religious sense, should accept a *ghar wapsi* in politics too.

Do you feel *ghar wapsi* will disturb the peace of the nation?

What is the purpose of *ghar wapsi*? The Constitution gives the freedom to choose any religion, practise and propagate it. If I want to be a Hindu, I can. If I want to be a Christian, I can. If I want to be an atheist, I can.

Why should some group solemnise the whole thing in front of the media? It sends out the wrong message.

Christians have the service of baptism, initiating someone to the Christian faith. How would you react if the Christian community does baptism like *ghar wapsi*? I would say, all this is wrong.

What do you think the government should have done when *ghar wapsi* happened at many places?

The government should say stop, if any statement or incident disturbing and embarrassing people happens. Not only the physical destruction of a temple or a church or a mosque but spoken words can also cause destruction. These are under the purview of the government, and it is their duty to see that all citizens are safe.

The home minister, when quested about *ghar wapsi,* said there shouldn't be any conversion at all in the first place. What does the Constitution say? It provides freedom to the individual to choose Hinduism or Christianity or Islam as his faith. How can a responsible person like the home minister talk like this? You cannot say that you do not have the freedom to choose your religion.

My simple question is: Will all of India's social and ethnic problems be over if you stop conversion? We need to address the issues that concern the well-being of the nation.

The issue of conversion is a little exaggerated, I will say. When we have the police, the legal system and the government machinery to ensure justice and punish the miscreants, why do you worry about this?

My question is: How was such a Constitution written and accepted when majority of Indians are Hindus? It only reflected the mindset of the people. India is a country where citizens have the freedom to choose any religion, any political party....

Can we make a rule, for example, that after 2016, there will only be three political parties in this country, and nobody has the right to change their political party?

India is a democratic and secular country. We respect all religions and among the Hindus itself, there are many movements. Nobody should forget the cultural ethos of this country.

The Constitution is the book of the nation, the guideline of the nation and it has to be respected. I think this will take a back seat when the most important issue takes the front seat, that is, to uplift the millions of poor who are deprived of many things and bring development to the entire nation.

It is said that conversion generally happens at the time of pain, despair and poverty. Is it true?

Let Indians speak. I read in the papers that a German couple came to Varkala to have a Hindu wedding. Would you say it was because of poverty or pain that they embraced Hinduism?

The yogacharyas from India have many followers in the West. Is it because of poverty or pain that they follow these gurus?

When someone embraces Christianity or Islam, you cannot say that it is only because of poverty. Every individual is free to choose what she wants to practise. It is a personal choice, and he has the personal freedom to do so. But the act of choosing should not disturb the serenity of community life.

Recently, Mother Teresa was dragged into a controversy by a comment that she was more interested in converting poor people than serving them. I think India's poor know her better than anybody else. How she lived, for whom she lived and for what purpose she came to Calcutta are well known to everyone. Indira Gandhi, the iron lady of India, always stood with her head bowed in front of the Mother, and that reflects the kind of respect she had for the Mother. Jyoti Basu used to call her, My Mother. Why did the country honour her with the Bharat Ratna? Because of her selfless service. Nobody should forget all this.

She only converted thousands and thousands of people to God's love and not to Christianity.

Some observers are of the opinion that the attacks on churches were an agenda by the ISI to disturb communal harmony and thus defame India....[1]

If that is so, what is the role of the Government of India? Is it not the duty of the government to protect all its citizens? If somebody is doing that, should the government not be taking adequate measures to stop this? If somebody has identified the reason, the government should be more alert and responsible.

What are you most disturbed about?

Not only the attacks on churches and persons at regular intervals, irresponsible comments coming one after another from responsible, learned, people, and also the constant silence of the responsible people.

What will be your message to the Prime Minister?

India has space for everyone, from the religious minded to those who do not believe in any religion. Don't bring in anything that is against the Constitution and culture of this country. That will spoil the equilibrium and serenity of our community life. If something untoward happens, it is the duty of the responsible people to see that it doesn't get repeated.

People who can disturb the country are powerful, but more powerful are those in control of the country. Remember your promise to the nation that there will be a moratorium on communal violence. It is high time to prove the promise.

Walk the talk; that is the demand.

[1] ISI: Inter- Services Intelligence or ISI is the premier intelligence agency in Pakistan.

Though ghar wapsi *has taken a back seat, eating beef and banning beef are still a topics of discussion in India.*

That is why Cardinal Cleemis's question is still relevant. 'Should this be the priority of India? Should we be spending our time and energy on such an issue when on another side, you are talking about India becoming a superpower in 2020 or 2030?'

After Ghar Wapsi, it is Award Wapsi

Close on the heels of the series of attacks on churches happened the chilling lynching of a Muslim man in Dadri, a village in UP, for allegedly slaughtering a cow. It was in 2015, a year after the BJP-led NDA came to power that a mob attacked and murdered 52-year-old Mohammed Akhlaq when he was at home, on the suspicion of cow slaughter.

The incident, that came to be infamously known as Dadri lynching, happened in the BJP ruled UP, and not just shocked but outraged many people. Protesting against the growing intolerance in the country, and the complete silence on the part of the Prime Minister, around 50 writers decided to return their Sahitya Akademi awards, and one of them was well known Malayalam writer ***Prof Sara Joseph****.*

A politically and socially active writer, Prof Sara Joseph chose to return her award in protest against the Dadri lynching and the 'cultural Talibanisation' that was happening in the country.[1]

1 Taliban is a political-religious grouping in Pakistan and Afghanistan. Those who propagate 'back to the root' social dictums at the cost of death are said to 'Talibanise'. The word Talibanisation comes from this.

Nayantara Sahgal (an Indian writer who writes in English who is also the niece of Jawaharlal Nehru), Shashi Deshpande (an Indian writer who writes in English) and you were the first writers to protest by resigning from the Sahitya Akademi Council and returning your awards. Was the Dadri incident the reason behind you returning the award?

It was not the Dadri incident alone that prompted me to return my award. Dadri was not an isolated incident; it was an extension of the cultural fascism happening in the country. I would like to call it cultural Talibanism, and not just fascism.

It all started in 2013, with the murders of writers Narendra Dabholkar (an Indian physician, social activist, rationalist and author from Maharashtra) and Govind Pansare (of the Communist Party of India and a writer in Marathi), who had different opinions. The latest victim was M M Kalburgi, an excellent writer and a great human being from Karnataka. Now, there is this threat on the life of writer Prof K S Bhagawan (Kannada writer).

A writer like Perumal Murugan (Tamil writer) was asked to withdraw all his books. What is more painful than that for a writer? Ghulam Ali (Pakistani ghazal singer of the Patiala gharana) was not allowed to perform in Mumbai because he was a Pakistani.

More heinous and unpardonable was the lynching of an innocent man because somebody thought he had stored beef in his house.

Added to all these are the offensive and crude statements against a certain religious community by some members of the ruling party.

If you remember when the BJP came to power, there were several attacks on churches though they claimed they were never behind the attacks. If you look at the number of attacks on the minorities, it is only going up and not coming down.

Is your protest against the Narendra Modi government or the Sahitya Akademi?

I am protesting against the silence of the Prime Minister and also against the Akademi. A prime minister represents the entire country, but he refused to react to what was happening to so many writers. He did not even react to what happened at Dadri. Only after the President (Pranab Mukherjee) reacted that he quoted him, that too, nine days after the incident.

Even then, did he directly speak about the Dadri incident? As part of the Bihar election campaign, he spoke in passing about the incident. Is this what we expect from a prime minister who speaks eloquently on all issues?

When a writer is silenced, when a writer is murdered, what did the Sahitya Akademi do? The Akademi should have done so many things condemning Kalburgi's murder, but there was not even a condolence meeting or a message condemning the writer's murder.

The Sahitya Akademi is a cultural and literary organisation and now it is under the BJP government. Though it is supposed to be an autonomous body, the funds come from the government. The appointments of the administrators are also done by the government.

Have all the previous governments not been doing the same thing?

I agree all governments install their people in institutions like the Sahitya Akademi, the Sangeet Natak Akademi, the

Lalit Kala Akademi, etc That is why when the government changes, either the members resign, or they will be replaced by the new government's nominees.

We have been victims of this whenever the government changes in Kerala, but there were exceptions too. Once I was the member of the Kerala Sahitya Akademi that had M T Vasudevan Nair (the Jnanpith award winning Malayalam writer) as the chairman. Before our tenure got over, the government changed, but they didn't replace MT. That was only because there was no one in Kerala who could replace MT (Vasudevan Nair).

But the general rule is, whenever there is a change in the government, we see the administration of all the institutions also changing. This happens both at the Centre and the State.

Today, we see that an Akademi that should have been there for writers and languages, has become a stooge under the government. This is how so many writers feel today.

When you decided to return the award, was it the writer in you or the politician in you that protested?[2]

Both. Though I am a writer, there is politics inside me. My beliefs tell me that just like I have the freedom to express, the other person also has the same freedom to express.

When the other person loses his freedom to express himself, eat what he wants and live as he wishes, even if I have all this freedom, I will not consider myself living in a free India.

We have lost religious tolerance and secularism in today's India.

---

2 Professor Joseph had joined the Aam Aadmi Party and even contested in the 2014 general elections.

You said the situation today is worse than the Emergency.

The Emergency was a bad period in the history of India. None of us will praise those days. But the Emergency happened because of a dictator, but what we see today has communal colour. All the people in the country suffered under the Emergency, but now we see one community not only trying to crush the other community, but even murdering them.

Today, they are indulging in such heinous acts. Do they know what is brewing in the minds of the other side? Do you think they will sit quiet? What is happening today can boomerang and lead to a very dangerous situation in the country.

The question that was asked by many to Nayantara Sahgal was, why she didn't return the award when thousands of Sikhs were butchered in 1984....

She must have felt like reacting now. The question, why didn't you react then, and why do you react now has no relevance. I am happy that we are reacting now.

I want to ask, who suffers when a writer returns his/her award? It is the writer's loss and nobody else's. People tell me that I should not show disrespect by returning the award. My book *Aalahayude Penmakkal* has won around 12 awards, but the Kendriya Sahitya Akademi award is my favourite award. And if I am returning my favourite award, I must be feeling awful inside; still I am doing it.

In a way, this protest has no violence in it; only suffering and it is only mine and nobody else's.

Do you feel the influence writers had on society, has waned of late?

I agree that today, writers do not have the same kind of influence yesterday's writers had. Those who influence society are film stars and such celebrities. With people who have no deep knowledge commenting on serious issues, society also looks at issues in a superficial way.

Those were the days when books and words dominated our lives, and there was no other distraction. There was no visual medium to distract people from reading though serious readers were few even then. With the advent of social media, everybody is a writer and everybody expresses his/her views.

Do you agree with what writer Shashi Deshpande wrote, that writers were not doing their duty properly? Is it because they are no longer unbiased or independent?

Their silence is scary. I agree that they are biased and most of them are part of some political party or the other.

In your case, after you joined the Aam Aadmi Party (AAP), did the party's political beliefs affect the writer-activist in you at any point?

Never. I will never be part of a political party that will stifle the writer and writer's freedom in me. So far, I have not had any such experience and if at all it happens, I will have no problem leaving the party.

The only reason why I am with AAP is because it is an open house. Even now, when I decided to return my award, the party's central leadership only appreciated me.

Before Narendra Modi came to power, many writers had said he would be a dictator. What is your opinion of him now?

I remember U R Ananthamurthy (Jnanpith award-winning Kannada writer) now. He said he would leave the country if Modi ever came to power. It is another matter he left the world itself. But how prophetic were his words! He had this prophetic vision to see what would happen if a person like Modi came to power.

Ever since Modi came to power, we see his followers following a dangerous path. On one side, he goes all around the globe talking about development while the hardcore elements in the party indulge in all these fascist activities.

Modi has not yet uttered a single word against anyone and not shown any communal agenda, but he silently supports the hidden fascist activities.

Do you think the government will wake up now?

I have no hope in the government waking up.

> *Today's writers' 'silence is scary. I agree that they are biased and most of them are part of some political party or the other', noted Prof Sara Joseph.*
>
> *In 2022 we see that majority of Indian writers have chosen to remain silent and not react to any of the violent happenings in the country.*

The Journey to Mission Mars

India may be described as a developing country but it is one of the top five countries in the world in its space programme.

One such advanced space programme was the Mars Orbiter Mission or the Mission Mars or Mangalyan, launched on 5 November 2013.

After a 298-day transit to Mars, when it was put into Mars orbit on 24 September 2014, India became the first Asian nation to reach the Martian orbit, and also the first nation in the world to do so on its maiden attempt.

It was in this background that I spoke to ***R Aravamudan****, one of the pioneers in India's space programme.*

He was among the very few scientists handpicked by Dr Vikram Sarabhai to start the Indian Space Research Organisation (ISRO) at Thumba in Thiruvananthapuram in 1962.[1]

Former President A P J Abdul Kalam was also part of the elite group of scientists along with Aravamudan.

---

1 Vikram Sarabhai: physicist and astronomer who initiated India's space research and also helped develop nuclear power in India.

In 1962, when Dr Vikram Sarabhai handpicked a few of you to start India's space programme, what was the dream all of you had?

I was just 25 and had already spent two years in the Atomic Energy Establishment, Trombay working in the Reactor Control Division.[2]

Hailing from Madras (now Chennai), I could not get adjusted to crowded and noisy Bombay (Mumbai*)* and wanted to get back to the South. This was when Dr Sarabhai picked me for the programme which involved training in sounding rockets in NASA, and eventually being posted in Thumba.

In 1962 the outlook was pretty simple: To establish a modest sounding rocket launching facility at Thumba, which happened to be under the Magnetic Equator, and provide facilities to the international scientific community to gather relevant data.

There was no mention of developing satellites or launching vehicles at that time, although Dr Sarabhai must have had it in his mind all the time. This programme was articulated a few years later. It was then that the dream took shape.

Most of the scientists who went to Thumba at that time were working outside India. It was said that nobody could say 'no' to Dr Sarabhai.

I was among the very first to join the group. In fact, all of us in the original group were from India. In the subsequent years, say by mid-1960s, the active recruitment drive started and whenever Dr Sarabhai went abroad, he used to meet scientists

---

[2] AEET, founded by Homi Jehangir Bhabha, which later became the Department of Atomic Energy, DAE.

and engineers working in this area, and tried to describe to them his vision of the Indian space programme and what the future would hold.

I am sure his earnestness and sincerity would have drawn people to decide to come back and have a shot at it. I would say, the majority of the scientists recruited for the Indian space programme came from India.

Many of them were from small towns and had studied in local universities.

What was your first impression of Vikram Sarabhai when you met him?

I was a young electronics engineer working in the Reactor Control division of the Department of Atomic Energy at Trombay, when word got around that Dr Sarabhai was looking for fresh electronic engineers to form a core team to set up a small Rocket Launch Pad in south Kerala.

I was asked to travel to Ahmedabad and meet Dr Sarabhai to get to know the details first hand. I took the Bombay-Ahmedabad train and checked into a seedy hotel. I took an autorickshaw to Navrangapura where the Physical Research Laboratory was situated.

The first person I met was (Professor) E V Chitnis (space scientist), a handsome young man who said that Dr Sarabhai would meet me shortly.

As I was hanging around in the corridor waiting, a Standard Herald car with an open top stopped at the portico, and a fair and dashing looking young man dressed in white shorts and shirt stepped out and asked, 'Are you Aravamudan?' I said 'yes' and he immediately asked me to hop into the car. He drove up a short distance to an instrumentation trailer from NASA

(The National Aeronautics and Space Administration in the US) parked in the campus. Later I learnt that this was called the Microlock Receiving Trailer.

He led me inside and personally explained to me the workings of this trailer and how it received signals from scientific satellites. He then went on to explain how he was planning to do scientific experiments from Kerala, perhaps from near Trivandrum, using rockets carrying measuring instruments. He also described the launch pad, telemetry receiving station, radar and Doppler velocity, and the position system he hoped to install.

It all sounded like science fiction to me, but I was quite interested mainly because if I took the assignment, it meant my moving down south. Also, it involved a spell of training at NASA which sounded quite exciting.

But more than anything else, it was the charisma of Dr Sarabhai, the gleam in his eyes when he described his plans and his sincerity which attracted me.

What comes to your mind when you think of 21 November 1963 when a rocket took off from Thumba which marked the birth of the Thumba Equatorial Rocket Launching Station (TERLS)? Will you please describe the days before 21 November and after that?

We were at the final stages of our training at NASA when preparations for the first launching from Thumba were at their peak. The Nike Apache Rocket had been flown to Trivandrum and the Vapour Cloud payload had been reached. Being hazardous items, the transportation of these from the US was in itself a pioneering effort, and many a tale could be written on this.

We were thrilled when an announcement came on the Wallops Island intercom that India had successfully launched its first sounding rocket.

The orange vapour trail was visible from all over Kerala and parts of Tamil Nadu. This created great excitement. Since the public had never seen such a sight before, it also gave rise to some hilarious newspaper reports.

In fact, the Kerala legislative assembly, which was in session, then apparently adjourned temporarily to have a good view of the bright vapour trail in the western sky!

NASA personnel who had gone to Thumba for the launch had nice stories to tell us about the beautiful Thumba beach with coconut trees all over. They also claimed that they launched the Nike Apache, with the help of bullock carts for transportation and their own pocket knives for tools.

How do you describe the initial rocket launches?

I cannot, for instance, forget the day when we were launching a small rocket, which required a siren to be sounded three minutes before the launch. When one of my colleagues pressed the siren switch, a thundering noise was heard and the rocket zoomed up.

Fortunately, it was pointing in the right direction, and no one was hurt and no harm was done to anyone or anything. The Test Director, Mr Murthy was heard asking anxiously, what the big sound was about.

We learnt that day, how important it was to isolate the ground leads of the firing circuits from the general ground.

Then there was the series of Nike Apache launchings with Vapour Cloud payloads, triggered by locally designed ignitors.

The rockets were to be fired successively. The first launching took off well, but there was no payload release.

Determined not to be deterred by a single failure, an order was given to go ahead with the next firing. But, alas! that was also a failure.

It then occurred to us to carefully examine the ignitor in the laboratory. To our dismay, we found that the ignitor did not work in a vacuum, while it was fine under normal pressure. The ignitor design was modified and then it started functioning well in actual flights.

There were, fortunately, no major accidents during the launchings, although there were cases when the rockets went astray and parts were picked up from the surrounding areas.

We also worked out a regular system of compensation for fishermen who claimed that their nets had been damaged by rocket debris.

How difficult was it for you to live in a small town like Thiruvananthapuram?

Although I was born and bred in the South, I had never visited Kerala before. I had always lived in big cities. First Madras, then Bombay and finally Washington. The contrast between these big cities and Trivandrum was quite stark.

Although Trivandrum was the State capital, it was a sleepy and slow town with 19th century tiled houses lost amidst coconut palms. The roads were narrow and curvy with sharp turns and fast changing slopes.

For young bachelors like us, who knew no cooking, there were hardly any eating places. All we had were lodging houses with minimal facilities.

At the Rocket Range, the Launch Pad and the Block House had been built and the main roads were laid. But the approach to Thumba was very circuitous. The present road via Veli was not laid and there was no bridge over the Veli lake.

We had to make use of public transport as there were no official vehicles yet. And no canteen. So, our day began with a quick breakfast of idli sambar at the railway station canteen, which was the only place where we could get food to our taste.

We would then pack some snacks and lunch from the same canteen and go to the bus stand, to catch a moffusil bus to Kazhakkutam. We would get down at the bus stand there and walk about a kilometre or so to the range. The whole trip took about an hour.

Our first office was in the Bishop's House and the Church Building. The range was quite large in the area and the only means of transport within the range was by bicycle. Those like Kalam, who could not cycle, had to hitch rides with others.

Soon the range acquired a Jeep in addition to a Standard van, and these were pressed into round the clock duties. When we got the first bus a few months later, it was a major relief to the employees. There were no strict working hours and work went on around the clock.

In the early days in Thiruvananthapuram, did you, A P J Abdul Kalam and Professor Satish Dhawan (a mathematician and an aerospace engineer) talk only about the space programme or did you all also have fun? Were you people boring scientists or fun-loving young men?

While Kalam and I reached Trivandrum in the early '60s to start the rocket activities, Professor Satish Dhawan was not in the initial team and was never posted in Trivandrum.

He came into the picture much later, in 1972 and took over as the chairman on the death of Dr Sarabhai. He was until then in Bangalore as a professor in the Indian Institute of Science (IISc) and later its Director. As a matter of fact, he was responsible for moving the ISRO headquarters to Bangalore.

The initial days were quite hectic since we were establishing the facilities and we hardly had any time to ourselves. Trivandrum also was much less developed and was little more than a small town.

But we had a nice beach in Kovalam which we used to visit often, and it was tough to reach there by the rickety buses. Of course, this was before the days of the 5-star hotels. Kalam was particularly fond of a dip in Kovalam, since he was born in Rameswaram!

The other possibilities of diversion in Trivandrum were the Padmanabhaswamy Temple and the odd cinema theatres, including one showing old Hollywood movies.

Several years later we formed our own recreation club named the Rocket Club in Kowdiar where we used to play badminton, cards etc As the tempo of activities increased in the '70s and '80s, our time for recreation contracted to the great unhappiness of our families, some of us by this time had become family men.

It was written that after the training at NASA, you had no proper facilities available at Thumba and had to manage with whatever was available. Did any of you feel demotivated at the time?

Not at all. We were all very young and full of energy, and the frequent interactions with Dr Sarabhai and other colleagues kept us going.

As ISRO grew, did the dream of you people also change? If so, in what way?

Yes. The programme grew in magnitude. The most important milestone was when on the unfortunate death of Dr Homi Bhabha in an air crash (an Air India 101 flight crashed near Mont Blanc on 24 January 1966), the mantle fell on Dr Sarabhai to take over the Atomic Energy Department and Space Research. This meant direct access to the prime minister and adequate funding.

What was the biggest challenge you faced in the initial days?

The main challenge was that we had to develop everything from scratch. Rocket technology being defence related, was not available from abroad for love or money. You may recall the US embargoes and Russian Cryogenic imbroglio (imbroglio over the sale of cryogenic engines to India)!

Aravamudan while speaking to me on the early days of India's space programme had said, 'The most noteworthy feature of the Indian space programme is that all the unique achievements have been made by engineers from small towns who have had a non-elite upbringing and who have grown with the programme'.

It continues to be so.

Aravamudan passed away on 4 August 2021. And his colleague from the initial days of ISRO, A P J Abdul Kalam, the former President of India died on 4 July 2015.

Planning Commission Becomes NITI Aayog

Though Mokshagundam Visvesvaraya, better known as M Visvesvaraya, is described as the Father of India's Economic Planning, India's first Prime Minister Jawaharlal Nehru's name is synonymous with the Planning Commission.

The first Five-Year Plan was launched in 1951, focusing mainly on development of the agricultural sector. After two subsequent Five-Year Plans were formulated, there was a break in 1965, because of the Indo-Pakistan conflict. Two successive years of drought, devaluation of the currency, a general rise in prices and erosion of resources disrupted the planning process between 1966 and 1969.

Then the fourth Five-Year Plan happened in 1969.

As if the BJP wanted to erase the name of Jawaharlal Nehru from India's history, and also have Hindi names for all institutions, in his first Independence Day speech in 2014, Prime Minister Narendra Modi announced that his government would replace the Planning Commission with NITI Aayog.

***Dr T M Thomas Isaac**, a well-known economist, and the finance minister in Kerala's Left Democratic Front (LDF)* *government from 2006-2011 and 2016-2021, strongly opposed this move by the Modi government.*

DO you agree with the BJP's view that the Planning Commission had lost its relevance in the post-reforms era?

It all depends upon your ideological perspective. Those who believe in the market economy and want the market to be the supreme, unquestioned decision-maker, and expect it to produce optimal outcomes, would say the Planning Commission had to be done away with.

But there is an equally important opposite view. Now that the neo-liberal reforms are taking place, it is important to have certain control over the market forces. There has to be at least some social concerns built into the process.

Dismantling the Planning Commission is tantamount to giving up even the modicum intervention in the decision-making process.

That is because there are many social objectives which the market does not take into consideration like regional inequalities, inter-sectoral and intra-sectoral inequalities, rural-urban inequalities and so on. All these inequalities have been worsening ever since reforms began. These are issues that the market cannot take care of.

You spoke of inequalities. As representatives from all the States are on the NITI Aayog, they say planning relevant to each State will happen.

This is (the NITI Aayog) simply a governing council of an institution, and do not have binding decision-making power. The actual power lies with the finance ministry which controls the money.

Earlier, the Planning Commission was linked to the National Development Council (NDC), in which all States were represented. Our demand has been that this bond must be strengthened, and the Planning Commission made accountable to NDC.

Now, the NDA government wants to constitute a council where States will get representation in turn, which I don't think, will address the concerns of the States in any way better.

The criticism earlier was that the Planning Commission was more centralised. When I interviewed the former Kerala Finance Minister K M Mani, he had said, though the priorities of each State were different, the decisions taken by the Planning Commission never reflected that.

It has always been the criticism of the Left that the Planning Commission's decisions do not correspond to the spirit of the federal structure of the country, and the priorities of each State are not given much attention. That is why we wanted the NDC to play a key role in the Planning Commission.

Now, the Planning Commission is dismantled, and a new body has come. In what sense this is going to be more decentralised? Merely by saying the needs of each State are different, and that one hat will not fit everyone, will not make the new council different, as long as arbitrary powers remain with the finance ministry and the objective norms are done away with.

In the new situation, the finance ministry is going to be the decision-maker in allocating funds to different States. Earlier, at least there was a body that was to an extent, independent of the finance ministry. I feel this new set up is going to be even more centralised.

Why do you feel so when there are representatives from each State in NITI Aayog?

There may be representatives from the States, but their decisions are not binding. Who takes the final decision on the financial matters? It is the finance ministry. So, there will be more centralisation in the allocation of funds.

Generally, the allocation of funds for the State governments are through three routes: The Finance Commission, the Planning Commission and the discretionary allocation made by the finance ministry.

All the studies have shown that the discretionary allocations have mostly been arbitrary and iniquitous while the Finance Commission is more equitable and less arbitrary. Given this experience, the reasonable conclusion that we can draw is that greater powers to the finance ministry is going to make resource devolution from the Centre more arbitrary and iniquitous.

After Independence, long-term planning for a young country was necessary. Today, in the globalised economy, when the economic scenario and markets change almost every day, are long-term planning commissions redundant?

I, for one, am opposed to the unfettered market economy. What is demanded is total freedom for business houses with respect to natural resources and investment decisions.

The recent global crisis and the deepening global environment crisis underlines the need for long- term planning and relevance of social intervention.

A whole lot of studies in the post-liberalisation period on global economy have shown that inequality has increased to frightful proportions, so much so that even the liberalised economies have understood the need to have market intervention either through redistribution of taxation to the poor and other such measures.

I would argue that in India, it is much more relevant because of the diversity of the Indian subcontinent and the regional differences. There is a renewed relevance of social intervention.

So, there is relevance for an institution like the Planning Commission that has gained certain reputation and established certain norms. Therefore, what is required is a major overhaul, making it autonomous under the NDC.

So, disbanding the Planning Commission was not a right decision?

Definitely not. It is a move to give global investors unfettered freedom in their decisions and access to the natural resources of the country. The change that is taking place in the Planning Commission is an additional fillip to the globalisation process.

We should not forget the experience of centuries of colonialism. The objective of national movement was precisely for having a national say in the development process.

What will be the ideal decision-making body that a country as diverse as India needs?

We need a Planning Commission that is more democratic, and in tune with the federal nature of the country. Therefore, it must be made an adjunct of the NDC. If you want to change the name, change it. There must be greater scope for decentralised planning; there must be a multi-level planning structure going down to the local level.

The Planning Commission should have this perspective and ensure that there is planning at different levels.

Why were the States ruled by parties opposed to the party at the Centre, always unhappy with the Planning Commission?

That was because the Planning Commission never took the States into confidence. Its autonomy was imaginary. In reality, it was an institution under the central government. You will see that all the Planning Commissions reflected the thinking of the central government.

Yes, many States were unhappy because certain decisions were made without consultations with them. The demand was not to disband the Planning Commission, but to make it more responsive to the demands of each State.

Prime Minister Narendra Modi said, he decided to disband the Planning Commission because he felt it was discriminatory to many States. He felt the same when he was chief minister of Gujarat....

The facts speak otherwise. The larger States got better deals from the Planning Commission. In fact, the Finance Commission was fairer to the poorer States.

What makes the Prime Minister think his new body will not be discriminatory to non-BJP States? With concentration of power in the finance ministry, the Central government's decisions are going to be even more arbitrary.

The Congress says the NITI Aayog may lead to a strained relationship between the Centre and the States. Do you feel so?

Definitely. If the Prime Minister is serious about creating a right balance between the Centre and the States, which is his reason for doing away with the Planning Commission, then he should ensure greater share of revenues for the States. All the States are unitedly demanding 50 per cent of tax revenues, while at present it is only 37 per cent.

Let him design a goods and service tax system which will ensure a higher rate for the States than the rates of the Central government.

It is true that the same hat will not fit everyone, but then who will decide the size of the hat? If it is left to the finance ministry, it will lead to serious conflict between the Centre and the States and between the States.

My fear is this (NITI Aayog) is going to be used as a political tool by the BJP.

What is your opinion on the talk that the Constitution has to be amended so that States get more power, especially in planning?

Absolutely. The fiscal autonomy of the State governments in budgetary policies is being undermined, because the Centre is making a fiscal devolution conditional upon the State government adhering to certain norms which the Central government has adopted, and it is unconstitutional. The Constitution doesn't envisage any conditional transfers between the Centre and the State.

Also, India is a quasi-federal country. It was at a peculiar situation of Partition that our Constitution was framed, and now it is high time to restructure it by making necessary amendments to the Constitution.

The position of all States has been that they should get high allocation of funds. It is high time we restructure Centre-State fiscal relations. The new institution the Prime Minister is bringing in is not going to contribute to this outcome at all.

Do you think the NDA is following the same economic policies adopted by the Manmohan Singh government?

The NDA is more aggressively following the economic policies of the UPA in terms of foreign investment and structural reforms of the economy. The UPA was handicapped by the fact that the Congress did not have majority in Parliament. It was amenable to pressures from various quarters.

Now Modi has a relatively greater autonomy because of the good majority his party has in the Lok Sabha. Therefore, he can follow the reform policies more aggressively.

In the Left-supported first UPA version, the UPA had greater focus on the social sector. Modi now wants the market to take care of the social sector problems. He has already cut the health budget and is seeking to undermine MGNREGA.[1]

Where do you see India in the next few years?

There will be social unrest in India. Growth is predicated on the misery of the large sections of people. So, one cannot predict what kind of social condition India will have in the future.

Maybe Hindutva will be used to suppress any such unrest. Maybe this is the agenda of rising fascism in India.

What is required is a broad united front of Left and democratic forces. See the changes that are taking place in Latin America during the past decade. I am more inspired by Latin America of the 21st century.

---

[1] MGNREGA: The Mahatma Gandhi National Rural Employment Guarantee Act, 2005 started by the UPA government is an Indian labour law and social security measure that aims to guarantee the 'right to work'.

'Now that the neo-liberal reforms are taking place, it is important to have certain control over the market forces. There has to be at least some social concerns built into the process', said economist T M Thomas Isaac.

In its new avatar, NITI Aayog has developed a Strategy for New India@75 'to improve the policy environment in which the private investors and other stakeholders can contribute to their maximum towards propelling India towards a USD 5-trillion economy by 2030 by achieving the goals set out for New India 2022.'

Has *achche din* come?

Narendra Modi came to power promising achche din *for the people of India.*

So, one question everyone asked after a year of Modi's rule was, has achche din *come?*

I spoke to **Dr Krishnamurthy Subramanian** *who was a professor of Finance at the Indian School Business (ISB).*

After graduating with top honours from the Indian Institute of Technology (IIT), Kanpur, and the Indian Institute of Management (IIM), Calcutta, he did his MBA and PhD from the Booth School of Business, University of Chicago.

DO you think *achche din* is here for the Indian economy?

There are good signs and bad signs. The bad sign: there is more noise than action. Take for example, the *Swachch Bharat* and 'Make in India' campaigns. From an economic perspective, the Make in India campaign is very important as it has the potential to have a positive impact on the manufacturing industry. Manufacturing forms just 15 per cent of India's GDP while it is 25 per cent in China, and we have a long way to go.

What has been described as a demographic dividend can be a demographic liability.

How can it be a liability?

In India, the working group between the age of 22 and 40 years forms the largest section of the population. There is a vast pool of potentially skilled labour, which can come into the workforce. This is the demographic dividend.

But if these people do not get the jobs, there is plenty of evidence that shows that disgruntled youth turn to crime, Naxalism, etc So, what could be a dividend can become a liability. If not treated well, it can also become a threat.

In that context, growth in the manufacturing sector is quite important.

How important is growth in the manufacturing for India's GDP?

Very important. Until 2008-09, we were growing at 8.5-9 per cent despite not doing that good in manufacturing. We can grow at high rates with services contributing a lot. But manufacturing is much more important as far as job creation is concerned.

Back to the question on *achche din*, the good signs are that the results of the efforts to think big will not show immediately. Even the *Swachch Bharat* campaign will show results after 10-15 years.

These good decisions are that of a visionary, and they will not bring votes for Narendra Modi or the BJP. I see a leader who thinks of the nation, and not just votes.

But the 'Make in India' campaign can bring in votes, if it translates into jobs. It is something that may not have an impact on the stock market but can transform the country, provided there are changes in the labour laws.

They are trying to put the ducks in line for the transformation to happen. This is a government that means business while the UPA was the most impotent, most corrupt and most incapable government I have ever seen. Compared to that, this is a breath of fresh air.

On one hand Modi started the 'Make in India' campaign, on the other the huge Nokia plant in Sriperumbudur, Tamil Nadu, closed down. What signal will this send?

I will not read too much into the Nokia plant closing down. In a capitalist society, it is the survival of the fittest. In India, we have the problem of too many living dead. If you are not good, you should close down. You can't keep the living dead on ventilator support all the time. Plants getting closed are not bad news at all.

Do you feel we should take the PSUs (public sector undertakings) **also off the ventilator?**

That should happen, and I advocate closure of all sick companies whether they are in public sector or private sector, more so in the public sector as the number of living dead is more there. I say, all power to those who close down sick companies.

I connect this with the comment the Reserve Bank of India governor (Dr Raghuram Rajan) made. According to him, one of the biggest problems in India is that the big promoters here borrow money and do everything not to repay. The big promoters are like leeches, sucking resources from the system.

The signal that should go out is, you cannot suck blood like leeches from the system. If there is a leech in the system, it should get killed.

The perception all over the world about products from India is not that good when you compare them with what is made in China, for example….

If you ask me about the perception of Chinese goods, I will say, cheap and below quality.

But Chinese products are sold all over the world....

Yes, they are there all over the world. When you read Made in China, you don't infer it as a good- quality product, it is inferred as a low-priced product. So, that is not what India should be doing.

The reason why 'Made in China' became ubiquitous was because they provide a really low-cost manufacturing base, right from setting up a factory to labour. That is why everybody is setting up manufacturing base there. China gets five times more foreign direct investment than India.

I don't think it is a good idea to be a low-quality, low-cost manufacturing destination. We can become a good quality, low-cost manufacturing base, the same quality that Germany produces but at a lower cost, and that is what we should be aiming at. The cost of manufacturing should be low for people to come to India.

In India, the most controversial aspect of setting up a factory is land acquisition….

In the case of land acquisition, the farmer should have the share of the upside. Without the land, an industrialist cannot do anything. Without the industrialist, the value of the land will not go up. The land needs both. That is why the farmer should get the upside.

Whatever price an industrialist gives, there will always be a feeling of injustice. So, the farmer's ownership should not be taken away and every time the price appreciates, he should get a share of it. The share should be such that the farmer gets the upside, an equity kind of payoff and not a debt kind of payoff. This is a good way to acquire land.

This is what I have been advocating, and I have written quite a few articles on this.

Are you happy with the 'single window' clearance the government is talking about?

The worrisome part about single window clearance is how well the Cabinet Committee, bureaucrats and common man will work in tandem to enable investment. The problem is, even if the Cabinet clears it, the guy at the bottom of the pyramid asks for a share. As a result, the projects cleared at the higher level do not get ground-level clearances.

The 'single window' clearance is not only at the level of the Cabinet but should reach the last inspector who has to sign the document. Only then, it really becomes single window. For this, all the officials associated with a project should come together and give clearance to the industrialist. This is the second obstacle that needs to be cleared to make 'Make in India' a reality.

Third is finance. If financing has to be provided, fiscal deficit has to go down. As of now, the government is the biggest borrower. If there is Rs 100 to lend, and the government is going to take away Rs 45, the private sector is left with only Rs 55. If the government reduces its fiscal deficit and borrows Rs 35 instead of Rs 45, then the extra Rs 10 will go to the private sector. If that Rs 10 is lent to an unscrupulous promoter, it all goes to waste.

So, governance of the public sector banks should be proper so that the money gets deployed in good projects.

What changes do you want in Indian labour laws?

As much as 85 per cent of the jobs are in the unorganised sector, and that is because of the draconian labour laws. Politicians must realise that they need to stop listening to the unions, who are just 15 per cent of the workforce from the organised sector. They just want to preserve their privileges.

Labour laws need to be made a lot simpler. The argument that labour laws are for workers is wrong. They don't help workers, they only hurt them. They help only the incumbent workers.

You need to bring down wages to include a lot more workers. Wages should be directly proportionate to your skill level. You should be paid according to how much you contribute to the economy.

If these things – land acquisition, single window clearance, change in labour laws and financial distribution – are followed well, they will create the necessary environment for corporates to manufacture in India.

The brand of 'Make in India' will not change overnight. If you change the enabling conditions, the manufacturing sector will see a change, as our manufacturing sector is pretty okay.

Should manufacturing be the driving force in the economic growth of the country?

It can, if the four things I said are taken care of. It has the capability and the potential and only needs a good environment. After all, we have the Tatas, the Birlas and the Godrejs who supply to the world but today, many of them are setting up base in China because it is low-cost there. We need to provide the environment so that they invest and create jobs in India.

While the large corporates are efficient, the small and medium are very inefficient. Inefficiency affects the cost. For 'Make in India' to be really successful, apart from the four things I have mentioned at the macroeconomic level, the SME (Small and Medium Enterprises) sector has to become more efficient. It shouldn't be a high margin but a high-volume sector.

Which sector has to grow for India to achieve a growth rate of up to, say, 8 per cent? Is it manufacturing?

I would say agriculture, manufacturing and services have to grow and not just one.

If I have to choose one, I will concentrate on manufacturing now, because that is the one that will create jobs. The first priority should be on manufacturing. If manufacturing grows at 10 per cent and not at, just 1 per cent, India can hit very high single digit or even double digit growth rate, that is, if we take care of the problems.

Yes, our agriculture sector is really stagnated. It has to grow; however, the services sector is doing fine.

For a country of more than a billion, is there anything like an ideal growth rate?

Research show that developed countries like the US, Europe, etc cannot grow at 10 per cent. But the level of growth we are in, irrespective of our population, in the next 20-25 years, we can grow at close to 8-9 per cent. We have the potential to do so. If we grow at 6 per cent, we will be doubling incomes in, maybe, 15 years comfortably. If we grow at 8 per cent, we will double incomes in the next eight-nine years.

Where do you see India in the next five years?

It is a hazardous job to predict the future. I see an optimistic and also a pessimistic scenario.

The pessimistic scenario happens when tough calls are not made, and harmony doesn't prevail and there is only noise and no action. If we don't get our acts together in five years, it is going to be tough for the country.

This year's (2015) Budget will be a path-breaking one where you expect the government to remove many bottlenecks so that the initiatives like 'Make in India' become a reality. If that happens and also reforms in the labour laws, we may achieve more than 6 per cent growth in the next year and 7 per cent or so two years later and maybe, in another year's time, we may see 8-8.5 per cent growth and stay there till the fifth year.

Though I am cynical on many things, I am an incorrigible optimist.

When Jawaharlal Nehru initiated the process of social economy, he spent a lot of time in communicating to the masses on why we needed to do that. Somewhere down the line, our politicians have stopped communicating with the people, maybe because they were not as smart as Nehru. They only communicated through symbols.

What we need now are difficult decisions, but they need to be communicated to the people. And politicians need to understand economics very well in order to communicate it to the masses.

Interesting comment! 'When Jawaharlal Nehru initiated the process of social economy, he spent a lot of time in communicating to the masses on why we needed to do that. Somewhere down the line, our politicians have stopped communicating with the people, maybe because they were not as smart as Nehru'.

In December 2018, just before the 2019 Lok Sabha elections, Dr Krishnamurthy Subramanian was appointed as the Modi government's Chief Economic Advisor (CEA). In August 2022, he has been appointed India's Executive Director at IMF.

De-Mon!

8 November 2016, 8 pm.

Narendra Modi, the Prime Minister of India came live on the national television and announced to the country that the Government of India had demonetised all Rs 500 and Rs 1,000 banknotes with immediate effect. He also announced that new Rs 500 and Rs 2,000 banknotes would be issued in exchange for the demonetised banknotes.

This announcement created chaos in the Indian economy. Though it was done to bring black money into the open, what it achieved was killing the micro and small industries which operated on cash.

Even in 2022, we find that entrepreneurs in the MSME (Micro, Small and Medium Enterprises) sector have not recovered from the shock of demonetisation.

No wonder demonetisation has come to be known as De-Mon, despite the government's stated intention.

According to ***Venkatesh B Athreya****, a left-leaning Economist who had held faculty positions/fellowships/visiting scholarships in various universities like the University of Wisconsin and*

Bucknell University in the US, Oxford University and the University of Cambridge in the UK, Lund University in Sweden, the Scandinavian Institute of Asian Studies in Copenhagen, demonetisation was an economic disaster.

WHAT is your reaction to demonetisation?

They claim demonetisation will help in four areas: Curbing black money, eliminating counterfeit notes, stopping terrorist funding, putting an end to corruption. I find all these claims unsustainable.

Corruption is an ongoing activity, and it will continue to occur in all activities in the future too. You cannot end it by taking out some currency notes from circulation.

Second, terrorist funding does not come only from counterfeit notes or black money.

It is said that stone-pelting stopped in Kashmir after demonetisation....

It has nothing to do with demonetisation. Stone- pelting is an ongoing process, which has its ups and downs. Defence Minister Manohar Parrikar (October 2014 to March 2017) claimed that in the border areas, all terrorist activities have stopped. I am amazed by the frivolousness of such statements. Terrorists get money through proper channels too. This has become an important propaganda weapon for the BJP.

Let me put this in perspective: Black money is not just idle money kept under mattresses and inside pillows. Black money constantly is engaged in economic activities like buying and selling of shares, in stock markets, etc

For example, the whole issue of participatory notes. The Foreign Institutional Investors who are not registered here, can operate with participatory notes without having any disclosure requirements. You won't even know where the funds are coming from and who owns them.

This plays an important role in terrorist funding too. There have been repeated requests for banning participatory notes. I remember (then national security advisor) M K Narayanan used to describe this as the route for terrorist funding.

If you look at the black money issue separately, my point is that black money is flowing all the time.

Is it a parallel economy?

It is not a parallel economy alone; it can intersect also. There is no Chinese wall between the parallel economy and the so-called legal economy because money is generated for legal activities. So, the activity may be legal, but the income may not be reported and hence black.

Then, there are all sorts of ways to change black into white and the government was facilitating this activity. For example, when they (the government) gave the six-month window to deposit and pay tax at 45 per cent without having to disclose the source of income. This was an open encouragement in the Union Budget for tax evasion. This was done in 1997 by P Chidambaram (the then Finance minister), and in 2016 by Arun Jaitley (the then Finance Minister).

In this country, the governments are unwilling to politically confront black money power and bring them to book. Instead, they prefer to offer them time to time amnesties. They say that they got Rs 69,000 crore income and Rs 29,000 crore in taxes. This is trivial in front of the outstanding taxes. So clearly, this government's credibility on the issue of black money is suspect looking at the tax concessions given to tax evaders in the past.

Now, the question is: How much of black money is held in cash?

If you look at the income tax raids conducted in 2012-2013, what emerges is roughly 6 per cent of the undisclosed income is held as currency notes. So, 94 per cent of the wealth is in other forms and it keeps generated in activity and reinvested.

What should the government do to attack this 94 per cent?

I would quote (then RBI governor) Raghuram Rajan. He had said this much earlier, and not in connection with this. When he was asked on demonetisation, he had said, the perception that high value notes taken out of circulation to control black money is misplaced. He said if you did something like that, the rich would find a way around it and that they would have their people to manage. He also said that India now had a reasonable tax rate. The way to make people pay tax is doggedly pursuing it through the regular channels.

As the bulk of the black money is in the form of jewellery and real estate, if you look for the transactions and find the source of income, you can pursue them. Yes, it is painstaking work. This was what the British administration was famous for – they kept pursuing.

The same view was expressed by a Government of India M C Joshi committee.[1] The committee said, the perception among the public that taking away high value notes would curb black money was misplaced as only a very small proportion

---

[1] Under M C Joshi, who was then the chairman of the Central Board of Direct Taxes, a committee was constituted in June 2011 to study the generation and curbing of black money. The committee finalised its draft report on 30 January 2012.

was held as currency. The way is to do with normal taxation channel carefully. Ultimately, that is the only sustainable way of doing it and not dramatic gestures.

I am very convinced that only a very small fraction of black money will come out by this exercise.

In the case of counterfeit notes, it is also found that counterfeit currency is only around Rs 400 crore out of Rs 17 lakh crore, which is 0.0008 per cent or so. So, the argument that the move is to find counterfeit money appears to be completely bogus.

Do you feel the idea is good, but the execution has been quite bad?

I am not saying the idea is great. What I am saying is this is a very poor way to address the black money issue. Yes, something might still come out of this as 6 per cent of black money is held in currency. Suppose half of that 6 per cent comes out, it is something, but not a big sum.

The State Bank of India says the bank collected Rs 1.14 lakh crore as deposits in the last one week....

But why should that be black money?

People have been asked to deposit money in the banks, so you are forced to deposit money and they are limiting the amount to be taken over the counter.

On one hand, the government wanted to stop high denomination currencies to stop black money, but why come out with the Rs 2,000 note?

The government has not given any satisfactory explanation. That is why it looks ludicrous in the eyes of the intelligent public. This is a completely silly and illogical measure. In fact, it is causing a lot of inconvenience to people.

If you can print such a large number of Rs 2,000 notes, why not more Rs 100 notes instead? The move towards lower denomination notes is always a good thing.

Nobody is opposing banking, plastic and all that, but we are very far from achieving cash-less economy. Whatever said and done, 90 per cent of transactions in India is through cash and not plastic.

Only 46 per cent of adult India has bank accounts and many of them are dormant Jan Dhan accounts. Only 22 per cent of India has Internet penetration. As many as 19 per cent of Indian households do not have access to electricity.[2]

What you are dealing with is, this is the kind of economy. The numbers of rural India will be worse as these are averages.

According to me, it has no logic, and it need not have been here. High denomination notes may not encourage but facilitate illegal activities.

Let me say again: Black money is not stationary like a piece of furniture; it keeps moving. One major black money activity other than jewellery and real estate is *hawala* operations where money is taken out of the country and brought back through the Mauritius route, turning black into white. The other is the participatory notes in the market.

What kind of economic impact will this exercise have?

There are serious consequences because of this. What has it done?

It has taken out 86 per cent of the currency in circulation. There will be a very sharp reduction in liquidity. This will have

---

[2] Pradhan Mantri Jan Dhan Yojana started by PM Narendra Modi is a financial inclusion programme to ensure financial access to all citizens, like banking services, insurance, pension, etc

a big negative impact on demand. Purchases will run dry. At the level of consumption, lot of transactions will stop. So, the immediate impact will be on consumption. There will be a demand reduction in the economy and a collapse of the market.

But the more serious is its impact on production. Suppose I have a unit in Tirupur (in Tamil Nadu), and I pay Rs 10 lakh as weekly wages. I can draw only Rs 50,000 from my current account in a week. So how does an honest businessman give wages to the workers and purchase raw material?

Do you call this *kadvi chai* or poison for the masses?

It is bitter tea for the masses, and sweet for the corrupt. Anyway, the government's policies are like giving poison in small doses every day. I have a very dim view of the government's free market policies. This is just an addition to it.

This is not a surgical strike against black money, this is the surgical strike against the working poor and farmers. The real distress is right now happening in rural India.

As a measure, this is ill-advised and extremely ill-implemented too. For example, if they had confined to just Rs 1,000 notes, it would have been far better as two thirds of the notes in circulation are Rs 500 notes. Imagine, removing 86 per cent of the notes in circulation one fine day. You are causing a huge liquidity squeeze in the economy, and an artificial crisis in the economy.

You feel this move was completely unwanted?

Completely unwanted and poorly designed.

They shouldn't have done this at all. There are better ways to clean up black money.

All over India, this was the common sight; people queuing outside banks to deposit the demonetised notes. https://sabrangindia.in

Venkatesh B Athreya had said, 'this is not a surgical strike against black money, this is a surgical strike against the working poor and farmers'. The fact is, what he had predicted came true.

A study by the All India Manufacturers' Organisation (AIMO) found that micro and small scale industries suffered 35 per cent jobs losses and a 50 per cent dip in revenue in the first 34 days of demonetisation. Industries engaged in export-oriented activities reported 30 per cent job losses and 40 per cent revenue fall. In the manufacturing sector, medium and large scale industries reported a revenue hit of 20 per cent.

Even after more than five years, the small businesses have not recovered from the surgical strike called De-Mon…

Then, the GST!

Though it was the UPA that came out with the idea of implementing a 'one tax' system for the whole of India called the GST (Goods and Services Tax), they could not do so.

The Modi government claimed that only they had the guts to introduce the 'biggest tax reform' but the implementation was so faulty that even in 2022, businesses, especially the small ones, are struggling with the GST.

Perhaps the Modi government had a fetish for midnight decisions; the roll out of the GST happened on the midnight of 30 June 2017.

Despite his endorsement of the Narendra Modi government, ***M R Venkatesh****, a chartered accountant turned lawyer and political analyst, was a vehement critic of the Goods and Services Tax.*

This was how he described GST, 'When the government was supposed to create a majestic animal called the elephant, they decided to have the body of an elephant with the tail of a goat, the hump of the camel, one leg of a jackal, one head of a mouse and the intestine of a python'.

FROM the Prime Minister to the Commerce and Industry Minister Nirmala Seetharaman, the Bharatiya Janata Party government is talking about GST as if India is set to achieve economic niravana from the midnight of 30 June. Do you still maintain that we are not going to achieve any such thing?

Nirvana has dual connotations – spiritual as well as physical – when one is stripped completely. I do not know which nirvana they are talking about – spiritual or physical.

Do you still feel it is going to be a self-goal by the BJP?

I pray that it is not a self-goal, but the chartered accountant in me says it is a self-goal for all businesses; from large to medium to small.

If my understanding is correct, one has to file not less than 37 returns per year for every ordinary business, and that too per State. If you are doing businesses in Chennai, Bangalore and Hyderabad, you have to file 37x3 returns every year!

The problem is, if something goes wrong, the GST assumes that it is a wilful default. So my worry is, people can be held to ransom for even a simple mistake, by the revenue department.

If the clerk in any organisation makes some mistake while uploading the information, the owner will be held responsible, and believe me the consequences are draconian. And that in my opinion, will breed corruption.

Alternatively, every businessman will be expected to pass the *agni pariksha* of the tax administrator, and then only he or she will be declared clean.

So, my worry is, in the first two years, there is going to be huge number of mistakes out of misunderstanding or lack of understanding. The consequence will be chaos, confusion and possibly economic crisis.

Most citizens who do not understand the intricacies of GST are confused. Small businessmen and shopkeepers are confused. The government claimed that GST means 'one nation, one tax', but now, they are saying that there are four different tax rates. How exactly does GST work?

One nation, one tax has finally ended up as one hotel, three taxes!

Even for a restaurant, there are three tax slabs – ones with AC have one rate, without AC have another rate, and a third one for smaller restaurants. All this will result in utter chaos. It is not just four rates; you have eight rates of taxes. And multiple rates will be an incentive for evasion. Since the law and the rate encourages evasion, the revenue department will suspect every assessee.

From now on, it is a proverbial case of downward spiral; a race to the bottom.

To understand where GST went wrong, I have to quote a Tamil proverb, *Pillayar pudika poi korangu anathu*. If you go to any temple here, you will see that Lord Ganesha, that is *Pillayar* who will invariably be opposite Lord Hanuman. This is what has happened to GST.

The original GST is 180 degrees at variance with the GST we have got now.

The basis of GST is the Kelkar committee report of 2003. He wanted one tax from Kanyakumari to Kashmir and Kandla to Kohima, which meant that the States and Union Territories exist for every administrative purposes, but do not have the right to levy any indirect tax. Kelkar called it a 'Grand Bargain'.

Our politicians realised that if they brought in such a law, it would go against the basic structure of our Constitution. Our policy framers realised far too late in the day that we could not deny the States of their taxation power without altering the basic structure of our Constitution, which is impossible. So, what came about is a 'grand compromise of sorts' between the Centre and the States, but without the promised 'grand bargain'.

And whenever there is compromise, there is bound to be pitfalls. So, when they were supposed to create a majestic animal called the elephant, they decided to have the body of an elephant with the tail of a goat, the hump of the camel, one leg of a jackal, one head of a mouse and the intestine of a python.

This is what we have got as the GST! Naturally, it is not just ordinary citizens like you, nobody is able to understand what type of an animal this GST is.

They (the government) said this would be a very easy tax to administer, but the Institute of Chartered Accountants of India are conducting seminars after seminars to explain the GST, but after each seminar, chartered accountants are more confused than they were before the seminar started.

It is not only the rates, but the very DNA of the GST is flawed. Unless the States give up the right to tax, GST is impossible. What we have got is a spurious GST.

The Prime Minister said tax terrorism would end with the GST, but it appears what we are going to experience is something bigger than terrorism...

It is going to be tax jihadism. Terrorism is a mild word.

I would say lawyers and chartered accountants are going to benefit and society is going to suffer.

The Prime Minister told the CEOs in the US that GST would be a game-changer and they should come and invest in India....

I wish the Prime Minister was briefed properly on this. I sincerely hope what he says comes true but having known the tax administrators in the last 25 years as a practicing chartered accountant, all I can say is that the propensity of our bureaucracy is not to say, 2+2 as 4, but $\sqrt{16}$.

On top of this convoluted law and a bureaucracy that is behind the curve, we have a judiciary that will also find it difficult to cope with the new law. This situation could even lead to multiple problems. We are in for chaos.

The data that appears in the newspapers say citizens are going to pay more for things like tea, coffee, TVs, fridges, computers, AC travel in trains, air travel and even service tax. So, other than the confusion, chaos and cluelessness, are consumers going to pay more post-GST?

Exactly. Today, I saw an ad in the paper that says the prices of TVs, fridges, etc are going to increase post-GST, so buy before 30 June.

On the other page, there was Amitabh Bachchan telling us GST is a boon. These are the two totally contradictory ads in the papers.

I am not sure what it will be for the consumers. We have to wait and see. But I am not very hopeful of a price reduction.

Another cause for worry is the anti-profiteering clause that says dealers and manufacturers should not take profit out of GST. The rules are so complicated that it can lead to corruption.

Importantly, it shows that the mandarins of North Block still do not believe in the market, they believe in administered prices. They think they can micro analyse the books of every business.

Likewise, there are provisions on search, seizure, raid, inspection, and survey in this law despite providing so much of information. All this indicate a lack of faith in the system by the law makers. I would call this mindset, unadulterated jihadism.

The middle class have been supporters of the BJP. If this is going to affect them badly, won't it affect the BJP politically?

I don't want to look at this from a BJP or a Congress angle because even the Left supported the GST. Yes, if GST fails, probably the price will have to be paid by the BJP politically.

But I am looking at it from the national position. I feel the political parties should have the courage to alter the basic structure of the Constitution and say that the States should not tax. I may sound a bit outlandish, but if you want to have one nation, one tax, you have to do this. One nation, one tax does not mean 29 States and 29 laws for each State with several rate of taxes.

We have 36 GST laws now at the State and UT level which replaced 36 VAT laws. Then we had one Central sales tax which has been replaced by IGST. And instead of excise and service laws, we have one GST. So, under the GST regime, we have 38 laws instead of 39 laws under the present regime!

Last year, many people were telling us that GST will bring in 2 per cent more growth, additional revenue for the government, it will be anti-inflationary, and it will protect the dealers' margin. Mathematically, how is this possible? Two out of the above four is possible, but 4 out of 4 is a mathematical impossibility.

Businessmen think they will get more money. The consumer thinks it will be anti-inflationary. The government hopes to get more revenue. Economists think there will be 2 per cent more growth. As a student of economics, I know this is impossible.

Do you think the consumer will be the loser ultimately?

One cannot generalise. It will be a case where some consumers will lose and some gain, but prices will never come down, that's for sure.

In India, I have not seen a single instance of a single excise cut being passed on to consumers in the last 25 years.

Some experts also feel that GST may slow down the economy further.

My worry is, as development is rooted in confidence, if you are not confident of success, you will not invest. In this type of a diffused scenario where you are uncertain about the effects of the GST, you will decide to wait for one or two years till everything settles down before you invest.

The backbone of the Indian economy is the SME (Small and Medium Enterprises) sector and if you load them with this kind of a draconian law, they will not be able to stand up. You cannot treat a multinational company and a small business on par. So, because of the confusion and lack of clarity, there will be a slowdown.

What do you foresee politically and economically for India?

If it is successful, there will be many parties and people, from P Chidambaram to Manmohan Singh to Ashok Mitra to Mamata Banerjee to claim credit, but if it fails, unfortunately the axe will fall only on the prime minister.

Strategically, the BJP should not have showcased the GST as a priority. In my opinion, the reputation of the prime minister is not worth the political risk taken.

As far as economic growth is concerned, the investment cycle that is already in a dip, will remain so because of the confusion. Nobody will start a new factory or a venture soon. Everybody will be on a wait and watch mode. Also, GST will push us down further in the ease of doing business.

Ultimately, there will be chaos, confusion and possibly also crisis.

Why is the government projecting GST implementation as another tryst with destiny?

I don't know. But I know that traditionally this land has not believed in doing anything auspicious at midnight.

We consider early morning as *Brahma Muhurtham*. So, you cannot wake up God in the middle of the night and say, I am bringing in GST, so kindly bless me!

On a serious note, this is because of our obsession with the Moody's (an American credit rating agency) and the S&Ps (another American credit rating agency) and their rating. Our concern is not the tax payee or the assesse; our concern is some rating agency sitting 6,000 miles away. Why are we bothered so much about their ratings?

Only if you are obsessed with what London and New York say, you will indulge in this kind of a *tamasha*.

> *M R Venkatesh said, 'our economic niravana is not through GST. Post-GST, consumers would pay more! The consequence will be chaos, confusion and possibly economic crisis'.*
>
> *How true; chaos and confusion over GST still continue, and consumers are paying more!*
>
> *But the Indian government chose to celebrate 1 July as GST Day.*

A Man who Dedicated his Life to the Backward Communities

*There are not many people in today's India who have dedicated their lives completely to the marginalised and underprivileged like **P S Krishnan**, a retired Indian Administrative Service (IAS) officer.*

After three decades of service as an IAS officer, he retired as the secretary to the Government of India in 1990 but continued his work for the socially deprived classes in India.

Krishnan was a member of the National Monitoring Committee for Education of SCs, STs and Persons with Disabilities, and a member of the Central Monitoring Committee of the National Mission for Empowering Women.

One of his most significant initiative at the national level was the formulation and initialisation of the special component plan for scheduled castes in 1978.

One can say, he dedicated his entire life to the upliftment of the backward communities in India.

When I spoke to him in 2016, he was 84.

YOU said your fight for the socially deprived class in our society started 65 years ago. What was the turning point?

The turning point, when I look back, was a report I read in a daily newspaper about what Babasaheb Ambedkar had said, that one in every seven Indians was an untouchable. As an 11- year-old, I could not understand what he meant by 'untouchable'. I thought, how could anybody be untouchable?

As a child, I used to accompany my father every day to the Padmanabhaswamy temple (in Thiruvananthapuram) and when we walked through the long corridor, I used to ask him many questions, and we used to discuss many issues.

The day I read the report, I asked him, 'Why does Ambedkar say that one in every seven Indians is an untouchable?' My father explained very honestly about the conditions of untouchables in India. I asked him, 'Is it not unjust?' He said, 'Yes, it is'.

What kind of impact did the revelation have on you?

When I read the newspaper report, it puzzled me. When my father explained it to me, I understood what it was. It shocked me but I could not accept it. That day, I decidedly went over to the side that suffered, and my place became there. I continued to be on that side even today.

What could you do for them after you joined the IAS?

Even before I joined the IAS; as a student and later on as a teacher, I tried to do whatever was possible to break the caste barriers. As a lecturer, when I put across these ideas to my students, all of them were responsive; not one student was against the idea of ending inequality in society.

I joined the IAS in 1956. From the beginning of my career itself, I took up the issue of scheduled castes, scheduled tribes, backward castes, nomadic communities, scavengers, etc When

I went on tour to villages, I used to camp only in the localities where Dalits, scheduled castes and scheduled tribes lived. I gave importance to land and house distribution to scheduled castes. These two functions became a part of my everyday life, apart from opposing untouchability and any crime committed against them.

Sixty years have passed since you joined the IAS and you have seen first-hand the situation they were in then. Do you think changes have taken place in our society in the last six decades? If so, how much has it changed?

There are changes, which I would call quantitative, but changes I would call qualitative, are not yet to be achieved.

Scheduled castes continue to be agricultural labourers and they continue to be the bulk of the landless. If they move to the cities, they continue to be urban unorganised labourers. Untouchability continues to be practised. Atrocities are being committed on them.

The changes that are essential for their emancipation have not happened. For example, all scheduled castes should have viable agricultural land, and this land should have irrigation through combined, joined tube wells or bore wells.

This applies to scheduled tribes also, though they are not landless. They are people with land, but their lands are being grabbed even now. Unlike the scheduled castes for whom ownership of land was prohibited from one end of the country to the other, scheduled tribes are people with land.

What is more important for their emancipation, owning land or getting education?

Both are extremely important. It is not one or the other. Nobody can touch them if they have a viable irrigated land in a village. So, for dignity, security, and resistance to untouchability, ownership of land is important while education is required for advancement.

If you have irrigated land, you get the wherewithal to educate your children. When you don't have this, you have to fall back on child labour as they are also required to contribute to the family income.

But once they get some income through irrigated land, their children will be free to pursue education.

Is the Dalit agitation we saw in Una in Gujarat as a result of years of suppression that has reached a boiling point?[1]

This is not only a matter of Gujarat, it is a matter of all of India. There is no State that can say, we have succeeded in eliminating the indignities and deprivations on Dalits, Adivasis and the backward castes.

Even in Kerala?

Yes, even in Kerala. If you take the scheduled castes of Kerala, the old type of untouchability has largely disappeared. Once they were asked not to wear clothes, footwear, etc

This happened thanks to the efforts of leaders unknown to the world like Ayyankali, Karuppan Master, Narayana Guru. Of course, Narayana Guru is more known unlike Ayyankali.[2]

---

[1] In July 2016, seven members of a Dalit family were assaulted by a group of people under the pretext of cow protection in Una in Gujarat. This resulted in State-wide protests and unrest later on.

[2] Born in 1863, Ayyankali was a social reformer and revolutionary who worked for the progress of the oppressed in Travancore.
Born in 1885, Karuppan Master was known as the 'Lincoln' of Kerala because of his relentless crusade against untouchability. Born in 1856, Narayana Guru became a revered spiritual leader, philosopher and social reformer.

These are all great people who without any expectations in return, fought against these indignities and mobilised Dalits and backward castes in those days, as a result of which the old type of untouchability has largely disappeared. But it still exists in those parts of Kerala which adjoin Tamil Nadu and Karnataka.

But the consequences of untouchability like low level of education, low ownership of land, high presence in unorganised labour still continue to haunt the scheduled castes, the scheduled tribes and fisherfolk in Kerala.

Do you feel banning beef and cow slaughter acted as triggers for the Dalit outburst we saw in Gujarat?

Atrocities against scheduled castes have been going on for a long time. When Dr Ambedkar appeared before the Simon Commission (that came to India in 1928 to study constitutional reforms), he gave a graphic description of the atrocities perpetrated on the scheduled castes. So, it is not a new thing.

After Independence, there was this notorious Ramnad riots in 1957 which most people in India today have not even heard of.[3]

Then there was this Keezhvenmani atrocities in Tamil Nadu in 1968 where 62 people were burnt to death, mostly women and children.[4]

There were a series of atrocities in Bihar, Uttar Pradesh, Gujarat, and many other places in various States. A scheduled

---

[3] A series of violent caste clashes happened in the Ramnad district, Ramanathapuram or Rameswaram in Tamil Nadu.

[4] Kizhavenmani massacre happened in the Kizhavenmani village in Tamil Nadu on 25 December 1968 in which striking Dalit labourers were killed by a gang led by their landlords.

caste boy was burnt to death as he had the temerity to sing during Garba.

Atrocities are an unfortunate part of our otherwise great civilisation. Ours is a great civilisation, but this is a dark spot.

Periyar started the Dravidian movement in Tamil Nadu. It is the most literate State after Kerala, but there is discrimination based on caste even today. Dalits are not allowed inside temples and honour killings happen in villages.[5]

All social revolutions move up to a point and then stop. As soon as a particular class or caste reaches a certain level, they do not want the people below them to come up.

The Tamil Nadu social revolution brought the backward castes up and once they reached the top, they started treating the Dalits the same way they were treated by the upper castes.

The caste virus is virulent, and it damages the minds of even good people. Even normal good people behave in a criminal way in the caste context vis a vis the Dalits and other lower castes. That's why the caste system has to be annihilated, which was one of the goals of Ambedkar.

Do you blame Hinduism for discrimination against Dalits in Indian society?

This is perpetrated by those who do not understand religion. The Upanishads talk of the universal soul permeating all. How can there be untouchability then? So, I don't blame any religion for this; society is to blame. Even in Muslim and Christian society, there is inequality.

---

[5] Social Activist and politician Erode Venkatappa Ramasamy Naicker, respectfully called as Periyar or Thanthai Periyar, started the self-respect movement in Tamil Nadu.

The Dalit agitation has been going on for many years. Even the Buddhist movement was strengthened by the scheduled castes.

There were many saint reformers in medieval India. In the 13th century, there was a great man called Basaveshwara (12*th* century social reformer) who broke rules and encouraged the marriage between his sister and an untouchable. Nobody knows about him in India except in Karnataka and his followers have become Lingayats, another caste.

There was a saint called Sankardev (15th-16th century Assamese polymath) in Assam who brought tribals to the mainstream society. These counter narratives against the caste narratives are unfortunately not known.

You mean the Dalit movement we see today is not new, but a continuation of what had happened.

It is a continuation of many movements that had happened even before Independence. You saw the Nationalist Movement, the Communist Movement, the Socialist Movement and then the Ambedkar movement. We also saw many movements in different States like Narayana Guru in Kerala, Periyar in Tamil Nadu, etc

After this, the scheduled castes began to slowly organise, began to resist. In Kerala, Ezhavas were untouchables then and they could not just enter temples, they were not allowed to walk around the outer walls of the temples.

The Vaikom satyagraha was not about entering the temple, it was about the rights of the untouchables led by the Ezhavas for the right to walk on the road surrounding the outer wall of the temple. Because of all these movements and later on with education, Ezhavas came out of the situation they were in.[6]

Don't you think we need political leaders who are visionaries, who understand history as well as society to douse the fire?

Over the years, I have written letters to all the leaders including P Chidambaram, Dr Manmohan Singh, Amit Shah, and Narendra Modi. I have not spared any leader. Only if they read, will they understand.

I have explained why and what special measures are required for scheduled castes, scheduled tribes and backward castes and the justifications for them.

I have taught like a teacher, but no student was willing to learn. They feel that by giving a sop here and there and by symbolic actions, they can win votes. That's all they want. Just votes.

Is it lack of understanding of a social problem or lack of political will?

Indian political parties without any exception are dominated by upper castes. There are political leaders who themselves grab the land of scheduled tribes. How do you expect them to work for the same people?

I am not talking in general terms, I know the individuals and what they did, I know the harm they have done to scheduled castes and scheduled tribes.

Domination of political parties by the same castes that dominate society has not helped the cause in any way. Not all

---

[6] Vaikom Satyagraha was a social protest that happened in 1924 in the erstwhile Travancore against the untouchability and caste discrimination that was prevalent in the Hindu society of Kerala.

people behave like this, but those who are doing this are from the upper castes.

Irrigated land distribution and universal education are the two most important things to be done. Both these were there in the UPA's (United Progressive Alliance) Common Minimum Programme on my efforts, but the government did not do anything on this.[7]

Not only in the Common Minimum Programme, it was there in the Presidential address to the joint session of Parliament in 2004 too. The President saying in Parliament, and not doing it is the most undemocratic and unconstitutional thing.

Next are pre-school education through *anganvadi*s and reservation in residential schools of high quality. Money was provided for such schools throughout the country through my efforts in 2006, but the then finance minister (P Chidambaram) did not allow it to happen. Otherwise, we would have had schools in every district.

Unfortunately, the goal of politicians is only to get votes and not work for society. Getting votes has become an addiction for politicians.

The Maharaja of Kolhapur in 1902 started reservations, based on caste. Do you feel even after 70 years of Independence, it has not achieved its purpose?

Reservation is not the single medicine, which will cure all the diseases. In Malayalam, there is this word, *Ottamooli*, reservation is not an *Ottamooli*. You require an array of instruments of which reservation is just one.

---

[7] The Common Minimum Programme is a document outlining the minimum objectives of a coalition government.

Will there be any difference if leaders from the scheduled castes, scheduled tribes and backward castes lead major political parties?

The problem is who will allow them to lead a major political party?

If I am the leader today, I want my son or daughter to be the next leader, that's what we see today. Why should I allow a Bangaru Laxman (a former president of the BJP who was a Dalit) to come in?

You knew him very well....

He was a very good person and understood these issues. He was one of those rare politicians who knew a South Indian language as well as Hindi. In my opinion, he didn't deserve what happened to him.[8]

But the truth is no party will give its high position to a backward caste person. When P V Narasimha Rao was there, he tried to have an election for the Congress Working Committee, and even the most popular scheduled caste person could not get enough votes to get in.

You feel an eruption of the volcano is what we are seeing in Gujarat?

Only the smoke is coming out now. Let us prevent the lava from coming out by taking proper measures.

We have to recognise that a great injustice has been done to our own people who are of our own race, and that we have been so cruel to them.

---

[8] Bangaru Laxman was made to quit from the post of the party president after he was caught on camera accepting money from a purported arms dealer in a sting operation by a news portal.

We should apologise and then join them in this effort to help them be equal in all the parameters of life which the upper castes of society enjoy.

The last I spoke to P S Krishnan was in March 2019 and in November, he passed away.

Till his last breath, he spent his life for a cause he believed in.

Should there be a Retirement Age for Politicians?

Year 2019. India and the BJP under Narendra Modi began preparations to face people once again.

After Narendra Modi came to power in 2014, he had side-lined all the senior party members and gave cabinet berths only to those who were below the age of 75.

In 2019, he went a step ahead by not giving tickets to those above the age of 75.

The question the most debated after Modi's decision was, should there be a retirement age for politicians?

I decided to ask the question to ***O Rajagopal,*** *one of the senior-most Bharatiya Janata Party leaders, the first and the only BJP MLA in the Kerala assembly, who turned 90 in 2019.*

Rajagopal had also served as a minister of state in the Atal Bihari Vajpayee government.

Though age had not caught up with him, he said he was looking forward to 2021 when his term as an MLA ends and he could retire from political life.

He was of the opinion that there should be a retirement age for politicians.

IN 2014, when Narendra Modi came to power, he decided to have only politicians below the age of 75 as his ministers. This time, the BJP did not give tickets to those above 75 like L K Advani, Murli Manohar Joshi, Sumitra Mahajan, etc which was criticised by many. Do you feel politicians also should have a retirement age?

Certainly. If you can have a retirement age for all other jobs, it applies to this job also.

At 90, I am past all that! I am in fact, disqualified. I am happy that there is a retirement age now as there will not be any pressure on me to contest after this.

I am waiting for 2021 so that I can retire.

I feel it is a right decision taken by my party. In fact, I feel it should have come long ago. If it had come earlier, I would have been enjoying a retired life.

The criticism against Modi and Amit Shah (He was the party president from 2014-2020 and the chairman of the NDA alliance) **is that they want to keep the seniors away....**

Such criticism is unwarranted. When Modi decided to form the government itself, it was decided that people past 75 should not be in the Cabinet. They wanted to bring in more young people. It was a good decision.

When Amit Shah decided to contest from Mr Advani's seat in Gandhinagar (in Gujarat), it was portrayed as if he was insulting Mr Advani.

It was a right decision for a healthy party that was looking for young talent. After all, it is the youth that can deliver. Politics is not a post for retired people to enjoy, like a governor's post.

If an old person is fit and mentally agile, should his experience not be utilised for the betterment of the country?

I feel it is taking a great risk. Yes, there are exceptions where some old people are mentally agile. But if they go on continuing, when will the next generation get a chance? Whether you are healthy or not, it is essential for old people to give way to the new generation. That is how it should be. The young generation also should get an opportunity to work, it shouldn't be hogged by some old people alone.

To have a good social equilibrium, there is need for one generation to move back to give way to the next generation.

Also, after a certain age, your ability to disseminate goes down, thus affecting your decision-making ability. At the same time, raw youth without any experience is also not good. They should be trained well before giving an opportunity to function.

What would you say about Mr Advani's blog criticising those in the BJP who have been labelling people who do not agree with them as anti-nationals?

What Advani wrote was 100 per cent right. In a democracy, somebody who disagrees with you is not your enemy. There are different views in a society. I have always been of the opinion that different views should be accommodated, understood and respected. Nobody should think that what he says is always right.

Also, what you think as right today may not be right tomorrow. I will give you an example from my life. The very first protest I participated in was against the RSS (Rashtriya Swayamsevak Sangh).

It was in 1948. I was a college student at the Victoria College in Palakkad. I was playing badminton with my friends when the news came on radio that Mahatma Gandhi was assassinated. We stopped playing immediately and there was a gloomy atmosphere in the entire hostel.

There were two groups of students in the college then, the Congress and the Communists, and I kept away from both groups. But after the assassination of Gandhiji, these two groups joined together and said it was the RSS that killed him. We all believed them, and I joined the torchlight procession on the streets of Palakkad shouting, 'Down! Down! RSS!'

In those days, as a devotee of Swami Chinmayananda (a Hindu spiritual leader who founded the Chinmaya Mission), I used to attend his Gita classes regularly. One day, when Swamiji came to know that (then) RSS chief (Madhav Sadashiv) Golwalkar had come to Palakkad, he got excited and said, 'I must see Golwalkar'.

Swamiji was one person I admired and when he spoke so excitedly about someone, I got interested. I was shocked to see a saintly person because I was expecting a ruffian!

At that time, I didn't know much about the RSS. Later on, when I came into contact with many RSS people, my opinion of the organisation and its members changed.

Why are the BJP members so intolerant to criticism? They don't take criticism in the right spirit.

I don't think they are intolerant. When the Opposition says something like 'Narendra Modi is a curse to the country', those who know him, his views and what he wants to do for the country, may not relish it. They respect him for what he is.

But calling them anti-nationals....

That's not right. There is a point in what Advani said. There will be two views on every subject. Just because somebody won't agree with your opinion, you cannot call him anti-national.

Sometimes because of youthful exuberance, you tend to have such extreme views. That's not a mature viewpoint. The party also should not approve of such an attitude. Anybody can disagree and criticise.

After all, we have a system, a parliamentary democratic system which we have borrowed from the British, where the Leader of the Opposition has been given a prominent position as important as the Leader of the House. The Leader of the Opposition gets a Cabinet rank.

In the five years of Modi rule (2014-2019), two issues that dominated were beef politics and cow vigilantism. Is it right to lynch a person just because he had beef at home, or he sold beef?

What happened was not right. People have the right to take whatever food they like. At the same time, there was an organised effort to tarnish the BJP's image highlighting something that happened in some remote place in UP or Bihar, as if incidents of that sort were regularly happening in the country.

Those were isolated incidents. Not that I approve of even those isolated incidents; they should not have happened. But playing them up as a regular and common thing was not right.

Didn't the BJP leadership fail in making them realise what they did was wrong?

It was a group of rural people in a particular area who behaved that way. A section of the media wanted to play it up as if the BJP was responsible for it. The BJP may not have any hand in them. But the media should realise that playing up such isolated incidents creates a bad image of the country when that is not the real image of the country. It doesn't mean that we should ignore or tolerate even such isolated incidents.

Many people felt at that time that the party gave more importance to cows and cow shelter than Indians. Though the BJP has not spoken about cows in the 2019 manifesto, in the 2014 manifesto, cows got prominence.

In the 2019 manifesto, the party has not spoken about cows or cow shelter. It is not a priority item now. The priority now is a clean, efficient, administration with focus on development, development strategies involving people which is *Sab ka Saath, Sab ka Vikas.*

Many people feel Modi is not talking about *vikas* now, but on national security and patriotism because not much *vikas* has happened in the last five years. What do you say about that?

Please understand that you cannot repeat the same slogan again and again. It does not mean that you give up *vikas*. As time progresses, your focus also should shift and come up with new ideas.

About the criticism that no *vikas* happened in the last five years, it depends upon your view on what really is development. When Modi came to power, only 38 per cent of the people had toilets in India and for the first time, a prime minister spoke about the need to have toilets at an Independence Day speech.

In 5 years, 98 per cent of the population have toilets. This is a great achievement. Providing these basic facilities is also part of *vikas*.

O Rajagopal retired from politics at the age of 92, once his term as an MLA ended in 2021.

. . . .

The general elections were to be held in the months of April and May of 2019.

But before that....

On the 14th of February, a convoy of vehicles carrying Indian security personnel on the Jammu-Srinagar National Highway was attacked by a suicide bomber in a vehicle at Lethapora in the Pulwama district of Jammu and Kashmir.

On the 26th of February, Modi government ordered an airstrike on an alleged terrorist training camp in Balakot, Pakistan. Indian warplanes undertook a bombing raid but later on, it was revealed that there were no training camps there.

Whether the terrorist camps inside Pakistan were destroyed or not, people of India were happy to have a strong and decisive leader like Narendra Modi who was confident enough to order air strikes on the enemy.

Interestingly, during the election rallies, we did not hear slogans like Sab ka Saath, Sab ka Vikas *or* achche din.

The new slogans were Bharta Mata ki Jai *and* Vande Mataram. *When Modi ended his speeches with* Bharat Mata ki Jai, *crowds at all places roared,* Bharat Mata ki Jai!

They were not bothered whether achche din *came or not. Economy did not matter.*

So, it was advantage Narendra Modi again.

. . . .

PART 7

2019-2024

Ruling Party: National Democratic Alliance (NDA)

Prime Minister: Narendra Damodardas Modi (BJP)

Modi-Shah jodi win again!
Thank you, Outlook India.

A Victor Again

The general elections for the 17th Lok Sabha were held in seven phases from the 11th of April to the 19th of May 2019.

In the background of Indian warplanes bombing Balakot in Pakistan, the ruling party could arouse unprecedented nationalistic sentiments across the country, and as expected, Narendra Modi won the mandate to rule India again.

And this time by a huge margin.

The BJP increased its vote share from 31 per cent in 2014 to 37.36 per cent, the highest by any political party since the 1989 elections.

The number of seats also jumped from 282 to 303, the BJP winning a simple majority on its own.

On the other hand, under the leadership of Rahul Gandhi, the Congress could not even win 10 per cent of the seats to get qualified to be the leader of opposition. The grand old party won a mere 52 seats.

The NDA had 353 seats as against the UPA's 91.

That's the story in a nutshell of the 2019 Lok Sabha elections.

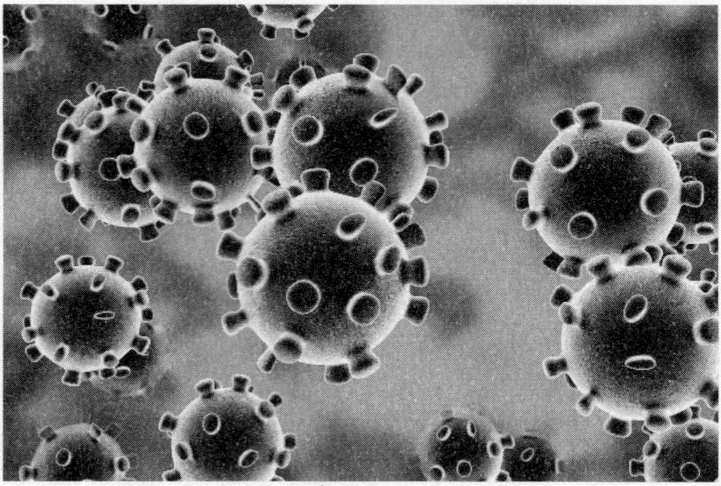

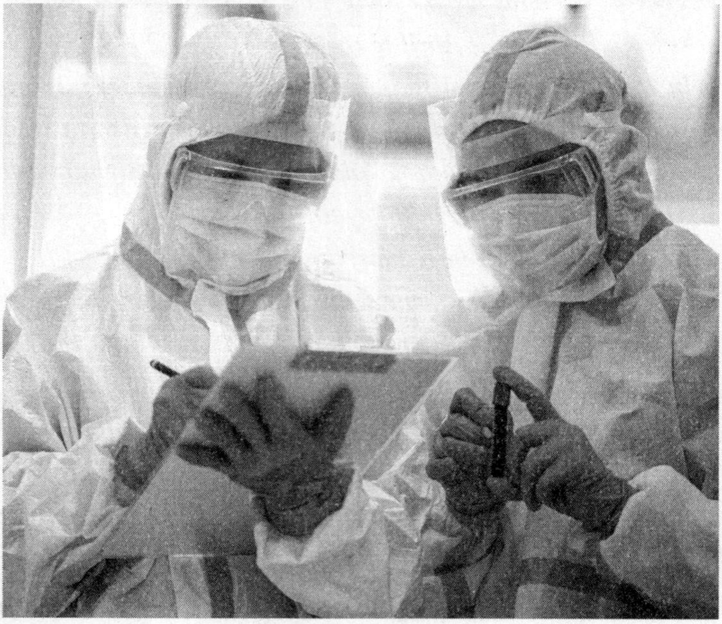

Corona virus strikes the world!
https://www.webmd.com
and
https://promptmd.com

Who Exactly is Narendra Modi?

There is no doubt about the fact that Narendra Modi won the 2019 general elections in style.

What is it about this man that works magic on people?

Who can talk about Modi better than someone who has known him for more than three decades?

And that one such person was ***Uday Mahurkar****, a journalist who is also an author of two books on Narendra Modi.*

AS the author of two books on Narendra Modi, and as a person who has known him for three decades, was his victory in the 2019 Lok Sabha elections a surprise for you, or was it on expected lines?

At least for me, it did not come as a surprise at all.

When I wrote my second book on the three years of governance of Modi, I understood the track he was on. People might say the Balakot attack was the trigger, but I would say Balakot was the icing on the cake. That is because he had already laid the foundation of good governance.

I would say the Direct Benefit Transfer (DBT) and monitoring of welfare schemes through geotagged photos were the two reasons that contributed to his success.[1]

DBT removed middlemen and money reached into the accounts of people directly. Before this, people had to grease the palms of clerks and others to get their cheque. If you remember, Rajiv Gandhi made an honest statement that out of every one rupee, only 15 paise reached the beneficiary.

DBT was a tool started by the Manmohan Singh government, but it was Modi who took it to its logical end. When he took over as prime minister in 2014, number of people under DBT was 2.5 crore. Today, the number is 55 crore.

When tools of technology came into governance, the success rate improved by 40 per cent. What was below 50 per cent before 2014 in the delivery of welfare schemes in the country, Modi has taken it to beyond 80 per cent to 90 per cent.

Under Modi's housing scheme, more than 95 per cent of the people got their houses at the same place with the same quality that was sanctioned by the government.

But the image of his governance was that of high unemployment rate, farmers' distress, etc.

It is a very complex phenomenon. Nobody can deny there is a problem in job creation. Nobody can deny there is a problem in the farm sector. But what overrode these factors was the Modi government's honesty.

---

[1] The scheme aimed to transfer subsidies given by the government of India directly to the people through their linked bank accounts.

Like what he told the BJP workers, that if the government could convince its honesty of purpose to the people, they will believe you. It is not that he has not committed any mistakes; he has. But people are willing to forgive you if you are honest.

Do you feel the Congress calling him '*chor*', (a thief) boomeranged as people believed in him and his honesty?

It definitely boomeranged. Those who have benefitted from his various schemes might have felt bad when the Congress was abusing Modi.

He started the '*Main Chowkidar Hoon*' (I am a watchman) campaign and totally demolished the '*Chowkidar Chor Hai*' (The watchman is a thief) campaign. It was like how he demolished Mani Shankar Aiyar's *chaiwallah* jibe with '*Chai Pe Charcha*' in 2014. He did the same thing in 2019 also. Basically, the Congress did not learn its lessons properly.

I was with Amit Shah on tour to UP, MP, Bihar, etc I saw a wave, but the margins of 3-5 lakh votes came as a surprise.

An incumbent prime minister emerging victorious with such huge margins is unprecedented....

It is unprecedented because if you compare Modi's victory to Jawaharlal Nehru's, you can say that Nehru had the advantage of being the leader of the freedom movement. So, this kind of victory is happening for the first time in independent India.

I have never seen such pro-incumbency in my life as a journalist. And it is built on multiple factors.

Which factor played the major role in his victory? Modi as a decisive leader or the welfare schemes?

All the factors played an equal role. Yes, Balakot attack certainly played a major role.

In December 2018, when many surveys predicted that the BJP would not win more than 200 seats, I did my own survey by talking to various sections of people. To my surprise, about 80 per cent to 90 per cent of people said, (they would vote for) Modi. This was before the Balakot attack.

When the liberals call him a Hindutva leader, people from all spectrum of Indian society, from tribals to backward communities to young voters to women, have voted for him. How do you explain this?

He has become the leader of the poor. The entire constituency of the poor which, the Opposition parties claimed as theirs, voted for him.

If you listen to his speech after the victory, you will see that he has emerged as a statesman. Let me say, he is emerging as a statesman in an Indian mould.

Nehru was also a statesman, but his statesmanship was rooted in Western concepts. Modi's beliefs are based on the liberality and spirituality of Hindu philosophy. So, we have a statesman now who is rooted in Indian philosophy.

A statesman has to be a very just leader, just to every section of society. But Nehru was always partial to the minority community because he believed that they were the younger brothers, and so needed pampering. He believed that if they committed something wrong, the majority should tolerate it.

Those who call Modi a right-wing Hindutva leader should look at the policies of the Modi government. Implementation of the policies has been without any discrimination. Muslims have got homes, scholarship, etc

The international media described Modi as a divisive leader even after he won more than 300 seats....

It is a very false campaign. I very strongly suspect it as a strong campaign driven by vested interests who do not want to see Modi as one of the world's leaders. They have exposed themselves totally now.

What is it about Modi that makes people either love him or hate him?

This election has proved that all those who are right thinking, all those who want India to rise above caste, politics and religion, are the ones who love Modi.

The Hate Modi brigade has their own agenda.

This election has been a great leveller in one sense. The margin of victory of the BJP candidates in the North Indian belt has been tremendous. It shows that Modi is an acceptable leader to all.

Modi's new slogan is '*Sab ka Saath, Sab ka Vikas, Sab ka Vishwas*'. Is it with real honesty that he is saying this? Or is it just a slogan for the election?

He truly believes in the slogan. He has dedicated himself to truthfulness. Even when he is hard on the Opposition, it is part of *Chanakya Neeti*. It is very clear in *Chanakya Neeti* that you have to be truthful to the people of the country.[2]

Muslim appeasement resulted in the Partition of the country and it was continued by the Congress party. The election result is also an anger against the Opposition parties and the Congress's Muslim appeasement.

---

[2] Collection of aphorisms selected from various sastras by Chanakya, an ancient Indian polymath.

But the criticism is that with this victory, India has become Hindustan....

No. India has become a truly secular country now. We were following pseudo-secularism till now, and Modi is moving towards real secularism. Real secularism is when the law of the land treats every caste, every religion equally.

How different will be Modi 2.0 from Modi 1.0? Will he take hard decisions this time, like building the Ram temple at Ayodhya?

He will take a very hard line on the issue of divestment.

He has promised to build the temple at Ayodhya, but he promised with a caveat, that it will be built with *Sarva Sammati* under the court's direction.

Do you think history will remember Modi as the strongest leader independent India has seen?

Certainly. I have no doubt about it. The way he reacted to the Pulwama attack, no leader has done so far. The way he has tackled China also. Nobody can deny that he put China in its place to some extent. Yes, much more needs to be done on the trade deficit front with China as it is still very high.

Will you place him above Indira Gandhi?

Bangladesh was a great feather in her cap, but she had many demerits.

Indira Gandhi was a strong leader, but then she allowed corruption, politics of nepotism and the Emergency to happen.

Narendra Modi is dismantling all these things. In April 2014 itself, just before he was elected to power, I had said that the arrival of Modi in Delhi would be a big shock for the favour-driven culture of Delhi.

Do you feel with this kind of win, the importance and influence of what Modi calls the 'Khan Market gang', or Lutyens's Delhi (who were critical of Modi) **will wane soon?**

It is already gone! In the last three months, nobody has used the word secularism. We are moving from pseudo-secularism to true secularism. Modi's USP is creating a sense of pride in our own abilities and the nation.

You have observed Modi closely for several years. How has he changed over the years as a leader and a person?

The trajectory of Modi is that he has learnt and moved forward, and thus, he has taken his level up.

I know him from the time he entered the BJP from the RSS, and I have been in touch with him from 1990 onwards. I have seen him as the chief minister of Gujarat and all those stories of good governance from 2003 to 2010, were mine. So, my criticism of Modi was also taken very seriously. When I criticise, it is taken as something quite objective as I am an admirer of Modi.

He has also changed a lot over the years. He was never a great listener before he became the chief minister. When you sit with him, he would like to talk more about himself and the topic of his interest. But now, he has become a great listener.

As chief minister, he used to tolerate ministers who could deliver, but were not very clean. He tolerated them for delivery. But after coming to Delhi, he has stopped tolerating anybody who doesn't pass the test of integrity. Every officer has to pass the test of integrity.

Has he become more confident and also impatient?

He has become confident, not impatient. When you want to reach the top in politics, you have to make small compromises in the beginning. If you aim for absolute perfection, you can't reach the top in politics. I would say he used *Chanakya Neeti* to reach the top.

Is he an ambitious politician who enjoys being in power?

He enjoys being in power, but he has linked his ambition to the good of the country, and not personally. That is the hallmark of a statesman; a statesman links his future with the future of the country.

An interesting observation from biographer Mahurkar: 'He (Modi) has also changed a lot over the years. He was never a great listener before he became the chief minister. When you sit with him, he would like to talk more about himself and the topic of his interest. But now, he has become a great listener.

As chief minister, he used to tolerate ministers who could deliver, but were not very clean. He tolerated them for delivery. But after coming to Delhi, he has stopped tolerating anybody who doesn't pass the test of integrity. Every officer has to pass the test of integrity.'

Recession in India?

When Narendra Modi government came to power the second time in 2019, it was said the Indian economy was slowing down.

At that time India was encountering major macroeconomic issues such as a sluggish GDP growth rate of 4.7 per cent which was the lowest since 2013, high unemployment rate, decline in industrial output of core sectors – the worst in 14 years.

But by 2020, many experts had started officially talking about a recession.

The question since then has been, where is Indian economy heading to?

***Professor K J Joseph**, director, Gulati Institute of Finance and Taxation, spoke about the direction in which the Indian economy was going.*

ARE we moving towards recession, or are we already in recession?

We are already in recession. How do you describe recession? When you clock declining GDP growth for six consecutive quarters, it is recession.

Anyway, it is by now well understood that the economy is slowing down. Economists have even termed it as the great decline. The question now is, where is this decline happening?

After India started liberalising in the 1980s and globalising in the 1990s, India's economic growth had steadily increased. India's growth rate from 1991 to 2000 was 5.5 per cent to 5.6 per cent, and from 2001-2010 it was 6.5 per cent. The growth rate accelerated by 1 per cent then.

But after 2010 till 2018, it was 6.8 per cent, which means that the growth rate was merely 0.3 per cent higher than the previous decade.

Coming to the present, the current year's growth rate is expected to be only around 5 per cent. It is quite likely that this decade is going to record a lower growth rate than the previous decades.

If it so happens, it also means India appears to have already peaked its performance. Deceleration has set in, which we cannot afford.

Peaking at less than 7 per cent? Does that mean it can only decline from now onwards?

If you are good enough, you may stabilise. Else, you will decline.

Now, we have to compare this performance with that of China. How has it been in the case of China? China registered a growth rate of 9.6 per cent from the 1980s till 2017. If you look at India's performance, you will see that it was never a steady growth. It had occasional downs.

For example in 1991, we had a growth rate of just 1 per cent, in 2000 it was 3 per cent. And in 2003, it was 3 per cent and now again, it is coming down to 5 per cent.

After growing at 3 per cent in 2003, it picked up to almost 8.1 per cent in 2016, which was the highest among many of the comparable countries at that time.

But the point is, today China is recording a growth rate of 6 per cent, which is after achieving 9.6 per cent for nearly thirty-seven years!

The Japanese economy doesn't grow now; even a growth rate of 1 per cent is great for them.

Can we afford to stagnate?

Exactly. And that is a point of major concern.

It is not for the first time after globalisation that the economy is facing this kind of recession. I will consider liberalisation as a 1980s phenomenon. In 1991, we had a slowdown, early 2000s we had a slowdown, and now we are experiencing one. What I want to argue is that Indian economic performance was never steady; it has always been fluctuating.

If you look at the annual growth rate from the 1980s, you will see that it always had violent fluctuations, unlike China. If at all China had fluctuations, it was much less violent as compared to India.

Why is it that we experience violent fluctuations? Has it anything to do with uncertain political situations?

No, it is not so much due to the political atmosphere. It can be due to endogenous and exogenous factors, that is something very specific to the economy and also something external to the economy.

I would like to compare this kind of economic situation to a human being. For example, what enables a baby to grow physically, mentally and intellectually strong? If the baby is malnourished, it catches cold and fever quite often. That is because it is not healthy. On the other hand, a healthy child can fight the viruses.

You mean the Indian economy is an unhealthy economy?

Precisely. That's why I said we had structural problems; when your fundamentals are not sound enough to sustain a growth that India badly needs. If you take the example of China, it has been shown that it is possible for large economies like India to grow steadily.

Compared to China, what is it that India lacks?

That is the question we need to answer. What generates growth? Growth does not come from the heavens. The basic thing you need is capability. And the most important capability is human capability. That human capability has to be manifested in terms of the capability of individuals and organisations to survive in the fiercely competitive global environment in which they operate. Today, it is more competitive than ever before. To survive in a highly competitive economy, you need the capability.

Does that mean people themselves are responsible for the violent fluctuations in the economy?

Exactly. Who are the agents of an economy? The labour force. They should be educated, they should be knowledgeable, they should be competent. These qualities make entrepreneurs. It is the people who make enterprises. Entrepreneurial capability is nothing but the manifestation of the overall capability of the people who manage them.

Today you are living in a world where knowledge is the key resource; not capital, not land. You can survive in a globalised open economy only if you are competitive. And that competitiveness depends upon your capability, and that capability is essentially a function of your knowledge and learning capability.

We are all the time talking about the large human capital that we have....

I will say that our human capital is used in a very wrong way.

For example, when you talk about learning capability, it can be in terms of science-based learning, research and development. It can be the number of scientists, engineers, R&D expenditure and patents you generate.

India has been talking about spending 2 per cent of the GDP on R&D from the 8th Plan onwards. But it is not even 0.9 per cent today. Compare this to the 2.1 per cent of the GDP in China (spent on science and technology). With respect to patents, India is nowhere near China.

Secondly, the experience-based knowledge, which is different from science-based knowledge. Perhaps you can describe it as scientific knowledge and synthetic knowledge.

In fact, under globalisation, India's strategy has been to make use of synthetic knowledge, by borrowing from others, by attracting FDI, by importing and other such means.

What about ideas like Startup India, Make in India, Skill India, etc? The intention was to encourage new ideas, and not synthetic knowledge.

These are all wonderful ideas. But unless you have a judicious mix of scientific knowledge with synthetic knowledge, none of this will succeed. This has to come from stronger Academia-Industry collaboration which is very much missing in India.

What is happening to the best brains? In fact, today India has been facing a brain drain of much more severe intensity than what we faced before liberalisation. Whether you succeed or not depends on the knowledge economy in the Fourth Industrial Revolution.

Compare India's software capability with that of China. Today, China has a software market of about $550 billion, and they export around $70 billion. That means $480 billion worth of software is used in the domestic economy. This domestic use of software, in fact, makes the Chinese economy in general more competitive and efficient. They are able to flood the world market with their products, so much so that they have generated huge employment in manufacturing.

Now, in the case of India, we have around $150 billion worth of software, out of which $100 billion is exported. Our domestic consumption may be around $50 billion only. This is as against the $480 billion in China.

Why are we exporting $100 billion worth of software instead of exploiting the huge domestic market?

The best minds of India do not work for India, but for other countries. By exporting, they are working for the companies outside this country. In an economy where there are no barriers to import, we are actually working against our own domestic firms and working for our competitors.

We hear about India's huge domestic market all the time, but why is it that nobody is really exploiting it?

Exactly. I would even go on to say that there may not be any county in the US which is working so hard for the American economy than Bangalore! I am not against software exports. In 1991, when India was facing a severe imbalance in the external sector, it was ideal to promote software exports. Today, we are sitting on a foreign exchange reserve of $450 billion. We should have changed our policies according to the needs of the time. What we miss is an ability to change according to the changing needs and contexts.

Do you think this is why China could produce an Alibaba while we have not been able to produce a single global company like that?

Do you know Alibaba has a domestic arm which has created 600 Taobao villages all over China? This is entirely for rural China. The turnover of Taobao villages is double that of Alibaba.[1]

How much have Indian IT companies done to make the Indian agricultural sector competitive, which is lagging behind by centuries? How much have they done to transform India's rural and agrarian economy which would have increased domestic demand? The truth is, they haven't done much.

For the last almost three decades, we have been hearing about the need to use technology in rural India and the need to have food processing units, but even today, we waste 16 per cent of our fruits and vegetables production, and 10 per cent of our oil seeds, pulses and cereal production....

Yes, in the case of agriculture, makers of value are not the takers of value. In enabling the makers of value to be its takers, IT has a huge role to play. Because of the dominance of the IT sector, there is reason to believe that other industries are also suffering because of competition for skilled manpower and the so-called resource movement effect. And it has affected India's manufacturing capability.

---

[1] Taobao village is a cluster of rural e-tailers where at least 10 per cent of village households engage in e-commerce or at least 100 online shops have been opened by villagers.

If we were to ask the question, why do we not have sustained growth, I would say it is because after globalisation, the kind of growth India has had only aggravated inequality.

Today, we have a services sector, including IT and software, that contributes 62 per cent of GDP which is produced by 33 per cent of the workforce. But take agriculture, 50 per cent of the population is involved in it, but it contributes only 17 per cent of GDP, indicative of very low productivity. This essentially is the first manifestation of inequality.

In the case of manufacturing, it contributes about 16 per cent of GDP and employs about 13 per cent to 14 per cent of the population. But this is the sector that is suffering the most.

In 1950-1951, India had 9 per cent of GDP coming from manufacturing which increased to 15 per cent by 1996. After 1996, despite new manufacturing policies, it has not gone up. It is only 16 per cent of GDP now.

What we need for the economy to grow is, there has to be a seamless transfer of people from agriculture to industry. It was made possible in China. And it was only because people got educated that they could move to industry.

Even today, our rural folks cannot be transferred to industry. Even if our agricultural contribution did not increase, industry's contribution should increase and for that, their productivity has to increase. 50 per cent of the people contributing only 17 per cent of the GDP is unsustainable.

Is it because they are not educated or skilled that the seamless movement of people from agriculture to industry not happening?

Yes, lack of skill. We should ensure that at least for the next generation, it happens.

Who is to be blamed, the policymakers?

Instead of blaming anyone, what we should do is change our approach.

We have one monetary policy for the whole country. One size doesn't fit all.

Further, simple reduction in interest rates will not induce investment, when investors don't find demand for their products due to low purchasing power on account of growing inequality.

India being a country that is more diverse than all the continents, we should have location specific, region specific and State specific policies with the States having the freedom to articulate policies.

Unfortunately, the fiscal federalism as it exists today hardly leaves any scope.

More autonomy?

Yes, more autonomy to the States. The States should have more freedom to decide the destiny of their people.

Would you say the problem the economy faces now is more structural?

I am rather puzzled to see the great divide among scholars of eminence. While one group considers it as an outcome of structural factors like labour market rigidity and inequity, others consider it as emanating from cyclical factors – slump in demand, demonetisation, GST etc

To my mind, the key ingredients in the making of the current economic problem are both structural and cyclical.

Since your child is already weak due to growing inequality and capability deficit, any external shock like demonetisation or faulty imposition of GST affects the child and it suffers more.

Further, slump in demand cannot be delinked from the increasing inequality in the distribution of income.

We are prematurely ageing. And we have to be careful about it.

What is the quality of growth we have? You take the problems faced by agriculture, manufacturing, they are all structural. Economies with structural problems are bound to have such cyclical problems. So, you have to address both cyclical and structural problems.

When you have both cancer and fever, you cannot have just paracetamol. You have to give paracetamol for the fever and chemotherapy for cancer.

'Unfortunately, the fiscal federalism as it exists today hardly leaves any scope for growth', said Professor K J Joseph.

Now fast forward to 2022. The problems are high inflation and high unemployment. The annual inflation rate in India was 7.79 per cent in April 2022, which is said to be the highest since May 2014.

Food inflation went up to 9 per cent in the second half of 2022, a new high since November of 2020. The cost of oils and fats soared by 17.28 per cent, and vegetables by 15.41 per cent. As per the CMIE report, the overall unemployment rate has increased to 7.83 per cent in April 2022 as compared to 7.60 per cent in March.

The UN Department of Economic and Social Affairs said in its World Economic Situation and Prospects (WESP) report released in May, India was projected to grow at 6.4 per cent in 2022.

Dementia, a Health Threat to Indian Society

After being labelled as the diabetic capital of the world with 74.2 million diabetic patients in India in 2021 which is likely to increase to 124.8 millions by 2045, what stares at Indian society is another terrifying disease called dementia, a disease connected to old age.

According to the Dementia in India report 2020, around 5.3 million people above the age of 60 suffer from dementia in India which is expected to go up to 50 million by 2050.

And by 2050, there will be more people above the age of 60 than those below the age of 15 years in India.

A frightening reality that is staring at India.

***Dr Sridhar Vaitheswaran**, consultant psychiatrist and head of the DEMCARES project at the Schizophrenia Research Foundation in Chennai, told me that Indian society needs to find answers to some of the questions like how to detect dementia early, and how to tackle it.*

A report says that people living with dementia has doubled from 1990 to 2016 globally. In fact, an increase of 117 per cent.

Is it because the world is ageing that the number has increased exponentially?

Yes. As the population gets older, all the conditions that are associated with old age increase, including dementia.

Is longevity the only reason?

No, there are a variety of reasons. The primary one, of course, is that we are better at treating infections and other diseases which makes people live longer.

For the first time in the history of humankind, there are more older people than young ones. Right now, we have the maximum number of older people living on earth.

Even in India, if you look at the number of people above the age of 60, it is anywhere between 100 to 130 million! It is also projected that we will have almost 300 million older people by 2025.

Would you say as our population is ageing, dementia is going to be one of the major challenges for the state, the doctors, society and families?

Absolutely. Anybody and everybody who is going to be dealing with older persons should be aware of the problems they would be facing starting with public transport, public services like post offices, banks, etc as we will have more and more elderly people accessing these services.

Yes, this is going to be a huge challenge for everybody; hospitals, doctors, nurses, physiotherapists, health workers and family members. And all of them should be aware of this reality.

What exactly are the challenges for the state and the community?

First and foremost, there is very little awareness about dementia. So, there are multiple issues.

It is not uncommon to see families bringing in patients with advanced Dementia. As the disease advances, patients will have more and more problems. Only then families realise that it is an issue that has to be treated.

Unfortunately, response to treatment is not fantastic at a very advanced stage. It is not that we cannot do anything, but it is better if the patients are brought in earlier; as soon as the family realises that they have something like a memory issue. But families don't bring in patients in the initial stages.

Due to lack of awareness?

Yes. Even among the educated population, families do not realise that the issues are because of dementia. Even when an elderly person complains of lack of memory or lack of concentration or direction, families brush it aside as old age.

There is also a negative image of dementia, and majority of the people think they can do nothing about dementia.

Can dementia be arrested or postponed or treated?

There is good treatment available which can slow down the advancement of dementia.

Can we say the treatment is palliative?

No. Palliative care is given towards the end of the life. For example, in the case of cancer, palliative care is given for six months to one year.

But when you are dealing with someone with dementia, you are not talking about such a short time period. The average age of survival of a person from the time of diagnosis of dementia till the end can be ten years. You cannot have palliative care for ten years.

So, what we are talking about is managing the illness. Yes, you need palliative care towards the end of life in dementia too. But then, that is towards the last stages.

In the early stages of dementia, a person can lead a very successful life and carry on with their day-to-day activities without any major problem at least till the mild and moderate stage.

With medicines?

With medicine and other treatment. There are also non-medicine treatments available which will help the patient continue to function as well as they can for a long period of time.

What are the symptoms that families and patients should look for?

There are multiple causes for dementia, depending on what type you have. The most commonly occurring symptom is memory loss. You get more forgetful than you normally are, like forgetting your spectacles, wallet, key, etc It doesn't mean that everybody who forgets has dementia.

The other most important thing is you may not be able to do things you were doing before, like going to the bank or any other routine you have been regularly doing. What I mean is you have trouble doing the routine activities which you were doing before. This is an early indication of something gone wrong. It is necessary that you get proper medical help at the right time.

There are many conditions which may look like dementia, but may not be dementia. It may be depression or hormonal disorder or a deficiency or some other clinical problem. If treated early, you can have complete reversal of the symptoms.

If it is dementia, and it is identified early and have the right treatment early on, patients can continue to function normally for a very long period of time and reduce the burden on their families.

Do you think more than the person, people around her/him should notice the symptoms early on?

Of course, though it can happen both ways. Sometimes, the person herself/himself may also be aware, but it is often the others who notice the symptoms.

Generally, by what age the symptoms appear in people?

Usually, dementia is common among people above 60 or 65, particularly in those who have high blood pressure or heart disease or any other chronic medical problem. They have the higher risk of developing dementia. So, they should be more aware of the disease and the symptoms.

Is there any difference between Alzheimer's disease and dementia? Are these two diseases connected?

Dementia is an umbrella term like fever. But there are different types of fever depending on the causes. Similarly, there are different causes and types of Dementia. And Alzheimer's is a type of Dementia, and one of the most common types of Dementia. There are other types of Dementia also like vascular dementia, dementia in Parkinson's disease, etc

Can dementia be prevented?

To an extent, yes. We talk about cancer prevention and the simple analogy is, smoking leads to cancer. But if you don't smoke, there is less risk of you getting cancer. It doesn't mean that you will not get cancer. It is not that non-smokers will not get cancer.

Following the same principle, if you do all the right things, you reduce the risk of getting dementia.

Doing right things means?

Generally, all the things that is good for the heart is also good for the brain. We all know about heart disease and what you should do to prevent it.

So, you follow the same principle; like exercise and proper diet, a healthy lifestyle, not smoking and drinking alcohol. Whatever causes heart disease also contributes to dementia.

Like I mentioned earlier, if you have high blood pressure, if you had a heart surgery and if you are diabetic, you run the risk of getting dementia. So, all these conditions have to be managed well as they increase the risk for dementia.

It is said that caregivers are the biggest sufferers taking care of people with dementia, working for more than ten hours a day. In what way can this situation be addressed?

There are multiple ways in which we can address this.

Because of lack of awareness, people seek help much later, when the problems become really bad. If they can identify the symptoms much early, we can prevent so many problems.

One of the most common problems you see at a later stage is, wandering. People with dementia tend to wander. They become restless and agitated. They lose the sense of direction even within the house; they may not know where the bathroom is, they may not know where the kitchen is.

In the very advanced stage of dementia, you see them quite often inappropriately urinating at all places. That is because they cannot identify where the bathroom is.

Many people come for help when the patients reach such an advance stage. By this time, it becomes very difficult to treat and it is difficult for the family members also.

To prevent them wandering away, you can use simple techniques like locking the gate. If it becomes too restrictive for the person, you can use a GPS tracker on the person.

And within the house, if they have difficulty in finding places, signages can help. Or leaving the toilet door open or leaving the toilet light on at night.

Dementia patients also fall down quite often. By making small changes in the house, you can prevent all these problems. If you make the changes earlier on, it will be easier for the family members and patients.

Is taking care of dementia patients tough for caregivers?

Any illness is tough for caregivers. Yes, taking care of dementia patients is a challenge. On an average, a family spends ten to ten-and-a-half hours looking after someone with dementia, which is more than a full-time job.

The University College in London has developed a programme called START that helps reduce depression and anxiety among the family caregivers of a person with dementia. This intervention has been found to be very effective in the UK. It has helped improve the quality of life of the caregivers and lessen the burden on them.

It is important that we address this particular issue also as in the longer term, it can have a huge effect on the country's economy. In the next few years, we are anticipating a large number of people with dementia in India.

It means, we are going to need as many or more number of young caregivers. It can create a huge problem for the family and the country.

So, we are going to adapt START and test it for use in India.

You spoke about humanoid robots that are used in Japan to take care of people with dementia. In a highly populated country like India, should we make use of people or use robots instead?

There is no one solution for this problem. Use of robots was necessary in Japan because of the huge demographic shift that has taken place in the Western world and Japan. There are more older people than younger people there.

India will reach that crisis point in 100 to 150 years. Then, we will not have enough human resources to look after people with dementia.

Right now, we are looking at 5 to 7 million people with dementia in India. It is going to reach 15 million by 2050 which is a huge number. Demand for support also will rise then. So, you have to develop human resources like an army of trained caregivers to address the issue. They alone may not be adequate.

We have to also take the help of technology and one technology we can explore is the use of robots. In the longer term, when we have more older people than younger ones, we have to depend on the use of technology.

I read about a study conducted at UCLA (University of California, Los Angeles) which says that the number of people with dementia is low in India because of the amount of turmeric we use in our food preparation. Can turmeric reduce the risk of dementia?

Maybe. Some studies say that the use of turmeric or coconut oil or the natural condiments we use in our food can have some positive effect. There are some other studies that say that a Mediterranean diet can prevent dementia, because people in the Mediterranean countries have lower risk of developing dementia.

Some studies show that pollution runs the risk of increasing heart disease, brain disease which will in turn lead to dementia.

It is not just diet that contributes to dementia, there are other factors also like the levels of stress people experience.

Another major factor that contributes in India to dementia is the use of alcohol. From the public heath perspective, use of alcohol needs to be addressed urgently.

You said by 2050, India is going to have 50 million people with dementia. Due to lack of awareness, is the situation going to be alarming?

Yes. It is going to be a major problem for the country. We have to make a lot of noise as we need to make everyone aware. We have to see that we don't miss the boat.

Yes, in future, this will be a major issue if we don't address the problem now.

'Indian society needs to find answers to some of the questions like how to detect dementia early, and how to tackle it', said Dr Sridhar Vaitheswaran.

According to the National Statistical Office (NSO)'s Elderly in India 2021 report, India's elderly population (aged 60 and above) is projected to touch 194 million in 2031 from 138 million in 2021, a 41 per cent increase over a decade.

The report also said that there would be 93 million males and 101 million females by 2031, up from 67 million males and 71 million females in 2021.

As per the report, Kerala has the highest elderly population (16.5 per cent) now, followed by Tamil Nadu (13.6 per cent), Himachal Pradesh (13.1 per cent), Punjab (12.6 per cent) and Andhra Pradesh (12.4 per cent).

A decade from now, that is by 2031, the same five States are projected to have the maximum proportion of elderly people in its population; Kerala (20.9 per cent) followed by Tamil Nadu (18.2 per cent), Himachal Pradesh (17.1 per cent), Andhra Pradesh (16.4 per cent) and Punjab (16.2 per cent).

Also, as age increases, prevalence of dementia increases. For example, nearly 20 per cent of people above 80 suffer from dementia.

In 2020, about 6.57 per cent of India's population were over 65 years of age. Also, the population aged 70 plus years increased by 3.73 per cent from 2019 to 2020.

The First Corona Virus case, in Kerala

February 2020. Life changed dramatically for not just India but the entire world.

Though the first corona virus case was first detected in late December 2019 in Wuhan in China, it was in early February that the first three cases of coronavirus (Covid-19) infection were confirmed in India, and all the three were in Kerala.

And they were medical students from Wuhan.

The Kerala State health machinery acted quickly in isolating and treating them, and all the three recovered from the attack. The most important aspect was that the State could contain the spread of the virus.

When the Nipah virus (a virus that can spread from animal to people) attack occurred in 2019 also, Kerala's healthcare system responded admirably.

And the person who was appreciated and complimented for swift action was the health minister in the Left Democratic Front (LDF) ministry, ***K K Shailaja,*** *popularly known as Shailaja 'teacher'. In fact, 'Teacher' has become her surname now.*

Her exemplary performance as the health minister during the Covid times won laurels all over the world; she was on the cover of many international magazines and the world nicknamed her as Rockstar minister.

It was in early March 2020 that I met her at her office. Several people were waiting in the lobby to meet her late in the evening too. It was after attending to the last person that we sat down to talk about how Kerala's health department successfully contained the corona virus.

When we spoke in March, we were unaware of what awaited us in the coming days and months!

IT is well known that hundreds of students from Kerala study medicine in Wuhan. So, when the coronavirus outbreak started there, were you concerned?

Of course, we were very concerned. From the moment we read the news online about the coronavirus outbreak in Wuhan, we became very vigilant. Because we had an experience with the Nipah virus, we knew that any virus could appear anywhere in the world.

So, when we read about the spread of coronavirus in China, the first connection that came to my mind was, China, Wuhan, medical university and students from Kerala. I knew they would fly back immediately, and they might even come carrying the virus.

When I called the health secretary, Dr Rajan Khobragade, he also said that we had to be very vigilant, for the same reason that came to my mind; that the students from Wuhan would come back any moment. So, the chances of a virus outbreak might appear in Kerala first.

Even before anyone landed in Kerala, we decided to set up a rapid response team and the team met immediately. We then sent messages to all the district medical officers to be ready. We also contacted Preeti Sudan, the health secretary in Delhi.

What kind of precautions did you take when you heard about the coronavirus outbreak in Wuhan?

We needed permission from the aviation department to have screening at the airport. Before we started the screening, a few students had come, and they were taken home by their parents. Because we had instructed people to inform us about all those coming from Wuhan, we could track them down immediately.

You must understand that this was much before the Indian government brought students from Wuhan by chartered flights.

We had already set up isolation wards in two districts.

The first girl we contacted already had sore throat and fever. So, there was not much resistance from her parents about the idea to keep her under quarantine. But they wanted to know why they had to be quarantined when only the girl had fever.

But we insisted they also come with us. We kept the girl in an isolation ward at the Trissur Medical College, and kept the parents under observation. We did this even before we got the test result from the virology department in Pune.

Then we caught hold of one of her friends who came with her, in Alappuzha, and he was also kept under quarantine there.

The third person had gone to Kasargod, and she was kept in isolation there.

Were you worried about an outbreak because these three students came from Wuhan?

Yes, we were extremely worried. In fact, 72 people came from Wuhan itself. We traced the addresses of all the people who were on the flight and contacted them through the local medical officers.

We isolated all those who came from Wuhan, and had slight fever. All of them were under our observation till they tested negative. We had sent the blood and sputum samples of all those who were isolated, to Pune.

When the results came from Pune, three students had tested positive. In fact, even before telling us, the virology department announced in the afternoon that the samples that came from Kerala were positive.

The moment we came to know the results, Rajan Khobargade and I went to meet the CM. When I told him that the situation was serious, he asked us about our plans.

We said, like what we did in the case of Nipah, it would be isolation, quarantine, and opening a control room in Trivandrum, and organising teams to take charge of each work.

The health secretary wrote 18 guidelines to be followed, and we called for a meeting of all the head of departments in the medical colleges.

Then we went to Trissur to oversee the work. By the time we reached Ernakulam, it was 12.30 at night. I called for a meeting with the doctors in the periphery, and also the HoDs (Head of the Department) in the medical colleges then itself. By the time the meeting got over, it was 2.30 in the morning.

I met the press after the meeting and told them that there was no need to panic, and everything was under control.

Why did you say there was no reason to panic when all of China had started panicking by then?

I said so because of the experience I had after the Nipah outbreak.

When we announced the Nipah outbreak, there was panic in the entire State. People from the village where there was the first outbreak, started leaving the village.

It was a panic reaction, and I didn't want such panic this time. If at all one of these people are carriers, they would be spreading the virus in another area. It was like a war zone moving to another area. That was why I said there was no need to panic. That was the only way we could contain the spread of the virus.

We had three positive cases, but our success was the three not going up to 30 or 100. Also, all the three survived the virus.

While you were planning all this, did you think of the magnitude of the situation in Wuhan?

Yes, I did. We only had three positive cases. There were hundreds of positive cases at that time in Wuhan.

What happened was, they did not grasp the situation in the beginning. By the time they understood, the virus had spread like wildfire.

In those days, I could not sleep at all. I could not even imagine something like that happening here.

I cannot but applaud the support given by our entire team. If not for Rajan (Khobragade) and the team, we would not have been able to contain it so well. There were many days when Rajan did not even sleep at night.

What about the students who were brought to India on special flights by the Central government?

That was a week or so after the first three people were tested Corona-positive.

When I came to know that the government was going to bring people from Wuhan, I called (Union Health Minister)

Harsh Vardhanji. I wanted to know whether they would send those people to their respective States soon after they landed. He said they would isolate them first in Delhi, and send them only if they tested negative. It was a good idea. Otherwise, we would be putting the entire country at risk.

Even after the 14 days of quarantine in Delhi, we decided to ask them to be in isolation at home for another 14 days. We didn't want to take any chance.

Now that Covid-19 is spreading to more and more countries, are you still vigilant?

Yes. We cannot relax now. I am still on mission mode. At night, I am still worried about the report that would be coming the next day. The satisfying part is that we could take immediate action and save those three children.

When I spoke to K K Shailaja in early 2020, neither she nor I imagined what was awaiting us in the coming days.

On the night of the 24 March 2020, in a televised address, Prime Minister Narendra Modi announced to the shocked nation that for the next 21 days, the entire country would be under complete lockdown to fight the corona virus.

He was following what Wuhan did – locking down the entire province and cutting it completely from the rest of China.

Life was not the same again for the people of India from the night of the 24th of March, 2020.

Corona Virus Strikes India

From March 2020 onwards, there was panic and chaos in the entire country.

According to the data from the Health Ministry, on the 25th of March, India had 618 confirmed cases of Covid-19, of which 562 were active.

There were 13 deaths with Tamil Nadu and Madhya Pradesh recording their first Covid deaths, and Gujarat reporting its second death.

By then, according to the WHO bulletin, more than 375,000 people were infected globally and 16,000 people had lost their lives to the virus.

In India, clueless doctors in PPEs and other armours were attending to the breathless patients who were admitted in the hospitals.

When I spoke to ***Dr Sudhir Kumar Verma****, an Associate Professor at the department of medicine, King George's Medical University, Lucknow, he had finished his one-week duty in the coronavirus ward and had started his 14-day quarantine at the hospital.*

I heard that none of the medical staff at KGMU has gone home since the first coronavirus patient was admitted.

Yes, the first patient, a doctor from Canada, was admitted on 9 March.

The whole team has been under active quarantine in the hospital in separate rooms for the seven days when they are on duty, and they are not allowed to go home.

After a team completes one week of duty, a new team takes over. The previous team will then undergo a quarantine of 14 days. In fact, they are given the option of quarantine at home or at the hospital premises itself.

They are given strict instructions to follow isolation at home if they choose to do home quarantine. But most healthcare workers have chosen to remain in the hospital quarantine area itself.

Is it because the virus is highly infectious, and they didn't want their family members to be under any risk?

Exactly. Most healthcare workers, including me, have elderly parents living with them. I also have a one-and-a-half-year-old child. Nobody wants to put the lives of their family members at risk.

Now that my active quarantine of one week is over, I have decided to undergo 14 days of quarantine in the hospital premises itself.

How did your family take the news that you were going to treat coronavirus patients?

When my family came to know that I was posted in the coronavirus isolation ward, everybody was very scared, especially my mother. She became less tense only after I explained to her that we go to the ward with proper protective gear.

I told her I was doing my duty when the entire nation is passing through this crisis, and that we needed to serve our people and country. Slowly, she realised that this duty is very important to me.

She would call me every day to check whether I was all right. You know how mothers are!

It is not possible to take calls when you are on duty as we did not want to contaminate the phone. So, I told everyone in my family and also my friends that I would not be able to receive calls during the day.

My mother became normal only when I told her that my active quarantine days were over, and I had no symptoms.

Please tell us how the one week in the coronavirus isolation ward was.

When we first got posted in the coronavirus isolation ward, what I did first as the team leader was, explain every detail about the virus, how we should avoid getting it, what precautions to take, how to wear and remove the PPE, etc to the entire team of doctors, residents, nurses and ward boys.

The protocol was that everybody underwent training which included knowing the illness and also psychological support, before they went to the ward.

I found that after the first day, everybody was relaxed, and I did not see any fear in any of them. Once you are taking care of the patients, nothing else comes to your mind; only the patient matters.

Our isolation ward has two areas; one for the suspected patients and another for confirmed cases. So, we also divide the team into two groups, and the groups rotate the position every day.

What was the mental condition of the patients when they got admitted there?

First, they were not ready to accept that they were coronavirus patients. When we explained to them that it was only a mild attack and there was nothing to worry, they relaxed.

Our first patient was a doctor who was a Canadian. She had come to Lucknow with her husband, in-laws and child on vacation. Though she was fully aware of the disease, we explained everything to her. She had only very mild symptoms. Among the family, only she tested positive first, and the others tested negative.

What was the condition of the patients when they were brought to the hospital?

They came complaining of fever, cough, sore throat, body pain, etc

Most of the patients who have come to our hospital were mild cases and they were young. The oldest patient was 56 years old. He has been cured of the disease and will be discharged very soon.

Luckily, we do not have any serious cases with serious pneumonia till now. So, we didn't have to use ventilatory support for anyone.

As per ICMR (Indian Council for Medical Research) guidelines, we have to test all acute respiratory illnesses for coronavirus. We got patients with severe acute respiratory illness, but on testing, we found they were all coronavirus negative. They were either community acquired pneumonia or swine flu or H1N1 cases.

Out of the ten cases, we have discharged three. In Lucknow there are twenty-five cases out of which twelve are who attended the Jamaat in Nizamuddin.

The last patient admitted was a two-and-a-half-year old child who is the son of our first patient, the doctor from Canada. When she was in our hospital, her two-and-a-half-year-old child was taken care of by her in-laws. Then, they also became positive. As the father-in-law was a former army officer, they went to the military hospital.

Finally, the husband and child also tested positive. Because she was treated here, she preferred to treat her child here. As she has recovered fully and has antibodies, she is with the child in the hospital. The child has only very mild symptoms and both of them are recovering in our coronavirus isolation ward.

What is the most challenging aspect of treating coronavirus patients?

As the transmission rate of the virus is very high, it is very important to protect ourselves while taking care of the patients. We had to follow the protocol very carefully, especially how we wear the PPE and remove it.

We have been very careful while dealing with the patients. We know that in Wuhan, three per cent to four per cent of healthcare workers and ten per cent to fifteen per cent of physicians got infected.

What is the medicine that you are giving patients?

The guidelines are changing almost every day.

We first started with chloroquine, but later we changed the medication to hydroxychloroquine when it became available. Now, we give hydroxychloroquine 400mg first day, followed by hydroxychloroquine 200mg twice daily for the next four days. Along with this, we give Azithromycin 500mg once a day. This is based on the recent ICMR guidelines.

How does hydroxychloroquine work in coronavirus cases?

Though hydroxychloroquine is used in malaria cases, it is predominantly used for inflammatory diseases like rheumatoid arthritis, systemic rheumatoid, etc Hydroxychloroquine has an immunomodulatory role, that is, it reduces inflammatory response and suppresses cytokine release.

Cytokine release is a kind of inflammatory response to the virus, and the main reason for acute respiratory distress syndrome which is the cause of respiratory failure leading to need for ventilatory support in many patients. This way, you can reduce mortality.

Uncontrolled studies – not randomised controlled studies – and also laboratory studies have shown that hydroxychloroquine is also able to reduce a significant amount of virus load. Thus, people recover faster. Yes, there are no randomised controlled studies done yet (at the time of the interview). It means, no authority has recommended this drug for coronavirus, but we are using it, based on the uncontrolled studies. ICMR has recommended this drug only for severe cases.

According to the ICMR guidelines, the treatment is, hydroxychloroquine 400 mg twice daily on day one, followed by 200mg twice daily for the next four days, along with Azithromycin 500mg daily, for at least five days in severe cases.

'As the transmission rate of the virus is very high, it is very important to protect ourselves while taking care of the patients', said Dr Sudhir Verma.

Debate on the Origin of the Virus Continues...

Year 2021. It was a little more than a year since the first case of Covid-19 was detected in Wuhan in China.

But the debate on the origin of the virus continued; whether it was man-made in a lab in Wuhan, or naturally originated in a wet market there.

World renowned virologist **Dr Shahid Jameel** *was of the opinion that it was unlikely the Covid virus was created in a lab.*

THE theory that the Covid virus originated in a lab and not in the wet market, is gaining momentum once again. Whichever scientist I spoke to in the last one year vehemently opposed the theory that it was a bioengineered virus. As a virologist, do you think it is created in a lab and leaked from there?

Knowing the methods that virologists use and the technologies that are available, it is unlikely (that it was created in a lab).

In science, you cannot say anything is impossible. But it is unlikely that this Covid virus is created in a lab.

There are diametrically opposite views floating around. One is that it jumped from a bat to a human.

Through an intermediary?

Maybe there is an intermediary. Maybe not. Because nobody has found the intermediary yet.

The second theory is that it was created in a lab.

There is also a third possibility, that it was not intentionally created in a 'gain of function' experiment. But it was possibly worked up in the lab and could have leaked, not intentionally but accidentally. Again, there is no evidence to prove the possibility. Then people ask, how can the virus jump to humans and directly infect them?

Is it possible to infect humans without an intermediary?

It is possible. You don't always need an intermediary. Viruses can jump directly to humans.

In fact, the same scientific group in China reported on the 27 May about another virus that was closer to SARS CoV2 than the RaTG13 bat coronavirus. The paper talks about the virus directly binding to ACE2 receptors on human cells.

This virus was not very well adapted to humans when it emerged in December 2019, but has since then evolved in humans to get better and better.

The first mutation that happened was D614G, which was first seen in January 2020 and from then on quickly became the dominant virus in the population. Almost all the present variants are derived from it. Several other variants have emerged as 'variants of concern' like the Alpha variant, the Beta variant, the Gamma variant and the Delta variant. And there are several 'variants of interest' circulating as well. All of these variants have improved the ability of the virus to infect humans and transmit between humans.

It is not a virus that was evolved in a lab to be the perfect virus to cause a pandemic.

You feel this conspiracy theory is more political than scientific?

It appears so. People do want answers but there are no clear-cut answers either way. Just because evidence is missing, doesn't mean evidence is not there. It only means that we haven't found the evidence yet.

Let's look at what the key arguments are on the lab-leak theory. It says that scientists collected the virus from animals like the bats, and kept it in the lab for study.

Or, they have bioengineered the corona virus genome in the lab. One argument in favour of that theory is, it is suspicious that even after a year and a half, the closest relatives haven't been found in any animal species.

Another point people make is that the virus contains some unusual features and genetic sequences, like a furin cleavage site, suggesting that it is engineered by humans.

Is that a possibility?

When you engineer a virus, you leave behind signatures, but such signatures are missing in this virus. Evolution does not leave signatures, but lab creations would.

Now, coming to the argument that just because no animal species was found as an intermediary, it must have been created in the lab, is wrong.

It took 14 years to find out that the Himalayan palm civet was the intermediary animal in the SARS epidemic of 2002 and 2003. The virus jumped from the bat to the civet cat, before reaching human beings. Here, we are talking about a short time period of over a year.

The problem is, animals are not often infected at a very high level and they also sometimes don't show the symptoms. And, how many animals are you going to survey to find an intermediary? In China, they have already looked at something like 80,000 wild and domesticated animals.

That is one argument that is used by some for the lab leak theory; that 80,000 animals have been tested and an intermediary has not been found. But 80,000 is a tiny fraction of the number of animals that are there in the country.

Do you think, because there is a virology lab in Wuhan and the first case was in Wuhan, this make people suspicious?

Yes, some ask, is it just a coincidence that the lab in Wuhan has corona viruses and the outbreak started there? I would say this is probably just a coincidence.

Virology labs are very specialised labs. They tend to be situated in places where there are sources of those viruses. China has a lab to study coronaviruses because you find a lot of coronaviruses there.

Similarly, there are influenza labs in Asia, Dengue fever labs in Latin America and Yellow fever labs in Africa. If a new Dengue virus emerges in Latin America, you can't say that a lab leaked the virus.

I don't think any of these arguments hold much water. They are not scientific. People who have written these articles are making arguments that it is lab created, because of lack of evidence.

Do you think these arguments are going around because China is very secretive about documents?

Forget about China. If India were asked to do it, would India do it? Would America do it? Would any independent country do it? I think it is too much to expect for them to make all their records open. Yes, people are demanding, but it is possibly not going to happen.

I don't think this situation is going to be resolved soon. The only way the origin can be established is, if China gives access to the complete record of that lab – if China opens the notebooks, the computers and the freezers. That is unlikely to happen.

Should they be secretive about how a virology lab works?

No, they should not be secretive but the world doesn't work in a simple manner.

Yes, they should open up their records to satisfy the world. But they are simply saying, who are you to ask? They are now saying that the virus was created in the US and brought to China through the military. And that is also without any evidence.

Do you think like the SARS 2002 and 2003 mystery, it may take decades to solve this mystery too?

I think so. All these arguments aside, whatever we know about this virus and the way it has evolved, it does suggest that it is a natural origin virus. It did not come into the human population heavily adapted. It continues to adapt through mutations.

This, I think, is a fairly good scientific argument; that here is a virus that possibly originated naturally.

Everything that people have presented so far is based on associations and coincidences with just circumstantial evidence.

'When you engineer a virus, you leave behind signatures, but such signatures are missing in this virus', pointed out Dr Shahid Jameel, saying that he did not think the virus was lab created.

The debate over the origin of the corona virus still continues....
And the virus continues to scare people by coming out with new mutations regularly....

Reforms in Agriculture to Continue

In September 2020, Prime Minister Narendra Modi introduced the Farm Bills in the Parliament as part of reforms in the agricultural sector. The Lok Sabha approved the bills on 17 September 2020 and the Rajya Sabha on 20 September 2020, amidst vociferous protests from the tiny opposition.

Narendra Modi described the passing of the farm bills as a watershed moment in the history of Indian agriculture. The three new farm bills — The Farmers (Empowerment & Protection) Agreement of Price Assurance and Farm Services Bill, The Essential Commodities Act (Amendment) Bill and Farmers' Produce Trade and Commerce (Promotion and Facilitation) Bill – became laws with the President's assent.

But the legislation has drawn fire not only from the farmers of Punjab and Haryana, but from other States as well.

Non-BJP ruled States soon made clear their intention to block the new laws.

It resulted in what is known as the Farmers' agitation with all the farmers' unions describing the laws as 'anti-farmer'.

*When I spoke to **Professor Ashwani Mahajan,** the co-convenor of the Swadeshi Jagaran Manch, aligned with the Rashtriya Swayamsevak Sangh (RSS) and the ruling Bharatiya Janata Party, he listed the changes that the Manch wanted in the laws.*

WHEN the Prime Minister said the passing of the farm bills was a watershed moment, why is it that farmers are unhappy and rioting, and burning the effigy of the prime minister?

What we at Swadeshi Jagaran Manch feel is, the intent of the farm bills is good.

If the farmers are unhappy, it is the duty of the people and society at large to indicate what changes are needed. That is why, we are raising certain issues to be addressed.

The problem in present-day agriculture is that farmers are subjected to various types of exploitation.

The major problem farmers face is, they do not get a good price for their produce. So, what the government has done by announcing an MSP (Minimum Support Price) which is the cost of production plus 50 per cent or more, is wonderful. It was mainly to encourage agricultural production and improve the economic condition of the farmers in the country.

In fact, the government had announced in 2017 to increase the farmers' income by 2022.

Now, to the Bills. When you look at the Essential Commodities Act (Amendment) Bill, it is taking out some agricultural items from the Essential Commodities Act. Agricultural products were placed under the Essential Commodities Act to stop the prices of some of the products from going up due to black marketing, hoarding, etc That was because we were living in an era of shortage of agricultural products.

Today, we have surplus production....

Yes, because we have surplus production, the problem has shifted to storage. To encourage people to create infrastructure for storage, you need to change the law that penalised people for storage. So, such a law doesn't serve any purpose now. That was why the Essential Commodities Act has been amended. It is a welcome step.

The next bill is about the *mandi*s, the APMC (Agricultural Produce Market Committee) *mandi*s. Earlier also, farmers used to sell their produce outside the mandis. But those who were purchasing could not buy in large numbers as they had to purchase through APMC. In the APMC *mandi*s, there are various charges the farmers had to pay, which in turn reduced the income of the farmers.

The new bill intends to keep the mandis intact, while allowing the farmer to sell outside if he wants to do so.

When the trade outside the APMC *mandi*s goes unregulated, will it not destroy the level playing field between the APMC market and other traders?

When farmers can sell outside the APMC *mandi*s, even if they are selling at the same price as in *mandi*s, they will, in fact, be getting 6-7 per cent higher price. That is because they do not have to pay the mandi fees, commission, etc

Yes, the cause of concern for us is that there won't be a level playing field. What we are saying is, when the procurers work outside the mandi, the interest of the farmers should be protected.

When the number of *mandi*s come down, it will be an incentive for the buyers to buy outside the *mandi*. In turn, the farmers will be forced to sell outside the *mandi* because buyers are only there.

Won't this lead to exploitation of the farmers?

Yes. Since farmers have very little bargaining power, there are chance of them getting exploited. So, the Swadeshi Jagaran Manch feels that we must ensure at least a Minimum Support Price (MSP) to the farmers outside the mandis also.

Till now, the procurement is done only by the government, and they were given a minimum support price. Even while passing the bill, the government went on to say that MSP will continue. Our concern is, the procurement by the government is only 6 per cent of the total agricultural production. For the rest 94 per cent, it will be outside the *mandi*s and outside MSP.

So, we feel that the laws should be with those who have less bargaining power, and those who are economically less privileged. And farmers come in this category. Therefore, we need to protect them.

The corporates sell products at a price decided by them, which is irrespective of the cost of production. And consumers purchase at the MRP decided by them, even though there is no justification for that MRP. Every authority, from the government to the income tax department, accepts this. Deals are made on MRP which has no scientific basis.

Is that not how free market works?

Yes. That is exactly what we want to stress upon. The very first resolution we passed was that corporates or companies should announce their cost of production because they don't announce the cost of production and they decide the MRP.

If this is how free markets work, how do you expect a farmer, who has a small holding, to know the moods of the market? Those who have the money, govern the market.

What should the government have done; announce more APMC markets and restrict the trade outside the *mandis*?

No.

There are two ways. One is, farmers should have more options. Sometime ago, the government had announced the opening up of 22,000 farmers' markets where farmers can sell their produce. More of these markets should be developed by the government. They should not be left to the mercy of the corporates.

What is happening today is, traders may come or may not come, they may buy or not buy. They may give a price decided by them.

Totally unregulated....

Yes, unregulated. So, the SJM has requested the government to bring a change in the law which will ensure MSP as the floor price for all farmers, below which nobody should buy anything from them.

It means, whether it is the government or the private entity, everybody is obliged to pay the MSP when they buy a product from the farmers.

I will give you an example. Australian wheat comes at Rs 1,600 per quintal after paying all the taxes. In India, the government purchases wheat at Rs 2,000 from the farmers. If free market is allowed to function, more and more Australian wheat will come to India, and Indian farmers will be forced to sell their produce at less than Rs 1,600.

Since the farmer is less privileged, the government should fix a minimum floor price which will be a scientific one.

You should also remember that the corporates are allowed to sell agri-produces at a price that is not scientifically decided. Nobody knows how they decide the MRP. But the MSP is scientifically calculated, because the government can calculate each and every element of the cost.

Such an MSP is more egalitarian, pro-farmer, pro-poor and scientific. So, you should put it in the law that anybody purchasing any produce from a farmer has to pay the MSP, and anyone purchasing below the floor price should be penalised.

The way the laws are right now, they give the corporates an upper hand, and the farmers and the consumers are at their mercy. Is that the reason why many people say the bills will give rise to crony capitalism?

I would say the intent of the government has been to empower the farmers, but the outcome is giving upper hand to the corporates. If they add a small paragraph that no purchase will be allowed below the MSP, the government has a winner on its hands.

That is why we say that the new bills are good, but you need to make these changes to make them effective for the farmers to get the real benefits.

Would you say that in the current form, the corporates have the advantage?

We are yet to see how it will turn out though it looks like that right now. Because of the weak bargaining power of the farmers, the buyers will be in an advantageous position.

The MSP can even be mentioned in the contract signed before contract farming.

The Bill also allows contract farming agreement between farmers and corporates or the buyers of the produce. Since a majority of the farmers in India are small farmers, do you think there are more chances of them getting exploited?

I don't disagree with you. At the same time, I would say it has two sides.

Yes, ours is a country of small farmers. Sometimes, they find it difficult to continue with farming and go on to do some other work. Sometimes, like in Kerala, only 20 per cent of the cultivable land is used for cultivation. So, for the full utilisation of the cultivable land that we have, it is a good option to make use of those who have the resources. That's why I said, it has two sides.

But you should make sure that the contracts signed are in such a way that the farmers are not exploited by the private parties.

Also, the current system of dispute resolution is not up to the mark. There is no clause about the company going back on its words and not buying the produce.

In the present law also, there is no safeguard mechanism for the farmers except the dispute regulation option the government has made, so that arbitrators can be appointed. And that, if their decision is not in favour of the farmer, he can approach the SDM (Sub-Divisional Magistrate).

Again, the decision of the sub-divisional magistrate is final. If that also goes against the farmer, where will he go?

Yes, the SDM has been given all the powers in the whole game. And this is not a very good dispute regulation mechanism. Moreover, farmers are also pointing out the same thing.

So, there should be a better dispute resolution mechanism like farmers' courts on the same lines of consumer courts. The farmers' courts will also reduce the litigation in the general court.

Since it is advantage corporates in whatever that is in the new bills, are we going to see a new form of zamindari system?

No. I don't see that happening because the farmer can say no to the contract any time. His land will not be taken away by anyone at any time.

What I am saying is, to maximise the benefits from the present law, it is essential to make these changes.

Another thing we want is, at present the farmer is given money only after the farming is over. Instead, he should be given money in 2-3 instalments at different stages of the crop. This will have many advantages; for example, the farmer doesn't have to go to the moneylenders for loan.

We also want to highlight that there is no registration of traders or buyers now; anyone can purchase the produce. We feel there should be a registration of traders to safeguard the interests of the farmers.

Also, anybody purchasing at the farm gate should make the payment immediately.

The reality is, last year PepsiCo penalised the potato farmers of Gujarat for using the same seed variety, and the farmers' organisations had to agitate and approach the court.

They could not penalise the farmers because Swadeshi Jagaran Manch was there!

When Pepsi filed a case against the potato farmers, we made a statement that Pepsi was wrong and its act was illegal because seeds, lives and plants, cannot not be patented as per the law of the land.

Then, according to the Plant Variety and Farmers Right Act, farmers have the right to produce, exchange and sell seeds. Nobody can take away this right from the farmers.

When Swadeshi Jagaran Manch made this clear, Pepsi in the US instructed the Indian arm to withdraw the case, and they withdrew it.

'The cause of concern for us is that there won't be a level playing field', feared Professor Ashwani Mahajan, the co-convenor of the Swadeshi Jagaran Manch.

On the 12th January 2021, the Supreme Court of India ordered an interim stay on the implementation of the farm laws. By then, six State governments – Kerala, Punjab, Chhattisgarh, Rajasthan, Delhi and West Bengal – had passed resolutions against the farm acts.

After protesting against the Farm laws for two months, thousands of farmers, mainly from Punjab and Haryana started a Dlli Chalo movement and started marching towards Delhi when the nation was going to celebrate the Republic Day on 26 January 2021. After eleven months of protests, on 19 November 2021, the Modi government decided to repeal the Farm laws. While addressing the nation, Modi said, 'Today, while apologising to the countrymen, I want to say with a sincere and pure heart that perhaps there must have been some deficiency in our efforts, due to which we could not explain the truth like the light of the lamp to some farmers. We have decided to repeal all three farm laws, will begin the procedure at the Parliament session that begins this month. I urge farmers to return home to their families and let's start afresh.'

Sedition Charge against Shashi Tharoor!

Filing FIRs (First Information Reports) against dissenting voices, and critics against the government and establishment, and labelling them as anti-nationals, was happening at regular intervals from 2014 to 2021.

But there was shock and disbelief when an FIR was filed against Member of Parliament (MP), ***Dr Shashi Tharoor,*** *on the 30th of January, 2021 along with some very senior journalists over their allegedly 'misleading' tweets on the violence that happened at the farmers' tractor rally in Delhi on Republic Day.*

The cases invoked IPC sections of sedition, criminal intimidation, promoting enmity, provocation to break public peace, criminal conspiracy, outraging religious feelings, etc

Shashi Tharoor spoke to me on these shocking developments.

VOICES of the protesting farmers are muzzled, anyone who support them is silenced, young activists are arrested….

Are you worried about the kind of terror that has been unleashed in the country?

Of course I am troubled by these developments, and saddened that my country is walking down this dark path.

I am also concerned that these incidents once again illustrate this government's stark immaturity, when it comes to leading the nation.

At a time when we are facing several challenges – an economy that has hit the doldrums on account of the pandemic and accelerated by this government's ineptitude, the threat of Chinese incursions on our sovereign territories, the persisting effects of the Covid-19 virus and a lacklustre rollout of our vaccination programme and the widespread agrarian distress – our government has chosen to direct its attention and energies to muzzling free speech, fundamental rights and individual liberties in the name of a purported national interest, that is unbecoming of our rich democratic ethos. It is a betrayal of the hopes and aspiration of our citizens who expected comprehensive solutions to these serious problems.

Don't you think a weak opposition is one of the reasons why all this is happening?

I don't think that is fair. The Opposition has certainly been at the forefront in highlighting the assortment of serious challenges that the country is facing – whether it is highlighting the genuine concerns of our farmers, or arguing for greater support towards our Armed Forced so that they are better equipped to handle Chinese aggression on our borders or even articulating a more fundamental need to preserve the freedom of individual liberties and rights that are the cornerstone of any democratic nation.

To blame the Opposition for what is taking place in our country is a simplistic and convenient approach that does not take into account the actual track record and performance of all of us who have demanded greater governmental accountability.

As far as I am concerned, the only reason why these troubling developments are taking place is because of a certain arrogance of power displayed by this government, that hopes to clamp down on those voices which have repeatedly pointed out that their bloated rhetoric and grandstanding is not matched by their insipid and tepid response in matters of governance.

Why do you think the government slaps sedition charges on anyone – from political leaders like you to young activists and journalists – who criticises its policies?

These attempts stem from a pronounced insecurity and authoritarianism that drives many of this government's actions.

At the same time, this government's dramatic responses to tweets by a pop star, a climate change activist, and the recent incident of putting a 21-year-old in jail has resulted in an implosion of India's image globally, in a manner that has no similar precedent.

India was a country admired across the world for the manner in which it celebrated its diversity (including of political ideology and opinion), that protected the fundamental rights of our citizens and managed to govern a chaotic and vibrant democracy through consensus, rather than conformity.

That is no longer the case in BJP-ruled India which has presented itself as a country headed by a government that is, paradoxically, not just authoritarian but characterised by a meek and fragile mindset.

We should not be surprised. After all, this government traces its political lineage to a group that not just stood by while our colonial overlords clamped down on the leaders of the freedom movement in a similar manner, but actively aided and benefitted from the British suppression of people, who wanted a free and independent India.

The tradition that started with the Hindu Mahasabha continues today with the BJP government.

What came to your mind when an FIR was filed against you, an opposition leader, citing sedition and spreading disharmony?

I was upset, of course, because after decades abroad I gave up a great deal to return to serve my country and would never have dreamed in my worst nightmares that anyone would ever accuse me of sedition!

But given the conduct of our ruling party, I realised that I should not be unduly troubled or particularly surprised.

For one, I have faced similar instances of plain harassment by surrogates for the government who have taken me to court on various grounds over the years, including for merely quoting statements that already exist in the public domain.

At the same time, the recent attempts to intimidate and suppress my voice is almost like a badge of honour that I am proud to wear. It shows that the ruling party considers the arguments I have been making publicly a serious challenge to their campaign to promote a bigoted and exclusionary idea of India.

What they want from all of us is total submission, obedience and the willingness to roll over and let their nativist campaign succeed. I am simply not prepared to do this nor am

I willing to compromise in fighting for that pluralist, inclusive and accepting idea of India that our forefathers gave their lives for during the Independence struggle.

Even though it is clear the legal troubles and inconveniences will persist, I will continue to fight for these ideas today, in the hope that by not cowering before tyranny I will encourage more people to join the fight for India's soul tomorrow

Is this what happens when a political party thinks it is the country and not just a party elected by the people to rule the country for a certain period?

The BJP government and their surrogates have deemed themselves to be the ultimate guardians of our 'national interest'.

With this kind of mindset, it is only natural that other trademarks of their style of governance becomes apparent – an inability to develop national consensus or unity, a pronounced unwillingness to engage in dialogue and negotiations with stakeholders who have a different worldview, and a tendency to resort to tools of suppression and harassment to intimidate and silence those courageous and patriotic enough to question and expose this government's underlying chauvinism.

The ruling dispensation always talks about the entire world conspiring to destroy India. Do you think the government and the ruling party suffer from persecution complex?

We must recognise that this government has systematically attempted to portray themselves as the guardians against a distinctive 'Other', which represents individuals and communities that the government claims can threaten to derail the progress of our nation.

Accordingly, terms like 'anti-national', 'urban Naxals' and '*tukde-tukde* gang' became regulars in the political lexicon employed by the ruling dispensation, to define the apparent threat posed by an assortment of players ranging from Muslims, the Opposition, comedians satirising the work of the ruling party, journalists who dared question the government, students from JNU and other universities who participated in campus politics – in short, anybody who opposed the government.

The Modi regime has done this through the aggressive assertion of a belligerent form of nationalism in which the government's ideological agenda is portrayed as synonymous with the national interest.

The corollary to this assertion is, inevitably, that any opposition to it is anti-national, if not treasonous; this explains the trigger-happiness with which BJP-ruled States slap sedition cases on their critics, since clearly their criticism itself is proof that they are betraying the nation.

Critics are routinely urged by government ministers to 'go to Pakistan', the mere choice of destination itself pointing to the traitorousness of their opposition.

The new nationalism essentially redefines loyalty to the country as loyalty to the ruling party, rather than the country, sentimentally defined as patriotism by the liberals.

The conflation of the nation with the government, the government with both the ruling party, and with the prime minister, has given India, for the first time, a larger-than-life ruler who literally embodies the nation and looms above its democratic institutions.

Do these actions remind you of anything from history?

These actions have parallels with events that took place at the height of the freedom struggle, where the British slapped our Nationalists – leaders and workers alike – with the same sedition charges and penalties that the government is resorting to today.

How ironic that a party that seeks to arrogate the mantle of nationalism to itself is actually behaving like the imperial oppressors.

But just like our forefathers did, we must be undeterred in our commitment and willingness to fight for India's soul and ultimately strive to liberate our nation from the intolerance and bigotry of the current ruling dispensation.

In fact, on the 13th of February, Disha Ravi, a 21-year-old climate change activist was arrested on sharing an online toolkit released by young climate change activist Greta Thunberg (the 19-year-old Swedish environmental activist) supporting the farmers' agitation.

Three days later, non-bailable warrants were issued against two more activists, Nikita Jacob and Shantanu Muluk for their involvement in the same toolkit.

Tharoor's words: 'What they want from all of us is total submission, obedience and the willingness to roll over and let their nativist campaign succeed. I am simply not prepared to do this nor am I willing to compromise in fighting for that pluralist, inclusive and accepting idea of India that our forefathers gave their lives for during the Independence struggle.'

Time to Remember the 'People's President'

July 2022. The term of Ram Nath Kovind as the President of the Republic of India ended and the 16th Presidential election happened on the 18th of July 2022.

For the first time in the history of independent India, the country got a president from the tribal community.

Droupadi Murmu, the new President of India, is from the Santhal community of Odisha's Baidaposi village. Before her entry into politics, she had taught children as a school teacher and worked as a junior assistant in the irrigation and power department for four years.

And it was also the right time to remember the one and only 'people's President' Dr A P J Abdul Kalam (2002-2007).

***S M Khan**, his Press Secretary, went back memory lane on his days with Dr Kalam at the Rashtrapathi Bhavan.*

YOU were the principal information officer for the CBI for many years. You were the director general of Doordarshan News. You were also President Kalam's press

secretary. Would you say this assignment was special in your career?

Definitely. Working with Dr Kalam was one of the most memorable assignments in my thirty-four years of service.

I can never forget the day I first met him; it was on the 5th of August 2002. Dr Kalam had become the president on the 25th of July.

Whatever I have learnt from President Kalam will remain with me forever. In fact, I have written a book also on my days with him. I have described those days as the most unforgettable, momentous and the best tenure in my career.

Was it because working with Dr Kalam was a unique experience that you decided to write a book?

Yes, working with Dr Kalam was such a unique experience that after his passing away, I decided that I should share my experience with the people.

Another reason was, I happened to meet Prime Minister Modi during the Independence Day celebrations at Rashtrapati Bhavan, soon after Dr Kalam passed away on the 27th of July 2015. That was the first Independence Day after his passing away.

As I conveyed my greetings to Prime Minister Modi, he said, '*Kalam Saheb par kuch likhiye*'.

His words were very inspiring, and I thought my best tribute to Dr Kalam would be to write a book on him. Later, I presented the first copy of the book to the Prime Minister as well.

We had Textbook Presidents, we had Rubber Stamp Presidents, but Dr Kalam was the only person who was called the People's President. What kind of a person was he?

Dr Kalam never felt or behaved like a president during his entire tenure of five years as the President. Not even a single day, he felt he was the first citizen of India, or someone different from the others, or the President of India.

Dr Kalam always used to say, 'I am just an ordinary person'.

When I first met him, he told me, 'I want to make this a people's place and not a presidential palace. So, you also work with that in mind'.

He interacted with people in such a way that people felt he was one among them. The most charming part of his personality was, he made whoever he met feel, whether he be the president of a country or an ordinary person of India or any other country, he was one of them. He liked to have direct interactions with people without any paraphernalia, without anybody else getting involved.

Also, on the first day itself, he made it clear that everybody would call him Dr Kalam and not His Excellency. In fact, there was a standing instruction to all the officers with the Government of India and State governments that they would only address him as Dr Kalam.

There is a practice that wherever the President goes, a limousine will go before him, and Dr Kalam was totally against it. 'What a sheer wastage of money and people! Why should a fleet of cars be flown from Delhi to Chennai or Pune or Patna for my visit?' he exclaimed. He asked them to stop the practice immediately. He said, 'I will use the vehicle provided by the State government'.

In those days, Ambassador cars were used by all the government offices and Dr Kalam would happily travel in those Ambassador cars.

Another practice he stopped was having separate chairs for the president on the dais, whenever he addressed a function.

He insisted on having the same chairs as the others, and not the ornate ones kept for the president. His argument was, 'Why should I sit on a different chair when all the others use same kind of chairs?'

Another thing I will never forget was this. It has been a long-standing practice at Rashtrapati Bhavan that every year, when the flowers bloom in the Mughal Gardens, it will be open for the general public in February and March.

During his time, thousands of people would visit the garden. He would go there unannounced and talk to the visitors, asking them, from where they came, which flowers they liked, whether they liked walking around, etc

He was never worried about security...?

Never. He would meet and talk to people even on New Year's Day, Independence Day, Republic Day, etc

On festival days like Christmas, Eid and Diwali, he would keep the gates of Rashtrapati Bhavan open throughout the day, and anybody could go in without any pass. All of them could meet him personally and talk to them.

This was how Dr Kalam conducted himself as the President of the country.

Was everyone working at Rashtrapati Bhavan surprised initially to see a President behaving like an ordinary person?

Yes, the entire staff was surprised. The security forces used tell him about the Blue Book. He would then tell them, 'You just treat me as Dr A P J Abdul Kalam and not as the President of India. This is not a presidential palace to have a Blue Book; this is just the headquarters of the President of India in a democratic republic, who is answerable to the people of India! We are not living in a monarchy'.

As you know all the protocols of Rashtrapati Bhavan came into existence during British times, when the Viceroy was answerable to the British monarchy. It was never changed. He always used to say, 'Change to what is suitable for a democratic country'.

With his attitude, he must have won the heart of all the people working there....

Every single person working there loved him. For everyone, right from the secretary to the peon, working with him was a different kind of an experience.

Interestingly, Dr Kalam treated everybody so well that every person felt he was very close to him. He made each person feel special.

Another important part of Dr Kalam's personality was that whenever he introduced us, he never used to say, he was this officer or that officer; he would say, this is my colleague. He was such a great person that not even once I had heard him say, my press secretary or my PA will do this. He would say, my colleague will do it.

Even when we went abroad, he introduced all of us as his colleagues. These are very small things, but it shows the character of the person and how he treats other people.

Thousands of students used to visit him every month and he used to interact with each and every student. In fact, when he became the President, he had told me that his target was to meet at least 5 lakh students personally during his tenure. And I was asked to keep a record of that.

Actually, he met more than 5 lakh students from various schools and colleges from all over India in those five years. He met them not to sign the autographs or let them take pictures, he wanted each interaction to be meaningful. He would tell the students, 'You ask any question to me, I will answer'. He was of the opinion that when they went out after meeting him, they would have learnt something.

What do you remember about the travels you had with him outside India?

An interesting thing was, whenever he met intellectuals or political leaders or academicians, he would have a power point presentation for them. He worked hard to prepare the power point presentations.

I will never forget our visit to Switzerland. The government over there had declared it as Science Day, as a scientist president was visiting their country. They had arranged a function in his honour in at the Zurich Institute, which had the distinction of producing a large number of Nobel Laureates. The Institute also invited many Nobel Laureates to the function, and twenty of them attended the function.

Dr Kalam addressed them with a power point presentation. And once it was over, all those Nobel laureates gave him a standing ovation! That was the kind of respect he got from the scientific community even outside India. I will never forget that moment.

What aspect of his personality made people love and respect him so much, irrespective of where they belonged?

The very fact that he was a very simple person and very inspirational. He was extremely popular among the youth of India. In fact, the Government of India had awarded him a Bharat Ratna, before he became the President.

He had no material possessions; no house, no car, no property, nothing. That was the first time in my life that I was meeting a person who did not own anything. He was not there to earn money, position or power; he genuinely wanted to do a lot for the country, but never expected anything in return.

People believed in his vision of making India a developed country. It was his mission to make India a developed country. After he became the President of India, he used to say, 'Now that I am the President, I will be able to market India to the world in a better way'.

What was his approach while dealing with politicians and political matters?

As far as government matters were concerned, he made his decisions totally on merit. He was not influenced by any considerations. I have seen him scrutinising in detail all the government proposals that needed the President's approval, and assessing them like a professional. If the proposals were against the Constitution or law, he had no hesitation in disagreeing with the government.

You may remember him returning the Office of Profit bill without signing, though all the parties together had passed the bill in Parliament. He did so as the Constitution says that an MP cannot possess any office of profit.

Similarly, there was a bill on the disqualification of Members of Parliament for not declaring what was stipulated by the Election Commission at the time of filing their nomination. This rule by the EC came during his tenure, when the NDA under Atal Bihari Vajpayee was ruling the country. Even though all the parties came together and wanted the rule to be struck down, he did not agree. The credit must go to Dr Kalam that the ordinance which was brought in by the Election Commission in 2002, is continuing even today.

One thing he always used to say was, 'I have taken up this post to preserve, protect, and defend the Constitution and I will do it during the time I am here'.

You should also remember that he worked with both the NDA and the UPA. From 2002 to 2004, he worked with the NDA and from 2004-2005, it was the UPA government with Dr Manmohan Singh as the Prime Minister.

He might not have been a politician, but he did not sign everything that came to him.

He knew the post of the President was not just ceremonial; the Constitution gave immense powers to the President where he could really be the person to ensure Constitutional morality and see that the government functioned in accordance with the Constitution for the benefit of people.

Do you think India will ever get a President like Dr Kalam?

I don't know. I can't say about that. Anything can happen.

But when he passed away, many people said, he was a President for life!

As India celebrates 75 years of independence, it got its first Adivasi President, Droupadi Murmu.

I am reminded of what C Subramaniam, who was a member of the Constituent Assembly that drafted the Constitution, told me in 1997 when India was celebrating 50 years of independence:

'The President's powers also have to be reviewed. He can't just be a dummy. The President should have more power in the formation of the government. Now, even when you have a ministry which does not have a majority in the Parliament, the President is bound by the advice of the Cabinet which has no parliamentary backing.'

Also what S M Khan said on Dr Kalam:

'He (Dr Kalam) knew the post of the President was not just ceremonial; the Constitution gave immense powers to the President where he could really be the person to ensure Constitutional morality and see that the government functioned in accordance with the Constitution for the benefit of people.'

A Hindu Built 111 Mosques, Four Churches and One Temple

At a time when people are fighting in the name of religion, here is the story of a Hindu who built 111 mosques and 4 churches.

The first mosque he built was with money coming from a Christian. Of course, this happened not now but almost six decades ago!

In 1962, when ***G Gopalakrishnan*** *achieved this rare feat, times were such that nobody felt it worth writing about or talking about it.*

But today, 85-year-old G Gopalakrishnan is looked upon as a symbol of universal brotherhood and religious harmony.

HOW did you get the chance to build a mosque in Kerala, and that too a landmark at the Palayam junction (in Thiruvananthapuram)?

The first and the most memorable experience I had was building the Palayam Juma Masjid.

As you know, the Palayam junction in Thiruvananthapuram is famous all over the world for having a church, a mosque and a temple close to each other.

The year was 1962.

I am a self-taught architect. Because my father, K Govindan Contractor, was a builder and a designer, I learnt the art of designing mostly from his sketches, and clearing my doubts from the person who designed for him.

When P P Kuttiamu Sahib (the first Chief Engineer of the PWD department in Kerala) noticed that the Palayam mosque was in a very pathetic condition, he formed a committee to reconstruct it. He showed the picture of the façade of the Safdarjung Mausoleum in Delhi to the then Chief Architect, J C Alexander. Though the mausoleum did not have a minar, Kuttiamu Sahib wanted a minar in the structure.

The mosque committee called for a tender, and what my father quoted was the lowest. Though we won the tender, we didn't have enough money to start work.

It was exactly at the same time that I had got a contract to build a house for one P C Chummar, who worked at the Accountant General's office in the city. He had also given me a cheque for Rs 5000 as advance to start the foundation work.

My father felt we should do both the house and the mosque simultaneously, and use the advance given by Chummar for building the mosque. I opposed it, saying we couldn't use Chummar's money for any other purpose. Then my mother intervened and asked me to get Chummar's opinion on this. When I narrated the situation to Chummar, he said, 'Why not? You can use it for the mosque. Anyway, it will take some time for me to get the loan from my office'.

That was how the fund to rebuild the mosque came from him, a Christian. And we were Hindus involved in building the mosque. And the architect was J C Alexander, another Christian.

When I realised this coincidence, I started believing in the idea of universal brotherhood. Of course, nobody wrote about this aspect then. Perhaps it was not that significant in those days.

Though we started work in 1962, the work got over only in 1967, and it was then inaugurated by the then President of India, Dr Zakir Hussain.

Was it the first mosque with a Minar in Kerala?

Yes. Following the traditional Kerala architecture, all the mosques and churches in Kerala had slopping tiled roof, just like the Kerala temples.

It was after the reconstruction of the Palayam Juma Masjid, that mosques in Kerala moved towards the Indo-Saracenic style of architecture with minars in place of slopping tiled roof.[1]

After we rebuilt the Palayam mosque, so many people contacted Kuttiamu Sahib to change the style of the existing mosques to Indo-Saracenic style. Because I was involved in the Palayam Juma Masjid reconstruction, he made me design and rebuild many mosques after that.

In the case of the Palayam Juma Masjid, you were reconstructing the old structure by adding a minar. Later on,

---

[1] Indo-Saracenic architecture, also known as Indo-Gothic, Mughal-Gothic, Neo-Mughal, or Hindoo style was a revivalist architectural style mostly used by the British architects in India in the later 19th century .

you started designing also. How did you get the chance to design a mosque?

I had designed many mosques at many places but all of them wanted me to design on the lines of Palayam Juma Masjid.

But in 1966, even before the inauguration of the Palayam Juma Masjid itself, I got the chance to independently design a mosque. It is the now-famous Beemapally Masjid.[2]

After seeing Palayam Juma Masjid, they approached Kuttiamu Sahib to reconstruct this one too with a minar at the top. He asked architect Rahim Sahib to design the new mosque.

What made Beemapally Masjid with its tiled roof different was the presence of two shrines or *Kabar* of two saints inside. And the problem with the sketch drawn by Rahim Sahib was, the shrines would be in one corner of the hall when they should have been at the centre.

When I pointed this out to him, he asked me to draw. I have no words to say how excited I was when he said so. I couldn't believe that I was getting a chance to independently design a mosque when I didn't have a degree in architecture, when I didn't have any qualification to do so except that I had built quite a few mosques!

So excited was I that I worked day and night without any rest or sleep for a week. In those days, we didn't have electricity in our house. So, at night I would have a lantern lit to continue working.

---

[2] Beemapally, the coastal town on the outskirts of Thiruvananthapuram, became widely known after a communal riot erupted there in 2009, followed by a police firing resulting in loss of lives.

We were very poor, but we made sure that whatever work we did, we did with utmost sincerity and dedication. Our father had taught us that work was more important than making money. When we knew how the committee members went around collecting small amounts of money, the thought of making money did not come to our mind also.

They liked my design and I started building Beemapally Masjid in 1967, but we could finish it only in 1984! You can say I dedicated 17 years of my life, my youth in building this mosque. Of course, I was doing other works for Kuttiamu Sahib along with this, and he paid me Rs 400 a month.

Once Beemapally Masjid was ready for inauguration, the unanimous verdict was that it was the best mosque in Kerala! I was thrilled beyond words.

You spoke about the lotus on which the domes of the mosques rested….

The Indian touch in the Indo-Saracenic style is the lotus on which the domes of the mosques rested! I had always felt that the presence of lotus in the Persian designs showed how heartily we had accepted the Persian architectural style, when it made its appearance in India.

Lotus under the domes was accepted till the Babri Masjid demolition. After that, I have been asked by people not to have any lotus in the structure. Anyway, from 1992 onwards, lotus disappeared from all the Kerala mosques.

The Vavar Juma Masjid at Erumeli in Sabarimala must be one of the most important mosques for you….

Yes, building Vavar *pally* (masjid) was an unforgettable experience because it symbolised what I believe in; universal brotherhood and religious harmony.

As you know, Lord Ayyappa devotees have no religion and all of them pray at the Vavar *pally,* before embarking on their journey to Sabarimala.

I consider it my good fortune to build a religious place like Vavar *pally*.

You also designed a mosque like Taj Mahal in Kerala.

I feel extremely fortunate to have built this mosque in Karunagappally in Kollam district, which has come to be known as the Taj Mahal of Kerala.

Kuttiamu Sahib had this dream to build a structure that looked exactly like Taj Mahal in Kerala, but he couldn't realise his dream when he was alive. So, this mosque was my tribute to Kuttiamu Sahib.

Why do you build only mosques?

When so many of my friends asked me, 'Gopalakrishna, why is it that you build only mosques? Why don't you build a church?', it kindled a desire in my mind. I wanted to build a church too.

It so happened that one day, a priest along with two others visited my office. The priest said, 'We know you have only been building mosques, but we want you to build a church. It should look like a church and not like a mosque! Even if it looks like a temple, it is okay with us but it should not look like a mosque!'

I told him, 'When I design a mosque, it will look like a mosque. When I am designing a church, it will be a church, and it will follow the Gothic style!'[3]

---

[3] Gothic architecture is an architectural style that was prevalent in Europe from the late 12th to the 16th century. It evolved from Romanesque architecture and was succeeded by Renaissance architecture.

Then I asked them why they came in search of me, someone who had been building only mosques! They said, a retired chief engineer called K C Alexander had suggested my name.

So, I went to see the site at Chandanapally in Pathanamthitta district along with him, and the place looked heavenly, perfect setting for a religious place.

When the church was inaugurated in 2000, I was fulfilling a wish of mine, and also answering the questions of my friends. I went on to build three more churches.

When did you build a temple?

Though I am a Hindu, I got a chance to build only one temple.

It is the one next to our house, which is more like our family temple. I designed it like a chariot.

As a person who has built so many mosques, what did you feel on 6 December 1992 (when the Babri Masjid was demolished)?

I am a creative person, and I believe only in creations. I abhor destruction, destruction of any sort. Not only in India, I don't like anyone destroying any creation anywhere in the world. So, the destruction of Babri Masjid saddened me.

More than the religious aspect, what affected me was the destruction of a creation.

Till 1992, not many knew that I, a Hindu had been building many mosques in Kerala. But in 1992 after the demolition of Babri Masjid, a newspaper wrote about me under the title, 'Builder of an emotional bridge'.

After studying the texts of all religions, I believe that there is an unwritten agreement between God and man. As per the agreement, the man is supposed to only improve the beauty of earth created by God and not destroy it.

But what you see today is abuse of nature, abuse of the planet itself. And we are suffering the aftereffects of our destructive deeds, in the form of floods, wildfires, drought and even the corona virus. Nature is teaching man a lesson for breaking the agreement.

To me, India is like a garden that has plants and flowers of all colours and hues in it. Do you think a garden with just one plant or one type of flower will be appealing? No. It will look drab, uninteresting and lustreless because a garden would be captivating only if it had many flowers of different colours.

The Palayam Juma Masjid redesigned by Gopalakrishnan.
Thank you, keralaonline.

Let me end the book with this heart-warming story as people like Gopalakrishnan give us hope in humanity, hope for a peaceful and harmonious tomorrow!

....

In 1997 when India celebrated 50 years of independence, it had an unstable coalition government. Twenty-five years later, the country is ruled by a majority government that has won 353 seats.

In 1997, the political instability had its repercussions on the economy, and it grew at just 4.4 per cent. But today, despite the pandemic and high unemployment rate, it is a $3.05 trillion economy, the fifth largest in the world and growing at the rate of 7.8 per cent.

Unfortunately, Indian society is divided on religious lines like never before….

....

15 August 2022.

It is India@75.

I am quoting NITI Aayog's Vision for India: 'When India turns 75 on 15 August 2022, it will mark a moment that comes but rarely in history, when we step out from the old to the new. It will be the era of a New India; an era where India begins its journey to become a global leader in thought and action.'

....

Acknowledgements

The first thank you note goes to Renu, my publisher. I am lucky to have a publisher who would ask on the day of my book launch, what is your next book?

Thanks always to Papri, my friend and the editor of this book.

Without Rediff.com, this book would not have happened at all. I have to thank Ajit Balakrishnan for founding Rediff, for being the first reader of the manuscript, for his valuable suggestions and also for all his support.

Thanks to Nikhil Lakshman, the Editor in Chief of Rediff.com, for believing in me and giving me the opportunity to do all these interviews.

Thanks to all the people who spoke to me on various subjects.

Big thanks to Saraswathi for her support.

Thank you, Siddhu.

And… Som for cheering me from somewhere out there in the universe….

This is a drawing by 8-year-old Maya. Little Maya's vision of what the cover design should have been.

Dreamchasers: Entrepreneurs from the South of the Vindhyas, and *Dreamchasers: Women Entrepreneurs from the South of the Vindhyas.*

As an interviewer, Shobha has established a reputation for her gentle yet incisive style of questioning, which often brings out aspects of the interviewee that are otherwise missed and draws out thoughts that are otherwise left unsaid.

As a writer, she has an evocative style that brings to life the poignant stories of people, especially those at the margins of modern India whose stories are otherwise left untold.

Shobha Warrier

Shobha Warrier has been a journalist and writer for over forty years, during the course of which she has been witness to and chronicler of the many seismic shifts within India.

Currently the Senior Editorial Director of Rediff.com, she has been associated with Rediff.com from its inception in 1996.

Prior to that, her writing, on a variety of subjects, has featured in the Sunday Observer, The Independent, The Hindu, The Asian Age, and Eve's Weekly.

In addition, she is a prolific and award-winning author, having been awarded the Lalithambika Antharjanam award for Best Young Woman Writer in 1996 for her book *Jalavidya*. She has published three short story collections in her native tongue Malayalam (*Ramakundam, Meghana, and Jalavidya*). Her short story was featured in the anthology of short stories by women writers from Kerala, titled *The Inner Spaces*.

Battlefield India is her fifth book in English; the others being *The Little Flower Girl and Others, His Days with Bapu,*